Praise for Ann Douglas and the previous books in this series

The Mother of All Pregnancy Books

"Comprehensive, informative, up-to-date, and brazenly neutral.... A must have primer."

— *The Toronto Star*

"Not preachy and bossy...it's upfront and fun."

— *The Toronto Sun*

"A book that lives up to its name.... Incredibly comprehensive yet easy to follow."

— *Chicago Tribune*

"The must-read pregnancy book! Ann Douglas has created the most comprehensive guide to pregnancy we've ever seen."

— DENISE AND ALAN FIELDS, authors, *Baby Bargains*

"At long last, a new pregnancy bible for women of my generation and younger has emerged in the form of *The Mother of All Pregnancy Books*. With humor, sensitivity, an easy, no-jargon style, and a million 'extras' that the leading pregnancy books don't cover, Ann Douglas holds nothing back. Not only do I love this book, but I will use it as a valuable tool in my own work as a women's health author."

— M. SARA ROSENTHAL, author of *The Pregnancy Sourcebook* and
The Breastfeeding Sourcebook, and founder of www.sarahealth.com

"Start reading this treasure trove even before you get pregnant so you can make it through every jam-packed page before your baby arrives."

— PAULA SPENCER, "The Mom Next Door" columnist,
Woman's Day Magazine; author of *Everything ELSE You Need to
Know When You're Expecting*

"Finally, a pregnancy book that includes essential pre-pregnancy concerns, such as planning and physical and emotional preparation! Ann Douglas has written her masterwork *The Mother of All Pregnancy Books* in the same unpretentious, concise style as her *Unofficial Guide*. She also stays true to her goal of informing parents and prospective parents as completely as possible, so they will be well-equipped to sort through the pros and cons of their own life choices as they see them. Not one to forgo difficult issues, her chapter entitled 'When Pregnancy Isn't Perfect' is one of the best I've read, both for its sensitivity and for its emphasis on coping and prevention. This is a book that will serve women and their families well."

— A. CHRISTINE HARRIS, Ph.D., author of *The Pregnancy Journal*

"This is truly 'the mother of all pregnancy books'—an intelligent resource that covers every pregnancy-related topic imaginable in a fun, reassuring way. Ann Douglas has done an exceptional job of arming parents-to-be with the facts they need to make the healthiest possible choices from preconception through postpartum. A must-have!"

— SUSAN NEWMAN, Ph.D., author of *Parenting An Only Child: The Joys and Challenges of Raising Your One and Only*

"*The Mother of All Pregnancy Books* is a comprehensive and incredibly informative resource about pregnancy (and what comes before and after!). Ann Douglas tells all in her witty style, entertaining readers along the way. Unlike other pregnancy books, Douglas combines thorough research and reporting with the human touch, offering her own experiences and insight while educating her readers at one of the most important times in their lives. This book is not to be missed!"

— ELISA AST ALL, Editor-in-Chief, *Pregnancy Magazine, Baby Years Magazine,* and iParenting.com

"If you're looking for an all-in-one 'Tell me everything, and tell it like it is' book for your pregnancy, *The Mother of all Pregnancy Books* is it. Not only is this hefty volume filled with facts about fertility, pregnancy and birth, it also contains hundreds of anecdotes from moms who lived—and maybe even loved—pregnancy. Author Ann Douglas knows her stuff, and is wise but not preachy, friendly but not overbearing. Keep this book close at hand for instant guidance through the highs and the lows of this extraordinary time!"

— NANCY PRICE, ePregnancy.com

"Here's a book that's packed with up-to-date information and practical advice on almost every aspect of pregnancy—from prenatal testing to proper nutrition, from infertility procedures to financial planning, from bedrest to breastfeeding. Yet despite its breadth and depth, the text is not dry or dull. Instead, Ann Douglas's reassuring style and insightful anecdotes make readers feel like they're chatting with a savvy, smart, sympathetic friend."

— TAMARA EBERLEIN, coauthor of *When You're Expecting Twins, Triplets, or Quads* and *Program Your Baby's Health*

The Mother of All Baby Books

"Ann Douglas, Canada's own Dr. Spock, gives us the manual Mother Nature forgot to include."

— *Flare Pregnancy* Fall/Winter 2001

"A great gift for anyone who's pregnant or whose baby is a few months old."

— MARILYN LINTON, Health Columnist *Toronto Sun,* December 10, 2001

"Indispensable! Every mom and dad should be issued a copy of this book at the hospital!"

— DENISE AND ALAN FIELDS, authors, *Baby Bargains*

"With humor, sensitivity, an easy, no-jargon style, and a million 'extras' that the leading baby books on the shelves don't cover, Ann Douglas holds nothing back. Finally, a baby book written for women of my generation!"

— M. SARA ROSENTHAL, author of *The Breastfeeding Sourcebook*, and founder of www.sarahealth.com

"Down-to-earth, informative, empowering and entertaining, this book holds your hand when you're uncertain, hugs you when you're discouraged, makes you laugh when you're aggravated, and inspires you when you're pushed to your limits. Also,this book doesn't shy away from looking at the issues around childbearing losses. So if you're a mother with special circumstances, you can pick up this book with ease, knowing that your experiences are reflected and gently acknowledged "

— DEBORAH L. DAVIS, Ph.D., co-author of *The Emotional Journey of Parenting Your Premature Baby: A Book of Hope and Healing*

"*The Mother of All Baby Books* is an amazing resource that all new mothers will love. Brilliantly presented, the book is both practical and inspirational, and no topic is left unexplored. Ann Douglas is the kind of savvy and reassuring guide that you'll want by your side as you embark on the monumental journey into motherhood."

— CECELIA A. CANCELLARO, author of *Pregnancy Stories: Real Women Share the Joys, Fears, Thrills, and Anxieties of Pregnancy from Conception to Birth*

"*The Mother of all Baby Books* provides excellent advice for topics that are easily overlooked during the pregnancy/baby adventure. The real life examples do a superb job supporting these topics in addition to giving you creative ideas on how you can implement these helpful suggestions into your life."

— SANDRA GOOKIN, co-author of *Parenting For Dummies*, and *Parenting For Dummies, 2nd Edition*

"There's nothing like another 'Mother' to help you navigate the amazing first year with a new baby. *The Mother of All Baby Books* has advice for almost everything you'll encounter."

— PAULA SPENCER, "The Mom Next Door" columnist, *Woman's Day Magazine*; author of *Everything ELSE You Need to Know When You're Expecting*

"A major thumbs-up goes to *The Mother of All Baby Books*—a fabulously written, comprehensive guide to baby care that is definitely a must-read for any parent or caregiver. Full of real-life experiences and wonderful tips, this book answers all those nagging little questions that plague parents, as well as providing scads of valuable ideas on how to do a bang-up job of baby care. It covers the whole spectrum-everything from getting prepped for the magical moments (meeting/greeting your brand-new baby), to brass-tack practicalities, such as choosing a baby carrier. (I'll definitely keep this book close at hand for my own new-baby questions this year!)"

— JENNIFER SHOQUIST, M.D., author of *Potty Training For Dummies*

"Ann Douglas has done it again! Like her pregnancy books, this new baby-rearing guide is comprehensive yet easy to read. Parents will find answers to all their questions, from big decisions ('How do we choose a pediatrician?') to minor matters ('Which wallpaper for the nursery?'), from age-old anxieties ('Is my baby eating enough?') to contemporary concerns ('Should we bank the umbilical cord blood?'). Plus, the book is reader-friendly and fun, with its practical suggestions reinforced by lively anecdotes from savvy, experienced parents."

— TAMARA EBERLEIN, coauthor of *When You're Expecting Twins, Triplets, or Quads* and *Program Your Baby's Health*

"As the old saying goes, 'Babies don't come with instruction manuals.' Well, Ann Douglas' *The Mother of All Baby Books* is really the next best thing! Covering everything imaginable—from newborn care to bathing basics, babyproofing your home to coping with sleepless nights—you will find ways to nurture this amazing new little person in your life while still keeping your sanity. Ann's wise ideas, researched information and real-life tips will help you make this time even more magical and memorable."

— NANCY PRICE, Editor, GeoParent.com, ePregnancy.com and *ePregnancy Magazine*

the
mother
of all

An All-Canadian Guide to Your
Child's Second and Third Years

toddler
books

ANN DOUGLAS

wiley.com

John Wiley & Sons Canada Ltd
22 Worcester Road
Etobicoke, Ontario
M9W 1L1

National Library of Canada Cataloguing in Publication Data

Douglas, Ann, 1963-
    The mother of all toddler books : an all-Canadian guide to your child's second and third years / Ann Douglas.

Includes bibliographical references and index.
ISBN 1-55335-016-2

    1. Toddlers—Care. 2. Toddlers—Health and hygiene. 3. Parenting.
I. Title.

RJ61.D685 2002   649'.122   C2002-903678-X

Production Credits
Cover and text design by Sharon Foster Design
Cover photograph/illustration by Karen Whylie/Coyote Photos
Illustrations by Kathryn Adams

Printed in Canada

10 9 8 7 6 5 4 3 2

*To Joan, Robert, and the
other members of the CDG Books
publishing "dream team":
Thanks for the memories.*

Acknowledgments

Writing a book of this magnitude is truly a team effort from start to finish. So I hope you'll bear with me as I run through the laundry list of people who contributed to the making of this book....

First of all, I'd like to thank the parents who agreed to be interviewed for the book. It's your stories and words of wisdom that truly bring this book to life. I owe each and every one of you a huge thank you: Molly Acton, Rita Arsenault, Aubyn Baker, Christina Barnes, Sue Beaulieu, Debbi Beiko, Candice Bianic, Brandy Boissonneault, Janet Bolton, Vicky Boudreau, Elisa Brook, Kelli Cale, Karen Chamberlain, Laura Ciarallo, Jennifer Clarke, Brandy Conlin, Stacey Couturier, Marguerite Daubney, Brenda J. Davie, Kara Doerksen, Julie Dufresne, Stephanie Estabrook, Jane Fletcher, Anne Gallant, Julie Gardiner, Leslie Garrett, Danielle Gebeyehu, Yvonne Gilmour, Jo-Anne Gomes, Joyce Gravelle, Julie Grimaldi, Sandra Grocock, Sue Guebert, Terri Harten, Karen Hayward, Monica Hecht, Andrea Illman, Debbie Jeffery, Cathy Jones, Trish Kennedy, Cindy Legare, Sharon Louie, Stephanie MacDonald, Catherine Marion, Heather Martin, Jennie Maynard, Lori Mcgonigle, Melanie McLeod, Joan MacNeil, Robin MacNeil, Colleen MacCuaig, Sidney Ellen Mckay, Colleen Mielen, Alyson Miller, Jedidja Nawolsky, Tami Overbeck, Kerri Paquette, Anita Paradis, Diane Pepin, Maria Phillips, Catharine Piuze, Bernadette Pratt, Cynthia Pugh, Kerri Quirt, Rose-Marie Racine, Myrna MacDonald Ridley, Lisa Roberts, Lisa Rouleau, Caroline Rosenbloom, Jeannine St. Amand, Loree Siermachesky, Rochelle Simon, Cathy Smale, Kimberlee Smit, Janice Smith, Janie Smith, Jennifer Smith, Christy Sneddon, Sherry Sollows, Helena Steinmetz, Susan Stilwell, Elizabeth Taylor, Lynda Timms, Melinda Tuck, Lise Van Beilen, Kristina Vienneau, Lori Voth, Kelly Wall, Cathy Watson, Tanya Weiner, Judith White, Stephanie Whyte, Joanne Wilson, Julia Wolst, Lynn Woodford.

I'd also like to thank the book's technical reviewers for the time and effort they put into reviewing various portions of the manuscript:
- Richard Whatley, M.D., a brilliant and compassionate family physician whose insightful comments contributed a great deal to the book
- Laura Devine, R.N., a caring and committed nurse who also happens to be one of the most "together" parents I've ever met!

- Lorrie Baird, a faculty member in the early childhood education program at Sir Sandford Fleming College and home daycare provider extraordinaire whose insightful comments on the chapters on child development, play, and creative discipline contributed tremendously to the book
- Cathy L. Kerr, M.A., psychologist and early childhood consultant, who suggested some excellent additions to the chapters on child development and play
- Brenda Wines-Moher, R.D., a dietitian and metric conversion whiz kid whose comments on the nutrition chapter were extremely helpful and who saved me from making a grievous error (encouraging parents to serve their toddlers "chopped children" as opposed to "chopped chicken")

As always, I am grateful to my husband, Neil, and my children, Julie, Scott, Erik, and Ian, for putting up with the usual book deadline insanity (think takeout, takeout, and more takeout!), and my research assistant and friend Diane Wolf for going above and beyond the duty on many occasions while I was busy researching and writing this book. (How can you say a proper thank you to someone who will drop everything to make an emergency run to Tim Horton's on your behalf?)

I also owe a huge debt of gratitude to Canada's most patient editor, Susan Girvan, who never let on how crazy I was making her when I needed to request a month-long extension for this book. Susan, a career in the theatre and/or the diplomatic service awaits you!

And as for the rest of the unsung heroes at the now-defunct CDG Books—Joan Whitman, Robert Harris, Jennifer Smith, Tom Best, Jamie Broadhurst, Scott Mitchell, and countless others—what can I say except, "Thanks for the memories." It's been a privilege and pleasure working with you.

Table of Contents

CHAPTER 7
Will the Sandman Ever Come? 325

Introduction

YOU'VE JUST BEEN THROUGH an intensive year-long training program designed to build your patience, increase your stamina, and test your ability to survive with little or no sleep. The goal of all this training? To prepare you for The Mother of All Challenges—surviving the toddler years!

While raising a toddler certainly isn't for the faint of heart or the squeamish, it isn't nearly as difficult as some people would have you believe. The very same people who had you scared silly about going into labour are doing a similar number on you right now, convincing you that parenting a toddler is guaranteed to be an exercise in torture. Their eyes positively gleam as they bombard you with hair-raising tales of temper tantrums, hunger strikes, and the perils of potty training. The end result? You're left with this sinking feeling that you've just signed up to be a contestant on the most frightening reality television show to date: Toddler TV!

Fortunately, the scaremongers are about to fall off your radar screen for the next 10 years or so, patiently biding their time until they can terrorize you with even scarier tales about teenagers. Until that happens, tune them out. After all, you've already figured out that their stories about 15-pound newborns, 96-hour labours, and foot-long episiotomy scars were, well, a little overblown. So it hardly makes sense to buy into their toddler tall tales, now does it?

A toddler by any other name

BEFORE WE GET too much further into the book, we'd better tackle an important terminology issue: the definition of the word *toddler*.

If you pick up an armful of parenting books, you'll see that child development experts aren't exactly in agreement about the term. Some experts insist that toddlerhood begins at age 12 months; others don't grant a baby toddler status until age 18 months or until he's actually walking. But where the *real* disagreement arises is in deciding when to mark an end to the toddler years. Some experts claim that toddlerhood lasts until a child starts school (around age five). Others argue that the toddler years come to an end as soon as a child turns three, at which point he becomes a preschooler (ages three and four).

I tend to buy into this last school of thought. The reason is simple: I can't imagine lumping one-year-olds and four-year-olds together into the same category. It's hard enough to talk about one- and two-year-olds in the same breath, given the lightning speed at which developmental breakthroughs occur during the toddler years. I mean, preschoolers are practically civilized beings in many ways, while toddlers—toddlers—well, let's just say toddlers are not. So there you go: that's my rationale for focusing on one- and two-year-olds in this book and leaving the three- and four-year-olds for the next book in this series: *The Mother of All Parenting Books*.

Made in Canada

NOW THAT WE'VE pinned down the definition of a toddler, let's get another important bit of housekeeping business out of the way: my rationale for writing a Canadian toddler book.

As you've no doubt gathered by now, the vast majority of toddler books—and parenting books in general—are written by American authors. While some might argue that there's no need for an all-Canadian parenting resource, I happen to disagree. If you flip through a typical American parenting book, you'll find pages and pages of material that simply doesn't apply to Canadian parents, like tips on shopping for juvenile products that may not even be available in this country. (In many cases, these products aren't available because they fail to measure up to our more rigorous product safety standards.) Even the chapters that are relevant to Canadian parents suffer from a major shortcoming: the expert sources cited time and time again in the book are almost exclusively American.

What Canadian parents need is a book that reflects the reality of raising a toddler in Canada—a book that zeroes in on the unique challenges that Canadian parents face (the doctor shortage that plagues many communities across the country, for example) and that contains up-to-the-minute advice from such respected Canadian health authorities as the Canadian Paediatric Society and Health Canada. (Believe it or not, health authorities on both sides of the border don't always see eye to eye on key pediatric health issues.)

Of course, it wouldn't be possible—or even advisable—to write a book that completely ignores what's happening south of the border. After all, some of the most significant breakthroughs in pediatric health in recent years have occurred in research laboratories in the U.S. What Canadian parents need, however, is a book that looks at that information through Canadian eyes and interprets it for a Canadian audience.

My publisher and I think we're on to something with this all-Canadian focus. After all, the response to the first two books in this series—*The Mother of All Pregnancy Books* and *The Mother of All Baby Books*—has been nothing short of phenomenal. But enough with the flag waving for now! Let me tell you a bit about what *The Mother of All Toddler Books* has to offer.

A one-of-a-kind toddler book

As you've no doubt noticed by now, books about toddlers tend to fall into one of two distinct categories: books that focus on toddler behaviour and books that focus on toddler health. *The Mother of All Toddler Books* covers both topics in exhaustive detail, doubling as a parenting book and a pediatric health reference book. (Hey, we didn't call it *The Mother of All Toddler Books* for nothing!)

If you take a quick flip through the book, you'll find a smorgasbord of valuable information, including

- a frank discussion of the joys and challenges of parenting a toddler;

- detailed information about the key developmental milestones for the toddler years;

- the facts about how your toddler's play style will evolve over the next two years;

- money-saving tips on choosing toys that will deliver the most bang for the buck;

- nitty-gritty advice on coping with all the toddler-related clutter in your life: storing toys, organizing art supplies, taming your toddler's stuffed animal collection, and so on;

- the facts about discipline: what works and what doesn't;

- parent-tested advice on coping with temper tantrums, biting, whining, and other frustrating types of toddler behaviour;

- sure-fire techniques for brushing your toddler's teeth, washing his hair, and otherwise keeping the dirt and grime at bay;

- nitty-gritty advice on choosing clothing and doing battle with the most common types of toddler-related stains;

- potty training do's and don'ts from parents who've survived this toddler rite of passage;

- the dirt on training pants, musical potties, and other potty-training paraphernalia;

- the secrets to serving up nutritious, toddler-pleasing meals;

- important information about choking, allergies, vitamin supplements, and other food-related health concerns;

- tried-and-true methods of coping with night terrors, bad dreams, the transition from crib to bed, and other nighttime parenting challenges;

- practical guidelines for coping with fevers and other toddler-related health concerns that can have you hitting the panic button (and speed dial!) at 3 a.m.;

- the facts on ear infections and antibiotic use;

- the inside scoop on travelling with a toddler;

- helpful suggestions on preparing your toddler for the birth of a new baby and practical advice on a variety of other family-related challenges;

- detailed information on potentially life-saving first-aid procedures;

- highly comprehensive safety checklists designed to help you toddlerproof each room in your home;

- a detailed glossary of pediatric health terms;

- a directory of Canadian organizations of interest to families with young children;

- a directory of Internet resources of interest to Canadian parents;

- toddler growth charts;

- immunization schedules;

- a list of recommended resources.

Of course, what makes *The Mother of All Toddler Books* really special are the contributions of the more than 100 Canadian parents who agreed to be interviewed for this book. I pulled together their best advice on weathering the biggest challenges of the toddler years and sprinkled their funniest and most touching anecdotes throughout. It's their from-the-trenches words of wisdom that really bring the book to life. After all, who better to turn to for advice on potty training than a mother who's just cleaned up her toddler's third puddle of the day?

You'll also find plenty of other bells and whistles as you make your way through the book:

Mom's the Word: insights and advice from parents of toddlers.

Mother Wisdom: little-known facts about toddlers, including some really fun pop-culture tidbits.

Toddler Talk: research updates and other important toddler-related information.

Fridge Notes: leads on resources of interest to parents of toddlers.

As you've no doubt gathered by now, *The Mother of All Toddler Books* is unlike any other toddler book you've ever encountered. It's comprehensive, it's fun to read, and— best of all—it's 100% Canadian-made!

I hope you enjoy the book.

Ann Douglas

P.S. My editors and I are determined to make *The Mother of All Toddler Books* the best toddler book available, so if you have any comments to pass along—good, bad, or ugly—we'd love to hear from you. You can either contact me via my Web site at www.having-a-baby.com or contact me via my publisher: John Wiley & Sons Canada Ltd., 22 Worcester Road, Etobicoke, ON, M9W 1L1.

CHAPTER 1

The Truth about Toddlers

"People always warn you about the terrible twos.
I prefer to call them the terrific twos."
—JULIE, 30, MOTHER OF ONE

"I think the term 'terrible twos' is dreadful because
it puts a negative twist on a beautiful experience.
Why not call them 'the wonder years' instead? My son
is in a daily state of wonder."
—KIMBERLEE, 28, MOTHER OF TWO

WELCOME TO THE toddler years—that exciting tight-rope walk that bridges the gap between babyhood and the preschool years. As any veteran parent can tell you, the toddler years are the best of times *and* the worst of times in one exciting yet exhausting package. There will be days when you're so head-over-heels in love with that wide-eyed, chubby-cheeked toddler that the mere thought of him ever growing up and moving away will bring tears to your eyes. And then there will be days when it's all you can do stop yourself from strapping all your toddler's worldly goods to the back of his tricycle and listing him for sale on eBay.

In this chapter, we're going to talk about how you may be feeling as your baby celebrates that milestone first birthday—whether you're more inclined to fumble for a tissue box or pour yourself a glass of champagne. Then we'll look at how parenting a toddler is different from parenting a baby. (I know, I know: just when you had the baby thing down pat, Mother Nature had to go and throw you a curveball!) Finally, we'll wrap up the chapter by getting down to the real nitty-gritty: the joys and challenges of raising a toddler.

From baby to toddler

THERE'S NO DOUBT about it: your child's first birthday is a major milestone for him and for you. How you feel about reaching this milestone will largely be determined by your parenting experiences during your baby's momentous first year of life. If you have fond memories of pushing a happy, gurgling baby around in a carriage, you may be reluctant to say goodbye to those baby days; if, on the other hand, you keep having flashbacks to all those endless nights spent pacing the floor with a colicky infant, you may be positively overjoyed to leave the baby stage behind.

"I was happy to have the first year over with," confesses Christy, a 38-year-old mother of two. "For me, it was one of the toughest years I had ever been through. I find having a baby a lot of work with very little reward."

"I personally found it a struggle when my daughter was a baby," adds Suzette, a 29-year-old mother of two. "She didn't sleep well, I was exhausted, and I felt very guilty because I didn't think I was living up to what society expected me to be as this baby's mother. Once she became more mobile and more communicative, I found her much easier to interact with. Not all mothers do well with the baby stage, and I was one of them."

Parents of higher-order multiples—triplets, quadruplets, and more—may be particularly eager to watch their babies celebrate that momentous first birthday. Yvonne—a 36-year-old mother of six—remembers feeling a tremendous sense of relief when her quintuplets reached that stage: "It was a huge milestone for us to know we'd made it through that first year. I'd been told by other mothers of higher-order multiples that nothing is as hard as the first year."

Of course, not every parent feels totally euphoric about having their baby's first birthday roll around. Many experience a mix of emotions: excitement about watching their child move on to the toddler stage, but sadness at leaving those special baby days behind. "I felt an incredible sense of joy and awe watching my daughter gazing at her birthday candles," recalls Laura, a 33-year-old mother of one. "I was very excited about her moving into her toddler years. She was already walking and speaking and I couldn't wait for her to start telling me how she felt about her day. And yet, at the same time, I was feeling a little sad. Over the course of a year, she had grown up so much."

MOM'S THE WORD

"I experienced a few moments of sadness as Alexis turned one, realizing that the completely dependent stage was over for good. She would never again need me in that baby way. And from this point forward, she would need me even less in her eagerness for independence."

—Karen, 33, mother of three

Watching your child blow out the candle on his birthday cake can be particularly poignant if you feel fairly certain that you aren't going to be having any more babies. Catherine, a 32-year-old mother of four, explains: "When the twins' first birthday came up, I remember watching them making a mess in their high chairs, thinking to myself, 'We made it!' I was so proud at that moment to know that they were healthy and well. But I also had a nice long cry that night when all our guests had left, knowing that these were the last babies I would ever have. I would never again have a baby, nurse a baby, and do all those things that mommies do with their newborns. That was difficult—and yet, at the same time, I knew we were entering a whole new stage of life. Our youngest children were now entering the toddler years and things would get easier (or at least we hoped they would!) and our life would now revolve around all the fun things you can do with older kids. And so I wrote a little goodbye note in each of my twins' diaries that night, saying goodbye to their babyhood and welcome to the big kid years. I was proud to have known them as babies, and would be even prouder to help them grow into strong, good-hearted boys and men."

While you may find yourself feeling a little wistful as your child's babyhood comes to an end, it's important to remind yourself that equally magic moments await you and your child in the months—and years—to come. "Sometimes I think to myself, 'This is incredible. I wish I could freeze time right here,'" says

---

MOM'S THE WORD

"I was thrilled to celebrate my daughter's first birthday. I think I felt somewhat heroic. I had survived! With my son, who will likely be my last child, I found myself in tears when the company cleared and the house was quiet again. I'm not quite as enthusiastic about the passing of time now."

—*Kimberlee, 28, mother of two*

Kimberlee, a 28-year-old mother of two. "And, of course, time rolls on and once again it seems perfect."

Helena, a 32-year-old mother of one, agrees that it's important to focus on what lies ahead: "I think that if you always look back then you don't enjoy what you have—and toddlerhood has its wonderful moments, too."

Getting psyched for year two

THERE'S NO DENYING IT: the rules of the game have just changed forever. You're no longer responsible for caring for a baby; you've just become the parent of a toddler. Here's the scoop on how your role as a parent is likely to change during the exciting and sometimes exhausting months ahead:

- **You'll spend less time taking care of your child's physical needs and more time attending to his other needs.** While you won't have to attend to your child's physical needs to quite the same degree as you did when he was a baby (he'll become more skilled at feeding himself during the months ahead, and—if the potty training gods are with you—he may even show some interest in toilet training), you'll spend a lot of time and energy trying to satisfy his almost insatiable hunger for new experiences. While many parents find this to be the most enjoyable aspect of raising a toddler, others find the pace to be a little overwhelming. "I'm at a constant loss as to how to keep my two-and-a-half-year-old son stimulated," confesses Elizabeth, a 27-year-old mother of three. "Some days, it's tempting to just leave him in front of the TV, especially when there are things around the house that need to be done and other children to tend to. I think we've done every activity ever invented a hundred times."

MOM'S THE WORD

"I definitely prefer the toddler stage over the baby stage. The toddler stage gives you the opportunity to teach and guide your child through so many things. You can play and engage a toddler in so many activities and then enjoy them along with your child. The baby stage doesn't offer the same opportunities, and sometimes you feel like nothing more than a slave to the baby's schedule and needs."

—*Tanya, 30, mother of two*

- **The way you relate to your child will change.** "Parenting a baby is so much about keeping them safe and dry and fed and happy," says Lisa, a 36-year-old mother of two. "Parenting a toddler is about that and so much more. It's about helping them take those steps away from you—both literally and figuratively. It's about watching to see what interests them most and then helping them to explore that more." Karen, a 33-year-old mother of three, agrees that there are many new challenges associated with parenting a toddler: "Parenting a baby is about giving time, giving love, giving energy, giving of self. Parenting a toddler is harder because you're giving space. Space for that toddler to attempt and fail and attempt again. Space to learn. Space to explore. Space to grow."

- **You'll get a clearer sense of your child's personality.** Your child's had a personality of his own right from day one, of course, but it's during the toddler years that you start to get a strong sense of who he is as a person—whether he's happy and easygoing or the ultimate control freak. As Heather, a 23-year-old mother of two, notes: "I prefer toddlerhood because I love watching my son's little personality blossom. Toddlers truly become 'little people.'" And once you have an idea about what makes your child tick, you can start figuring out which types of parenting strategies will work best with him. After all, there's no such thing as "one size fits all" in the often weird but generally wonderful world of parenting.

- **You'll be able to download some of your childrearing responsibilities to other people, including your partner.** While babies tend to view anyone other than the keeper of the breasts (a.k.a. Mom) as second-rate, toddlers are ready to open their hearts to a growing number of people. At the top of their list? Why, Daddy, of course! Whether he realizes it or not, your baby's father is about to become your toddler's favourite toy—something that will mean a little more freedom for you. Jo-Anne, a 43-year-old mother of seven, explains: "Toddlers turn to their fathers more often than babies do. They can go off in the car together without worrying about being nursed in an hour. They can run around in the park and enjoy more physical games. In this sense, it's less intense for me, the mother, than the baby stage." And it's not just moms who are relieved to share the star billing in their toddlers' hearts: dads seem to appreciate their new role at centre stage, too. As Kelly, a 31-year-old mother of two, explains: "Now that my twins are toddlers, my husband feels more like a parent and less like 'Mommy's assistant.'"

- **You may feel more confident in your parenting abilities.** It's not just your partner who is likely to be feeling more confident about this parenting thing: chances are you are, too. After all, you've survived a whole year of baby boot camp. Your confidence can also be boosted by the simple fact that your child suddenly seems a whole lot less breakable. As Helena, a 32-year-old mother of one, puts it: "Toddlers seem sturdier—not as fragile as babies."

- **You may feel increased pressure to do a good job as a parent.** Being a parent is hard work—the most difficult job in the world, in fact. And what makes it even tougher is knowing

MOM'S THE WORD

"The move from babyhood to toddlerhood is difficult from a social perspective. Babies are welcome almost anywhere. Everyone wants to see and hold them. Toddlers, on the other hand, are sometimes seen as a nuisance."

—*Joan, 35, mother of five*

that you're under constant scrutiny from others around you—scrutiny that tends to intensify during the toddler years. "If your baby starts crying at the mall, most people smile sympathetically and say, 'Someone needs a nap,'" explains Terri, a 34-year-old mother of three. "But if that same child is a little older, people give you a look that says, 'What a brat!' Dealing with a toddler's emotional outbursts is difficult enough without the glares and stares of strangers."

- **You'll get a taste of your "old life" again.** After a year of stumbling around in a sleep-deprived fog, you'll finally get a taste of some of the perks that come along with parenting a slightly older child—small but sanity-preserving things like sleeping for more than two to three hours at a stretch and eating your dinner while it's still warm. If you've got a particularly vivid imagination and/or are into self-delusion, you may even be able to convince yourself that you've got your old life back. (But, frankly, for most of us, that's a bit of a stretch.)

As you can see, there will be plenty of noteworthy changes during the months ahead as your baby makes the transition from baby to toddler—proof positive that becoming a parent is the ultimate personal growth experience! Now let's talk about how some of those changes are likely to play out in the months to come.

The challenges and joys
of raising a toddler

YOU'VE NO DOUBT heard plenty about the challenges of raising a toddler: after all, that's the stuff of which parenting magazines and really bad sitcoms are made. What you might not have heard as much about are the joys of parenting a toddler—something that should go a long way toward explaining one of the greatest mysteries of our time: why some parents sign up for more than one tour of duty through toddlerhood! But just so that we can hold onto that mystery a little longer, we're going to tackle this thing in reverse order, starting out with the challenges and then working our way back to the joys. (What can I say? I've always been a sucker for happy endings.)

The challenges

As promised, here's a whole laundry list of reasons why parenting a toddler is not for the weak of heart—to say nothing of the weak of stomach!

- **Toddlers are fiercely independent.** If toddlers had their own theme song, it would have to be Frank Sinatra's "My Way." But whether they're prepared to admit it or not, they still need a lot of help from you. Unfortunately, that help may not always be welcome: "My two-year-old is very independent

---

MOM'S THE WORD

"It's not all sunshine and roses. The temper tantrums can be horrendous. Trying to reason with a 26-pound time bomb in the middle of a packed shopping mall can be a very delicate operation."

—*Myrna, 34, mother of one*

and wants to do everything himself," says Tanya, a 30-year-old mother of two. "Any assistance you give that wasn't requested leads to a huge fit."

- **Toddlers are easily frustrated.** At the root of this frustration is the fact that their abilities can't keep pace with their ambition: your toddler is determined to make a tower with his blocks and becomes enraged when he lacks the manual dexterity to do so. The upside to this drive to achieve is the fact that toddlers are extraordinarily persistent. One day soon your toddler will amaze you with his tower-building abilities.

- **Toddlers are highly volatile.** It takes years for children to learn how to cope with strong emotions, and toddlers simply aren't there yet. As Terri, a 34-year-old mother of three, puts it: "If someone had told me that toddlerhood was like PMS, mood swings and all, I think I would have had a better idea of what to expect."

- **Toddlers are highly impulsive.** Rather than slowing down long enough to weigh the pros and cons of eating dirt or climbing on top of the TV, toddlers just do it. That's why you have to keep such a tight watch on them: they can get themselves into trouble when you're not looking—and sometimes even when you are! One of the moms interviewed for this book thought her toddler was having some innocent fun with a bucket of water until she noticed the empty Kool-Aid package beside it. In the blink of an eye, her daughter had managed to dye her hands green. And as any parent who has tried to wash Kool-Aid off a child's skin can tell you, the dye in Kool-Aid is powerful stuff indeed. It sticks to skin like crazy glue.

- **Toddlers operate on their own time clock.** "Toddler time" can either be extremely fast (when your toddler is magnetically pulled toward the closest hazardous object) or painfully slow (when he shrieks "Me do it!" when you're trying to get him dressed in a hurry). When your toddler dawdles over breakfast, he isn't the least bit worried about whether he's going to make you late for work: he's having too much fun floating his crusts in his juice! And if you try to rush your toddler, you'll only end up frustrating yourself and him. "The biggest challenge for me is to give my toddler the time he needs to stop and smell the roses," admits Maria, a 32-year-old mother of two. "Too many times I'm after him to move faster, go quickly, hurry up, don't dilly-dally. But all he wants to do is explore. Who can blame him? His world is fascinating to him and he's just now learning how to communicate all the wonders of the world through words and actions. I need to stop and let him just be a toddler, stop and let him take his time, stop and let him explore and learn."

- **Toddlers have a limited attention span.** They don't stick with any one task for very long. "Once children move into toddlerhood, the days seem to get divided into smaller and smaller chunks," explains Jo-Anne, a 43-year-old mother of seven. "Toddlers want to do everything, but only for a short time. Time moves incredibly quickly and the pace can be exhausting."

- **Toddlers are highly egocentric.** They have not yet learned how to take other people's thoughts and feelings into account, and they're driven to find out just how much power they have over other people by constantly testing the limits. The child development experts stress that a toddler's self-centeredness is a good thing: it means that your toddler is developing a strong sense of himself. That doesn't necessarily mean, however, that it's easy to deal with a member of the "me generation." It can be frustrating and exhausting, to say the least.

- **Toddlers demand your undivided attention.** Gone are the days when you could flip through a magazine while your baby was having a romp in her bouncy seat: your toddler wants you to make eye contact with him every second of the day! And as for heading down the hall to use the washroom on your own—you really are dreaming in technicolour, now aren't you? While it's nice to be the centre of someone's universe, it's also a little bit exhausting. I swear, parenthood is the only job on the planet that doesn't guarantee you a coffee break or a lunch hour!

The joys

Fortunately, it's not all gloom and doom on the toddler front. Raising a toddler can also be tremendously rewarding. Here's why:

- **Toddlers are highly affectionate.** They're generous with their heartfelt hugs and wet kisses. And when they manage to utter their first soulful "I love you"—well, that's pretty much as good as life gets. "Toddlers bring more joy simply because they give love back," says Janie, a 33-year-old mother of one. "Babies are a bit of a one-way street in that regard."

- **Toddlers are fun to be with.** Whether they're stringing words together with hysterical results or hamming it up for the camera, it can be a lot of fun to spend time with a toddler. "I know how to make my daughter laugh and jump and dance," says Debbie, 33, mother of one. "She always wants to play" and it's easy to make almost anything into a game."

- **Toddlers have a passion for learning.** They're eager to explore every inch of their world. "Madison learns something new every hour of the day," insists Sidney, a 33-year-old mother of one.

- **Toddlers find joy in little things.** "One of the biggest joys is seeing the world through a toddler's eyes," says Terri, a 34-year-old mother of three. "Things that seemed so ordinary suddenly become new and exciting. This is the first year my one-year-old has taken notice of the leaves falling from the trees. It gives me a chance to teach him about the changing of the seasons. I can't wait for the first snowfall so that I can see the look on his face."

- **Toddlers are learning how to communicate.** This is the age at which language development really explodes. "For me, the biggest joy of parenting a toddler is being able to communicate with your child," says Janet, a 34-year-old mother of one. "When Malorie was a baby, she was able to communicate her basic needs, but I had no idea what she was thinking about. Now that she can speak, she's able to tell me about the hundreds of little discoveries she's making each day. I feel like I'm discovering her personality through our interactions."

Do toddlers get a bad rap?

AS YOU'VE NO DOUBT noticed by now, toddlers tend to get a bad rap in our society. Instead of celebrating their growing independence and the accompanying stubborn streak, we tend to treat their quest for autonomy as some sort of counter-revolutionary activity. On those particularly frustrating days—

the days when you realize you've heard the word "no" a dozen times already and it's not even 7:00 a.m.—it can be helpful to remind yourself that your toddler isn't trying to undermine your authority; he's just trying to assert his own. As Selma H. Fraiberg notes in her book *The Magic Years,* "It's a kind of declaration of independence, but there is no intention to unseat the government."

Like many parents, Janet, a 34-year-old mother of one, feels that toddlers are greatly misunderstood. "Society leads us to believe that toddlers are terrors and that it's a huge burden to be a parent of a toddler," she explains. "In fact, once you understand that a lot of your child's 'bad' behaviour can be explained by developmental issues (she screams and cries while pointing at something because she doesn't have the words to tell you that she wants to touch it; she cries when she can't put her own shoes on because she lacks the coordination to do so and yet she really wants to help out; she cries when you're busy in the kitchen because she can't see what you're doing above the counter), then it becomes a challenge to help your child overcome the developmental obstacles and to channel his or her energies positively. This doesn't always work and there are times when the child is really a handful, but most of the time it's an exciting challenge to be raising your own little human being, particularly as you

---

MOM'S THE WORD

"Everyone talks about how unruly toddlers are and how difficult it can be to get through this stage, but I think toddlers are the most wonderful people. I'm not saying they're angels, but they're so busy exploring everything—their environment, themselves, their emotions, other people—that they treat life as one big adventure. I love this age. It's so exciting to watch."

—*Candice, 28, mother of one*

MOM'S THE WORD

"I'm glad I don't remember my toddlerhood; I'd probably be having nightmares about it!"

—*Catherine, 32, mother of four*

discover more about your child's personality, his or her likes and dislikes."

Catherine, a 32-year-old mother of four, believes that a lot of parent–toddler conflicts could be avoided if parents made a greater effort to try to understand what life must be like for a toddler. "Imagine what it would be like to be a couple of feet tall and trying to find your place in the world. You're not permitted to touch anything, you can't go where you want, you can't eat what you want, everything is so big, everyone else makes decisions for you, and people don't always notice that you're there—unless you do something bad. It must be terribly confusing, perhaps frightening, and we as parents need to help them through this time so that they can learn to trust themselves and the world around them. Speak to them with respect. Listen to their opinions. Acknowledge their fears and feelings. And finally, love them as they deserve to be loved."

CHAPTER 2

The Incredible Growing Toddler

*"I love the fact that parents and kids grow together. You don't
suddenly find yourself with a toddler; your baby turns into
a toddler and you both move through the stages together."*
—LISA, 36, MOTHER OF TWO

MOTHER NATURE WAS very wise indeed to schedule a little pre-season training before sending you off to the big leagues (a.k.a. toddlerhood). After all, the powerful bond that you've been forging with your child right from day one will serve you well during the exciting and action-packed toddler years.

The toddler years are, after all, a time of amazing firsts for both you and your child—a time to learn and grow together. You'll have the opportunity to look on in wonder as your toddler adds to her repertoire of skills week by week, day by day, sometimes even hour by hour.

And in between the major milestone achievements that the child development books pay so much attention to—the moment when your child utters her first words or takes her first steps—there will be a million and one other mini-milestones to celebrate as your child makes her journey through toddlerhood. The first time she manages to steer the spaghetti fork from the bowl to her mouth. The first time she remembers to pat the cat *gently*. And, of course, the first time she pees in the potty!

In this chapter, we're going to focus on toddler development. We'll start out by talking about what developmental milestones can—and can't—tell you about your child. (Hint: Walking on your first birthday doesn't necessarily guarantee you a spot in the Harvard Medical School class of 2025.) After we've talked about the limitations of developmental milestones in predicting your toddler's future career path, we'll run through a laundry list of the specific developmental milestones that you can expect your toddler to achieve at various points during the next two years— give or take a couple of months, of course. Next we'll zero in on the two most dramatic milestones your child is likely to achieve during the toddler years: learning how to talk and learning how to walk. Then we'll wrap up the chapter by touching upon a perennial hot topic for parents of toddlers: when and how gender differences come into play.

Milestones revisited: Why it's not a good idea to compare toddlers

FORGET ABOUT KEEPING up with the Joneses when it comes to superficial things like how big a house you live in or what kind of car you drive. If you want to indulge in the ultimate game of one-upmanship, try comparing kids instead!

As you've no doubt noticed by now, parents tend to get very competitive when comparing the achievements of their offspring, constantly looking for evidence that their child is genius material. As Judith, a 33-year-old mother of one, notes ruefully: "Each and every child in the daycare that I direct is 'gifted'—at least according to their parents!"

So what drives parents to compare every detail about their toddlers' development, timing the achievement of the most bragworthy milestones right down to the minutes and seconds? According to Lori, a 31-year-old mother of five, this urge to compare stems from a desire to reassure yourself that your child is progressing on schedule: "It's very tempting to compare one child to another—either to another one of your children or to a friend's child, which can be upsetting for one or both parents. Even though logically we know that all children develop at different rates, it's worrisome when your child isn't doing all the same things as the neighbour's child who's the same age. Parents always want to know if their children are progressing 'normally.'"

Understandable or not, sometimes the endless comparisons can be a little hard to stomach—particularly if you know some- one who seems determined to keep proving how much smarter her toddler is than yours. "A friend of mine is constantly telling me how gifted her son is at absolutely everything," complains Kelly, a 31-year-old mother of two. "I resent the implication that my children aren't as special as her child is. It's starting to cause problems in our friendship."

Of course, comparisons aren't always a bad thing. Sometimes they can alert you to the fact that your child may be lagging behind in a particular area of development. Brandy discovered that her older child was experiencing some developmental delays

---

MOM'S THE WORD

"I have two close girlfriends with children the same age as Joey. Each one of the three children has reached some developmental stage before the other two children, so it evens out eventually."

—*Alyson, 37, mother of two*

MOM'S THE WORD

"My daughter has excelled in almost all areas. In fact, when she was 18 months old, our pediatrician recommended that we start reading about gifted children. My only concern for her is that although she's advanced both intellectually and physically, she's still just a 22-month-old child. People perceive her to be older than she is, and this can be frustrating both for her and for us. I have to remind myself and others around her that she's still just a baby and needs time to cuddle and to cry and to be a little person."

—*Sidney, 33, mother of one*

---

only when her second child began to surpass him in language abilities, social skills, and so on. "It was only then that I knew there was a problem," the 24-year-old mother of two explains.

Still, there are times when comparisons can do more harm than good—a lesson that Kelli, a 32-year-old mother of one, learned the hard way. "I spent most of my daughter's first year of life fretting about the fact that she didn't seem to be developing as quickly as other children her age. She sat, crawled, and walked much later than all my friends' children and she was also a bit smaller. Suddenly, she turned one and is now off the chart for height and weight, running around with ease, and talking up a storm. I spent too much time worrying about what she wasn't doing and not relishing all the wonderful and fascinating things she was doing."

The tyranny of timelines

What parents like Kelli can temporarily lose sight of is the fact that no two children follow the exact same timeline in growth and development. The fact that your child is lagging a little behind is not necessarily cause for concern. As Dorothy Corkville Briggs notes in her book *Your Child's Self-Esteem*, "Every child has an inner timetable for growth—a pattern unique to him.... Growth is not steady, forward, upward progression. It is instead a switchback trail; three steps forward, two back, one around the bushes, and a few simply standing, before another forward leap."

While it can be helpful to look at timelines summarizing the point by which your toddler can be expected to have achieved particular developmental milestones (see Table 2.1), it's important to keep in mind that what you're looking at is a rough sketch rather than a rigid blueprint for development. So take heart: the fact that your toddler isn't progressing at quite the same rate as the other kids at daycare when it comes to potty training doesn't necessarily mean that she's sentenced to a lifetime of being an "also ran." It simply means she has other things on her mind than perfecting her toileting techniques!

That's not to say that charts outlining the key developmental milestones for the toddler years are entirely without merit. If they were, I would hardly have chosen to include such a detailed one in this book. What these charts can do is give you an indication of the rough order and the approximate age at which toddlers tend to master particular skills and an approximate idea of when these milestones are generally achieved by a "typical" toddler (although who that mythical toddler is, I have no idea).

MOM'S THE WORD

"My twins were slow to walk, slow to talk—just basically behind when I compared them with their two older siblings. I should never have compared them. That was my first mistake. And having family members constantly asking if they were doing this or that yet drove me nuts! Finally, I decided to do a little research and found that, in many cases, twins develop at a different rate than singletons. Once I knew that for sure, I was able to reassure concerned family members that there wasn't anything to worry about."

—*Catherine, 32, mother of four*

While most toddlers make minor deviations from the developmental timeline, if a toddler is consistently missing milestones it could be an indication that her development is lagging behind that of her age mates for some reason. According to Statistics Canada, developmental delays occur in approximately 17% of boys and 11% of girls under the age of three, so it's important to be alert to the warning signs of a developmental delay. (See Table 2.2.)

In some cases, the reason for the delay may be apparent. If your baby was born prematurely, for example, your doctor will encourage you to think in terms of her developmental age rather than her chronological age when you're trying to figure out where she should be at. "I think that when you have preemies, you're even more acutely aware of milestones," says Jennie, a 32-year-old mother of two. "We were always working to help the boys meet their milestones."

And if your child was born with a serious medical condition, you may have to take that into account as well. "Our second child had a serious heart defect, which made it impossible to compare her to her older sister," explains Karen, a 33-year-old mother of three. "She didn't reach 10 pounds until her first birthday. So we learned how to accept each child as she was and to celebrate her achievements individually."

Of course, the same thing applies if your child has been identified as having some sort of developmental delay, such as Down Syndrome. In this case, you should forget about fixating on your child's chronological age and focus on her developmental age instead. Your baby's doctor will be able to give you an indication of where your baby should be at given any medical conditions or developmental challenges she's dealing with.

Regardless of when your toddler achieves a particular developmental milestone—whether it's sooner rather than later, or vice versa—you can expect to experience tremendous pride and

MOTHER WISDOM

Sometimes development in one area slows down when a toddler is busy mastering other types of skills. Bottom line? If your toddler is absorbed in learning the mechanics of walking, she may not be much of a conversationalist right now!

---

joy. Jennie, 32, reflects on what it's been like to watch her twin with cerebral palsy master the walking-related milestones that came much easier and sooner to his able-bodied twin: "We thought Matthew's first steps were miraculous, and they were, but Andrew's first steps are a wonder to behold. He has yet to take unassisted steps, but in the past 12 months he's gone from being a child who may never take a step to a child who's capable of moving his legs forward, bearing weight on them, and who is very, very close to taking a step." Jennie feels particularly joyful when she recalls what it was like to watch Andrew start using his walker: "The smile on his face when he realized that he was mobile for the first time and face-to-face with the other kids was worth all the frustration and struggle to get him to that point."

Developmental milestones of the toddler years

THE TODDLER YEARS are a very exciting time to be a parent. Every time you turn around, your toddler has mastered another new skill. Here's what to expect every few months in terms of the physical, cognitive, language and social/emotional development of your incredible growing toddler.

TABLE 2.1

Physical, Cognitive, and Social/Emotional Highlights

	Your 12-Month-Old
Physical Development (Gross Motor and Fine Motor Skills)	↑ Either already walking or is about to take her exciting first step—the Mother of All Kodak Moments! Her wide-legged gait makes it very clear why one-year-olds are known as toddlers. (From a functional perspective, the gait actually makes a lot of sense: it lowers her centre of gravity and helps to improve her stability.) You'll also notice that these first efforts at walking require a tremendous amount of concentration. During the weeks ahead, your toddler will constantly be checking where her feet are in relation to objects around her.
	↑ Capable of stacking blocks and working with very simple frame-style puzzles (the kind where a piece with a handle fits into a wooden or plastic frame of the same shape). She's also becoming a pro at placing objects inside one another (e.g., nesting cubes) and can grasp a crayon and use it to make a mark on a paper. Her self-feeding skills are improving and she enjoys helping you turn the pages in her books.
	↑ May be starting to show a preference for one hand over the other but still uses both hands freely.
	↑ Can use her index finger and thumb (pincer grip) to pick up small objects like peas or Cheerios on her high-chair tray. This new-found skill also allows her to pick up screws, pebbles, and other tiny—and hazardous—objects that she happens to find lying around, so you'll need to watch her extremely carefully.

continued on p. 32

Your 12-Month-Old (continued)

Perceptual/Cognitive Development

↑ Able to use some very basic methods of sorting toys (e.g., grouping them by colour or shape).

↑ Enjoys "dump and fill" play (e.g., dumping all the blocks out of a container and then filling the container up again).

↑ Can take apart a set of stacking rings and can use a basic shape-sorter.

Language Development

↑ May understand as few as three words or as many as 100 words, but it's unlikely that she's able to say more than a dozen words at this stage—likely "mama," "dada," some explanatory expressions (e.g., "oh-oh"), and a few names of objects.

↑ Can follow simple one-step directions (e.g., "Go get your boots.")

↑ Understands the meaning of the word "no"—but may not always listen!

Social/Emotional Development

↑ Becoming increasingly independent—insisting on feeding and attempting to dress or undress herself. Her catchphrase will soon become an indignant "Me do it!"

↑ Enjoys exploring her environment and testing your reactions.

↑ Enjoys showing you her toys and will sometimes agree to hand the toy over if you ask for it.

Your 15-Month-Old

Physical Development (Gross Motor and Fine Motor Skills)

↑ Continues to use the wide-legged gait so characteristic of children her age, but her walking skills are improving by the day. She hardly ever falls now, and when she does she just picks herself up and tries again. She's got places to go and people to see!

↑ Has mastered the art of walking, and now has a new trick up her sleeve—climbing. Suddenly she's ready to climb anything and everything in sight. Don't be surprised if she manages to climb out of her crib one morning or if you find her standing on the kitchen counter one day, pointing proudly at the chair she used to climb up. (Of course, it's a lot more difficult to get down than up, so you may get summoned to rescue your little climber countless times each day.)

↑ Balance is still imperfect, but is improving by the day. By the end of this month, she should be able to stand on one leg for brief periods of time.

↑ Enjoys splashing around in water, but may become upset if the beach where she's playing is too crowded or she keeps getting splashed. (Many adults react the same way!)

↑ Fine motor skills are improving by leaps and bounds. She's becoming quite masterful at using cups, spoons, and crayons; building towers that are up to three blocks high; and turning the pages of books. She's also capable of holding two small items in each hand at the same time—something that opens up a whole new world of play possibilities for her.

↑ Enjoys playing with pull-toys.

↑ Hand preference may be becoming apparent. She's likely to start favouring one hand over the other when she's feeding herself or holding a crayon.

↑ May get annoyed or upset if her hands are dirty, which may put a damper on your efforts to introduce her to "messy" crafts like fingerpainting. This stage tends to be short-lived, however, so don't assume you'll be getting off scot-free in the mud puddle department just yet!

Perceptual/Cognitive Development

↑ Learning how to use different types of skills at the same time: e.g., concentration, memory, hand–eye coordination, and problem solving to figure out how to tackle a complex task such as a puzzle or how to rescue a toy that's stuck under the couch. Her increased attention span makes more demanding tasks possible.

continued on p. 34

Your 15-Month-Old (continued)

Perceptual/Cognitive Development (continued)	↑ Learning how to classify objects. For example, if you show her a plastic truck and a wooden truck, she'll understand that they have something in common, even though she may not yet know the word for truck.
	↑ Starting to take note of where she leaves her favourite toys so that she can find them again—a major breakthrough in perceptual/cognitive development.
Language Development	↑ Ability to understand what she hears is growing by leaps and bounds. Some studies have indicated that toddlers this age may be able to comprehend many hundreds of words, particularly names of household objects, toys, clothing, people and pets, and the verbs they're exposed to most often. Nonetheless, your toddler is likely to be frustrated by the fact that there's a huge gap between the number of words she understands and the number of words she's able to say. Many early childhood development experts believe that this helps to explain why there tends to be a sudden increase in the amount of crying in toddlers this age.
	↑ Relies on both gestures and words to communicate with you. Almost all the words she can say at this point are nouns used to label people and objects.
Social/Emotional Development	↑ Can be laughing one minute and crying the next. Mood swings are the norm for toddlers this age. You may also notice that she's a little extra-clingy: while she's eager to explore the world around her, she wants to keep you in her sight at all times.
	↑ Beginning to assert her independence, which can lead to temper tantrums when she doesn't get her own way.
	↑ Becoming increasingly interested in including you in her experiences. If she sees something exciting, she wants to show it to you right away. A toddler's needs are immediate, intense, and personal.

↑ Becoming more tuned in to your emotions and may even try to comfort you if you seem to be distressed.

↑ Starts engaging in functional play (play that imitates the types of things she sees you doing, like using a computer or pushing a vacuum cleaner around the house). She's also very interested in cause-and-effect toys like jack-in-the-boxes.

↑ Beginning to acquire some rudimentary social graces, like passing a toy to another child. Don't expect her to share her toys consistently, however. She's not ready to do that quite yet.

↑ May be very possessive insofar as you're concerned. If you pay attention to another child, she may become quite jealous. It's her way of telling the world that her mommy or daddy is "Mine, all mine!"

Your 18-Month-Old

Physical Development (Gross Motor and Fine Motor Skills)

↑ Has mastered the mechanics involved in walking, running, and climbing. Now she's working on her balance—a skill that will serve her well when it comes time to start walking rather than crawling upstairs.

↑ Able to tackle more than one task while she's on the go: for example, dragging a pull-toy behind her as she walks.

↑ Fine motor skills are improving by leaps and bounds. She can now pick up small pieces of bread or cereal smoothly and accurately. She's also likely to be a pro with her spoon by now, but chances are she often reverts to finger-feeding since it's still easier.

† Enjoys playing with modelling materials such as playdough, clay, or sand. She's no longer quite as freaked out about touching wet or sticky substances (assuming, of course, she was freaked out in the first place: some kids are born to love messy play!)

continued on p. 36

Your 18-Month-Old (continued)

Physical Development (continued)	↑ Becoming increasingly coordinated in her play: she can pour water from one container to another without too much spilling or splashing.
Perceptual/Cognitive Development	↑ Developing a stronger sense of self and is able to recognize herself in the mirror.
	↑ Attention span is increasing and her recall memory is improving. She'll amaze you with her ability to point to the various parts of her body as you name them.
	↑ Can differentiate between round and square shapes, a skill that comes in handy when she plays with her shape-sorter toy. She can also recognize a growing number of colours by name.
Language Development	↑ Language comprehension skills continue to improve. She's able to understand such simple commands as "Put the cup on the table." Her language production is also increasing rapidly: she's picking up about five or six new words each week and may even be using a few two-word sentences. Of course, language abilities at this age vary tremendously. One study involving 20-month-olds found that the size of their vocabularies ranged from one word to 400 words!
	↑ Uses her own name to refer to herself rather than using the appropriate pronoun.
	↑ Attempts to sing songs with words.
	↑ Imitates noises that she hears in her environment (e.g., a police siren or the sound of a dog barking).
Social/Emotional Development	↑ Has developed a much stronger sense of self. She soaks up praise like a sponge.
	↑ Has turned into a social butterfly, freely giving out hugs and kisses to the people she cares most about. (On the flip side, it's pretty easy to tell from her body language when she doesn't want anything to do with a particular person—which can prove a little embarrassing for you if the person she's determined to ignore is Grandma or Grandpa!)

↑ More willing to accept help when she's having difficulty with a particular task, which helps to minimize the amount of frustration she experiences over the course of a day.

↑ Starting to learn how to socialize with other children her age, but these interactions tend to be brief and she tends to communicate using eye contact and facial expressions rather than words. This type of play is known as parallel play. (See Chapter 3 for more on play.)

↑ May show a sudden attachment to a blanket, teddy bear, or some other transitional object (the term psychologists use to describe objects that provide comfort to a child). Research has shown that 60% of toddlers form an attachment to some sort of transitional object.

↑ May be restless and stubborn and prone to tantrums—pretty typical behaviour for a child her age. She's likely to protest decisions she doesn't agree with—like when you announce it's her bedtime.

↑ Enjoys your company and is eager to have your undivided attention, so don't be surprised if she interrupts you constantly if you try to carry on a conversation with another adult, whether in person or over the phone.

Your 21-Month-Old

Physical Development (Gross Motor and Fine Motor Skills)

↑ Able to squat while playing. She may also be able to walk down the stairs holding the railing, and may have enough coordination to kick a ball and/or throw and catch it from a standing position.

↑ May enjoy zooming around on a ride-on toy, but it's unlikely she'll have much luck pedalling her tricycle just yet. That will come in time.

↑ Can balance herself well on a swing. Of course, she's still using a toddler swing as opposed to a "big kid swing" at this stage of the game.

continued on p. 38

Your 21-Month-Old (continued)

Physical Development (continued)	↑ Hand control has become increasingly precise. This makes it easier for her to do crafts, but also makes it easier for her to get herself into trouble. She's now got the coordination to attempt more precise (and dangerous) manoeuvres, like trying to shove cutlery and other objects into electrical outlets.
	↑ May be a master at undressing herself, but she's still likely to need some help dressing herself again. Some children this age can manoeuvre large buttons or zippers, but they tend to be the exception rather than the rule.
Perceptual/Cognitive Development	↑ Can now tell the difference between circular, square, and triangular shapes, and is beginning to spot those shapes in her storybooks.
	↑ Has a new-found interest in textured objects, and may take particular delight in fingerpainting, playing in the sandbox, and squeezing mashed potatoes through her fingers.
	↑ Understands that she can learn more about objects by manipulating them (e.g., opening lids to see what's inside something).
	↑ Enjoys dancing to music and making rhythmical sounds using simple musical instruments such as drums and tambourines.
	↑ Enjoys watching you carefully and then copying what you're doing—her way of "apprenticing" to learn a new skill.
	↑ Actively uses trial and error to solve problems.
	↑ Has a million-and-one questions about her world and is increasingly able to understand your answers to those questions. Don't be surprised if she asks the same question over and over again. She wants to see if your answer will remain constant over time!

Language Development	↑ Able to construct two-word sentences and enjoys experimenting with new—sometimes incorrect—word combinations. She is also able to imitate slightly longer phrases (e.g., three- to four-word phrases) if you model them for her.
	↑ Now able to refer to herself when she speaks. "Me" and "mine" have become two of her favourite words (but, of course, they still don't quite rank up there with "No.")
	↑ Uses language to express needs and desires.
Social/Emotional Development	↑ Becoming increasingly autonomous. She's increasingly determined to do things for herself.
	↑ Still becomes upset when she's angry, afraid, or frustrated, but in general she's experiencing fewer temper tantrums than she did even six months ago. She's even starting to make some attempts to control her negative emotions, but, of course, it'll be a while yet before she's totally tantrum-free!
	↑ Capable of demonstrating two or more emotions at the same time (e.g., fear and anger).
	↑ Finds routines reassuring and comforting.
	↑ Showing increased interest in playing with other children her age, but when it occurs, play tends to be rather short—hardly surprising given that two toddlers may have difficulty understanding each other and/or taking turns.
	↑ Loves dress-up play, particularly if the object she's playing with happens to be something of yours. (My parents still have a photograph of my little sister Sandra strutting around the house in a pair of my mother's high heels while dressed in little more than a diaper!)

continued on p. 40

Your 24-Month-Old

Physical Development (Gross Motor and Fine Motor Skills)	↑ Much more coordinated than she was a few months ago and enjoys active play. She's now using a more mature heel-to-toe walking motion rather than the waddling gait of a younger toddler. And she's able to do other things while she's moving, like talking, looking around, or carrying something in her hands.
	↑ Can jump a short distance off the ground and, with practice, may even be able to jump over small objects in a single bound. (It's a bird. It's a plane. It's Super Toddler!)
	↑ Fine motor skills have improved to the point that turning pages, building a tower with blocks, and sticking pegs in holes are all tasks that she can perform with ease.
	↑ Is capable of catching a large ball.
	↑ Makes her first spontaneous designs on paper rather than copying lines and shapes that you've drawn.
	↑ Can now open doorknobs, unscrew jar lids, and hold a cup with one hand. Look out world, here she comes!
Perceptual/Cognitive Development	↑ Beginning to understand the concept of quantity (some, more, gone), spatial relationship down/behind, under, over), and time (now, soon).
	↑ Understands what objects are used for and enjoys grouping objects by colour or other distinguishing characteristics, which helps to lay the groundwork for an understanding of basic mathematical concepts.
	↑ Enjoys threading large beads on a string and threading laces through her lacing toy—two excellent ways of putting her increasingly polished fine motor skills to good use.

↑ Can identify herself in a family photo. Just a few months ago, she would have been more inclined to point to herself and say "baby."

↑ Likes to test the rules to see how you'll react. One researcher discovered that a typical toddler breaks five family rules every *hour!*

Language Development

↑ Can follow simple commands—when she's in the mood to cooperate!

↑ Can now associate a single word (e.g., grocery-shopping) with a whole series of events (getting in the car, driving to the store, buying groceries, and coming home again).

↑ Vocabulary has grown to about 50 words.

↑ Has graduated from one-word sentences to two-, three-, or four-word sentences. Still, her speech is not always easily understood by others. Strangers are able to decipher only about 25% of what she says.

↑ Capable of using the past tense, making simple verbal requests, and answering simple questions.

Social/Emotional Development

↑ Likes to please adults.

↑ Starting to recognize other people's emotions.

↑ Starting to demonstrate cooperation when she's playing with other children, but heated disputes over possessions still occur.

↑ Will try to cheer you up if you're in obvious distress.

↑ Enjoys helping you with routine tasks, like picking up socks and throwing them in the laundry.

↑ May become extremely upset if major changes are made to her routine. Toddlers this age are definitely creatures of habit.

continued on p. 42

Your 30-Month-Old

Physical Development (Gross Motor and Fine Motor Skills)	↑ Can jump in a forward direction.
	↑ Can jump from a small height—e.g., a small stool—and land on her feet without losing her balance.
	↑ Can dress and undress herself independently.
	↑ Can walk on her tiptoes and is steady on her feet. And she can run quite well and glance over her shoulder without losing her balance.
	↑ Can pedal her bicycle and play on age-appropriate playground equipment.
	↑ Learning how to cut paper using child-safe scissors, but may become frustrated if the scissors jam or the paper rips.
	↑ Is capable of copying a circle if you draw one first.
	↑ Can make a block tower that's eight or more blocks high.
Perceptual/Cognitive Development	↑ Beginning to demonstrate an understanding of routines that occur in places other than the home (e.g., at daycare). She continues to thrive on routine.
	↑ Able to anticipate the consequences of her actions. She understands that if she tips her plate sideways while she's carrying it across the room, her food will fall on the floor.
	↑ Able to accurately copy movements and fully participate in action songs such as "If you're happy and you know it, clap your hands."
	↑ Can do simple jigsaw puzzles. She'll have the most success with chunky wooden puzzle pieces with handles.
	↑ Can match up pictures that are identical.
	↑ Able to correctly identify pictures in books that depict objects and events that are familiar to her.

↑ Beginning to remember people, places, and events. She has started to use the words "yesterday" and "tomorrow," but may not fully understand their meanings.

↑ Able to use her imagination to make up simple stories.

↑ May assign human qualities to inanimate objects (e.g., she may worry that her teddy bear feels lonely if he's left in her room by himself all day).

↑ Able to commit words to memory by repeating them to herself.

Language Development	
	↑ Has 1000 or more words in her vocabulary. She's always curious to learn the meaning of an unfamiliar word—one of the reasons her vocabulary is growing by leaps and bounds.
	↑ Understands that people have names. She has also grasped the concept of numbers, although it will be awhile before she actually learns how to count.
	↑ Understands a growing number of verbs.
	↑ Beginning to use words to express her emotions: happy, sad, mad, scared, and so on. She's also a lot less moody than she was a few months ago. She's passed through the drama queen stage—for now.
	↑ Makes some attempts to correct grammatical problems in her speech when she's aware of them, but she may or may not be successful in fixing the problem.
Social/Emotional Development	
	↑ Loves to please others and is thrilled when you praise her.
	↑ May play alongside other children, but she's not really playing with them just yet. (See Chapter 3 for a detailed discussion of how a toddler's play style evolves over time.)
	↑ Has a distinct sense of where she fits into the world and is fiercely protective of both her possessions and her personal space. Her new favourite word? Mine!

continued on p. 44

Your 36-Month-Old

Physical Development (Gross Motor and Fine Motor Skills)

↑ Now an accomplished climber. (She should be: she's been getting plenty of practice!)

↑ Can walk up and down stairs, using alternating feet.

↑ Can kick a ball, pedal a tricycle, and bend over to pick up an object without falling.

↑ Can make towers that are six to eight blocks high and string half-inch-sized wooden beads.

↑ Can use a fork to feed herself.

Perceptual/Cognitive Development

↑ Able to understand the physical relationships between objects (e.g., "on," "in," "under").

↑ Understands the difference between what's pretend and what's real.

↑ Beginning to associate some activities and possessions with members of a particular sex and can easily sort photographs of men and women by gender.

↑ Can match an object in her hand to a picture in a book and is able to do three- to four-piece puzzles.

Language Development

↑ Can recognize and identify most common objects and understands most sentences.

↑ Can tell you her name, age, and sex.

↑ Using sentences of four, five, or even six words. She's also starting to use pronouns correctly ("I," "you," "me," "we," "they") and, of course, she has a solid grasp of the concept of possession ("his/hers" versus "mine").

↑ Can respond to two- or three-component commands (e.g., "Get your coat, your boots, and your umbrella").

↑ Speech can be understood by people who don't know her particularly well. They're able to understand approximately 75% of what she says.

Social/Emotional Development

↑ Becoming more confident in handling new situations and in forming relationships with people outside the immediate family. She's also beginning to spontaneously demonstrate affection for familiar playmates.

↑ Sometimes able to settle disputes with other children her age without having to call on you to intervene, and she's learning how to take turns in games. Of course, she still tends to be a little bossy.

↑ More willing to follow family rules—something that dramatically reduces the frequency of her temper tantrums.

↑ Enjoys picking out the clothes she wants to wear—one of the many ways she's beginning to assert her autonomy.

↑ Able to experience feelings of both pride and shame, which is why you have to be sensitive in choosing a method of discipline.

↑ Developing a wacky sense of humour—something that's fun for both her and for you.

MOM'S THE WORD

"We knew Sean would be the last baby, so I think I was content to let him be a baby longer rather than wanting him to grow up and hit all the developmental milestones."

—*Susan, 37, mother of two*

TABLE 2.2

When There May Be Cause for Concern

It's a rare child who manages to achieve each and every developmental milestone right on target. While there's generally little cause for concern if your toddler is a little bit late achieving the odd milestone, you should let her doctor know if she's consistently lagging behind or if she's significantly late in achieving any of the key developmental milestones. As a rule of thumb, you should at least consider the possibility that your toddler may be experiencing some sort of developmental problem if the following apply:

Your toddler is 13 months of age and she ...

➜ still doesn't have the ability to grasp objects or transfer objects from one hand to the other;

➜ still can't sit on her own;

➜ can't pull herself to a standing position;

➜ isn't creeping or crawling;

➜ doesn't differentiate between people she knows well and complete strangers;

➜ doesn't pay any attention to gestures;

➜ is unable to follow simple directions;

➜ is totally uninterested in social games;

➜ has yet to start making any vowel or consonant sounds;

➜ doesn't imitate sounds;

➜ doesn't blink when fast-moving objects approach her eye;

Your toddler is 18 months of age and she ...

➜ still isn't showing any interest in people or toys and doesn't seem to understand the functions of common household objects (e.g., telephone, toothbrush, spoon);

➜ is unable to stand without assistance;

➜ is not walking yet;

➜ doesn't appear to recognize any underlying patterns in your family's day-to-day routines;

→ doesn't appear to understand anything you say;

→ has fewer than 15 words in her spoken vocabulary;

→ isn't making any attempts to imitate your actions or your words;

→ doesn't demonstrate any sort of attachment to you;

→ doesn't exhibit a variety of emotions, including anger, delight, and fear.

Your toddler is 24 months of age and she ...

→ does not yet recognize herself in the mirror;

→ doesn't show any interest in pictures or familiar objects;

→ has not yet developed a mature heel-toe walking pattern (e.g., she tiptoes rather than walks);

→ is not able to feed herself;

→ is not able to take off her own clothes, shoes, and socks;

→ is not yet using two-word sentences;

→ doesn't understand how to classify or group objects;

→ doesn't engage in any imitative play;

→ doesn't demonstrate any sense of achievement in her accomplishments.

Your preschooler is 36 months of age and she ...

→ drools a lot or has very unclear speech;

→ isn't speaking well enough for other people to be able to understand her;

→ is not yet using three- to four-word sentences;

→ is not yet asking questions;

→ is unable to understand and follow simple commands and directions;

→ is unable to say her own name;

→ doesn't seem to enjoy playing near other children;

→ doesn't engage in any sort of "pretend" play;

→ is unable to focus on an activity that she enjoys for even 5 to 10 minutes;

→ is unable to build a tower using more than four blocks;

continued on p. 48

Your preschooler is 36 months of age and she ... (continued)

→ has difficulty manipulating small objects;

→ is unable to draw a circle;

→ falls often or has a great deal of difficulty with stairs;

→ is unable to jump up and down without falling;

→ is unable to balance on one foot;

→ still needs help dressing herself;

→ has an extreme difficulty being away from you.

If your child is diagnosed with some sort of developmental delay, you'll want to find out as much as you can about the challenges that he is facing and to connect with other parents whose children are facing similar challenges. Information and support are crucial.

Here are some other important points to keep in mind if your toddler is diagnosed with a developmental delay:

- Deal with your feelings head-on. Some parents experience a tremendous amount of guilt and sadness when their child is diagnosed with a developmental delay, wondering if they are somehow responsible for their child's difficulties. It's important to remind yourself that your child's delay is not your fault.

- Focus on what makes your toddler similar to other children the same age rather than on what makes him different. Rather than zeroing in on what sets her apart, stop to consider all the things she has in common with other children the same age.

- Be prepared to modify activities to make them more relevant and useful to your child. You may wish to choose slightly different types of play materials or to introduce shorter, more frequent opportunities for play to take advantage of your child's interests, abilities, and attention span.

- Accept the fact that the toddler years may be extra frustrating for your child. Your toddler may be cognitively ready to master a particular task, but may lack the physical skills required to carry it off—something that can lead to tremendous frustration for her and for you.

- Celebrate your child's achievements large and small, and be patient and persistent even if your child's progress is frustratingly slow.

- Stay grounded in the here and now rather than worrying about the future. Your child may surprise you with her progress over time.

Encouraging your child's healthy development

WHILE IT'S IMPORTANT to provide your toddler with a stimulating environment, you don't have to go to such extraordinary lengths that you end up developing a full-blown case of Super Parent Syndrome. Contrary to popular belief, it's not necessary to painstakingly program every minute of your toddler's day to maximize the number of learning opportunities—nor is it necessarily helpful (or healthy!) to bombard her with flash cards at every turn.

A more sensible approach is to look for natural opportunities to incorporate learning into your child's day—so-called "teachable moments"—and to recognize the fact that your child is going to learn a great deal simply by being part of the hustle and bustle of a typical household. (Just think of the language acquisition opportunities alone if she happens to be within earshot when you or your partner hit your thumb with a hammer!)

Ideally, you want to provide your child with enough stimulation to keep her interested and entertained, but not so much that she becomes overstimulated and exhausted. Like you, she needs some downtime to relax and unwind.

Here are some additional tips on promoting healthy development without driving yourself—or your toddler—crazy:

- Tap into your toddler's interests. It only makes sense to put that powerful toddler drive and determination to work for you! Find out which activities, toys, and games have the greatest appeal to her and then use them as the launching pad for other learning opportunities. If, for example, she's crazy about animals, you might decide to use Eric Carle's book *Brown Bear, Brown Bear, What Do You See?* to start teaching her about colours.

- Encourage your child to play with a wide range of toys and to attempt a variety of different types of activities, but don't force her to do things she genuinely detests. Instead, keep reintroducing the less popular activities every so often to see if she's more willing to give them a chance. Who knows? She may have conquered her Fear of Fingerpainting since the last time she sat down at the craft table!

MOTHER WISDOM

It's important to give your child the opportunity to learn how to entertain herself. Otherwise, you could unwittingly be creating yourself a job for life as her social director! So rather than attempting to program every minute of every day, offer her a choice of activities so that she can assume some of the responsibility for deciding what she'd like to do. It'll be a few years yet before she'll happily play for an hour or two on her own—for now, she'll still want you to help her build a block tower or play with her train set—but at least you'll be starting to plant some of the seeds of independence.

MOTHER WISDOM

Don't feel like you have to fill your child's world with so-called "educational toys." Any toy that is of interest to a child will have educational value for her.

- Be encouraging and supportive when she's tackling a new task. It takes courage to try something new, so compliment her whether or not she manages to get stellar results. She needs to know that you're proud of her for trying.

- Give her time to puzzle things out on her own, but don't be afraid to step in if her frustration level is building to the point where she's likely to experience a meltdown. Allowing her to experience this much frustration won't magically allow her to master a particular task any sooner; if anything, it may make her reluctant to tackle that particular task again.

- Allow for repetition. Practice makes perfect, so don't let it drive you slightly bonkers if your toddler wants to climb up and down the same set of stairs over and over again.

- Provide your toddler with plenty of opportunities to engage in open-ended activities rather than activities that follow a predetermined course.

- Take advantage of each developmental breakthrough. Once your child masters the pincer (thumb and forefinger) grip midway through her second year she'll be able to pick up small objects, which will allow you to introduce her to all sorts of new play opportunities.

- Take time to celebrate each of your toddler's achievements. Don't be so busy sprinting toward the next major milestone that you fail to savour the mini-achievements along the way.

MOTHER WISDOM

Your toddler comes pre-wired to favour a particular hand. As her fine-motor skills improve and she begins to engage in single-handed activities such as colouring, it'll become increasingly apparent which hand she favours. While the vast majority of children are righthanded, one in 10 boys and one in 12 girls are lefthanded and one in 200 children is ambidextrous (equally comfortable using either hand).

If your child ends up favouring her left hand, you'll want to supply her with left-handed scissors and other left-handed tools to make her life easier. And when you teach her how to tie her shoes, you'll want to do so facing her so that she can mimic your movements using the opposite hands.

Whatever you do, don't try to fight her hand preference. Forcing her to use her other hand could lead to hand–eye coordination problems down the road, so this is definitely one of those situations where you'll want to let nature take its course.

On the move

AFTER A YEAR of dress rehearsals, it's finally curtain time! Your toddler is ready to take those momentous first steps. Better make sure you've got your camera handy: this is one of those moments you'll want to capture on film. "When I saw Victoria walk for the first time, I felt unbelievable pride," recalls Laura, a 33-year-old mother of one. "You would have thought she'd won a gold medal!"

Baby steps

Of course, there is a lot of behind-the-scenes work to be done before your toddler is ready to start walking. Here's what needs to happen first:

- She needs to grow out of her "baby body" and into the body of a toddler. A newborn baby's head is huge in relation to the rest of her body, which puts her centre of gravity smack dab in the middle of her chest. And then there's the fact that her nervous system has not yet matured to the point where it can orchestrate all the complex movements involved in walking. That's why most children don't learn to walk until after their first birthday: it takes that long for them to acquire the necessary "equipment" to become fully mobile. And while we're talking body types, here's a bit of trivia to share the next time you're having coffee with a group of moms: babies with bigger heads tend to start walking later than their smaller-head peers (no, it's not because these supposedly smarter babies are busy hanging out at the library); and babies with leaner body types tend to become mobile before their chubbier counterparts.

- She needs to build up the strength in her legs—something she accomplished during all those months of kicking her feet, putting weight on her legs, and cruising around the furniture.

- She needs to be able to balance herself on one foot for brief periods of time—the basic skill involved in walking. (Think about it: you're not going to get very far if you tip over the moment you put all your weight on one foot.)

- She needs to have the confidence to start walking. If you've tried your hand at any adventure sports, you'll know that there's a bit of a leap of faith involved in hang-gliding or white-water rafting for the very first time. Well, if you think about it, walking is the ultimate adventure sport from a toddler's perspective: despite the fact that you're feeling kind of shaky standing in one spot on two feet, you somehow have to find the confidence to lift one leg and—yikes!—try to take that first step. It's hardly surprising, therefore, that risk-taking tots

TODDLER TALK

Here's a rather humbling statistic to share with that obnoxious parent at playgroup who keeps bragging about her toddler's walking abilities: newborn zebras are able to stand 10 minutes after birth, walk well within half an hour, and break out into a canter within 45 minutes. Guess you could say they're busy earning their stripes! (Groan.)

tend to master the art of walking months earlier than their more cautious counterparts. (Who knew there was such a thing as an X-treme toddler!)

And even after your toddler finally takes the plunge by attempting to take those awkward first steps, she'll still be honing her walking skills for another two years. The first order of business? Losing that lurching Frankenstein-style walk! Over time, she'll learn how to keep her feet a little closer together and to point her toes straight ahead rather than outward while she walks. She'll also learn how to get to a standing position by bending one knee and pulling herself. Initially, her key method of "launching" herself will be to spread her hands on the floor, straighten her arms, lift her bottom in the air, and use her hands to push herself into a standing position. It may not be the most graceful manoeuvre, but it tends to be highly effective. Note: See

MOM'S THE WORD

"Brendan waited until he was almost 17 months to walk on his own. He'd been cruising around furniture with barely a finger holding on since around 12 months, but I guess he chose not to take the big step until he was ready. He's always been cautious about things, so maybe he simply didn't feel confident enough to try walking on his own."

—Julie, 30, mother of one

Table 2.3 for a breakdown of the key walking-related milestones that most toddlers achieve between one and three years of age.

TABLE 2.3

Look Who's Walking!

Here's a summary of the key walking-related milestones for the toddler years. Studies have shown that 90% of toddlers will be able to

→ walk while holding onto a parent's hand or by "cruising" along a piece of furniture such as a couch by age 12.7 months;

→ stand alone briefly by age 13 months;

→ stand alone well by age 13.9 months;

→ walk alone well by age 14.3 months;

→ begin to run by age 18 months;

→ walk up steps by age 22 months;

→ run with ease by age 24 months;

→ stand on tiptoe by age 24 months;

→ step backwards by age 24 months;

→ jump by age 30 months;

→ kick a ball forward by age 30 months;

→ climb a low ladder by age 30 months;

→ lean forward without losing balance by age 30 months;

→ pedal a tricycle by age 30 months;

→ hop by age 36 months;

→ climb stairs using alternating feet by age 36 months.

Walking the walk

Wondering what's behind that classic toddler waddle? Here's the scoop from a physiological standpoint. When toddlers are first learning how to walk, they find it difficult to keep their balance.

That's why they like to walk with their feet wide apart, their toes pointed either out or in, and their arms spread out to either side. It provides them with a little added stability.

While most toddlers quickly outgrow the pigeon-toed (toes pointed inward) stance, some children are born with a twist in the foot or the leg that causes them to favour sitting positions that may perpetuate the problem (e.g., sitting on their feet or in a "W" position). If this is the case with your child, you'll want to encourage her to use other sitting positions and you'll want to talk with her doctor about whether any additional treatment is likely to be required.

There's also no need to worry about your toddler's flat feet. It takes until around age six for a child to develop a full arch. And here's another noteworthy statistic: according to the Canadian Paediatric Society, 97% of children under age 18 months have flat feet—mostly because they have a fat pad on the underside of their feet. (I know: they should refer to this condition as "fat feet" rather than "flat feet"!) In most cases, flat feet are only a temporary phenomenon. By age 10, only 4% of children will still have flat feet.

There are some foot-related oddities, however, that can be cause for concern. If your toddler prefers to walk on tiptoes rather than on flat feet, you'll want to point this out to her doctor because this could be an indication of a neurological or muscular problem. And if your child is still bowlegged (i.e., there's a noticeable gap between the knees when she walks) at the age of three, you'll want to get an opinion on this as well because it could be a sign of vitamin D deficiency or some other medical problem.

Growing pains

Of course, walking is more than just a physical challenge for your toddler; it can be emotionally challenging as well. She may need time to come to terms with her new-found walking abilities. On the one hand, she may have an almost insatiable desire to explore the world around her now that she's mobile; on the other hand, she may miss being carried around by you and may signal her ongoing need for closeness by becoming extra-clingy. She may decide to treat your lap as "home base," periodically returning for a reassuring cuddle as she repeatedly orbits around the room!

And now that she's mastered the art of walking, she may be motivated to set more challenging goals for herself. (Forget walking! She wants to hop, skip, and jump, too!) While this is great in principle—after all, every parent wants a motivated kid—sometimes it doesn't play out quite so neatly in real life. Your toddler is likely to experience a great deal of frustration when she discovers that she can't accomplish everything she sets out to do.

To make matters worse, her frustration level will also be fueled by the large number of tumbles she's likely to experience during her early days as a biped: a wrinkle in the carpet or a slight incline in the floor may be all it takes to cause her to trip and fall. You can help to minimize the number of tumbles by taking steps to make her environment safer, but it's impossible to prevent every single fall: you can expect your toddler to sport a goose egg or two and numerous other bumps and bruises while she's learning how to coordinate the mechanics of movement. And, of course, if there's a Murphy's Law that applies to toddlerhood, it goes something like this: if there's only one item in your room that could injure your toddler, she'll be magnetically drawn to it just as it starts to fall—and the size of the resulting goose egg will be inversely proportional to the number of hours until your doctor's office reopens.

This stage can be emotionally challenging for you, too, of course: not only do you have to contend with your toddler's see-sawing emotions, but you may also be experiencing an emotional tug-of-war yourself. While you may be bursting with pride at your toddler's achievements on the walking front, you may also feel downright weepy about her babyhood winding to a close. Catherine, a 32-year-old mother of four, remembers feeling thrilled but also a little wistful when her toddlers started walking: "Those baby steps were the first steps they took toward independence."

MOTHER WISDOM

Don't rush to squeeze your toddler's feet into a pair of shoes. According to the Canadian Paediatric Society, there's growing evidence that wearing shoes in early childhood interferes with the development of a normal longitudinal arch. Your toddler needs to graduate to shoes only when she starts walking around on surfaces that could injure her feet. At that point, you'll want to take her to the shoe store to invest in a brand-new pair of shoes. (While hand-me-down clothing is great, it's best not to rely on hand-me-down shoes.)

When you're shopping for shoes, you'll want to look for a pair that features square rather than pointy toes, that is flexible enough to allow for full movement of the foot, and that provides just the right amount of traction (enough to keep her from slipping, but not so much as to cause her to trip).

You'll also want to make sure that the shoes you buy fit your toddler's feet properly. That means checking to ensure that

- there's enough room for her toes to wiggle (there should be about 1.5 centimetres of wiggle room at the front of the toe when she's standing up);
- the shoe is wide enough to fit comfortably (there should be a bit of space on either side of her foot);
- the heel won't slip and cause blisters (make sure you can fit your pinky finger in between the back of your child's shoe and her heel).

Here's a bit of additional from-the-trenches advice on how to test-drive shoes in the shoe store. Have your toddler walk around in a new pair of shoes for a minute or two. Then remove them and yank your child's socks off, looking for any red pressure marks on her feet. That should provide you with a pretty good indication of whether or not the shoes are pinching her feet.

And, if you dare to admit it to yourself, you may also be hit with a totally irrational fear: the kind of fear that creeps up on you in the middle of the night when you're at your most vulnerable. This crazy but oh-so-common worry? That you're on the verge of becoming obsolete! After all, your toddler is growing more and more capable by the day. Surely it won't be much longer until she no longer needs you at all!

Fortunately, I can offer you a truckload of reassurance on this front. It'll be years before your child's burgeoning abilities do you out of a job. While your toddler will inevitably need less and less hands-on help as the months march on, she's still nowhere near ready to ask to borrow the car keys—unless, of course, she wants to chew on them or use them to play in her toy car! Bottom line? Don't be afraid to allow yourself to relax and enjoy this exciting stage of your child's life: your child will still be your "baby" for a very long time.

Talk, talk, talk

LEARNING TO TALK is the other key developmental achievement of the toddler years. After months of wondering what your child has been thinking about, you finally get a window on her world! Of course, she won't be speaking in complete sentences overnight. Language acquisition is, after all, a gradual process.

TODDLER TALK

According to researchers at Stanford University, it takes a 15-month-old about a second to process a word—even a familiar word like "baby." By age 18 months, however, a toddler's brain is able to start processing that word before she's even finished saying it!

MOM'S THE WORD

"Brianna's first real word came at 14 months. We were putting up the Christmas tree, and as I was putting on the lights I told her not to touch the bulbs because they were hot. Of course, she pinched one between her fingers, looked up at me, and said, clear as day, 'Hot.' My jaw just about hit the floor."

—*Susan, 37, mother of two*

Say anything ...

It can be difficult to predict in advance when your toddler is going to utter her first words, but researchers have identified some factors that influence when a child is likely to start talking:

- **The number of languages spoken at home.** Children who are born in families in which more than one language is spoken may be slower to talk than children who grow up hearing only one language. Still, there's no need for concern that growing up in a language-rich environment will prevent your child from learning how to speak English: studies have shown that bilingual and multilingual children eventually catch up with their peers.

- **Gender.** Girls tend to speak and form phrases earlier than boys, and they're more likely to use words that express emotion. They're also quicker to use language as a problem-solving tool during play. (Little boys, on the other hand, are more likely to try to work through the same problem with action.) These gender differences in language tend to become less pronounced over time, so don't despair that your two-year-old is doomed to spend his life wrestling with other children for toys! This too shall pass. (Or at least that's the theory.)

- **Genetics.** Children tend to follow in their parents' footsteps in language acquisition. If you were an earlier talker, your child may be, too. Have your parents dig out your old baby book so that you'll know for sure whether you were talking up a storm at a very early age or were more the strong, silent type!

- **Birth order.** This shouldn't be a surprise to anyone who grew up with siblings: birth order is another important factor in language acquisition. First-born children are more likely to have larger vocabularies during the second year of life than children with older brothers and sisters, and are more likely to reach the 50-word vocabulary milestone (the point at which toddlers typically begin to use two-word sentences, incidentally) a little sooner. It's not difficult to figure out why this is the case. While baby number one has the limelight all to herself, younger children don't have quite the same opportunity to enjoy their parents' undivided attention, something that can slow their rate of speech development. All is not lost for second and subsequent children, however: studies have shown that they make better conversationalists than first-borns. Because

---

TODDLER TALK

It's hardly surprising that toddler girls tend to do better in the language department than toddler boys. Studies have shown that mothers tend to use more open-ended questions and longer, more complex sentences when they're speaking with two-year-old girls as opposed to two-year-old boys. They vary their speech patterns in other significant ways as well: studies have shown that mothers are likely to use "motherese" (the exaggerated speech patterns that mothers around the world use with their infants) when communicating with girls this age, but that their conversations with boys the same age are likely to be more matter-of-fact, focusing on whatever the boy happens to be doing at the time.

they've had more experience with multi-person conversations, they learn at an earlier age how to tell when it's their turn to speak and when it's their turn to listen.

- **Whether or not the child is a twin or other multiple.** Twins and other multiples sometimes spend so much time communicating with one another that they can be quite literally in their own world. Consequently, they may be less tuned into the world of adults, which can make it a bit more challenging for them to master the fine points of communicating with someone other than their fellow multiples.

- **Your child's overall development.** Toddlers with developmental delays can also be slower in learning how to talk. Children who have been born prematurely, for example, tend to achieve particular speech milestones around the time that would be expected for their adjusted rather than their chronological age.

- **How your toddler's attempts to communicate are met.** All other things being equal, a child who is encouraged to communicate will develop language skills more quickly than a child who doesn't receive the same amount of encouragement or the same opportunities to test-drive her speaking abilities on the adults in her life.

TODDLER TALK

Contrary to popular belief, sibling conversation isn't an adequate substitute for one-on-one conversations with Mom or Dad. According to speech development experts, older siblings tend to give their younger brothers and sisters orders rather than engaging in a lot of heartfelt conversation. (Like it or not, being repeatedly ordered to go get the remote ain't going to turn any toddler into a modern-day Shakespeare!)

TODDLER TALK

Sibling squabbling at the dinner table may be giving you indigestion, but it could be giving your kids the developmental edge. According to British psychologist David Cowell, children learn such skills as self-assertion, negotiation, and compromise as a result of these heated mealtime discussions.

The 15 most important things parents can do to encourage language development

Wondering what you can do to encourage language development in your toddler? Here's what the experts suggest:

1. Set aside time to have one-to-one conversations with your toddler. While she's likely to be exposed to plenty of language over the course of her day, she'll benefit tremendously by having focused conversations with an adult. The best way to get the conversation started is to talk about what she's doing and seeing at that very moment. This type of conversation will help to keep her attention, and will also make it easier for you to decipher her messages. (Remember, you'll be initially relying on a combination of gestures and words as you try to make sense of what she's saying.) If your child's language skills are still pretty rudimentary, you may end up serving as her narrator, helping her to put her thoughts and ideas into word.

2. Keep the TV off. While you might think your child's speech and language skills will benefit from all that chatter on the tube, even the very best children's shows require very little verbal input from the child. Bottom line? TV can't hold a candle to a face-to-face conversation with Mom and Dad. And besides—as you'll find out in the next chapter —TV isn't

really recommended for very young children anyway. Time to lose that remote once and for all!

3. Make eye contact when you're speaking to your toddler. This will allow you to see if she's still focused on the conversation as well as help to hold her attention. It will also help to reassure her that she's got your undivided attention (e.g., she's not competing with the newspaper!).

4. Speak slowly and deliberately, making a point of pronouncing your words carefully, using good grammar, and expressing your thoughts in complete sentences. How is your child supposed to learn how to understand the "rules" of spoken language if such language isn't modelled appropriately at home? Note: Your child will also be exposed to good grammar if you get in the habit of reading to your child every day.

5. Aim for a language level that's just above your toddler's and make a point of exposing your toddler to a wide variety of words. (Don't feel as though you've got to sit there and read the dictionary to her, however! This language exposure will happen naturally if you simply make a point of talking to her about what she's seeing and doing over the course of her day.) While you want to use grammatically correct speech that's

---

TODDLER TALK

Human beings aren't late bloomers when it comes to speech; they're just born a little too soon. Because human babies have large heads and women's pelvises can only accommodate babies with heads up to a certain size, babies need to be born before their brains are fully "cooked." Besides, as Steven Pinker—a professor of psychology at the Massachusetts Institute of Technology and author of *The Learning Instinct*—noted in an interview with *Baby Talk magazine*: "Language has to be coordinated with other people; babies can't just be born speaking Esperanto!"

clear and simple enough for your child to copy, don't be afraid to throw in the occasional "big word." Your child may not be able to repeat the word back to you, but over time she'll learn how to decipher its meaning.

6. Keep your messages brief. If you speak for too long, your toddler will lose track of what you're saying. And take advantage of these conversational pauses to ask for some sort of feedback from your toddler: perhaps a nod "yes" to indicate that she has understood what you were saying.

7. If your toddler's attention starts to wander, instead of speaking more loudly, drop your voice to a whisper to force her to listen more attentively. Obviously, you'll want to be realistic about how long you expect her to stay engaged in the conversation. She's not exactly the world's greatest conversationalist yet!

8. Expand on your toddler's single-word utterances. If she says "ball," expand her thought for her; for example, say "Yes, that's a big red ball. Would you like to play with it?" You'll be helping her to build her vocabulary as well as letting her know that you understand what she's saying.

9. When you ask your child a question, try to phrase it in such a way that it requires more than a yes or no answer. After all, shaking her head "yes" or "no" doesn't allow for the most exciting conversational possibilities! Instead of asking her whether she'd like an apple, ask whether she'd like an apple or a banana. She'll get the chance to practise saying "apple" or "banana" as well as the satisfaction of deciding which type of fruit she'd like to eat. (And, as you'll discover in Chapter 4, toddlers love nothing more than feeling as if they're the ones in charge!) Of course, it's unrealistic to expect your child to utter a crystal-clear "apple" or "banana" the first time around:

she'll likely mumble something and then point to the piece of fruit she wants. That's okay. What's important is that she's trying to communicate. So be sure to heap on the praise. If you don't understand what your toddler is trying to tell you, ask for clarification. ("I know you want me to get you something down off the shelf. Do you want the cup or the bowl?") Then wait for her to continue the conversation by using words and/or gestures.

10. Rather than correcting your toddler if she makes an error in her speech, simply use the word in a sentence and repeat it back to her in a natural way. There's no need to point out that she's made a speech error or to ask her to attempt to say the word correctly. Speech errors are extremely common in young children, and you'll drive her—and yourself—crazy if you insist on perfection each time she opens her mouth!

11. Don't expect your toddler to be a great conversationalist when you've got visitors over. She may lose her confidence when asked to speak in front of an audience of strangers.

12. Make sound play a part of your toddler's day. Make up simple sound patterns (e.g., beep, beep, beep) and encourage your child to imitate you. Then wait for her to come up with a sound pattern and mimic her, too. Or make sounds as you play with toys or listen to the sounds that you hear as you take a walk around the neighbourhood. (You can turn this into a

---

TODDLER TALK

Don't be alarmed if you catch your toddler talking to herself. She's simply honing her language skills. Whether she's talking to a favourite toy or giving an impromptu monologue directed at no one in particular, what she's doing is perfectly normal and will only help to improve the quality of her speech.

bit of a game if you take a portable tape recorder with you and make a tape of the neighbour's dog barking, someone's car alarm going off, and so on. Then you can go home, turn on the tape, and encourage your toddler to remember what made the different sounds.)

13. Look for opportunities to play with language, too. Here are a few ideas:
    • Teach your child nursery rhymes and then, once she's familiar with them, pause so that she can fill in the blanks.
    • Teach your child some fingerplays (simple poems accom panied by hand movements, such as "The Eensie Weensie Spider" and "Twinkle Twinkle Little Star"). If you want to add a few more fingerplays to your repertoire, pick up a fingerplay book or visit a fingerplay Web site.
    • Get in the habit of naming objects in books or magazines, or when you're venturing around the community. This can be a real vocabulary builder for your child. Then, as your toddler begins to acquire a solid repetoire of nouns, you'll want to start introducing plenty of verbs, too.

14. Create a picture file for your toddler. Cut interesting pictures out of magazines, cover them with adhesive paper, and stick them in a shoebox or a photo album. Encourage your child to look through the box or photo album with you and tell you about the pictures.

15. Familiarize yourself with all the key language-related mile stones so that you'll be able to pick up the signs of any speech and language delay early on. (See Table 2.4 for a list of the warning signs of a speech and language delay in a two-year-old.) At the same time, try not to drive yourself crazy with worry. While a "typical" toddler can be expected to utter her first word around the time of her first birthday, a child who

achieves that milestone at any point between 10 and 24 months is still considered to be within the normal range. And, as for having crystal-clear speech every moment of every day, that's a bit much to ask of any toddler: studies have shown that a typical three-year-old is intelligible just 75% of the time.

TABLE 2.4

Warning Signs of a Speech and Language Delay

You should at least consider the possibility that your toddler may have a speech and language delay if the following applies:

She's two years of age and she ...

→ doesn't seem to be making much progress from month to month;

→ doesn't react normally or consistently to sounds;

→ uses mostly vowels as opposed to a mix of vowels and consonants;

→ uses one catch-all sound or syllable to refer to large numbers of objects (e.g., "duh" or "duh-duh");

→ is sticking to single-word utterances rather than full sentences;

→ doesn't use common words like "bye-bye" or seem to enjoy basic speech-and-language games like peekaboo;

→ doesn't integrate new words into everyday speech (e.g., she uses a word once but then seems to forget that the word exists);

→ doesn't point to common objects in books when you ask her to identify them;

→ gives up easily if she's not able to communicate a message to you.

She's three years of age and she ...

→ is unintelligible to others;

→ has a very limited vocabulary;

→ can't produce words or phrases spontaneously (i.e., she can only repeat back what you're saying);

→ can't follow simple directions;

→ has a highly nasal sound to her voice or some other unusual voice quality.

Diagnosing a speech and language delay

Approximately 5 to 10% of children are diagnosed with some sort of speech and language delay. Fortunately, most speech problems can be resolved if they are caught early on.

If your toddler shows signs of having a speech and language delay, her doctor may want to send her for a hearing check. This is because hearing problems are responsible for a significant number of speech delays. Your child may have been born with some sort of hearing problem or there may be lingering fluid from a middle ear infection—something that can interfere with your toddler's ability to hear. If fluid in the ear turns out to be the problem for your child, tubes in the ears and/or a dose of antibiotics to clear up the infection may be recommended. (Note: You'll find detailed information about ear infections in Chapter 8.)

Your child's doctor will also want to evaluate her motor skills to see if an inability to coordinate the muscles in the mouth and the throat is at the root of her problem. Speech involves the coordination of more than 100 different muscles in the vocal tract. If a motor skills problem is diagnosed, speech therapy will likely be recommended.

TODDLER TALK

Don't assume your toddler has a speech problem just because she happens to stutter from time to time. Stuttering is very common in toddlers—so common, in fact, that most speech-language professionals recommend that parents wait until after a child's third birthday before becoming overly concerned. Most children go through a stuttering phase at some point. It's most likely to be a problem if a child is tired, excited, or upset. That said, if the stuttering lasts for longer than three to six months or continues past age three, you may want to have your child's speech checked.

Stuttering occurs in 5% of children and is four times as common in boys as girls.

MOTHER WISDOM

If your two- to three-year-old's speech is so unclear that you're unable to decipher what she's saying at least half of the time, a coordination problem may be to blame. You can help your child improve her speech coordination by singing and repeating rhymes together (which will give her a chance to practise formulating words) and by playing sound games together (e.g., making snake sounds and crawling around your belly to practise the letter "s").

Your child's doctor will also attempt to determine whether some underlying medical condition may be responsible for her difficulties. Cerebral palsy and other neuromuscular disorders, severe head injuries, strokes, viral diseases, mental retardation, and physical impairments such as cleft lip or palate are all known to contribute to speech difficulties. In many cases, however, the cause of a speech and language delay is unknown.

Speech and language delays can be divided into six basic categories:

1. articulation impairments, which occur when a child cannot make a particular speech sound or sounds (either because of a structural problem in the mouth or nose or an abnormality in the functioning of the muscles and nerves involved in the production of speech);

2. phonological impairments, which occur when a child makes speech errors such as leaving certain sounds off the starts or ends of words or incorrectly using one sound in the place of another;

3. dyspraxia, a communication problem that is defined as an inability to produce the fast and skilled mouth and tongue movements required for speech when there are no other obvious causes (e.g., hearing or other perceptual problems, motor

MOTHER WISDOM

Some toddlers have difficulty speaking because their mouth muscles are underdeveloped. Your doctor may suspect that this is the cause of your child's speech problems if she prefers soft food that requires little chewing, lets food fall from her mouth when she's eating, drools a lot, breathes through her mouth, and is extremely difficult to understand. While you're waiting for formal speech therapy to begin (and thanks to the shortage of speech-language pathologists in many parts of Canada, that wait can be considerable), you may want to try the following exercises to help develop your toddler's mouth muscles:

- Give your toddler opportunities to practise blowing: Bubble-blowing is a perennial favourite with toddlers, particularly if you put a few drops of food colouring in the bubble-blowing solution. Blowing a feather across the kitchen table or blowing on a harmonica or a whistle are other great ways of getting your toddler to give her mouth muscles a workout.
- Sucking straws: Encourage your child to put his lips near the top of the straw and purse his lips as much as possible. Other variations that work the same muscles? Sucking on a strand of cooked spaghetti.
- Humming: Humming can also help to develop muscle strength, so put on some hum-worthy tunes and start humming along with your toddler.

---

problems, and structural problems involving the mouth and/or the tongue);

4. voice disorders, such as hoarseness, voice loss, and highly nasal speech;

5. communication problems caused by brain disorders, which can interfere with speech production and speech and language comprehension (e.g., aphasia—the loss of speech and language abilities resulting from stroke or head injury);

6. speech language delays, which occur when a child exhibits a delay in the onset or development of speech and language skills (e.g., less fluency than what would be expected in a child of a particular age).

Boys are from Mars, girls are from Venus

RESEARCHERS HAVE DISCOVERED that toddlers begin to clue into gender differences around the time of their first birthday, and from this point forward it's a source of endless fascination to them. As psychologist Carole Beal, Ph.D., author of *Boys and Girls: The Development of Gender Roles*, told *Parenting* magazine, "Toddlers see the world as divided into two camps. Once they know which camp they belong to, their sense of self quickly becomes tinted pink or blue and they begin to infer how to fit in."

By the time toddlers reach three years of age their behaviour becomes noticeably gender-specific: girls tend to become less aggressive and start playing with dolls and other "girl toys" while boys engage in more rough play and gravitate toward "boy toys" such as trucks and action figures.

All this can have you hitting the panic button if you were determined not to steer your child toward gender-specific roles. If you're feeling that you've somehow failed as parent because your daughter insists on playing with her dolls 24/7 and your son won't play with anything more "girly" than his Lego blocks, it's time to cut yourself some slack. After all, this is typical toddler behaviour.

So, certainly, do what you can to encourage your child to think more broadly about gender roles (e.g., give the car a tune-up while your partner whips up a batch of muffins). And go

---

TODDLER TALK

The differences between the sexes can play out in some other fascinating ways during the toddler years. While boys tend to be more adventurous than girls, girls tend to achieve the major developmental breakthroughs sooner than boys, and boast superior social skills and concentration abilities to boot. Clearly this "girl power" thing starts young!

ahead and shop for gender-specific toys. Just promise not to do a number on yourself if you still end up with a "girly" girl or a boy's boy. Some of these gender differences are hard-wired right from day one, like it or not.

Now that we've had a lengthy chat about child development, let's move on and tackle another important topic: the importance of play in your toddler's world.

CHAPTER 3

Fun and Games

*"For a small child there is no division between
playing and learning; between the things he or she
does 'just for fun' and things that are 'educational.'
The child learns while living and any part of
living that is enjoyable is also play."*
—PENELOPE LEACH, *Your Baby and Child*

FORGET ALL THOSE spoilsports who like to hammer home
the point that play is "a child's work." By making it all
about work, they tend to lose sight of the fact that the key
ingredient in play is fun! Is your toddler motivated to work away
at that block tower because he's "on the job"? Hardly. He's sticking with the tower building because he's having a good time.

Playing and learning are as natural to your child as breathing.
And as his repertoire of skills increases, his play possibilities
increase exponentially. While he had to content himself with
reaching for or batting at toys when he was a very young infant,
now he's got both the physical and intellectual abilities to decide
what toy he wants and then toddle across the room to get it!

In this chapter, we're going to talk about toddlers and play:
why it's important and what you as a parent can do to encourage it. We're also going to talk about how your toddler's play style

will evolve over time, what you can do to help him navigate his way through the "mine" field (remember, sharing isn't likely to become your toddler's forte for some time yet!), what types of activities and games are likely to be a particular hit, what you need to know to encourage his love of reading, what factors to keep in mind when you start stocking the toy box, and what every parent needs to know about computers and TV.

Playing with your toddler

IF YOU ASKED your doctor to give your toddler a prescription for a happy and healthy life, she might be tempted to reach for her prescription pad and simply scrawl the world "play." After all, play is good for toddlers!

Just in case you haven't cracked open any child development textbooks lately, allow me to give you a crash course in the benefits of play. Studies have shown that play allows toddlers to

- interact with other people;

- develop their gross and fine motor skills;

- experiment with language;

- improve their creative thinking abilities and problem-solving skills;

- heighten their powers of concentration by allowing them to focus on a particular task for an extended period of time;

- tap into their natural curiosity about the world around them.

Your child's play style

Child development specialists have determined that toddlers tend to be kinesthetic and tactual learners. (See Table 3.1.) Simply put, they learn best when they're given the opportunity for hands-on exploration. It therefore makes sense that so much of the learning that occurs during the early years happens through play.

How your toddler's play style will evolve

Your one-year-old hasn't shown any interest in playing with other children. In fact, you've noticed that he'd rather play quietly with his blocks in the corner than join in any group activities. Should you be concerned?

Probably not, say the play experts. It takes time for a child to master the art of playing with other children. Most children don't demonstrate a lot of social behaviour before the age of two. So don't assume that your toddler is doomed to spend his childhood standing on the edge of the playground, watching while the social butterflies in the toddler crowd romp around together. Chances are, it won't be long before he decides to get in on the fun, too. Table 3.2 on page 79 highlights some important milestones to watch for as he matures.

TABLE 3.1

The Four Basic Learning Styles

Psychologists have identified four basic learning styles: infants and toddlers tend to be both tactual and kinesthetic learners, whereas older children and adults are more likely to be auditory and visual learners.

Learning Style	What It Means	What Parents Can Do
Tactual Learning (based on touch)	A child with a tactual learning style needs to touch objects in order to understand how they work.	Provide your child with a variety of learning materials so that he can experiment with different shapes and textures. Note: A child with a tactual learning style may have difficulty following directions. Instead of telling him what to do, show him what to do (e.g., show him how to tip his sippy cup to get the juice to flow rather than offering verbal instructions)
Kinesthetic Learning (based on movement)	A child with a kinesthetic learning style learns best through movement.	Take advantage of your child's love of movement by encouraging him to role-play, play active games, and engage in activities that encourage him to develop both his gross and fine motor skills.

continued on p. 78

Learning Style	What It Means	What Parents Can Do
Auditory Learning (based on hearing)	A child with an auditory learning style will have no trouble memorizing the words to stories and songs, following directions, and repeating phrases and comments he's overheard— even those phrases and comments you'd prefer he didn't!	Take advantage of your child's auditory learning style by exposing him to songs, rhymes, and conversation and by reading books to him.
Visual Learning (based on seeing)	A child with a visual learning style learns best through seeing.	Provide your child with picture books and other learning materials that are ideally suited to a visual learner.

TABLE 3.2

How Your Child's Play Style Evolves as He Matures

Type of Play	What It Means and What You Can Do to Promote It
	Younger toddlers (under 13 months of age)
Onlooker play (observing others at play rather than participating themselves)	Onlooker play helps your toddler learn how to relate to others and gives him an opportunity to acquire language. He also starts figuring out how others are likely to respond to various types of social behaviours (e.g., smiling versus hitting) and what he can do to get the other children's attention.
	Allow this learning process to unfold naturally, but be prepared to help your toddler if he seems eager to play with the other children but unsure about what he needs to do to indicate that he wants to join in the fun.
	Note: Older children often engage in this type of play, too.
Solitary play (your toddler plays by himself, but is still in close proximity to other children; this type of play can be seen in older children, too, but tends to become less frequent)	Solitary play helps your toddler develop a wide range of skills and learn about the world around him. You'll want to stay close by so that you can intervene if the other children start to crowd your toddler. You want the experience of playing near other children to continue to be a positive one for him, which is unlikely to be the case if a rambunctious four-year-old keeps kicking over his block towers!

continued on p. 80

Type of Play	What It Means and What You Can Do to Promote It
	Older toddlers (18 months to age three)
Parallel play (your toddler may appear to be playing with other children his age because they're playing in the same part of the room, but if you look closely you'll see that there's no actual interaction between them)	Provides your toddler with opportunities for role playing, such as dressing up and pretending to pour tea. It also helps him gain an understanding of the concept of property rights ("Mine!"). Sometimes toddlers will engage in imitative parallel play: two toddlers will make eye contact and imitate what each other is doing, even though they aren't actually playing together. Note: Some psychologists question the existence of parallel play, arguing that toddlers *do* interact with one another: adults just don't understand the nature of those interactions.
	Preschoolers (ages three to four years)
Associative play (very loosely organized play, e.g., a group of preschoolers may be sharing a box of blocks, but they're each making their own constructions)	Provides a preschooler with opportunities for socialization and teaches him the do's and don'ts of getting along with others (e.g., don't be too bossy). Teaches young children the art of sharing. Encourages language development, problem-solving skills, and, (in the case of cooperative play) cooperation, too. Note: Children this age tend to be socially awkward at first. Their way of indicating that they want to play may be to walk up to another child and grab what that child is playing with. If this occurs, recognize that your preschooler simply wants to play with the other child. Try to defuse the situation by telling the other children that your child wants to play too, while suggesting to your preschooler that he find something similar to play with nearby.

School-aged child (age six and up)

Competitive play (games have rules and there's a clear "winner") Note: There's no room for this type of play with younger children, as they will only find it frustrating.	Gives the child the opportunity to develop special friendships with one or two playmates while enjoying the stimulation of being part of a group. Fosters creativity and self-esteem.

MOM'S THE WORD

"I've been to playgroups, but often found that the parenting philosophies of the other parents were very different from my own. How could I explain to my youngster that we do not allow hitting in our family when a mother is swatting her child for hitting another child? It was too stressful, so we stopped going to that group and I started my own play-group and invited like-minded moms and children to join us."

—*Kerri, 36, mother of six*

The play's the thing

PLAYGROUPS CAN BE a lot of fun for parents and toddlers: parents get the chance to compare notes on the joys and challenges of raising toddlers, while the little ones get the chance to check out one another's toy collections. If you aren't able to find a group in your area to join—or if the playgroup you check out doesn't seem to be quite right for you and your child—then you might want to consider starting your own group instead. Here are a few tips on organizing a playgroup:

- Decide how large you'd like your group to be and start issuing invitations to other mothers you know who have young children. If you dig out your class list from prenatal class you'll have a ready-made group of moms to invite. (Don't worry, you can "accidentally" forget to invite Supermom and her baby genius.)

- Choose a location for your group. You might want to have the group meet in members' homes—rotating from one house to the next—or you might prefer to have your group meet at a community centre or other public space such as a playground. Obviously, you'll have to make sure that group members are willing to chip in a few dollars for the cost of renting a room if you decide to go the community centre route, and, what's more, each family will have to assume responsibility for toting along a few toys (unless, of course, the community centre happens to have a collection of its own). Nonetheless, sometimes it can be easier to meet at a community centre than to psych yourself up for the arrival of a dozen moms and tots at your house the week when you're the host mom!

- Choose your time of day with care. As you've no doubt discovered by now, toddlers tend to be at their best first thing in the morning, when they're most rested. Having an afternoon playgroup can be risky business because it may mean that some of the toddlers in the group will miss out on a much-needed nap—not exactly the best way to guarantee playgroup success!

- Decide what to do about snacks. The simplest approach is to have the host family provide the snack that particular week, taking into account any food allergies within the group. If you're hosting your group in a public place, you can either take turns bringing the snack or put one person in charge of bringing the snack each week. (In this case, you'll want to pass around an envelope and ask everyone to chip in a few bucks.)

- If you're hosting the playgroup in your house, make sure that the area where the children will be playing has been adequately childproofed. If some of the children in the group are significantly older or younger, you'll want to ensure that the environment will be safe for them, too. Similarly, if one of the toddlers is showing potential for a future career as a trapeze artist, make sure that you've childproofed the environment to his standards, too!

- Move your toddler's favourite toys from the family room to his bedroom before the guests start filing in. That way, your

MOTHER WISDOM

"Thou shalt make plenty of play toys available, but not go overboard with a series of let's-make-fantastic-castles-out-of-garbage-bags pro-
jects. You'll just make me look bad when it's my turn."

—Paula Spencer, "Playdate Rules for Parents," Parenting, September 1998

toddler won't be forced to share his most prized possessions.
"If I'm hosting a playgroup at my house, I put some of Joey
and Maggie's favourite toys away because I've found that
they—like most children—get a bit territorial about their
favourite toys," says Ally, a 33-year-old mother of two. "I also
put away toys that tend to be difficult to share because that
helps to avoid problems."

- Encourage the other children attending the playgroup to
  bring along a toy to share (ideally a duplicate of a toy that
  some of the toddlers in the group have found particularly difficult to share in the past). That way, the "host toddler" won't
  be the only one who has to share his toys.

- When you're planning activities for the playgroup, be sure to
  include some neutral ones that don't involve the sharing of
  toys, e.g., playing with playdough, chasing bubbles, or doing
  crafts together as a group.

- Make sure that everyone is in agreement about the ground
  rules for the playgroup, e.g., whether sick kids are allowed to
  attend or not, when it is and isn't appropriate to discipline
  someone else's child, whether the mom who's hosting the
  playgroup is responsible for planning a craft or other group
  activity, and so on.

- Be sure to supervise the toddlers closely. It's unrealistic—even
  dangerous—to leave two toddlers unsupervised during a playdate. So make sure that the area where the moms congregate

for coffee will allow for proper supervision and that you don't all become so caught up in the conversation that you fail to notice that one of the toddlers has gone AWOL.

- Come up with creative solutions for dealing with the inevitable tug-of-war over a toy. A kitchen timer can work wonders: toddlers quickly learn that the telltale "ding" means it's time to hand over the toy. (Note: You'll find additional tips on coping with toddler behaviour challenges in Chapter 4.)

- Give your child a five-minute warning before it's time to go home. That way, he'll have a chance to get used to the idea that the fun is winding down before it's time to put his coat on and leave. Springing the news on him at the last second will result in an unhappy toddler—and consequently an unhappy mom, too.

The "mine" field: The perils of sharing

HERE'S A REASSURING fact to tuck away in your brain for the next time your toddler starts shrieking "Mine!" According to the child development experts, claiming ownership of an object is a major intellectual breakthrough.

MOM'S THE WORD
"Our caregiver had an idea that worked well right from the beginning: 'count to 10 turns.' When the children can't be distracted in any other way and there's only one of a particular toy, the person holding it has to count to 10 and then hand it over. Then the other child has a 'count to 10 turn' and hands the toy back again. Usually, this is enough to satisfy both children, but if it's not, they go back and forth a few more times until one of them gets tired of it and finds something else to do."

—*Joan, 35, mother of five*

MOTHER WISDOM

Start encouraging your toddler to spend short periods of time playing on his own. Learning how to entertain himself will encourage his independence, self-confidence, and creativity.

Of course, given how frustrating this particular toddler trait can be to deal with, you're unlikely to be cracking open the champagne to celebrate the fact that your toddler has achieved this major milestone. Here are some tips on making your way through the "mine" field until your toddler masters the art of sharing:

- Don't expect a young toddler to understand the concept of sharing. He's not yet capable of seeing things from another person's perspective, so it may not even occur to him that someone else might like to play with the same toy that he's playing with.

- Don't expect your child to share his very favourite possessions (e.g., the teddy bear he sleeps with at night). Would you be willing to lend your brand-new car to your sister or your best friend? Would you be willing to hand the remote to your partner seconds before your most favourite (and his least favourite) TV show is about to start? Maybe, maybe not....

- Make sure that your child has plenty of opportunities to play with other children. The more practice he gets with sharing, the easier it will become. Catherine, a 32-year-old mother of four, was surprised when her two-year-old twins came up with a sharing system on their own: "If one of them wants something the other is playing with, he makes an effort to find another really interesting toy to offer his brother in the hope of making a successful exchange. Believe it or not, it usually works!"

- Come up with creative strategies for resolving disputes over toys. Brandy, a 24-year-old mother of two, finds that giving each child a short turn with the toy works well for her family: "If Austin and Ceilidh are fighting over a toy, we use the five-minute rule: one person gets the toy for five minutes and then the other person gets the toy for five minutes. We go back and forth until they agree to share the toy or one of them moves on to something else." Note: An egg timer works well in this situation because it allows a mechanical device rather than a human being to play the role of the "toy police."

Ideas unlimited:
Activities that you and your
toddler can enjoy together

LOOKING FOR SOME ideas for activities that you and your toddler can enjoy together? You'll find plenty of inspiration in this part of the chapter as we zero in on the following types of activities:

- arts and crafts;
- sensory play;
- music;
- dramatic play;
- excursions and outings;

- active play;
- math;
- science;
- reading.

Of course, it would be impossible to list every possible activity for toddlers. There are entire bookshelves full of books on this topic, after all. The best book I've come across to date is *Creative Learning Activities for Young Children* by Judy Herr (Delmar/Thomson Learning, 2001). So when you run through the list of ideas here, you might want to pick up a copy of Herr's book. And, of course, you can find all kinds of great craft

activities by visiting some of the Web sites listed in Appendix C
that feature databases of children's activities. That should help
to keep you and your toddler busy for a while!

Arts and crafts

Arts and crafts activities provide toddlers with the opportunity to
experiment with various types of materials, learn about colours
and shapes, experience different textures, figure out how to use
tools like scissors and paintbrushes, develop pride in their own
creative abilities, express their feelings through art, and work on
both their small muscle coordination and their hand–eye coordination skills.

Stocking the craft cupboard

Of course, before your toddler can start reaping all those arts and
crafts–related benefits, you'll need to have the necessary supplies
on hand. You may end up spending a fair bit of money on basic
tools and supplies, but you can supplement your purchases with
all sorts of inexpensive or free materials—things that would otherwise end up in the trash or the recycling bin (see Table 3.3).

Here are a few important points to keep in mind when you're
shopping for art supplies for your toddler:

MOTHER WISDOM

Index cards are just the right size and thickness for a toddler
who is just learning how to use scissors, so be sure to keep some on hand.
Besides, they come in all kinds of great colours, providing your toddler with
a rainbow of craft possibilities! For best results, cut them in half horizon-
tally. That way, it'll only take your toddler a couple of snips to cut across the
index card.

TODDLER TALK

Don't throw away your toddler's broken crayons. Shorter pieces help to promote a more mature pincer grasp because they cannot be held in the fist-like palmar grasp that young toddlers tend to use when they're holding on to a long crayon.

- Make sure that you avoid art supplies that contain toxic ingredients. Even if your toddler is unlikely to try to chow down on a crayon or to drink liquid paint, art materials are still likely to get on his hands and consequently into his mouth at some point.

- Seek out toddler-sized art supplies to minimize your toddler's frustration. Slightly chunkier markers, paintbrushes, and pencils will be easier for him to manoeuvre than the skinnier versions of these products that are designed for use by older children.

- Some parents purchase small paintbrushes from hardware stores rather than the standard long-handled paintbrushes from craft supply stores because shorter-handled brushes tend to be easier for toddlers to manage.

- While markers tend to produce spectacular results—your toddler can get an explosion of colour without having to apply the same amount of pressure that a crayon demands— they aren't without their problems. Caps tend to get left off or misplaced entirely, and—even worse—they can pose a choking hazard. Add to that the fact that toddlers like to suck on markers or colour themselves with them and you can see why using markers requires a lot of close supervision. (Trust me, there's nothing yuckier than watching a mouthful of green drool ooze down your toddler's chin!)

- Make sure that the child-safe scissors you purchase actually work. (Some child-safe scissors are so safe that they won't cut anything, including paper!) Ideally, you want a pair with a rounded tip, sharp metal blades, and a special little spring that keeps the scissors from closing all the way. (Toddlers can get frustrated when they're using scissors because they get the scissors jammed on the paper and then they can't get them open again. The little spring thing helps to alleviate this particular frustration. If only all toddler problems could be solved this quickly and easily!)

- Rather than purchasing regular "skinny" crayons that tend to snap in two if a toddler applies a lot of pressure, stick to "chunky" crayons that resist breakage. Or, even better, look for the ultimate in durability: hockey-puck-shaped crayons. (Talk about an all-Canadian art experience!) Note: You'll find a recipe in this chapter for making your own hockey-puck-style crayons using muffin tins.

- And speaking of crayons, some early childhood educators recommend that you peel the wrappers off crayons so that toddlers can use all surfaces of the crayon rather than just the tip. You'll have to be the judge of whether this will work with your toddler. If he has a strong perfectionist streak, he might go to pieces if he catches you messing with the labels on his crayons!

- Glue sticks may be the neatest way to dispense glue, but they can be incredibly frustrating for toddlers. Your toddler may

---

MOTHER WISDOM

If your toddler's paint tends to drip because it's too runny, thicken it up with a small amount of flour or cornstarch. (Note: Add flour or cornstarch only to the paint your child is using in this art session. Paint doesn't keep very well once you've added these ingredients.)

MOTHER WISDOM

Reluctant to fork over a lot of money for that nice glossy finger-painting paper? Shelf paper and tinfoil work every bit as well. And, of course, you can skip the paper entirely if you encourage your child to fingerpaint directly on a hard surface such as a mirror, a window, or a sheet of Plexiglas. Don't assume that you'll lose your child's masterpiece forever the moment you pull out a mop or a sponge. You can save the picture for posterity by making a print. Simply place a sheet of paper on top of your toddler's creation and gently rub a rolling pin over it. Voilà! You've now got another fingerpainting to add to your collection.

---

find it easier to use the glue if you pour it into a puddle on a small paper plate and provide him with Q-tips or cotton balls for spreading it.

- Liquid tempera paints are more convenient to use than their powdered counterparts and have a more appealing texture, but they tend to be a bit pricier. Fortunately, you can save money on liquid paints by buying them in bulk from craft supply stores. If you don't think your toddler is going to be able to use all that paint, split your order with another family.

- While you're loading up on paints, pick up an extra package of sponges. Then cut holes in the sponges to hold your child's paint jars in place when he's working at his easel. Not only do the sponges help to prevent the jars from tipping over, but they also help to catch any stray drips.

- Toddlers find it easier to paint at an easel than on a flat surface such as a table. This is because painting at an easel encourages a toddler to extend his wrist—something that provides a more stable position for painting. If you can't afford to buy an easel, make your own by removing one side of a cardboard box and then taping the remaining sides of the box together. You'll end up with a triangular-shaped easel that you can then tape to the tabletop. If that sounds too complicated, here's an even simpler solution: Use tape or magnets to stick a sheet of paper to the side of your refrigerator or steel door and let your toddler use that as his easel.

- Some people recommend letting toddlers fingerpaint with chocolate pudding, yogourt, whipped cream, and other foods. Others insist that this is a bad idea because it sends a mixed message to toddlers about playing with their food—proof positive that there's no element of parenting that's entirely without controversy!

- Something that's often recommended but not necessarily a great idea for toddlers is fingerpainting with shaving cream: not only is there a chance of skin irritation (most shaving creams are positively loaded with chemicals, including powerful colognes), but your toddler could rub some into his eye—which is likely to leave you with one unhappy kid on your hands.

- And speaking of getting stuff rubbed into your toddler's eyes, this is a good reason to "just say no" to glitter until he's a little older. It looks like tremendous fun—and it is, for older kids—but given how easily a bit of glitter can get into a toddler's eye, it's simply not a good choice at this age.

- Don't lose sight of the fact that you can make some of your own art supplies. You'll save money, and in many cases the product will end up being superior to anything you can buy in stores. See Table 3.4 for some recipes that work particularly well. (Note: I left out the yucky-sounding recipe for "Dryer Lint" playdough that I stumbled across while doing my research—my personal pick for this year's strange-but-true recipe award.)

TABLE 3.3

Stocking the Craft Cupboard

Here's a list of the types of art supplies you'll want to have on hand to nurture your budding Picasso's creativity. Note: Some of these materials may pose a choking hazard for younger toddlers, so keep your toddler's developmental stage in mind as you start stocking the craft cupboard.

Basic Tools and Supplies

→ Chalk (regular and sidewalk)

→ Crayons

→ Glitter glue

→ Glue

→ Glue sticks

→ Markers

→ Masking tape

→ Paints (tempera, watercolours, and fingerpaints)

→ Paintbrushes

→ Paper (white paper, construction paper, tissue paper, etc. in all shapes, sizes, and colours)

→ Pastels

→ Pencils (regular and coloured)

→ Playdough or modelling clay

→ School glue

→ Scissors

→ Sponges

→ Stamps and a washable pad

→ Stencils

→ Tape (Scotch Tape or masking tape)

Additional Materials to Collect or Purchase

→ Aluminum foil

→ Beads (large)

continued on p. 94

Additional Materials to Collect or Purchase (continued)

→ Berry boxes

→ Boxes

→ Buttons (large)

→ Calendars

→ Cardboard

→ Catalogues

→ Cereal boxes

→ Chalk

→ Cloth scraps

→ Clothes pegs

→ Coffee filters

→ Confetti

→ Cotton balls

→ Crayon pieces

→ Deodorant bottles (roll-on style for rolling on paint)

→ Doilies

→ Egg cartons

→ Fabric scraps

→ Feathers

→ Felt

→ Flower pots

→ Flowers, artificial or dried

→ Foam and wood shapes

→ Frozen juice cans (cardboard style)

→ Gift-wrap rolls

→ Gloves

→ Greeting cards

→ Hair rollers

→ Junk mail (especially the type with "stamps")

→ Lace

→ Lacing cord

→ Leaves, artificial or dried

→ Magazines and newspapers

→ Makeup brushes

→ Milk cartons

→ Mittens

→ Muffin papers

→ Napkins

→ Paper bags

→ Paper plates

→ Paper towel rolls

→ Paper towels

→ Pasta

→ Pie tins, aluminum

→ Pine cones

→ Pipe cleaners

→ Plastic containers

→ Plastic cups and bottles

→ Pom poms

→ Popsicle sticks

→ Postcards

→ Ribbon

→ Rice (uncooked)

→ Rocks

→ Seashells

→ Shells

→ Shoeboxes

→ Shoe polish applicators (they make great paint applicators)

continued on p. 96

Additional Materials to Collect or Purchase (continued)

→ Socks (for puppets)

→ Spools

→ Squeeze bottles (for paint)

→ Stamps

→ Stickers

→ Straws

→ Styrofoam trays

→ Tissue paper

→ Toilet paper rolls

→ Toothbrushes

→ Wallpaper scraps

→ Wood scraps

→ Wool or string

→ Wrapping paper

TABLE 3.4

Homemade Art Supplies

You don't have to be Martha Stewart to get great results from these craft recipes. (Trust me: I should know!) Note: I've never found a homemade paste recipe that I like, which is why you won't find one here. I think this is one art supply that should be purchased, not made.

Basic Cooked Playdough

→ 500 mL (2 cups) flour
→ 500 mL (2 cups) water
→ 250 mL (1 cup) salt
→ 60 mL (4 tbsp) cream of tartar
→ 30 mL (2 tbsp) vegetable oil
→ Food colouring

Combine the flour, water, salt, cream of tartar, and oil in a saucepan and cook over medium heat, stirring constantly. When the playdough begins to form a ball, it's cooked. Cool for five minutes and then knead in food colouring. Note: It's fun to add glitter and scents like vanilla to playdough as your toddler gets older, but it's best to hold off on this while he's still young enough to be tempted to eat the playdough.

Craft Clay for Homemade Ornaments

→ 250 mL (1 cup) of cornstarch
→ 500 mL (2 cups) of baking soda
→ 375 mL (1½ cups) of water

Combine these ingredients and cook in a saucepan until the clay has acquired a doughlike consistency. Then knead on a lightly floured pastry board. Objects made out of this craft clay can be painted once they've had a chance to air dry.

Fingerpaints

→ 1 L (4 cups) of water
→ 125 mL (½ cup) cornstarch
→ 60 mL (¼ cup) soap flakes
→ A few drops of glycerin
→ A few drops of food colouring

Gradually add water to cornstarch, stirring constantly. Cook until the mixture is clear and then blend in the soap flakes. Finish by adding a few drops of glycerin and food colouring.

Poster Paints

→ 250 mL (1 cup) water
→ 60 mL (¼ cup) flour
→ Dry tempera paint (available at craft supply stores)
→ 3 mL (½ tsp.) liquid dish detergent

Combine the water and flour in a saucepan, heating the mixture over medium heat and stirring constantly for about three minutes. When it starts to thicken, it's time to remove the mixture from the heat. Add the paint and the dish detergent and, if necessary, an additional 30 mL (2 tbsp.) of water.

Goop

→ 250 mL (1 cup) cornstarch
→ 250 mL (1 cup) water
→ Food colouring

Combine ingredients in a bowl and then pour onto a cookie sheet. You can vary the texture by adding more or less water. Your toddler will have fun "fingerpainting" in the goop.

continued on p. 98

Giant Crayons

→ Broken crayons (paper removed)
→ Tinfoil
→ Non-stick cooking spray

Line an old muffin tin with pieces of tinfoil and coat the tinfoil with non-stick cooking spray. Then fill each muffin cup with broken crayons. (You can either sort the crayons by colour or go for a multicoloured effect.) Place the muffin tin in a warm (not hot!) oven and remove the tin once the crayons have melted. Allow the mixture to cool and harden and then pop each giant crayon out and peel the tinfoil off.

Getting organized

Once you accumulate all these bits and pieces, you'll need to figure out what to do with the resulting avalanche of materials. You might find it helpful to set aside a kitchen cupboard for paint bottles, packages of paper, and other large items, and use a fishing tackle box or toolbox to hold smaller items. (The trays are ideal for pencils, crayons, and paintbrushes, while the larger storage area underneath is ideal for feathers, foam chips, and other art supplies.) Cutlery holders can also work well for organizing your toddler's art tools and supplies. The main thing to keep in mind is that the materials need to be easily accessible to your toddler so that he can quickly switch into art mode when a moment of inspiration strikes. That doesn't mean giving him

---

MOM'S THE WORD

"My husband and I have set up activity stations in our daughter's playroom. For example, at one station there are crayons and colouring books and stamps. At another station there are playdough, rolling pins, cookie cutters, and so on. She also has a play kitchen where she pretends to make meals, wash dishes, and feed her dolls."

—Kelli, 32, mother of one

immediate access to the super-messy supplies like paint and glue, but he should be able to get at washable markers, washable crayons, and other similar supplies relatively easily.

Mess patrol

You'll also want to give some thought to how to contain the mess, since even children's art supplies that claim to be washable don't always live up to their name. ("The product labels on the paints and markers may say 'washable,' but that doesn't mean they come out of all fabrics and surfaces," warns Anita, a 39-year-old mother of four.) But you don't want to be a total spoilsport when it comes to messes, of course: As Julie, a 30-year-old mother of one, notes, "Being messy is part of the fun!"

Here are a few tips:

- Designate a certain area of your home as the craft zone and let your toddler know that while it's okay to make messes when he's doing crafts, they're to be done only in that one particular location. After all, it's one thing to mop a bit of paint off your kitchen floor, and quite another to try getting that same blob of red paint off your living room carpet.

- To minimize the amount of cleanup and to prevent your child's art supplies from damaging your kitchen table, throw a plastic tablecloth or shower curtain or a green garbage bag that you've sliced open across the table before your toddler starts doing crafts. A quick wipe-down with a damp sponge is all that's required once your toddler is finished working his magic with paint and glue.

- Figure out what you need to do to protect your toddler's clothing. You can use a paint smock, an old raincoat (cut off the sleeves and put it on your child backwards), an apron-style bib, or some other sort of garment (e.g., an old dress shirt) to protect your child's clothing. Or, if the weather's nice, you may find it easier to simply strip your child down to his diaper.

- Get in the habit of adding a squirt of liquid soap or liquid laundry detergent to your child's liquid paints to encourage any paint-related stains to wash out more easily in the laundry. And if your toddler manages to get a blob of paint under

---

MOTHER WISDOM

You'll be less stressed about craft splatters and other toddler-related stains if your home is decorated to hide dirt. Here are some points to consider the next time you go into reno mode:

- Go with matte rather than glossy finishes on walls, countertops, and floors. High-gloss finishes tend to emphasize spills, scratches, and fingerprints—the last thing you need when you've got a toddler on the loose!
- Paint any exposed woodwork with semi-gloss paint that can be wiped down easily.
- When you're choosing paint colours, zero in on medium-tone rather than dark or light colours, since these shades do a better job of hiding dirt.
- Sponge-paint your walls or go for some other faux finishing technique that creates patterns within the paint. This will help to hide fingerprints, ketchup splatters, and the inevitable scribble mark or two.
- Think durability if you're in the market for wallpaper. Don't settle for anything less than a high-quality washable vinyl or your wallpaper will be damaged in no time. Toddlers tend to pick at wallpaper seams and have even been known to tear off large chunks of wallpaper. You might want to hold off on wallpapering until your toddler comes through the prime wallpaper-removal stage.
- Stick with easy-to-clean flooring in the high-traffic areas of your home. Remember, vinyl flooring is a mom's best friend! If you've got your heart set on carpeting, stick with highly textured berbers. Plush carpeting and toddlers don't make for a particularly winning combination.
- Avoid indented or embossed tile or floor coverings, unfinished wood trim, and carpet in the kitchen or bathroom, all surfaces difficult to keep clean.

his paint smock, rub some soap into the spot right away. Then, when he's finished painting, whisk the paint-splattered garment away and soak it until the paint stain starts to lift.

- Realize that less can be more when you're dishing out the art supplies. It's a lot easier to clean up a spill from a small container of paint or glue than a huge, litre-sized bottle! To minimize the disaster potential, put small amounts of glue or paint in small containers or on pie plates. Your toddler can then apply the glue using a cotton ball, a Q-tip, a small paintbrush, a Popsicle stick, or a small piece of sponge held by a clothes peg.

- Supervise your toddler closely when he's doing crafts. "We ended up with charming green handprints permanently stained onto our kitchen wall for two years, and a row of craft paper glued to the wall for the month—the result of a couple of minutes of inattention," says Anita, a 39-year-old mother of four.

- Hang wet paintings to dry on a clothesline in your basement or bathtub. That way, your toddler is less likely to accidentally sit down on a wet, paint-covered masterpiece.

- If all else fails, check out The Mother of All Stain Removal Charts in Chapter 5 (for dealing with stains on clothing) and the craft stain removal chart (Table 3.5) for dealing with craft-related stains on various types of household surfaces.

Nurturing your child's creativity

The best way to encourage toddlers' creativity is to provide them with the necessary arts and crafts materials and then back off. "Don't show them how to do it, don't tell them how to do it, and don't label their creations," advises Brandy, a 24-year-old mother of two. "Let them use their imagination instead."

Julie agrees that it's important to take a hands-off approach to art activities. "I think it's crucial for parents to let kids do crafts their own way," the 30-year-old mother of one insists. "If they want to make a puppet with six eyes, that should be okay."

TABLE 3.5

Craft-related Stains

A few splatters and spills are inevitable when toddlers are doing crafts. Here are some tips on getting craft-related stains off some common household surfaces:

→ Use baking soda and a damp cloth to remove crayon marks or tempera paint from painted walls and wood. If that doesn't do the trick, you can also experiment with baby oil, liquid detergent, silver polish, or toothpaste.

→ If you're faced with a really chunky buildup of crayon, try painting a layer of rubber cement over the crayon mark. Once the rubber cement has had a chance to dry, you should be able to peel off most of the crayon mark.

→ Rub a slice of dry bread over your wallpaper to remove pencil marks.

→ Use white vinegar to remove ballpoint pen marks from walls and wooden surfaces.

→ To remove stickers from walls, saturate the sticker with white vinegar or vegetable oil.

→ To hide scratches in wooden furniture, reach for your toddler's crayon box. Then use a crayon of the appropriate shade of brown to "colour in" the scratches.

→ To remove crayon marks from carpeting, place a thick stack of paper towels on the stained area and use a warm iron to heat up the wax. The heat should help to draw the crayon up into the paper towels.

Note: The usual stain removal disclaimers apply! Tackle a less noticeable area first and then proceed with caution, using the least powerful stain removal technique first. And when you pull out that iron, be sure to keep the temperature low: The last thing you want is to melt or burn a hole in your living room carpet!

MOM'S THE WORD
"Isabel has never liked colouring books. She complains that 'the pictures are already there.'"
—*Stephanie, 29, mother of one*

Of course, that doesn't mean you should ignore what your toddler is doing for fear of stifling his creativity. It's okay to do crafts right alongside him provided you're prepared to follow his lead. Supporting his creativity in this way isn't merely fun for you, by the way: it's also good for your toddler. Studies have shown that children whose parents participate in their creative activities tend to develop larger vocabularies and more advanced cognitive abilities than kids whose parents sit on the sidelines.

That said, there's a fine line between being involved and taking over the activity. Contrary to what many parents believe, it's not necessary to "teach" your toddler how to do art by helping, correcting, or making suggestions to improve the quality of the final product. As Judy Herr notes in her book *Creative Learning Activities for Young Children,* "Given maturation and experience, his work will gradually become more refined." A better strategy is to comment on the process ("Wow, you're using a lot of different colours today!") and encourage your toddler to talk about his work ("Tell me about your painting"). After all, it's the process more than the quality of the final product that is likely to capture his attention during the toddler years.

And if your toddler comes up with unconventional ways of using his art materials, do what you can to encourage that free thinking. Let him know that you think his idea about painting with pipe cleaners is really cool! (Of course, there will be times when you have to gently redirect your toddler's artistic endeavours—like if he decides that the living room curtains would benefit from some colourful splashes of red paint.)

TODDLER TALK

Here's another important point to consider if you're tempted to show your toddler how to make the perfect paper snowflake: demonstrating craft activities for toddlers may set a standard that is too difficult to live up to. After all, it's a rare toddler indeed who can get picture-perfect results the first time he picks up a paintbrush or a pair of scissors.

And don't be afraid to suggest some alternative uses for art supplies yourself. Kelly, 31, finds that she and her two toddlers have more fun when they try something a little out of the ordinary—like painting, cutting, and gluing playdough. Ditto for Julie, a 30-year-old mother of one: "We paint with all kinds of things: fingers, spongers, fat brushes, thin brushes, Q-tips, apples cut in half, and potatoes with shapes cut into them," she explains. Kristina, a 32-year-old mother of two, is also a strong believer in encouraging toddlers to "colour outside the lines"— both literally and figuratively. "Fingerpainting on the kitchen linoleum floor is the best!" she insists.

Of course, a willingness to allow your toddler free artistic rein doesn't necessarily guarantee that he'll develop a passion for art. Some toddlers—particularly those of the exceptionally wiggly variety—don't want anything to do with crafts. "I have two non-crafty kids," says Jennie, a 32-year-old mother of two-year-old twins. "I've tried and tried, but they will not sit long enough to attempt a project—even something as simple as fingerpainting. They're just not interested."

If, like Jennie, you have a toddler who turns his nose up at crafts, your best bet is to wait a few weeks or months before trying to whet his interest in art again. You might, for example, try squirting a few different colours of liquid paint into a zip-lock bag along with a bit of cooking oil and then showing your toddler how to "fingerpaint" by squishing the paint around. Note:

This type of activity is likely to have greater appeal for a particularly active toddler than an art activity that absolutely has to be enjoyed while sitting down.

And, of course, the best way to encourage your toddler's creativity is to let him know just how much you value his art by displaying it in a place of honour in your home. There are countless ways to do this, but here are a few ideas:

- Hang his artwork on the refrigerator door where it can be admired each time someone is looking for a snack.

- Hang his artwork on the inner surface of any exterior steel doors in your home. (Four strategically placed fridge magnets can do a great job of holding artwork in place so that it doesn't blow away when someone opens the door.)

- Hang a miniature clothesline along one wall in your child's bedroom so that he can clip his artwork to it. Or turn one wall of his room into a gigantic bulletin board by applying a thin layer of cork. Of course, you'll need to hang your child's artwork for him and keep the pushpins out of his reach until he's a little older. You don't want him to end up putting a pushpin in his mouth.

- Buy some inexpensive picture frames or make some frames of your own out of cardboard or other materials. (You can get some pretty impressive results by simply painting a picture-frame-shaped piece of cardboard with gold paint and then decorating it with coloured pasta or glitter.) You can also mount a favourite picture on placque board.

- Laminate your toddler's artwork to make a special set of placemats. You might even encourage your toddler to make a second set to give to his grandparents or some other relative or friend on the next special occasion.

- Scan one of your toddler's creations and use the image as a screen saver on your computer. Or incorporate one of his illustrations into the family form letter you send out at holiday time. (You do send out a form letter, now don't you? You don't want to make the rest of us moms look bad by sending out—gasp—personalized letters!)

Some fun arts and crafts activities to try

Now that you've loaded up on art supplies and given some thought to how you're going to simultaneously contain the mess *and* nurture your child's creativity (no small feat, that), it's time to get down to the real nitty-gritty: coming up with fun ideas for activities to enjoy with your toddler. Here are a few ideas:

- Draw a thick line on a piece of paper using an extra-wide magic marker. Your toddler can practise cutting along the line. Start out with straight lines, progressing to curvy lines as your toddler becomes more skilled at handling the scissors. Hint: You might want to also give your toddler the opportunity to practice some "pre-cutting" activities like filling eye droppers and turkey basters with water or using plastic tongs to lift cotton balls. The manouevres used are similar to those involved in manipulating a pair of scissors.

- Help your toddler drizzle some glue on a sheet of construction paper. He can then sprinkle sand, cornmeal, or birdseed on top of the glue to make a picture.

- Show your toddler how to make a puppet by gluing a toilet paper roll to a Popsicle stick. Of course, you can also make puppets out of socks, paper bags, and other materials. (See the material on puppet-making later in this chapter.)

- Gather up textured objects like leaves and use them to make rubbings with crayons. (Place the leaf underneath the sheet of paper and rub the crayon on top of the sheet of paper. You should end up with an imprint of the shape of the leaf.)

- Unroll a sheet of MacTac and place it sticky side up. Then give your toddler a variety of art materials to stick on the MacTac. Apply a second sheet of MacTac or a piece of construction paper and—voilà!—you'll have some instant artwork.

- Trace your toddler's hand and feet on a sheet of paper or let him make handprints and footprints with paint. (This is a great outdoor activity for a warm summer day.)

- Let your toddler fingerpaint on a window or mirror or in the bottom of the bathroom sink. If he's not into getting his fingers dirty, he can use a paintbrush instead.

- Attach bubble wrap to a paint roller. Your toddler will enjoy observing how the bubble wrap affects the design he's able to produce with the paint roller.

- Give your toddler a bunch of fun alternatives to paintbrushes: sponges, feathers, old toothbrushes, combs, Q-tips, a potato masher, apple slices cut into shapes, and so on.

- Make a stamp pad by placing wet paper towels in a small bowl and covering the paper towel with paint.

- Give your child the chance to paint the house or the sidewalk with coloured water. (It won't actually colour these, but the water will look like paint while it's in the pail.)

TODDLER TALK

Contrary to popular belief, colouring books do not enhance creativity. They're the creativity world's equivalent to Twinkies—junk food for the brain! That's not to say that you should ban them from your house entirely: just make sure that you provide your toddler with a balanced diet of "nutrient-rich" art supplies, too.

TODDLER TALK

Don't make the mistake of assuming that your toddler's scribbles are nothing more than random doodles. Believe it or not, there's actually some order in that sea of markings. Toddlers start out by drawing a series of horizontal lines, eventually progressing to vertical lines, too. Then they move on to drawing incomplete circles, closed circles, and spider or sun patterns. So there you go: a crash course in the science of scribbling!

- Pop the ball out of an empty roll-on deodorant bottle and fill the bottle with liquid tempera paint. Snap the ball back into place and—voilà—your child will have a fun roll-on art tool. Just make sure to keep the bottle away from the bathroom or you could end up starting your day with neon-green armpits!

- Make pasta necklaces using large pasta. You can paint the pasta first using tempera paints or combine food colouring with a little water to dye the pasta instead. (Simply dip the pasta in the coloured water for about 10 seconds and then allow it to dry overnight. Note: Be sure to wear plastic or rubber gloves as this may stain your fingers.)

- Make paperweights by painting rocks. (Once your toddler has finished painting, you can seal the rock by spraying on varnish.)

- Roll a cob of corn in a shallow dish containing a thin layer of paint and then roll it along a piece of paper.

- Dip a plastic strawberry basket in a shallow dish containing a thin layer of paint and then press it on a sheet of paper. Hint: A frisbee or a tin pie plate tends to work particularly well.

- Place a blob of paint in the centre of a large sheet of paper. Drive a toy car through the puddle and watch how the wheels leave tracks on the page.

- Place a piece of paper in the bottom of a square cookie tin. Dribble a bit of paint on the sheet of paper and add a ping-pong or golf ball. Put the lid on tightly and show your toddler how to shake the container vigorously. The ball will end up "painting" the page.

Sensory play

Sensory play refers to any activity that stimulates your toddler's senses. It includes many of the art activities mentioned above as well as many of the music and movement activities we'll be discussing later in this chapter. What could be more sensory, after all, than squeezing playdough through your fingers, walking through puddles of paint with your feet, or listening to the beating of a drum?

Sensory play provides a fun and relaxing way for your toddler to learn about the world around him. It also gives him a chance to experiment with such basic mathematical concepts as volume and measurement and to encounter gravity and other scientific principles. Add to that the fact that sensory play allows him to improve his fine motor control and hand–eye coordination skills, and you can see that your toddler can learn a great deal through sensory play.

Here are a few of the most popular types of sensory play activities for toddlers.

Water play

It's no wonder toddlers and their parents love water play: water is readily available and it's free! While you might want to round out your child's water play by including funnels, pumps, and other types of water-play accessories (see Table 3.6), the key ingredient is nothing other than good old-fashioned H2O.

MOTHER WISDOM

Store your child's bath toys in a mesh lingerie bag and hang the bag from the tap so that the toys can drip dry between uses. Then, when it comes time to give them a more thorough cleaning, simply tie the bag shut and drop it into your washing machine or dishwasher. (Keep your dishwasher's heat setting on low so that you don't inadvertently end up melting some of your toddler's favourite toys!)

Your toddler has a prime opportunity for water play every time he hops in the bathtub, but you may wish to provide some additional water-play opportunities by either placing a bin of water and some water-play accessories on the kitchen or bathroom floor or putting a few inches of water in a wading pool, baby bathtub, or oversized plastic bin. (Obviously, you'll want to supervise your child carefully, since children have been known to drown in even a couple of inches of water.) Your toddler will also enjoy watering the grass, using squirt bottles, and pouring water through a water wheel.

TABLE 3.6

Water-Play Accessories: What to Have on Hand

→ Bottles

→ Bowls

→ Bubble-blowing solution (you can make your own by mixing equalparts of liquid dish soap and water)

→ Buckets

→ Cups

→ Eye droppers

→ Film containers (plastic cases)

→ Funnels

→ Ice cube trays

→ Ladles

→ Measuring cups

→ Measuring spoons

→ Pitchers

→ Plastic containers (including some with holes punched in
the bottom)

→ Plastic tubing

→ Salad spinner

→ Scoops

→ Shovels

→ Sponges

→ Squeeze bottles

→ Squirt bottle (trigger style)

→ Strainers

→ Straws

→ Styrofoam meat trays

→ Toy boats

→ Turkey baster

→ Watering can

→ Water piping (available from your local plumbing store)

→ Water pumps

→ Water wheel

MOTHER WISDOM

Here's something fun to try the next time you're helping your
toddler blow bubbles. Dip a plastic strawberry box in bubble-blowing solution and hold it in front of a fan. You'll both be delighted by the resulting
cascade of bubbles.

Sand play

Like water play, sand play can be enjoyed both indoors and out-doors. (Good thing, or Canadian kids would end up being a lit-tle short-changed in the sensory play department!) All you need is a large plastic container with a lid or sandbox. (If you go the outdoor sandbox route, a lid is *de rigueur*. Otherwise, your child's sandbox could quickly become the neighbourhood cat's favourite litterbox.)

As for what to put inside your child's sandbox, white play sand is the crème de la crème of sand, known for its fine, almost silky texture. You can find it at your local hardware store or department store.

If you'd like an alternative to sand, you can use rice, cornmeal, oatmeal, or birdseed instead. Just remember to discard it on a regular basis so that it doesn't become a breeding ground for dis-ease and/or attract rodents or bugs! And some parents choose to avoid using food products in the sandbox for the same reason they don't allow their children to fingerpaint with chocolate pud-ding or yogourt: they think it sends young children mixed mes-sages about food.

Here's some good news if you're on a bit of a budget: a lot of water toys can double as sand toys. (And, of course, a lot of water toys can be made from things you already have around the house—which makes them free or next to free.) You might also want to add a few bells and whistles, however: things like shov-els, spoons, coffee scoops, sieves, a flour sifter, some old plastic dishes, small fishnets, shells, twigs, rocks, gardening tools, and some sandbox-sized cars, animals, or people.

Snow play

And now we come to the ultimate Canadian sensory play expe-rience—playing in the snow! In addition to lugging your child's sand and water toys out into the backyard, you might want to try some of the following activities with your toddler:

- **Winter bubble fun:** If your toddler loves blowing bubbles in the summer, he'll have even more fun blowing bubbles when the temperature goes below zero. It's possible to catch the bubbles on the bubble wand and watch them freeze.

- **Ice cube surprise:** Place some toys in a milk carton and fill the milk carton with water. Place it outside until it's frozen and then bring it back inside. Then peel off the carton and place the ice block in a large bowl. Your toddler will enjoy watching the toys reappear as the ice block melts.

- **Frozen rainbow:** Here's a variation on the previous activity. Instead of freezing toys in the carton, freeze layer upon layer of water that has been coloured with food colouring. If you use enough colours, you'll end up with a rainbow effect. Your toddler will enjoy watching the rainbow melt before his eyes.

- **Snow painting:** Fill plastic squirt bottles with coloured water. Your toddler will have a great time "painting" the snow.

Other sensory play ideas

The sky is the limit in sensory play opportunities, but here are a few things you might want to try with your toddler:

- **Playdough fun:** Playing with playdough and other types of modelling materials (including goop) is a terrific form of sensory play. Your toddler will enjoy using a variety of accessories with his playdough, including cake-decorating tools (provided the playdough is extra soft), plastic dishes, a cheese slicer, cookie cutters, a playdough press (you can pick one up at a garage sale or buy one new), an egg slicer, a pizza cutter, plastic knives, Popsicle sticks, a rolling pin (you can make your own using wooden dowelling), and, as we mentioned earlier, a pair of toddler-safe scissors so that he can cut the playdough into pieces.

• **Silly Putty:** Whether you opt for the commercial variety or make your own (simply mix 250 mL [1 cup] of liquid starch, 250 mL [1 cup] of white glue, and a few drops of food colouring), your toddler will have fun exploring the properties of this strange, rubbery material. Just one word of caution: Don't allow your toddler to play with Silly Putty unsupervised. This is not the kind of thing you want him to be putting in his mouth.

• **Cooking:** Cooking is the ultimate sensory play experience because it can appeal to all of your child's senses—unless, of course, you make something "yucky" that his taste buds aren't willing to try! Because a toddler's attention span is pretty limited, you'll want to stick to "quick and dirty" recipes like applesauce rather than attempting more involved ones like a soufflé. (Besides, what do you think your odds are of having that soufflé rise just perfectly when you've got a toddler running around your kitchen?!!)

Music

Music is another form of sensory play. It helps your toddler develop his listening skills, promotes the development of auditory memory, stimulates the imagination, and can help him to relax and unwind.

Here are some fun ways to work music into your child's life:

• Invest in a CD player or a children's tape recorder so that you can expose your child to a wide variety of music: everything from lullabies to classical to rock. (You'll want to go easy on

TODDLER TALK

Don't allow your toddler to listen to music with headphones on unless you're monitoring the volume carefully. If he were to crank up the volume too loud, he might end up doing permanent damage to his hearing.

the rap, of course; otherwise your toddler's vocabulary may end up including some rather colourful four-letter words.)

- Sing with your child. According to Judy Herr, author of *Creative Learning Activities for Young Children*, toddlers find it easiest to master songs with strong melodies.

- Take your toddler to concerts and other live music events that are geared to very young children. Concerts for adults are sometimes too long and too loud.

- Make some homemade musical instruments so that your toddler can enjoy making some music of his own. (See Table 3.7 for instructions on how to make various types of home made musical instruments.)

- Find fun ways to enjoy music with your toddler. Flip on some music with a powerful beat and have your toddler lead your family "marching band" around the house. Light up one wall in a room and try "shadow dancing" together. Sing some familiar songs together using different types of voices: happy voices, grouchy voices, high voices, low voices, and so on. And make some props so that you can act out some of the actions in your favourite songs (e.g., help your toddler make monkey puppets to play with when you're listening to Sharon, Lois, and Bram sing "Five Little Monkeys").

TABLE 3.7

Homemade Musical Instruments

Type of Instrument	How to Make It
Pots and Pans	Time to organize your own in-house pots-and-pans band! This is the easiest type of homemade instrument—one that doesn't require any work on your part at all. Simply set your toddler loose in the pots-and-pans cupboard. He can bang on your pots with a metal or wooden spoon, bang pot lids together like cymbals, or turn a cookie sheet into a gong.
Shakers	Shakers can be made out of just about anything: containers with lids (e.g., film canisters, potato chip cans, popcorn and nut cans, coffee cans, empty dishwasher detergent bottles, or empty pop bottles); plastic Easter eggs that can be taken apart and filled; salt and pepper shakers; tin pie plates; and so on. Simply fill the container with something that will make a really satisfying noise when shaken—marbles, rice, pasta, beans, nuts and bolts, or small rocks, for example—and then glue the lid on tightly.
Washboard	Believe it or not, you can still purchase metal washboards in hardware stores. They make terrific musical instruments. All your toddler has to do is rub the washboard with a wooden stick or a metal spoon, and voilà—an explosion of sound.
Wooden Blocks	Cut two hand-sized pieces of wood for your toddler to bang together. You can either leave them au naturel or attach a small piece of sandpaper to each block so that they make a satisfying swooshing sound. (If you go the sandpaper route, you'll want to supervise their use extra-carefully to prevent any skinned knuckles and/or sanded furniture.)

continued on p. 117

Type of Instrument	How to Make It
Kazoo	Cover the end of a toilet-paper roll with a piece of tissue paper, holding the tissue paper in place with an elastic band. When your toddler blows against the tissue paper, he'll be rewarded with a kazoo-like sound.
Twanger	What toddler can resist a twanger—a musical instrument that consists of a doorstop attached to a piece of wood? Just one quick word of caution before you set your future pop star loose with his twanger: make sure that the rubber tip at the end of the doorstop is glued on securely to eliminate the risk of choking.

Note: While it's possible to make your own homemade drums, tambourines, and bells, you'll get better results by purchasing rather than making these items. So invest your creative energies in making some other type of homemade musical instrument. Steer clear of musical instruments like triangles and cymbals that require more advanced fine motor skills than your toddler is likely to have at this age. You'll succeed only in driving your toddler—and consequently yourself—crazy.

Dramatic play

As the name implies, dramatic play involves acting out scenes based on real life. Each time Mr. Dressup reached inside his tickle trunk to pull out a funny hat or wig, he was teaching Canadian kids the art of dramatic play.

Dramatic play isn't all fun and games, however. It's also highly educational. It allows toddlers to build their vocabulary, develop both their fine- and large-muscle skills, work on their hand–eye coordination, experiment with people and things, explore and learn to make sense of the world around them, face problems and come up with creative solutions, and express feelings they may not feel comfortable expressing in real life.

Since toddlers tend to be natural-born drama queens (and kings) anyway, why not encourage your toddler to put some of that flair to good use by engaging in some dramatic play? Here are a few tips:

- Provide your child with some props that will allow his imagination to soar. Table 3.8 lists popular dramatic play themes along with the types of props that can help to encourage such play. Note: You don't have to provide your child with each prop or introduce him to every single theme. You'd need a warehouse to store all the props! Instead, pick a few themes, dig up a few props, and leave the rest to your toddler.

- Don't assume you have to go broke trying to supply your toddler with all kinds of costumes and props. A little imagination can take your child a long way. A towel can be magically transformed into a magic carpet or a superhero's cape in the blink of an eye without you having to fork over a penny. And, of course, some of the best treasures of all can be found if you dig deep enough into your clothes closet. Who knows? You may finally have a use for that oh-so-tacky *Flashdance* wear that was all the rage back in the late eighties!

TABLE 3.8

Dramatic Play Themes and Props

Dramatic Play Theme	Recommended Props
Baby	Baby doll, doll clothes, baby bathtub, cradle, stroller, high chair
Beach	Towels, sunglasses, picnic basket, beach music, sandbox full of sand, pails and shovels
Camping	Tent, sleeping bags, backpacks, cooking utensils, plastic food, logs for the fire
Cleaning	Broom and dustpan, toy vacuum cleaner, pail with sponges and a duster
Construction	Wheelbarrow, pieces of wood, plastic pipes, tools, hard hats
Cooking	Plastic food, child-sized furniture, plastic dishes, apron
Doctor	First aid kit, bandages, a bed for the patient, a doctor's coat, a nurse's hat
Dress-up	Dress-up clothes, hats, wigs, shoes, purses, costume jewellery
Fairy Godmother	Magic wand, fancy dress, fancy shoes
Farm	Barn and plastic animals, animal costumes, animal puppets
Fireman	Fireman's hat and boots, yellow raincoats, fire hose (e.g., a vacuum cleaner hose or a garden hose)
Fishing	Boat (e.g., cardboard box), fish made out of cardboard, fishing rods (wooden dowels with string attached), tackle box, life jackets

continued on p. 120

Dramatic Play Theme	Recommended Props
Grocery Store	Plastic fruit and vegetables, play food, cash register, play money, paper bags
Gym	Workout mat, wristbands, headbands, aerobic class music, weights made from Tinkertoys
Hairdresser	Shampoo bottles, combs, wigs, hair ribbons, an old blow dryer or curling iron with the cord cut off
House	Large cardboard box for a house, dollhouse
Pet Store	Stuffed animals, toy cash register, play money, empty pet-food boxes
Picnic	Picnic basket, plastic dishes, plastic utensils, plastic food
Police Officer	Police hat and badge, whistle, walkie-talkie, handcuffs
Princess	Crown (cardboard and tinfoil), fancy dress, fancy shoes
Post Office	Mailbox, old junk mail, letter carrier's hat and bag, postage scale
Restaurant	Child-sized table and chairs, tablecloth, plastic dishes and utensils, menus
Tea Party	Plastic tea set, table, chairs, and dolls or stuffed animals to serve as guests
Village	Miniature buildings, people, and cars (either homemade or bought)
Workshop	Measuring tape, tools, a tool box, a carpenter's belt
Zoo	Tiny plastic animals, plastic berry baskets for cages

- If there are some props that you'd like to add to your child's collection, take heart: you're likely to find plenty of treasures by hitting the thrift shops and garage sales or the post-Halloween sales. And if you're lucky enough to have a toy-lending library in your community, you may even be able to borrow costumes and other dramatic play props for free.

- Don't make the mistake of thinking you have to be Martha Stewart in order to whip up a costume or prop for your child. You'd be amazed by the great things that can be made out of cardboard, tinfoil, and old clothing.

- Keep your toddler's safety in mind when you're buying and making costumes, and have some family rules about where costumes can be worn. Keep the strings on costumes short and don't allow your child to wear capes and other dangling types of clothing on playground equipment.

Puppets

Puppets also allow for all kinds of fabulous dramatic play possibilities. You can purchase ready-made hand or finger puppets or—if you're feeling inspired—you and your toddler can make puppets at home. Here are a few ideas to get you started:

- **Paper bag puppets:** Paper bag puppets are, without a doubt, the easiest type of puppet for a toddler to make. You simply decorate a paper lunch bag with crayons or markers, glue on a few construction paper accessories, and voilà!—you've got a puppet to play with. The only drawback to paper bag puppets is that they can't withstand a lot of abuse, like being dipped in your toddler's milk or smooshed into a plate of spaghetti, and, what's more, they can rip easily if your toddler is putting a lot of gusto into a puppet performance.

- **Paper plate puppets:** Paper plate puppets are almost as easy to make as paper bag puppets and tend to be a bit more durable. Simply fold a paper plate in half and decorate it. Unfortunately, your toddler may have a bit of difficulty getting your puppet's mouth to open and shut, so you may have to play puppeteer with this type of puppet.

- **Sock puppets:** An old sock can be transformed into a puppet by gluing or sewing on pieces of fabric, felt, wool, vinyl, or paper. (Of course, you'll want to avoid buttons, googly-eyes, and other hard objects for now in case your toddler manages to pull them off and swallow them.) You can either leave the sock loose and floppy so that your toddler can insert his hand all the way to the end of the sock or you can stuff part of the sock with paper or fabric to give the puppet a more stuffed animal-like appearance. Note: If you stuff part of the sock, you'll probably want to mount the puppet on a wooden dowel to make it easier for your toddler to manipulate.

- **Finger puppets:** Cut the fingers off an old pair of gloves and you'll be able to whip up a whole family of finger puppets for your toddler. You can glue on small pieces of fabric, embroider on some eyes using a bit of wool, or draw a face on the paper using a permanent marker. (Obviously, you'll want to maintain total control over the permanent marker rather than share it with your toddler.)

- **Papier-mâché puppet faces:** Papier-mâché puppets are easier to make than you might think. Simply blow up a balloon and papier-mâché it. (Combine 125 mL (½ cup) of all-purpose flour with 500 mL (2 cups) of cold water. Add this mixture to a saucepan containing 500 mL (2 cups) of boiling water. Remove the mixture from the heat, stir in the sugar, and allow the mixture to cool. Then dip newspaper strips into the paste, using your thumb and forefinger to squeeze off any extra paste, and apply them to the balloon, leaving a small opening around the knot of the balloon.) Allow the papier-mâché to dry completely (it will take about 12 hours) and then apply another two or three layers. Once those layers have also had a chance to dry, pop the balloon. (Important: Get rid of the popped balloon immediately so that your toddler can't accidentally choke on it.) Then insert a wooden dowel through the opening at the bottom of the balloon and papier-mâché the dowel into place. Once the papier-mâché has dried completely, you and your toddler can paint and decorate the puppet.

Once you've finished making puppets, you may want to make some sort of puppet theatre. The easiest thing to do is to hang a baby gate across the bottom half of a doorframe and cover the gate with a towel. Your toddler can crouch behind the gate and give a puppet show. If you'd like to come up with something more elaborate, you can make a puppet theatre by carving a hole in a large cardboard box or by constructing a puppet theatre out of plywood or particle board.

Excursions and outings

Starting to develop a case of cabin fever? Why not plan a few outings with your toddler? Not only will the two of you have a lot of fun exploring the neighbourhood, but you'll also be helping your toddler learn about his world. Of course, you'll want to take your toddler's likes and dislikes into account when planning your itinerary: if he's absolutely petrified of animals, you might want to postpone that zoo trip for a while.

In addition to everyday destinations such as the post office, grocery store, and drugstore, you might want to plan some extra-special outings to such destinations as the park or playground, a nursery or a garden store, the beach, a nature sanctuary, a children's museum, an aquarium or a zoo, a farm, a library or bookstore, a

MOTHER WISDOM

Planning a trip to a zoo or other attraction? Here are a few tips to ensure that you survive the outing with your sanity relatively intact:

- Give some thought to the timing of your visit. It's best to hit the attraction a few minutes after the gates open: not so early that you have to wait in line with the rest of the crowd, but early enough to be able to take advantage of the cooler early-morning temperatures. There's nothing more exhausting than trying to walk through a zoo at 12:00 p.m. in the blazing sun.

- If your toddler is out of diapers, find the location of the washrooms in the park the moment you walk through the front gates. That way, you'll know exactly where they're located if your toddler needs one in a hurry. Hint: If there's a washroom near the zoo gates, encourage your child to use it before you start exploring the attraction. That should help to eliminate at least one impromptu sprint to the washroom.

- Be realistic about how much of the attraction you intend to take in. If you're visiting a large zoo or museum, you may need to make a number of different trips on different days if you're determined to take in each and every exhibit. Toddlers aren't exactly known for having long attention spans, after all!

- Avoid any exhibits that your child is likely to find particularly scary. If, for example, your toddler is deathly afraid of cats, you might want to bypass the lion cage or the tiger exhibit until he's a little older.

- Consider the temperament of your kids. If you've got a toddler who loves to run away, confine that toddler to a stroller or backpack or—if he insists on walking—use some sort of toddler harness or safety strap system instead.

- Make a point of bringing an umbrella stroller with you even if your toddler is usually determined to walk. He may welcome the chance to hitch a ride in the stroller after an hour or two of running off steam! Besides, if you've got older children who are frustrated by the way their younger brother dawdles, popping him in the stroller every now and again will allow the rest of the family to pick up the pace a little.

- If you're bringing along a picnic lunch to enjoy—a great way to cut down on the cost of your excursion, by the way, provided you're actually allowed to bring your own food and drinks past the front gates—make a point of including some frozen juice boxes. They'll help to keep your toddler's sandwich chilled and, as an added bonus, by the time lunchtime rolls around your child will have an icy cold drink to enjoy. Note: If you use the refillable plastic kind of juice box, don't overfill it or the container may crack when you freeze it.

- Decide on a family colour when you go on outings and have every family member wear T-shirts and ball caps of that colour. Try to stick to something bright and eye-catching like yellow, red, or green so that each member of the family will stand out in a crowd. That way, if you momentarily let go of your toddler's hand and he disappears from sight, you'll be able to find him again in a flash.
- Tape your toddler's contact information to the inside of his shoe—information that could prove invaluable to the zoo or park staff if your toddler were to become separated from you. And if you happen to own a cellphone, be sure to include that number, too, and then make a point of bringing your cellphone with you on your outing.
- Play games or sing songs while you're waiting in line for an exhibit so that your toddler will be less tempted to wander off. More often than not, it's boredom that causes toddlers to wander.
- Maintain reasonable parent–kid ratios. One adult per kid is the ideal if you're hitting a busy attraction. Hire a teenager or invite along an extra relative or two if you've got more kids than grown-ups in your group. This is one of those situations where you don't want to be outnumbered.

---

construction site, a firehall or police station (call ahead to make sure they welcome young visitors), and/or an airport or train station. If your toddler doesn't get to travel by bus very often, you might want to make that part of the adventure, too.

Active play

Looking for a reason to make physical activity an important part of your toddler's daily life? The latest statistics on childhood obesity should help to convince you. According to the Canadian Fitness and Lifestyle Research Institute, only 38% of girls and 48% of boys aged five to 17 are active enough to achieve optimal growth and development.

This is nothing short of a national tragedy in the making. More than half of kids stand to miss out on the benefits of physical fitness, and according to the latest research those benefits are considerable. Physical activity helps to build strength, flexibility, and stamina; reduce the risk of heart disease, diabetes, and obesity; and promote the development of muscles and bone mass. It also improves the quality of sleep; minimizes aggression, anxiety, and depression; and boosts self-confidence. It can even help to boost creativity and concentration!

Fortunately, there's plenty you can do to prevent your toddler from joining the ranks of the next generation of couch potatoes. The key is to make active living a part of his life from a very early age. Human beings are, after all, creatures of habit: soon that daily walk around the block will seem as natural to him as brushing his teeth and listening to bedtime stories.

Here are some fun ways to get your toddler hooked on being physically active:

- Flip on some of your favourite tunes and dance with your toddler. You'll both get a terrific workout and have a lot of fun.

- Place a child-sized climbing gym in your living room or dining room so that it'll be possible for your toddler to fit in some physical activity on even the coldest or rainiest of days. Install a hockey net in your fireplace. Or try something really fun and creative—like Kimberlee, a 29-year-old mother of two, who turned her family room into the deck of a ship!

TODDLER TALK

Encourage activities and games that give your toddler the chance to work on his balance and coordination skills, e.g., stooping and retrieving toys from the floor while maintaining a standing position; walking while pulling a toy; kicking a ball or rolling it back and forth; and throwing a ball or a beanbag.

TODDLER TALK

By the time a toddler celebrates his first birthday, he should be able to skip, run, and jump with both feet. Within a year, he'll be able to handle more complicated manoeuvres, like abruptly changing his direction without losing his balance.

- Play "Jack in the box." Show your toddler how to curl up into a tiny little ball and then spring up like a jack in the box. Not only will he have fun yelling "pop" and trying to surprise you; he'll also be strengthening his legs, improving his balance, and increasing his spatial awareness.

- Make an indoor obstacle course using pillows, cushions, cardboard boxes, tables, chairs, and other common household objects. Then, on the next sunny day, put together an outdoor obstacle course instead.

- Teach your toddler how to play "over and under": crawl over couches and under tables. Or make a bridge with your body and have him crawl under your body or through your legs.

- Play "the zoo game." Pretend to be animals by imitating their movements: be a snake that's slithering across the grass, a kangaroo that loves to hop, or a bird that's flying around the backyard.

- Attach a large plastic beachball to an elastic string and hang it from a doorframe. Your toddler will enjoy batting this "tetherball" around, and since the ball is so lightweight you won't have to worry about it doing any damage.

- Have a family relay race. Instead of passing a baton from person to person, pass along a teddy bear or other favourite toy. (If you're in a goofy mood, you could even rename the event the teddy bear race.)

- Make an indoor hopscotch court by lining up hula hoops on the ground or sticking masking tape to your family room carpet. (When the weather gets nice, you can grab a box of sidewalk chalk and take the hopscotch fun out-of-doors.) Toddlers aren't yet able to manage a one-legged hop, but they'll have fun jumping from square to square with two feet.

- Organize a neighbourhood scooter-and-tricycle rodeo so that the preschool set can have fun riding around together while practising their "cycling" skills. Of course, you'll want to insist that each rodeo contestant is properly equipped with the necessary safety equipment: it's never too early to get your toddler into the helmet habit.

- Play a game of hockey using pool noodles and a beach ball. You can turn an oversized cardboard box on its side and use that as your goal. (Boy, does this book tell you everything you need to know to raise a Canadian kid or what?!!)

- Make a bean bag toss game or set up a pint-sized basketball hoop.

- Play "kick the can." It'll give your toddler a bit of kicking practice, and he'll get the satisfaction of listening to the deli-

---

FRIDGE NOTES

Fitness Canada and the Canadian Institute of Child Health have published a series of three booklets designed to encourage physical fitness in young children:
- "Moving and Growing I: Exercises and Activities for the First Two Years;"
- "Moving and Growing II: Exercises and Activities for Twos, Threes, and Fours;"
- "Moving and Growing III: Exercises and Activities for Fives and Sixes."

The cost is $5 per booklet or $12 for all three. To order, call the Canadian Institute of Child Health at (613) 224-4144 or visit the Institute's Web site at www.cich.ca.

MOM'S THE WORD

"In the wintertime, when there's enough snow, my husband makes a labyrinth in the backyard. Our kids love spending time wandering around in that labyrinth."

—*Catherine, 32, mother of four*

ciously loud noise a tin can makes as it bounces along the sidewalk.

- Teach your toddler how to play follow the leader. (Hey, your toddler is already naturally inclined to want to follow you around and imitate your every movement, so why not try to take advantage of the situation?)

- Show your toddler how to do a log roll by sticking his arms above his head and rolling along the grass. (Remember how much fun you had doing this when you were a kid?)

- Play a game of "Simon Says." Your toddler will have fun running and stopping, and will also get a chance to work on his listening skills.

- Forget fingerpainting; try foot painting instead! Put a large sheet of mural paper on the sidewalk. Pour nontoxic paint into a large shallow tray (an old Styrofoam tray or pie plate works well). Then have your toddler dance across the page. He'll get some exercise and will end up with a colourful mural to hang on his bedroom wall.

- "Shadow dance" outside on a sunny day. Make sure that the sun is behind you and your toddler and then watch how your shadow dances across the grass as you dance. If you're worried that the neighbours will think you've lost it, try doing this particular fitness activity in the backyard instead. Or better yet, invite the neighbours over for some shadow dancing, too.

- Show your toddler how to make "angels" in the snow by lying on his back and swishing his arms up and down and his feet from side to side. The motions involved in making a snow angel help to promote good coordination,—and provide excellent training for jumping jacks!

- Remind yourself that toddlers thrive on unstructured play—running, swimming, climbing, playing in the sandbox, and splashing around in the wading pool—so be sure to provide opportunities for this type of spur-of-the-moment fun, too.

Of course, encouraging physical activity is a moot point for some parents. Some toddlers spend their lives in perpetual motion. If only you could harvest a little of that energy for yourself!

One final thought before we wrap up this discussion on toddlers and physical activity. There's a world of difference between telling kids about the benefits of being physically active and showing them that fitness is a priority in your own life. If you're not physically active yourself, your words are likely to lose their impact. Bottom line? You have to be prepared to walk the talk—literally.

Math

Your child may not be ready to learn how to count, but he's already mastering some key mathematical concepts, like group-

---

MOTHER WISDOM

Here's a fun fitness activity to try once your toddler starts recognizing numbers. Show him how to bend his body into each of the 10 digits. If you're not quite sure to pull off all the necessary contortions ("4" may have you scratching your head for a while), cheat by printing out a copy of "Moving and Growing: Exercises and Activities for Twos, Threes, and Fours." You'll find this document online at www.cfc-efc.ca/docs/cich/00002_en.htm.

TODDLER TALK

You can introduce your toddler to the concept of counting by teaching him counting rhymes (e.g., "One, two, buckle my shoe") or by encouraging him to help you set the dinner table (over time, he'll figure out how many place settings of cutlery to take out of the drawer so that there's a set for each person). Just don't make the mistake of assuming that your toddler is Rhodes-Scholar material if he surprises you one day by counting to 10. At this age, he's most likely to be relying on rote memory rather than any true understanding of the concept of counting.

ing objects and measuring things. Here are some fun ways to build on these important mathematical building blocks.

Grouping and matching objects

- Have an indoor scavenger hunt. Give your toddler two different-coloured pails and encourage him to walk around the house collecting objects of the same colour (e.g., red things to go into the red pail and yellow things to go in the yellow pail).

- Use two or more different shapes of cookie cutters when you're baking a batch of cookies. Your toddler can then help you sort the finished cookies according to their shape.

- Encourage your toddler to help you spot objects of various shapes as you walk around the neighbourhood: square windows, round garbage can lids, triangular hopscotch marks, and so on.

- When you're folding the laundry, encourage your toddler to help you match up the different colours of socks. Not only will he be getting important practice with matching objects; he'll be proud that he's able to help with such an important job.

TODDLER TALK

Don't overlook the relationship between music and math. Researchers at the University of California at Irvine and the University of Wisconsin have found that keyboard and group-singing can help preschoolers improve their spatial-temporal reasoning (a skill that helps with block-building and puzzles as well as more advanced mathematical concepts such as geometry, fractions, and ratios).

- When you're unloading groceries, let your toddler help you to separate the items by category: canned foods versus fresh fruits and vegetables, for example.

- Collect pebbles or shells at the beach and then sort your treasures according to their texture, shape, or colour.

- Play matching games with your child. Either invest in a card or board game that teaches young children how to match up objects or make your own set of cards by cutting out photos from magazines and gluing them to pieces of cardboard or boxboard. (Hint: If you purchase two copies of the same issue of a magazine, you'll automatically end up with a matching set of photos and illustrations.) If you want your cards to last awhile, you should plan to cover them with some sort of clear adhesive plastic film (available for sale in most hardware stores).

Measuring games

- The best place to learn about measuring is in the bathtub, so make sure your toddler has measuring cups, measuring spoons, and containers of various sizes. (See the material on water play earlier in this chapter.)

- Show your toddler how to organize toys or blocks so that they range in size from smallest to largest.

- Make a cardboard handprint or footprint for your toddler so that he can use it as a tool for measuring common household objects—a fun alternative to a ruler.

Science

The universe is a living laboratory for your toddler—a fact you've no doubt observed on those days when he seems hell-bent on testing the principles of gravity and every other scientific principle known to humankind! Here are a few simple ways to encourage your budding Einstein's growing interest in the scientific principles at work in everyday life:

- Provide him with cause-and-effect toys (manufactured or homemade) so that he can start learning about the relationships between objects.

- Give him opportunities to experiment with sound. He'll be amazed to discover how loud and echoey his voice sounds, for example, if he shouts into a large concrete tunnel. And he'll be intrigued to find out just how different it sounds when you put sand as opposed to rice inside a homemade shaker.

- Plant a butterfly garden in your backyard so that you'll attract brightly coloured butterflies to your garden all summer long.

- Take a trip to the zoo to check out the animals or a walk in a nearby field to look for flowers and bugs. Or let him stay up really late one night to check out the stars in the sky.

Finally, make a point of nurturing your toddler's curiosity by encouraging him to ask questions about the world around him. If he's not much of a conversationalist yet, help to formulate his questions for him by responding to his gestures. If he's pointing to a brightly coloured bird outside your kitchen window, let him know that it's a bluejay. If he's amazed by the redness of the evening sky, let him know that the sun is setting. The important thing is to anticipate and answer his questions in terms he can understand. Remember, you've been entrusted with the job of serving as his interpreter until he's better able to ask those questions for himself.

Reading

One of the greatest gifts a parent can give a child is a love of reading. After all, early exposure to books can help a young child develop an array of skills, including listening, auditory memory, visual memory, and critical thinking.

Here are some other important reasons to read to your toddler:

- It's fun. What could be more enjoyable for you or your toddler than snuggling up on the couch to share a favourite book? For years and years I wrapped up the bedtime routine by reading my daughter the same story, a book that was rather appropriately called *I Love You, Goodnight*. A decade later, she still remembers vivid details of the story.

- It provides your toddler with additional exposure to language. He's in prime language acquisition mode these days, so he'll benefit tremendously from this exposure.

- It helps to improve your toddler's attention span. His interest in the story will encourage him to sit still, focus on the book, and tune out the rest of the world—skills that will serve him well throughout his academic life.

TODDLER TALK

Don't underestimate the power of those rhymes your toddler enjoys so much: researchers at Oxford University have discovered that children who hear rhymes the most often are quicker to grasp the idea that words are made up of individual sounds—a key building block for reading.

"One day when I was teaching my son his alphabet, we got to the letter 'u' and I said, 'This is the letter 'u.' He looked at me funny and said, 'The letter "me?"' It was the cutest thing ever."

—*Kristina, 31, mother of two*

- It teaches him how books work. He'll learn the mechanics of reading—in our culture, we read books from front to back and we read the text from left to right—and he'll also discover to his amazement that the same words leap off the page each time the book is opened—even if it's Daddy reading the bedtime story tonight instead of Mommy.

- It helps him develop his imagination by giving him lots of things to think about long after the book has been put back on the shelf. Just think of how often you end up reflecting back on something you read: that happens with toddlers, too.

What you can do to encourage your toddler's love affair with books

Looking for ways to encourage a lifelong love of reading? Here's what the experts recommend:

- Make storytime part of your child's daily routine. The more important a role books play in his life, the more likely he is to get hooked on the reading habit over time.

- Take advantage of opportunities to demonstrate how reading fits into your life. "I make a point of pointing out words that we see when we're in the car, such as the word 'stop' on a stop sign," says Brandy, a 24-year-old mother of two.

- Demonstrate your own love of books. Let your toddler catch you reading books as well as newspapers, magazines, and other print material on a regular basis. This is another one of those situations where it's important to walk the talk!

- Rotate your toddler's books so that there's always something new and exciting to read. A book that's just reappeared after a month-long sabbatical in the basement will feel like a new book to him.

- Find creative ways to make the book you're reading come alive for your child, whether by adding props, encouraging miniature play (giving your child some small figurines so that the two of you can re-enact some key scenes from the story) or dramatic play, and doing some related activities (e.g., making blueberry pancakes if you've just finished reading *Blueberries for Sal*).

- Turn storytime into a dramatic reading. Rather than droning on in a monotone, vary the volume and pitch of your voice to keep your toddler interested.

- Play listening games. Change a character's name to see if your child will notice, or pause at various points in the story to ask your toddler questions about the book.

- Give your toddler a chance to read the book back to you. It's great practice for him and can be a lot of fun for you, too.

TODDLER TALK

Don't feel compelled to drill the alphabet into your toddler. While most toddlers start to recognize letters of the alphabet between ages two and three, there's no evidence to suggest that early mastery of the alphabet will necessarily lead to advanced reading skills later on. So take a laid-back approach to teaching your toddler his ABCs and consider your mission accomplished if he's starting to recognize some of the letters in his name. Anything more than that is a bonus.

MOM'S THE WORD

"If I'm baking, I show Timothy how I read the recipe. I also show him labels on foods and words on TV. I think if he sees how reading is involved in everything we do on a daily basis, he'll realize how important reading is. Of course, letting him pick the book at night to read or offering to read it during the day helps as well."

—*Rita, 37, mother of two*

- Expose your child to a variety of different types of reading material: fiction, non-fiction, poetry, and—as his attention span increases—short "chapter books" that take a couple of nights to finish reading. On the other hand, don't get upset if your child has his heart set on hearing the same story night after night. Toddlers learn through repetition. Eventually, he'll move on to another book.

- Don't force your toddler to listen to the entire book if he loses interest halfway. You want reading to continue to be a positive experience for him—not an exercise in torture!

- If your child has a hard time staying still long enough for you to read him an entire book, try reading to him while he's sitting in the tub. Just make sure that any book you bring to the bathroom won't be any the worse for wear if it ends up getting hit with a wave of water: the book is likely to get as much of a bath as your toddler.

- Don't reserve books just for bedtime. Read to your child at other times of the day, like when he's sitting in his high chair, impatiently waiting for the microwave to ding, or when you're standing in line at the bank, waiting for a teller to become available. Not only will you be teaching your toddler that reading can happen anywhere, anytime; you'll also nip a lot of potential behaviour problems in the bud.

Homegrown words

Don't assume that every book you give your toddler has to be a book you've purchased in a bookstore, picked up at a garage sale, or borrowed from the library. Homemade books make a wonderful addition to any toddler's library. Here are some basic instructions on how to make them:

- **Zip-lock bag book:** Trim some pieces of cardboard or box-board so that they'll fit snugly inside a series of zip-lock bags. (Ideally, you'll want eight or more bags.) Decorate the cardboard or boxboard with photos from magazines, copies of family photos, and other eye-catching images that you think your toddler might enjoy. Then tape the ends of the bags together to form a book. (If you don't intend to make any

---

MOTHER WISDOM

Here are some important points to keep in mind when you're shopping for books for your toddler:
- Look for books with sturdy, tear-resistant pages. Anything less hardy simply isn't going to survive long enough in the hands of your in-house King Kong.
- Young toddlers don't have the attention span necessary to enjoy text-heavy storybooks, so start out with simple picture books featuring bright, eye-catching illustrations, little text, and one major idea per page.
- Make an effort to seek out books that will be particularly relevant to your toddler—books with clear illustrations or photos that your child will recognize. Remember, toddlers prefer books that accurately reflect their own life experiences.
- Look for books that celebrate all the possibilities of language by incorporating rhythms, rhymes, and just plain funny noises.
- Books on tape are terrific for keeping toddlers entertained in the car, but don't make the mistake of assuming that they can take the place of your regular storytime. Books on tape should supplement rather than replace that nightly bedtime story.

FRIDGE NOTES

Looking for an unbiased opinion on which toys are—and aren't—worth the money? Each year, the Canadian Toy Testing Council publishes a report evaluating hundreds of toys on the basis of design, function, durability, and play value. Toy reviews can be downloaded from the Council's Web site at www.toy-testing.org.

further revisions to the book, you can tape together the ends of the bags that are open. But if you do intend to update the contents from time to time, you'll want to tape the sealed ends of the bags together instead. Some moms like to go all out and sew the books together by hand or by using the zigzag stitch on the sewing machine, but that sounds like too much work to me. I mean, why sew when there's shipping tape or duct tape available?!!)

- **Photo album:** Stick family photos or photos you've cut out of catalogues or magazines into a photo album. You can use a full-sized photo album that can accommodate four or more photos per page or a smaller photo album that's large enough to accommodate only a single photo per page. Note: Magnetic-style photo albums work best because it's more difficult for toddlers to remove the photos.

- **Binder:** Glue magazine pictures onto a piece of cardboard or boxboard that you've trimmed to fit inside an undersized binder. Cover the pages with clear adhesive paper and you'll have a durable, spill-resistant book that can be added to over time.

Inside the toy box: Your best toy buys for the toddler years

FEELING OVERWHELMED BY the sheer number of choices you face each time you set foot in a toy superstore? You're certainly in good company. Many parents find it difficult to choose among the growing number of products competing for their toy-buying dollars. Is it any wonder that Canadian consumers collectively spend some $1.3 billion on toys each year?

The right stuff

The challenge, of course, is to learn how to sidestep all the gimmicky (and almost invariably battery operated) gizmos that promise to be a source of endless delight to your toddler. (That delight inevitably wears thin around the time the toy packaging hits the recycling bin.) Here are some tips on choosing toys that will entertain and stimulate your toddler—and without going broke in the process:

- Choose toys that are age-appropriate (see Table 3.9). Toys designed for younger children will bore your toddler, while toys designed for older children will cause him massive frustration. That said, be sure to take manufacturers' claims about the age range for a particular toy with a grain of salt.

MOM'S THE WORD
"Most electronic toys are a waste of money. The kids play with them for a short time and then the toys break. Besides, toddlers prefer blocks and dolls and cars and simple things. Ever notice how your kid likes the box better than the toy?"

—*Melanie, 38, mother of eight*

MOM'S THE WORD

"I think we as a society are developing an unhealthy preoccupation with 'entertaining' our children that's not only changing family dynamics, but the economy as well. I hope this trend comes to a screeching halt soon."

—*Anita, 39, mother of four*

Some of these toy claims appear to have been made by people who've never so much as laid eyes on a toddler!

- Zero in on toys that are durable and easy to clean. Otherwise, you'll be making constant trips to the dump and the toy store to get rid of and replace broken toys.

- Look for toys that are versatile and that can grow with your toddler, like a bucket full of brightly coloured wooden blocks. The beauty of toys like blocks is that they can be played with in many different ways and there's no "right" or "wrong" way to play with them.

- Look for toys that will stimulate your toddler's imagination and give him the opportunity to master new skills.

- Steer clear of toys that require little or no input from your child (e.g., talking toys that spit out the same old tired phrases over and over again).

- Don't fall into the all-too-common trap of automatically purchasing whatever toddler toy happens to be the Flavour of the Month. Instead, stick with classic toys that generations of toddlers have enjoyed.

- Purchase a variety of different types of toys for your toddler. Just as you aim to provide him with meals built around the four food groups, you should aim to stock his toy box with toys from the five "toy groups": active play toys, construction materials, manipulative toys, dolls and dramatic play toys, and arts and crafts supplies. So before you add another toy to your toddler's collection, ask yourself if it will complement or duplicate the other toys in his collection. Remember, your goal is to serve up a balanced "diet" of play materials.

- Don't limit your purchases to toys that are gender specific. Mix things up a little. Annie, 44, has made a point of providing her three-year-old son Tomas with both "girl toys" and "boy toys"—everything from helicopters and trucks to farm animals and dolls: "I kind of like seeing the soft and gentle side of him when he picks up one of his dolls. It's a nice contrast with his bashing and crashing and saving of creatures with his superheroes!"

- Exercise healthy skepticism when you're sizing up the merits of "educational" toys. Many toys claim to be educational, but they don't all deliver the goods. My husband still likes to tease me about the first "educational" toy I bought our daughter: a chew toy that featured five different textures of cloth for her to suck on. Did I get conned or what? (On second thought, this very same kid has turned out to be a rather brainy teen: maybe there was something to that educational chew toy after all.)

- Don't feel obligated to break the bank. It's not necessary to spend a small fortune on toys for your child. Your child can learn a great deal by playing with ordinary household items

---

MOM'S THE WORD

"Some of our best buys have been at garage sales and at the Salvation Army and Goodwill stores. We bring them home and clean them up. Then, when my daughter has played with them for a few months and is finished with them, we donate the toys to her daycare centre."

—Sidney, 33, mother of one

MOTHER WISDOM

Wondering how to clean up the toys that you've purchased secondhand? While good old-fashioned soap and water will get rid of most of the grime, here are some trade secrets from other moms on doing battle with squeaks, stains, and stickers:

- Use petroleum jelly to lubricate moving parts and eliminate squeaks in toys like tricycles.
- Use nail polish remover to get rid of marker and pen marks on hard plastic toys like balls.
- Use rubbing alcohol to get rid of glue residue left behind by labels and stickers.

such as pots and pans, funnels, basic art supplies, and so on. Besides, you can stretch your toy budget considerably by hitting garage sales or consignment stores (see Chapter 9 for some important safety tips on purchasing toys secondhand), joining a toy library (see Appendix B for the Canadian Association of Family Resource Programmes contact information) or forming a toy-buying cooperative with a group of friends (that way, you can share the costs of big-ticket items like large plastic climbers and play kitchens and then simply rotate these toys from house to house).

TABLE 3.9

Terrific Toys for Toddlers

→ Arts and crafts supplies (see Table 3.3)

→ Balls

→ Blocks

→ Board games (cooperative)

→ Books and books on tape

→ Building toys

continued on p. 144

Terrific Toys for Toddlers (continued)

→ Card games

→ Construction toys

→ Dramatic play materials (see Table 3.8)

→ Dump and fill toys

→ Lacing cards (for older toddlers only)

→ Magnetic letters and shapes (toddler-sized)

→ Musical instruments

→ Nesting cups and blocks

→ Nylon tunnels for crawling through

→ Pegboards (large pegs only)

→ Picture dominoes

→ Plastic beads (large, snap-together style)

→ Pull toys

→ Push toys

→ Puzzles (12 pieces or less)

→ Ride-on toys (wide wheelbase for added stability)

→ Sand and water toys (see Table 3.6)

→ Shape sorters

→ Soft dolls and puppets

→ Stacking toys

→ Tape recorders and music tapes

→ Tents and playhouses

→ Toy telephones

Toy storage smarts

Now that you've accumulated all those nifty toys, it's time to talk about how to tame the resulting toy-related clutter. And tame it you must. Never, ever let the toys get the upper hand!

TODDLER TALK

Think you're doing your toddler a favour by buying him that talk-ing shape sorter? Think again. Most child development experts make the case that low-tech toys are a much more sensible alternative for very young children. In fact, they argue that high-tech toys designed to be used in only one particular way can actually stifle a child's creativity and imagination. While an old-fashioned set of blocks can become a house, a tower, or a some-thing else entirely depending on what your toddler chooses to do with it that day, no "talking" bear or "interactive" shape sorter can make the same claim. Unfortunately, high-tech toys appear to be here to stay. In fact, they're start-ing to crowd out traditional toys on the toy-store shelves. According to the U.S. non-profit association Zero to Three, 60% of new toys introduced by Fisher Price in 2000 had some sort of computer chip embedded in them as compared with less than 10% three years earlier.

Toy boxes may look attractive and may help to hide the mess momentarily, but they're not your best bet for toy storage. They pose a hazard to toddlers, since toy boxes with heavy lids can bonk heads or crush fingers, while poorly ventilated toy boxes have been known to cause suffocation deaths. As well, the toys tend to get all mixed together, leaving your child with the rather daunting task of having to go digging through the entire toy box in order to find all the pieces of the puzzle he wants to do. (And, of course, he'll manage to empty the toy box in the process, which isn't going to make you terribly happy either!) Here are some saner alternatives:

- Keep your child's toys in easy reach—ideally on low, sturdy shelving units in his bedroom or your family room. That way, he can get them out when he's ready to play and he can start to assume responsibility for putting them away when he's finished with them.

- Store your child's multi-piece toys in see-through storage containers with lids. (If you use a non-see-through container, you'll want to cut out a picture of the toy from a catalogue or the original packaging or take a snapshot of the toy with your camera so that your toddler will know what's inside the plastic container.) He'll be able to see what's inside without having to dump everything out. Stackable plastic bins, plastic laundry baskets, plastic dish bins, tote bags, and mesh bags also work well. Hint: To ensure that the plastic containers stack properly, buy a large quantity of the same size and brand at the same time.

- Buy a bedskirt that matches your child's comforter and use the area under his bed for storing less-frequently-used toys. (If you've still got space left under the bed, use it to stash away some of his off-season clothing.)

- If you're reluctant to take out a second mortgage in order to pay for all those fancy (and sometimes pricey) storage containers, use empty baby-wipe containers or large plastic tubs instead. Use baby oil to remove any existing stickers and labels and then stick on a homemade label indicating what's in the box. Since it's unlikely your child will be able to read at this tender age—budding genius or not!—a picture of a toy car will mean a lot more to him than the letters "C-A-R"!

MOTHER WISDOM

Don't feel you need to keep each and every toy within easy reach at any given time. It's better to rotate your toddler's toys on a regular basis so that there's always something "new" and exciting for him to play with. If you notice that your toddler seems to have grown bored with a particular toy, pack it away for a few weeks. Chances are he'll be delighted to see it again a few weeks or months from now. If he still seems bored with it at that point, consider setting it aside to give away, swap, or sell. He's clearly outgrown this particular toy.

- Use clear shipping tape to reinforce the corners of new games and puzzles that come in cardboard boxes. The boxes will stand up a lot better. When the inevitable happens, however, and the box finally gives up the ghost, simply transfer the puzzle pieces into a zip-lock bag. If you're lucky, you'll be able to salvage the picture of the puzzle from the lid of the box. If it's too late for that, simply take a picture of the puzzle the next time your child completes it and then tuck that photo inside the bag along with the puzzle pieces.

- Get some of your child's least favourite stuffed animals off the floor by dropping them in a hammock, storing them in shoe racks in the bottom of his closet, or clipping them to a clothesline attached to the ceiling of his bedroom. Obviously, you'll want to keep his absolute favourites within easy cuddling distance.

Homemade toys

Looking for some practical tips on stretching your toy dollars a little further? Here are some terrific baby and toddler toys you can make at home using items that you're likely to have around the house:

- **Building blocks:** Baby-wipe container and oatmeal boxes make terrific building blocks. Milk cartons do, too, if you remove the triangular-shaped section at the top and fold down the side panels to make a rectangular or square-shaped block. If that sounds too complicated, buy some oversized sponges. Not only are they fun to stack; they're fun to toss around!

- **Pull toys:** String together spools of thread, cardboard boxes, or other objects to make a "train" that your toddler will enjoy pulling around the house.

- **Shape sorter:** Cut holes in the lid of a large coffee can or a shoebox so that your child can use it as a shape sorter. (Hint: Trace your child's blocks to ensure that the holes are the correct shape and size.) If you're using a coffee can, you might want to run masking tape around the lip of the can to prevent your toddler from coming in contact with any sharp edges.

- **Bubble box:** Use an empty plastic mesh-style strawberry box for blowing bubbles. Simply dip the box in bubble-blowing solution and have your toddler wave it in the air. (For a really fun effect, hold the box in front of a fan. You'll end up with a cascade of bubbles.)

- **Nesting cups:** Use margarine containers and yogourt containers of different sizes to create a set of nesting cups that fit inside one another.

- **Beanbag toss:** Fill a small zip-lock bag with rice, macaroni, or oatmeal and then seal it with plastic shipping tape. Tuck it inside an adult-sized sock, and then knot the end of the sock.

- **Mailbox:** Cut a mail slot into a large cardboard box and give your toddler all your old junk mail.

- **Giant lacing beads:** Give your child shower-curtain rings, rubber canning rings, or plastic napkin rings to thread onto a large piece of aquarium tubing. Then, as his fine motor skills improve, you can provide him with thread spools to string on a shoelace or piece of plastic lacing.

Note: See also the earlier sections of this chapter that talk about making your own craft supplies, musical instruments, and homemade books.

Toddlers and TV

WONDERING HOW much TV is appropriate for a toddler? No TV at all, according to the American Academy of Pediatrics, and no more than one hour a day, according to the Canadian Paediatric Society.

So why are these leading health authorities encouraging parents to wrestle the remote control away from their toddlers? Because young toddlers have a critical need for interaction with parents and other adults in order to foster healthy brain development—something that they're less likely to receive when they're planted in front of a television set. Add to that the fact that excess TV viewing has been linked to weight problems, a reduced ability to interact with adults, a lack of initiative for learning, and diminished creativity, and you can see why leaving the TV set off could be one of the biggest favours you do for your toddler.

Here's something else you need to know about toddlers and TV: your toddler doesn't have to actively watching a program to

---

MOM'S THE WORD

"I do use the TV as a babysitter occasionally, but I'm really making an effort to have them playing with playdough or colouring at the kitchen table when I'm making dinner or doing chores."

—*Alyson, 33, mother of two*

MOM'S THE WORD

"I limit the types of shows and the amount of time they spend watching television. But I have to admit that I've used the television to keep me from blowing a fuse on a 'bad mommy day.' But even then, they're only allowed to watch one of the agreed-upon channels. Or we put on a video."

—*Lisa, 36, mother of two*

be harmed by the effects of TV. Background noise from a television set can interfere with a toddler's ability to learn.

Surf's up: Introducing your toddler to the computer

OF COURSE, parents today don't just have to grapple with the issue of toddlers and TV. They also have to decide when it's appropriate to introduce a young child to the computer.

If you decide to expose your toddler to the computer, limit his computer time (most experts recommend a maximum of 30 minutes a day for two- to three-year-olds) and be selective about how you allow him to use that time. Pre-screen software and Web sites to make sure they're age appropriate and that they don't contain images that could be scary or otherwise disturbing. What's more, you'll want to treat your toddler's computer time as a shared learning opportunity for the two of you rather than as a babysitter.

Here's something else to consider. Many computer software packages for young children suffer from the same fatal flaw as those high-tech toys we talked about earlier: they tend to artificially limit opportunities for learning. So don't make the mistake of assuming that computer programs can replace real-world learning materials. Playing with "virtual" Lego is no substitute for getting down on the floor with bucketfuls of the real stuff.

CHAPTER 4

Who's the Boss?

*"If we expect toddlers to misbehave, they will live
up to that expectation. Terrible twos? Not in my house.
Yes, toddlers become wilful and stubborn and have
tantrums, but children of all ages have moments
like that. Some adults have moments like that, in fact!
But with toddlers, it's generally pretty easy to figure
out what the problem is and how to cope with it."*
—ANITA, 38, MOTHER OF FOUR

WE ALL NEED A friend like Anita—an experienced mom who's willing to take us aside on the eve of toddlerhood and whisper reassuringly, "You're going to be just fine!" You see, while raising a toddler may not exactly be a cakewalk, it's nowhere near as dreadful as the doomsayers would have you believe (you know, those helpful folks who make it sound as though it's nothing short of a miracle if you manage to make it through to your child's third birthday with your sanity relatively intact). How refreshing it would be to have someone like Anita to turn to when you needed help putting things in perspective. You could program her phone number into speed-dial and call her on those days when you need to be reminded that your toddler will eventually make peace with green vegetables, start using the potty, and stop throwing temper tantrums whenever she has to wear something on her feet. (Hey, a little bit of hope can take you a long way.)

As you've no doubt gathered by now, this chapter is all about discipline—what it means and why your toddler needs it. It's a rather a hefty chapter and one that covers a lot of ground—two years' worth of toddler behaviour, in fact. We're going to start out by talking about why toddlers are, well, *toddlers*—wilful, stubborn little beings who can have minor meltdowns over little things that may not even show up on your radar screen. (When was the last time you burst into tears because your cookie broke when you bit into it?) Then we're going to consider how individual temperament fits into the whole parenting equation— specifically, which methods of discipline seem to work best with toddlers of various temperaments. Next, we'll zero in on some of the most common problems parents encounter while dealing with toddlers: biting, whining, hitting, and, of course, temper tantrums. (Think of this section as an all-perils insurance policy.) With any luck, having a variety of different discipline techniques to turn to the next time your toddler goes into meltdown mode will help to minimize the amount of time you spend studying at the Parenting School of Hard Knocks. (Or at least that's the plan.)

MOM'S THE WORD

"All you ever hear about is 'wait until he or she hits the terrible twos.' I've heard this for two-and-a-half years. I honestly believe my son was born going through the terrible twos, so parenting has always been busy for me!"

—*Lisa, 37, mother of three*

Your toddler's declaration of independence

WHEN YOU'RE KNEE-DEEP in the parenting trenches (e.g., you're dealing with the 10th temper tantrum of the day and it's not even 8:00 a.m.), it can be easy to lose sight of the fact that your toddler's declaration of independence is actually something to be celebrated. The very behaviours that you find most frustrating to deal with—her stubborn streak and her desire to challenge your authority, for example—are proof positive that your toddler is developing a strong sense of who she is and where she fits into the world.

Toddlers don't mean to be tyrants. Really, they don't. They just happen to be embroiled in a developmental stage that requires them to repeatedly demonstrate their independence from you. (This early declaration of independence is, of course, a dry run for the more pointed version you can expect your child to make during the teen years.) Here's a quick snapshot of some of the key developmental factors behind many of those oh-so-challenging toddler behaviours:

- **Toddlers are endlessly curious about their environment.** Your toddler is eager to put her new-found mobility to good use by exploring each and every square centimetre of her universe. Sometimes her powerful curiosity gets her into trouble, however, which is why toddlers come equipped with parents.

- **Toddlers learn through experimentation.** Sometimes that means carrying out experiments that you'd rather your toddler didn't—like trying to find out if it's possible to colour on the family pet. A toddler who engages in this type of experimentation isn't trying to drive you (or the cat) crazy. She's simply in Einstein mode.

- **Toddlers need to demonstrate their independence from their parents.** Your toddler is busy proving to herself that she's separate and distinct from you—something that encourages her to rebel against you in crazy ways, like insisting on wearing her bathing suit in December or her snowsuit in the middle of July. She's not trying to push your buttons by being deliberately defiant; this is simply her less-than-subtle way of telling you that *she's* the one calling the shots.

- **Toddlers need proof that they're loved no matter what.** Your toddler may test the limits because she needs to reassure herself that your love is unconditional—that you'll love her every bit as much when she's getting into mischief as when she's in total angel mode. This is the game she's playing when she pauses to check out your reaction as she repeatedly drops your toothbrush into the toilet. She's not experimenting with the toothbrush; she's experimenting with you!

- **Toddlers are highly impulsive.** Your toddler doesn't have the impulse control to put the brakes on when her hand starts reaching for a cookie—which certainly helps to explain where the folks at *Sesame Street* got their inspiration for Cookie Monster! So don't expect very much from her in terms of self-control at this age. She hasn't got it in her just yet. Self-control is a skill she still needs to grow into.

- **Toddlers have not yet acquired the ability to look before they leap.** (Literally!) A toddler needs the adults in her life to set limits for her because her physical abilities are massively out of synch with her cognitive skills. As Penelope Leach notes in her book *Babyhood,* "The toddler begins to move around as fast as an older child, but without the older child's sense or memory." This is arguably a bit of a design flaw on the part of Mother Nature: your toddler is not yet ready to accept responsibility for herself, and yet she's programmed to reject control by you!

- **A toddler's memory is not yet firing on all cylinders.** Your toddler is not deliberately ignoring the impassioned plea you made yesterday about not putting crackers inside the DVD player; she's simply forgotten the discussion entirely. (Of course, that's assuming she was listening in the first place. As you've no doubt discovered by now, a typical toddler has a very limited attention span.)

- **Toddlers are highly self-centred.** Your toddler is not yet able to consider other people's feelings, which can make life extremely frustrating for others in her life, including you. It's not that she's trying to be a self-centred little monster; she simply lacks the ability to see the world through anyone else's eyes but her own at this stage of her development.

So there you have it: a quick rundown of the key reasons why disciplining a toddler requires so much time, energy, and patience. And, as you can see, this isn't just about you and your toddler. This is just the most recent episode in a drama that's been playing since the beginning of time! The forces you're battling

---

MOTHER WISDOM

"The 'terrible twos' is really a cognitive exercise. It's a toddler's way of exploring cause and effect, with her parents as the guinea pigs."

—*Andrew Meltzoff, Ph.D., quoted in "A Year to Cheer," Parents.com*

MOTHER WISDOM

"The fundamental job of a toddler is to rule the universe."

—*Lawrence Kutner,* Toddlers and Preschoolers

are, after all, the product of thousands and thousands of years of toddler evolution. We're talking pretty powerful stuff indeed.

But don't let that shake your confidence in your parenting abilities: you've been busy evolving, too. In fact, you're a member of the best-educated generation of parents ever. So don't let the theatrics of any two-foot-tall person throw you off your game. Toddlers are tough and parenting is tougher, but, trust me, you're more than up for the challenge.

Discipline: What it is and why your child needs it

ONE OF YOUR key responsibilities as a parent is to help your child develop an inner compass that will guide her through life, helping her to make the best possible decisions along the way. While you'll serve as her compass during the early years, your

MOM'S THE WORD

"The hardest thing about raising a toddler is knowing when something is a discipline issue and when it's a learning issue. It seems like she's always doing something that we have to come up with a family policy on: like when she feeds the dog food from her dinner plate, when she tries to climb the stairs, when she screams for attention, when she grabs another child's toy."

—*Debbie, 33, mother of one*

ultimate goal is to do yourself out of a job. Parenting is, after all, one of the few occupations in this world where having your position declared surplus is actually a good thing!

Of course, it will take many years for your child's inner compass to become fully functional, and there will be times in her life when you'll swear she's misplaced the damned thing entirely. But, with any luck, your hard work will pay off and your child will grow up to be a happy, healthy, and successful adult.

You can get there from here

Of course, when you're putting in long days—and nights—raising a young child, it may feel as though that day will never come—that you're doomed to spend the rest of your days reminding your child to brush her teeth, wash her hands, and pick up her toys. The job can be thankless and exhausting at times, but it's important to remember that most children do grow up to be fully functioning human beings. In other words, you *can* get there from here!

But how do you get started on this long and convoluted journey? It's a question that's befuddled parents from the beginning of time. Teaching a child self-discipline may be one of a parent's most important jobs, but it doesn't always necessarily come naturally or easily to every parent.

The challenge, of course, stems from the fact that there are two variables in the discipline equation: you and your toddler. Some parents feel confident about setting limits for their child and seem to have been blessed with an intuitive sense of how to do so in a loving and effective way. Others struggle with the whole concept of discipline right from day one, which inevitably triggers a battle of wills between them and their toddler. Similarly, some toddlers are naturally compliant and easy to discipline while other toddlers are not. So before we get down to the real

MOTHER WISDOM

"The child supplies the power, but the parents have to do the steering."

—*Dr. Benjamin Spock*, **Dr. Spock's Baby and Child Care**

---

nitty-gritty of discipline—which techniques tend to be most effective with children of this age group and which ones are not—we'll take a detailed look at the two important variables: your parenting style and your toddler's temperament.

Your parenting style

WHILE NO TWO parents are exactly alike, parenting experts have identified three basic parenting styles: authoritarian, permissive, and authoritative. (If you're a big fan of parenting expert Barbara Coloroso, as I am, you'll recognize these three parenting styles as the brickwall, jellyfish, and backbone schools of parenting she describes in her books.) Here's the scoop on each style:

- **Authoritarian:** As the name implies, authoritarian parents tend to be big on control. Their motto? "I'm the one in charge." They expect immediate obedience from their children and have a strict, unwavering code of conduct that offers little—if any—opportunity to question their edicts. And, what's more, they're prepared to enforce their rules through spanking or yelling. Children learn to obey authoritarian parents not because they believe their parents' rules are fair or reasonable, but rather because they fear the consequences of not obeying. These children have less opportunity to learn how to control their own behaviour and are consequently less independent and confident than children raised by less controlling parents. And because the focus of this particular discipline style is on stamping out the bad rather than celebrating the good, children raised in this sort of environment may not feel particularly loved by their parents, which can put them at risk of developing an array of self-esteem-related problems. Bottom line? This ain't exactly the formula for raising happy, well-adjusted children!

- **Permissive:** Permissive parents can be found at the opposite end of the discipline spectrum. Their motto? "Anything goes." They allow practically any behaviour so long as their child isn't in any immediate danger. Consequently, they don't have a lot of rules for their children, and what rules they do have tend to be enforced on a rather haphazard basis (e.g., whenever Mom or Dad can be bothered). Kids raised by permissive parents lack structure and don't have a clue about how society expects them to behave. They tend to be impulsive, self-indulgent, aggressive, and highly inconsiderate because their parents have always given in to their needs. And since they have yet to master any self-control or self-discipline, they're held hostage by their own needs and wants, doing anything and everything on a whim simply because they've got the urge. While they tend to be highly creative, even that can get them into trouble if they choose to exercise that creative streak in the wrong way, e.g., by colouring on the walls at Grandma's house, picking flowers from the neighbour's garden, or trying to upstage the bride at a family wedding. (You've encountered kids like this, now haven't you?)

- **Authoritative:** Most parenting experts agree that an authoritative parenting style works best for parents and kids. The motto that these types of parents choose to adopt? "We're in this together." They set clear limits and have high expectations of their children's behaviour, but—unlike authoritarian parents—they encourage two-way communication and tend to be a bit more flexible in applying the rules. They're known for being fair, consistent, and willing to discuss problems and work through solutions with their kids—a parenting approach that can reap tremendous dividends for the entire family. Authoritative parents tend to be rewarded with well-adjusted, self-confident children who respect themselves and others around them and who demonstrate good self-control. These children tend to be more achievement-oriented than those raised by other types of parents, and as an added perk they tend to be less rebellious during their teen years (reason enough to buy into this particular parenting style, in my humble opinion).

Your toddler's personality type

OF COURSE, YOU'RE not the only ingredient in that complex equation known as parenting: you also have to factor in your child's temperament—a trait that's pre-wired into your child before birth.

While every psychologist or medical doctor who's ever written a parenting book seems to have come up with a slightly different laundry list of terms to describe children's temperaments, linguistic nuances aside, they pretty much boil down to the same three types that psychologists Alexander Thomas and Stella Chess described way back in the 1950s:

- the difficult or spirited child (a child who doesn't adapt well to new situations and who tends to have a negative attitude much of the time);

- the slow-to-warm-up or shy child (a child who is very cautious and shy when faced with a new situation and who is slow to warm up to new people);

MOM'S THE WORD

"While babies seem to fall into fairly predictable 'types,' in my experience toddlers do not, and the generalizations about toddlers simply made me feel lousy. Sophie was not at all like the kids I read about in books, but she was still a really neat kid. It wasn't until I found the book *The Difficult Child* by Stanley Turecki and Leslie Tonner that I started reading about kids who sounded like my own—and got workable strategies for dealing with her."

—*Leslie, 37, mother of two*

- the easy child (a child who is upbeat, adaptable, and mild to moderate in intensity of response).

Now that you've had an entire year to get to know your child, you should have a pretty good idea of which type of temperament she was born with—whether she's a happy-go-lucky kid who pretty much goes with the flow or a kid who passionately protests even the most minuscule variation to her usual routine or one who shies away from new people or situations.

The "difficult" toddler

While disciplining "easy" children tends to be relatively, well, *easy* (you set limits and, over time, your child learns to respect those limits—or at least that's the theory), "difficult" children require extra calmness, patience, consistency, structure, and understanding from their parents.

If you happen to have been blessed with one of those higher-than-average intensity kids, try not to hit the panic button. You're not necessarily doomed to have a difficult run as a parent simply because you have a "difficult" child! Creative parents quickly learn how to find ways to use their knowledge of their child's temperament to their advantage.

Judith, a 33-year-old mother of one, is the first to admit that her daughter Meagan is a high-intensity kind of kid—one that requires a lot of patience and consistent parenting—but she doesn't consider parenting Meagan to be an insurmountable challenge: "We lovingly refer to Meagan as the ultimate drama queen. Everything she does has some sort of dramatic quality to it, including temper tantrums. I find that she's the kind of kid who will try to negotiate everything if you don't put your foot down and remind her that you make the rules for a reason."

Here are three basic survival strategies that may make life easier for you if, like Judith, you have a difficult (or "spirited") toddler:

- Help your toddler to anticipate transitions. Get in the habit of providing her with plenty of advance warning when it's almost time to wind up one activity and move on to the next. You'll find that your toddler is less likely to dig in her heels and refuse to cooperate if she has a bit of time to get used to what's coming. "One thing I do that I think really helps to keep tantrums at bay is give my son fair warning when we're changing activities," explains Julie, a mother of one. "For example, if my son is having a bath and it's time to get out, I'll say 'Five more minutes and then it's time to get out.' 'Two more minutes and

---

MOTHER WISDOM

"All toddlers are busy: they're climbing and jumping and throwing things. But the high-energy kid is the one who can get to the top of the refrigerator. All toddlers say no, but a spirited child's noes are louder and more frequent, his tantrums longer-lasting and more intense. You gradually realize that as a parent you're working harder than your neighbour, whose child is simply not as intense, persistent, and emphatic as yours. Your child is still normal, he's just more."

—*Mary Sheedy Kurcinka*, Raising Your Spirited Child, *quoted in an article at BabyCenter.com*

MOM'S THE WORD

"I don't think some people realize how frustrating it can be to deal with a high-energy toddler. I find it most frustrating when people tell me to shut my kid up when he's screaming in public because I've told him not to do something. They don't seem to realize that I'd like nothing more than for him to be quiet, but the more I try to get him to be quiet, the louder he becomes."

—*Christy, 38, mother of two*

---

it's time to get out.' 'Mommy is going to count to 10 and then it's time to get out.' This works really well for us. I know people who have used an egg timer to accomplish the same thing."

- Be clear and consistent when it comes to routines. The moment a spirited toddler gets wind of the fact that there might be a tiny loophole in a particular rule, it's game over for you! So make sure you spell out the rules in bulletproof language and that you stick with the same rules from day to day.

- Make a point of steering clear of situations that have caused her—and you—a lot of problems in the past. It's impossible to sidestep every single situation that could potentially set your toddler off, but you can minimize the number of meltdowns she experiences by learning to avoid situations that have caused her (and you) a lot of trouble in the past, e.g., dining out at establishments that are notorious for their slow service or trying to run a lot of errands during the time of day when she should be taking a nap.

The "shy" toddler

Some toddlers are highly cautious—even fearful—in new situations. They're the toddlers who can be found clinging to their mother's legs on the first day of nursery school or hiding behind the couch whenever someone new has been invited over for dinner.

Here are some tips on coping with a shy toddler:

- Try to understand what's at the root of the problem if she refuses to cooperate in a particular situation. She may be refusing to go to bed because she feels lonely or afraid when she's in her room. And she may be refusing to eat the casserole that you whipped up for dinner because it contains a vegetable she doesn't recognize. It's easier to deal with a particular problem once you've pinpointed the root cause. At that point, you can start brainstorming some creative solutions.

- Even if you're a natural-born extrovert who's never shied away from a new situation in your life, let your toddler know that you understand how she's feeling and that you're not angry at her for being shy or scared. Although it can be incredibly frustrating to sign your toddler up for a mom-and-tot gym class only to have her spend the entire session crying and begging to go home, she can't help the way she feels, so it's important to be kind and empathetic.

- Encourage your child's attempts at socialization. Continue to expose her to social situations even if she isn't willing to do anything more than tentatively observe the other children from the sidelines. Eventually, she'll become more comfortable with the idea of socializing with other children.

- Accept the possibility that your child may not outgrow her shyness any time soon. According to Lise Eliot, Ph.D., author of *What's Going On in There? How the Brain and Mind Develop in the First Five Years of Life*, the majority of toddlers who are highly inhibited continue to take a cautious approach to life: only 40% of shy toddlers overcome their feelings of inhibition by the time they start kindergarten.

The "easy" toddler

Think you're going to get off scot-free in the discipline department just because you were blessed with an "easy" toddler? You're dreaming in technicolour. All toddlers require discipline, easygoing or not!

Your key challenge in managing the behaviour of an easygoing toddler may be in finding a discipline method that works. Some toddlers with this sort of happy-go-lucky temperament may have trouble clueing into the fact that they're being disciplined!

"My kids are generally 'make lemonade' kinds of kids," explains Anita, 38, mother of four. "Nothing fazes them. If I send them to their rooms, they find a way to enjoy it. They take a nap or look at their books or sing for a while. If I take away a toy or a privilege, they get over it almost immediately. If I say they can earn a toy or a privilege, they find a reason not to need it. They are determinedly cheerful and optimistic and that makes them hard to discipline sometimes, but, on the other hand, I know that these very same characteristics will serve them well throughout their lives."

A mixed bag

Of course, it's one thing to deal with a child with a challenging temperament. It's quite another to deal with two or more kids with radically different temperaments!

That's the parenting challenge that Rita, 37, is facing these days. Her four-year-old son Timothy and two-year-old daughter Nicole are total opposites in temperament and consequently demand totally different approaches to discipline: "Timothy has a very laid-back, easygoing attitude. Nicole, on the other hand, is starting to turn into a bit of a control freak. I've tried to treat her the same way I treat him, but I have to come up with different strategies to manage her behaviour. This makes it difficult for Timothy because he sometimes thinks she's getting preferential treatment."

Like Rita, Lori, 31, has found that she needs to vary her behavioural expectations and discipline techniques when dealing with each of her five children: "I think you have to find the discipline technique that works best for your child. Some children are very sensitive and cannot handle blame. Other children are afraid to be alone and cannot tolerate being sent to their rooms. A child who is very emotional may need some time alone to cool down while a child who is shy or timid may need some quiet time with Mom or Dad. Sometimes a child who is very strong-willed may need a firmer disciplinary method than another child, and some children need to see the consequences of their actions or be involved in resolving the problem before the discipline can be effective. I think a child's temperament must be considered when parents are deciding what type of discipline to use."

The experts agree with Lori's take on the situation, stressing the importance of factoring a child's temperament into any discipline decision. That means considering whether a particular discipline technique is likely to be effective or not, given what you know about your child's temperament.

Just one final word of caution before I set you loose in the parenting laboratory: predictions about a child's behaviour tend

---

MOTHER WISDOM

Temperament isn't the only factor involved in shaping a child's personality. According to psychologists, the split between inborn and acquired personality traits is about 50/50, so you still have a major role to play in determining the type of person your child ultimately becomes. Since you have little control over the "nature" factors, you'll want to do what you can to influence all the factors on the "nurture" side of the equation, coming up with parenting strategies that tend to bring out the best—rather than the worst—in your child.

> **MOM'S THE WORD**
>
> "The twins are able to get into more trouble than my singletons ever did. One day, I used two wooden boxes to block the doorway out of the living room so that I could fold laundry without the twins disappearing. Claire was trying to climb over the boxes, but couldn't, so Saige got down on all fours so that her sister could use her as a step. Then Saige got up and gave Claire the last boost on her bottom to get her on top of the box and over the other side!"
>
> —*Kerri, 36, mother of six*

to be self-fulfilling. If you've labelled your baby as "difficult" right from day one, she may be encouraged to live up to the label. So while it's okay to acknowledge the fact that you've been blessed with an exceptionally challenging child, you don't want to saddle her for life with that label. Instead, you'll want to identify both her strengths and weaknesses and come up with practical strategies for bringing out the best in your child.

Mission possible

WHETHER OR NOT discipline comes naturally to you, it's important that you rise to the challenge. Your child is counting on you to equip her with the skills she needs for life. "Toddlers are looking to you to be their guide—the one who sets the boundaries and lays down the law when that needs to be done," explains Lisa, a 36-year-old mother of two. "You're helping them to become responsible people who nonetheless remain curious and excited about the world around them."

The art of discipline—and, trust me, it truly is an art—is in setting limits for your child while still allowing her the freedom to grow. As Stephanie, a 29-year-old mother of one, puts it, "The purpose of discipline is to keep her safe and teach her some acceptable limits, but to give her freedom within her boundaries."

While few parents would argue the benefits of discipline, they may struggle with what's required on a day-to-day basis to end up with a disciplined child. "Discipline is difficult because no one likes to be the heavy," explains Annie, a 44-year-old of one. "It's also demanding. It takes a lot of energy—often when there isn't much to spare."

And then there's the fact that parents are subjected to so much unwanted advice about discipline—comments that can leave you shaking with anger while secretly questioning your own fitness for parenthood and sizing up your odds of raising a megabrat.

"I wish we didn't have to do so much of our disciplining outside the home," says Sharon, a 29-year-old mother of three. "Children seem to always test our rules in new environments, which means strangers look on and judge."

Joan, a 35-year-old-mother of five, agrees. She confesses to having blown her top at a complete stranger in the grocery store when that stranger decided to volunteer some unsolicited discipline advice. "My daughter was having a tantrum in the store and an older woman came by and said, 'That's ridiculous. You're letting her control you. You should just give her a smack and get on with your shopping,'" the mother of five recalls. "My less-than-gracious response was to say, 'Maybe I should give you a smack for being so rude while I'm at it.' She huffed off, so I'm sure she didn't get the point, but the other woman in the aisle sure thought it was funny and stopped to commiserate with me for a moment about how hard it is to parent in public."

TODDLER TALK

Feel like you're butting heads with your toddler every couple of minutes? You may very well be right! Researchers have discovered that toddlers and their parents tend to have minor disagreements approximately once every three minutes.

And because discipline is such a tough issue for parents, it's easy to second-guess yourself and to conclude that you're not doing nearly as good a job of raising your kids as you should be. According to Anita, a 38-year-old mother of four, these insecurities can be fuelled by the one-upmanship that some parents choose to engage in—a dialogue that tends to go something like this: "'We spank our children if the behaviour meets certain criteria.' 'Oh, we could never hit our children; we only use time outs.' 'That's interesting. We feel that time outs lead to feelings of abandonment, so we suspend certain privileges.' 'Oh really? We want our children to have all the things we never had, so we never take anything away, but ....' It's no wonder we don't want to talk about it!" Anita insists.

Disciplining your child will seem a less daunting task if you're clear about your own values and what basic behavioural standards you want to set for your child. (Chances are you have a pretty clear idea in your head about where you stand on this, but it can be helpful to jot a few points down on paper.) It also helps to have age-appropriate expectations about your child's behaviour, since you'll drive yourself—and your toddler—crazy if you have unrealistic ideas about what toddlers are capable of (e.g., expecting your toddler to have perfect manners or a tidy bedroom by age two). Finally, it's important to ensure that you and your partner are on the same page when it comes to discipline. Otherwise your child will learn over time to exploit the differences between you and your partner. Here's what you need to know to get the dialogue between you and your partner started.

The art of co-parenting

WHILE IT'S UNREASONABLE to expect to agree with your partner on every possible parenting issue—you will, after all, have made thousands of parenting decisions by the time your child grows up and leaves home—it's important to come up with a game plan for managing those differences. Here are some tips on managing the types of day-to-day disagreements that can lead to marital meltdowns:

- Accept the fact that you're each going to have your own unique parenting style. Not only were you raised in different households; you're entirely different people. Perhaps your partner feels most comfortable taking a boot-camp style to parenting, while you prefer a much more laid-back approach—or vice versa. "I sometimes tease my husband about how he gets to be 'the hero' with Joey and Maggie," admits Alyson, a 33-year-old mother of one. "He tends not to discipline them as much as I do. He also has a higher tolerance for unacceptable behaviour than I do. And he's not home with them as much as I am and therefore doesn't want to spend what little time he has with them disciplining them."

- Identify those areas where you actually are in agreement. Chances are you and your partner don't go head-to-head on every conceivable parenting-related issue. And if you do, that's more of an indication of problems in the marital relationship than of differences in your parenting philosophies. It can be reassuring to discover that you and your partner are on the same wavelength with big-picture parenting issues and that your disagreements tend to centre on relatively minor points,

---

MOM'S THE WORD

"My husband and I don't see eye-to-eye on discipline matters at all. He's a much firmer disciplinarian than I am. I tend to give in too much, while he expects too much from the kids."

—*Lisa, 37, mother of three*

MOM'S THE WORD

"My husband and I often differ in our views on discipline. I guess we were raised differently. I used to state my opinion right away in front of the kids, but my husband felt he lost face with the kids when I did that. So now we discuss the situation after the kids are in bed and try to come up with a compromise. If one of us feels strongly about a situation, the other one will often give in a bit. That way, we present a united front to our kids. Even as toddlers, they'll take advantage of the situation if they know they can get away with doing something with one parent and not the other."

—Christina, 26, mother of three

---

like how to handle your two-year-old daughter's recent conversion to nudism.

- Come up with a parenting game plan that you both can live with. Kids are merciless in exploiting cracks in the parental armour, so it's important that you and your partner are in basic agreement about how to handle particular childrearing challenges. That means anticipating the perennial parent–child conflicts in advance and deciding how the two of you intend to handle them.

- Be clear about each parent's turf. Sometimes it makes sense to divide up the parenting responsibilities so that you each handle the same sorts of responsibilities from day to day: e.g., you get your child washed and dressed in the morning, while your partner oversees the bedtime routine. Not only does this help ensure that you both receive a bit of downtime from the rigours of parenting, but will also create greater consistency in your child's day-to-day routine.

- When in doubt, call a time out. If you're unhappy with the way your partner is handling a particular situation, wave the proverbial white flag. That way, you can discuss the situation out of earshot of your children and agree to a common solution. "If Lyle disciplines William in a way that I don't completely agree with, I wait until we're alone to discuss it with him," says Candice, a 28-year-old mother of one. "I don't contradict him in front of William. Not only would that undermine Lyle's authority; it would teach William that he could play us off against each other. And that's not a good thing."

- Give each other the benefit of the doubt. Recognize that every parent blows it from time to time. Don't hold your partner up to superhuman standards of parenting. And compliment him when he handles a situation particularly well. Everyone benefits from a pat on the back every now and again, including parents.

- Know when to call in the pros. Don't be afraid to seek out the advice of a neutral third party, such as a family therapist, if you're continually butting heads on parenting issues. Sometimes a single session with a highly skilled facilitator can help you and your partner really cut to the chase on an issue.

- Commit to an ongoing program of parental development, and encourage your partner to come along for the ride. If you find a parenting book or video that's particular helpful to you, share it with your partner. (If he's not the type to read

---

MOM'S THE WORD

"My husband is more demanding of our children. He often has a difficult time 'not sweating the small stuff.' We work to limit our battles, and he and I have developed a code word when we're in the midst of a difficult situation. This allows my husband to gracefully withdraw from his position without undermining his participation in the parenting team."

—*Kimberlee, 28, mother of two*

an entire parenting book, act as his clipping service: use Post-it notes to flag the parts of the book that serve up the most useful bits of wisdom.)

- Find ways to reconnect with your partner on a regular basis. It's hard to feel that you're on the same parenting page if you've lost touch with one another as a couple. Make "date nights" part of your routine by booking a high school or university student to come to your home on a particular evening each week or—at a minimum—every other week. Don't think of it as an expensive frill, but rather as an important investment in your well-being as a family.

- Remind yourself and your partner that this too shall pass. You won't always have young children underfoot. The childrearing years typically last for just one-third to one-quarter of a person's life. Chances are that in years to come you'll look back on these trying times with the fondest of memories. Parental amnesia is, after all, one of Father Time's greatest gifts.

Creative discipline

THINK DISCIPLINING A toddler sounds like total drudgery? Think again! Despite what you might have been told, disciplining a child is not about reinforcing the same old rules the same old way day after day.

While consistency is important—after all, you can't expect your child to learn the family rules if those rules change from day to day—disciplining a toddler can actually be a highly creative exercise: the ultimate opportunity to show off your ability to think on your feet!

Rather than allowing yourself to fall into a rut—which tends to reduce the effectiveness of your discipline techniques anyway—it makes more sense to constantly challenge yourself to come up with new and more effective techniques. It doesn't matter whether you come up with these ideas on your own, or by brainstorming with your partner, reading parenting books, or signing up for some sort of parenting class. What matters most is that you're constantly challenging yourself to "think outside the box."

Here are some important points to keep in mind regardless of what type of discipline method you end up using:

- Remind yourself that it's your job to set limits for your toddler and her job to test those limits. And test them she will! Since she's willing to hold up her part of the bargain, be sure to hold up your end, too, by setting—and enforcing—safe, age-appropriate limits. This will help her to feel safe and secure. She'll have a clear idea about what behaviour is and isn't acceptable. If you don't set any limits, she can't learn these important lessons and may feel as though her entire world is spinning out of control. It's important to let your child know that you're in control of the situation and that the

---

MOM'S THE WORD

"There have been times when I've fallen into discipline ruts where what I've been doing has ceased to work, but I haven't recognized that I need to rethink my reactions to certain behaviours to come up with a new way of handling the situation."

—*Kelly, 31, mother of three*

universe is unfolding as it should. Okay, there may be times when she wishes she lived in a universe in which only cookies were served, but over time she'll appreciate the fact that she can count on healthy foods for breakfast, lunch, and dinner each day.

- Keep in mind that actions speak louder than words. While nobody's expecting you to be perfect, it doesn't hurt to try to model the types of behaviours you want your child to learn. After all, it's pretty hard to teach your child the importance of putting her dirty laundry into the clothes hamper if there's a mountain of dirty clothing building up on your bedroom floor. Ditto for teaching her not to hit people: it's not terribly helpful to tell her that hitting is wrong, only to rush in and smack her for clobbering another child during a battle over a toy.

- Learn how to pick your battles. It's not necessary—or healthy—to do battle with a toddler every time she tries to assert her will. "Who really cares if she's wearing a dress with rubber boots?" asks Janie, a 33-year-old mother of one. "If it makes her happy, why not? Chances are that next time you offer her the dress and the same pair of boots, she'll pick the dress shoes!"

- Follow through immediately when discipline is required. Make it clear that you mean what you say and that you're going to ensure that your toddler follows through. Don't fall into the trap of giving your child endless chances. All you're teaching her is that she doesn't have to listen to you the first few times you ask her to do something—not exactly the message you want to get across!

- Make sure you have your child's attention before you start trying to discipline her. That means getting down to her level and ensuring that she's making eye contact and listening to what you have to say. It's not the least bit effective to simply start issuing orders from the other side of the room!

- Practise active listening when you're communicating with your toddler. Help her to put her thoughts into words, e.g., "You're really hungry" or "You'd like a snack right now." Not only will it help to reduce her frustration and possibly avoid a complete meltdown, but it will also encourage her to play an active role in solving whatever problem is frustrating her at the time.

- Teach your toddler the names for her various emotions so that she'll eventually learn how to verbalize what she's feeling. You may find it helpful to cut out pictures of people demonstrating various emotions and make a "feelings book" for your child. Until she masters the names for her various emotions, you can provide opportunities for her to express those feelings through play (e.g., kneading playdough or engaging in some active play) and let her know you understand how she's feeling by giving her the language to express those emotions: "You're feeling really angry right now because it's not your turn with the toy." Be kind but firm. Don't sound hesitant or unsure of yourself when you're giving your child an instruction or attempting to discipline her. It's important to come

---

MOM'S THE WORD

"At times I get busy doing something, and even though I can see that my child is misbehaving, I end up saying no to him from across the room rather than actually going over to him, distracting him, and telling him that he can't do something. Then my son thinks, 'Hey, I've got her where I want her. I'm the boss now!'"

—*Bernadette, 33, mother of one*

across as a confident, capable parent. But don't let things go too far the other way, either: there's no need to treat your toddler as if she's a new recruit at boot camp!

- Don't phrase commands as questions unless you're willing to give your child a choice. The moment you ask your toddler "Are you ready to go to bed?" you leave the door open for her to say no! Even a simple "okay" tacked on at the end of a sentence can be a problem: e.g., "It's bedtime now, okay?"

- Use a pleasant tone of voice when you're asking your toddler to do something, and making a point of saying "please" and "thank you" so that she can begin learning how these words fit into everyday conversation.

- Be specific about your expectations. Telling a toddler to "be good" won't mean much to her. She needs to know exactly what you mean in this particular situation: e.g., you want her to colour at the kitchen table rather than running through the house, red marker in hand. At the same time, you'll want to make sure that those expectations are realistic. (If this is your first child, you may have unreasonably high expectations, which could cause your toddler to rebel and fight back.)

- Don't expect your toddler to be able to dig deep into her memory vault in order to retrieve the instructions you gave her yesterday or last week. You may have to repeat the same instructions hundreds of times before she remembers what you said and uses that information to modify her behaviour. (I know—it's enough to make *you* want to throw a temper tantrum!)

- Don't overreact if your child makes a poor decision, like scribbling all over the newly painted wall in her bedroom. She may have assumed that it was okay to colour on the wall since you just spent the past week painting on it! Rather than losing your cool, simply explain what the problem is, clean up the mess, and take her crayons away. You may find it helpful to see yourself as playing the role of a coach—helping to guide her because she's still not quite clear about all the rules of the game.

- Be consistent with family rules, since knowing what to expect will make life easier for you and your child. Even though she may not like a particular rule, she'll feel safer knowing that the universe stays the same from one day to the next. And make sure that you and your partner are consistent in enforcing the rules. It's not fair to stick one partner with the bad-cop role while the other gets away with playing good cop.

- Make sure that you have a good answer if your toddler asks you to explain the reason for a particular rule. It's not enough to simply fall back on that catch-all parenting phrase: "Because I said so."

- If you decide to deviate from a family rule on a special occasion, make sure your toddler understands that it's a one-shot deal: that the only reason she's eating ice cream in the living room is because it's Great-Grandma's 80th birthday party! (Of course, you'll probably end up spending the next few weeks trying to reinforce the original rule, which may have you second-guessing your decision to hold Great-Grandma's birthday party in the living room in the first place!)

MOM'S THE WORD

"Sometimes discipline doesn't work out the way you think it should. A lot of times, just as soon as you think you've found the perfect way to get compliance on an issue—poof!—your toddler changes the rules without warning. It's hard to be consistent in your discipline when the response you get from your toddler doesn't remain equally consistent."

—*Annie, 44, mother of one*

- Avoid making promises you're not prepared to keep. If you're not going to follow through on a particular consequence, don't try to pretend that you will. Otherwise your toddler will quickly learn that you don't mean what you say.

- Make sure that your toddler has plenty of outlets for her frustration. Depending on her temperament or interests, she might be able to get rid of some of her frustration by running around, taking a bath, or working with modelling clay. And while she's busy working off some of her frustration, make a point of doing the same thing yourself, whether that means going for a walk, climbing in the tub, or picking up the phone to vent to a friend about the frustrations of being a parent.

The top 10 toddler discipline techniques

WHEN YOU'RE SHOPPING around for a method of discipline that will work well for you and your toddler, you'll want to zero in on one that

- is suited to your toddler's developmental stage and temperament;

- leaves your toddler feeling good about herself;

- leaves you feeling good about yourself as a parent;

- is effective at teaching your toddler appropriate behaviour;

- helps to build upon the bond between you and your toddler.

You'll probably find that you'll use different types of discipline techniques in different types of situations, and that you'll have to go back to the drawing board every now and again to come up with something entirely new. (Toddlers evolve over time, so your discipline methods need to evolve, too.) Fortunately, there are plenty of terrific discipline techniques to choose from. Here's the scoop on 10 techniques that tend to work particularly well with toddlers:

1. **Prevent problems from occurring in the first place.** An ounce of prevention is worth a pound of cure—actually, 10 pounds of cure, when you're dealing with a toddler. Since this is the easiest method of disciplining a toddler—not having to discipline at all!—I decided to put it at the top of the list. You'll find that you can greatly reduce the number of opportunities for conflict if you take steps to anticipate and avoid problems, e.g., keeping objects that she's not allowed to touch out of reach and running errands only at those times of the day when

---

MOM'S THE WORD

"Instead of telling kids what *not* to do, tell them what *to* do instead. If the kids are getting into a drawer they shouldn't be, instead of saying, 'No, don't go into that drawer,' I'll say, 'Claire and Saige, show Mommy how you can close the drawer.' That then gives me the opportunity to follow through with some positive reinforcement by giving them a pat on the back and saying, 'Good job, you closed the drawer.'"

—*Kerri, 36, mother of six*

MOM'S THE WORD

"Be creative when it comes to discipline. As your children grow older, the options increase. I really admire those parents who can be creative and witty on the spot while appearing calm and capable in the situation."

—*Kimberlee, 28, mother of two*

she's likely to be at her best (when she's well rested and well fed). While it's unrealistic to expect to be able to head off every possible problem, you'll be amazed at just how many you can avoid by using this technique on a regular basis.

2. **Find creative alternatives to saying no.** Toddlers tend to dig in their heels if they hear the word "no" all the time, so you'll want to find all kinds of creative ways to avoid using that particular word. Here are a few examples of how you can avoid saying no:

   - If your toddler starts throwing food, instead of saying "No throwing food," gently remind her that "Food is for eating."
   - If your toddler wants to get down from the high chair before you've had a chance to clean her up, don't tell her "No, you can't get down." Tell her, "You can get down as soon as I wipe your hands."
   - Use high-impact words like "stop," "hot," or "dirty," instead of "no." They'll get your message across more clearly and will eliminate the need to say no. (And, in the case of the word "stop," you'll actually be giving her something to do.)
   - Come up with some phrases of your own that you can use instead of "no," like "Not for Sam!"

3. **Offer a substitute.** This is another great way to sidestep a battle of wills. You simply defuse a situation by giving her

permission to do something other than what she's asking to do. Here are a few examples:

- If your toddler wants to scribble on the front of the fridge, give her permission to do something similar instead, e.g., she can draw on a piece of paper that's stuck to the fridge, play with a set of fridge magnets, or draw a picture of a refrigerator and colour it whatever colour she'd like. (As you can see, you can get really creative with this particular technique. I don't know about you, but I think this has the makings of a board game.)

- If your toddler wants to touch a breakable object like a china figurine, give her permission to look at it but not touch it. Or, if you're feeling particularly brave, agree to let her touch it while you hold onto it for dear life!

MOTHER WISDOM

Looking for creative ways to distract your child when she's about to have a meltdown in a restaurant or other public place? Here are some tried-and-true methods straight from the parenting trenches:

- Have a "treasure hunt." Ask your toddler if she can spot someone wearing yellow.
- Turn your toddler's hands into puppets by drawing faces on the back of her hands. Note: Don't do this if your toddler is a neat freak and will have a fit about the marker squiggles on her hands or you'll have one unhappy kid on your hands.
- Make sure you have a surprise or two tucked away in your purse so that you can find a quick distraction when your toddler is about to go into meltdown mode, e.g., junk mail that she can open (the kind with stamps or stickers can be particularly entertaining), an inexpensive plastic toy (the type that fast-food restaurants hand out), Wikki Sticks (bendable, wax-coated sticks that can be used to create sculptures), a flashlight, a magnifying glass, or an unbreakable mirror.
- Find ways to make your toddler laugh. Be goofy, make faces, pretend to be the tickle monster: do whatever it takes to distract her.

MOM'S THE WORD

"I have found that distraction works really well with my son. Sometimes it takes longer than other times to find that perfect fascinating distraction for him, but in the long run, it usually works."

—Brandy, 26, *mother of one*

- If your toddler wants to pour her milk on her cereal herself, put her milk in a small measuring cup. That way, if it happens to get spilled you'll be faced with ounces rather than cupfuls of milk to mop up.
- If your toddler wants a cookie before dinner, offer her some sliced or grated vegetables instead. Or give her permission to have that cookie after dinner.
- If your toddler wants to jump on her bed, give her permission to jump on the floor instead.
- Offer freedom with limits. Let her know that it's okay to play with the ball in the house as long as she remembers to roll it, not throw it.

4. **Offer a distraction.** Countless tantrums have been averted on the part of both toddlers and parents as a result of this amazing technique. It's the closest thing you're likely to find to a discipline magic wand. Here's how it works. If your toddler is about to shove her hand in the fishbowl because she wants to pet the family goldfish, immediately come up with something even more exciting to distract her. Sing a song, hand her a stuffed animal to pat (ideally a stuffed goldfish, if you can swing it!), pick her up and tickle her—do whatever it takes to get her mind off the goldfish.

5. **Give your toddler the opportunity to make choices.** As you've no doubt gathered by now, toddlers are control freaks. They like to be the ones running the show. So why not tap

into your toddler's powerful need to be in charge by allowing her to make some decisions? If, for example, she's refusing to brush her teeth at night, you can give her a choice: she can brush her teeth either before or after her bedtime story. (Obviously, you can't give her a choice about whether or not to brush her teeth at all or you'll get yourself in major hot water with her dentist.) The keys to making this technique work for—not against—you is to offer only those choices you can live with, to limit the number of choices (more than two tends to be paralyzing, not empowering, to toddlers), and to give your toddler a limited amount of time to make her choice. (If she refuses to make a choice within this period of time, you'll have to help her make her decision. For example, if she refuses to choose between the red cup and the blue cup, you'll have to give her an additional choice: "Do you want to decide or do you want me to decide?" If she still refuses to make a decision, then simply say "I see you want me to decide," and hand her one cup or the other.)

6. **Allow your toddler to experience the natural consequences of her actions.** Natural consequences are those that logically flow from the child's own actions (if you throw your cookie on the floor, it has to go in the garbage). They can be a powerful way to give your toddler the opportunity to learn from her mistakes. Obviously, natural consequences can't be applied to

---

MOM'S THE WORD

"Disciplining your kids does not mean having total control over your child. Kids need to feel they're able to make decisions. At first it may be which colour crayon to use or what type of cereal they want for breakfast. Later they may want to choose their own clothing. Often parents fall into the trap that says they're the ones who are always right."

—*Catherine, 32, mother of four*

MOM'S THE WORD

"If Joey and Maggie are being uncooperative about completing a task, I give them choices: either you do this or we won't do this. For example, either they put their coats and shoes on or they can't go outside and play. Sometimes the choices they make are harder on me than on them and I find this frustrating, but I have to stick to my words."

—*Alyson, 33, mother of two*

MOM'S THE WORD

"If Nicholas is hitting Jonathan with a toy, I take that toy away. That becomes the punishment. It's directly related to what was happening."

—*Catherine, 32, mother of four*

every situation: getting a concussion is too big a price to pay for learning that it's not such a great idea to swan-dive off the couch. In this situation, you may have to provide a logical consequence instead: for example, telling your diving enthusiast that you're going to boot her off the couch if she's keeps insisting on trying to dive off of it.

7. **Master the art of selective ignoring.** This technique becomes more and more effective as the years go on and is the ideal method of handling such annoying but non-life-threatening behaviours as making rude noises, acting silly, or having a temper tantrum. Basically, you pretend not to notice the annoying behaviour in the hope that your child will get bored and move on to something else. It tends to be highly effective— I mean, there's no point in having a temper tantrum if you've lost your audience, now is there?—and it allows you to save your energy for the battles that really matter: running on the street, biting or hitting other people, playing with electrical outlets, and so on.

8. **Be generous with your praise.** Positive reinforcement is the twin sister of selective ignoring, but, in this case, you're making a point of reinforcing praiseworthy behaviours. Your toddler is hungry for your approval and will be more likely to repeat good behaviour if she thinks she'll be praised for it. To be effective, praise should be as specific and descriptive as possible: "I like the way you put your books back on the shelf! You're really doing a good job of tidying up" rather than a rather bland and meaningless "Good girl!" Also, be sure to praise improvements in your toddler's behaviour rather than holding out for perfection, and try to work in some honest recognition wherever possible. (Honest recognition involves pointing out how her behaviour is genuinely helpful to you: "Now that the books are up off the floor, we don't have to worry about anyone stepping on them. You really know how to take good care of books.")

9. **Discipline your child verbally.** Verbal discipline will play an increasingly important role as your child grows older. While it's sometimes easier to physically redirect a young child who's refusing to cooperate by picking her up and carrying her out of the room, physical direction doesn't work nearly as well with a six-foot-tall teenager, so you may as well start honing your verbal discipline skills now. After all, you're going to need

---

MOM'S THE WORD

"Claire and Saige have discovered that no matter where we go, they can get anyone and everyone to look at them if they make a smooching sound and give each other a kiss. (Still works on me at home, too!) However, they also know that screaming at the top of their lungs works, too. I'm hoping that reinforcing the kissing and ignoring the screaming will cause them to kiss more and scream less!"

—*Kerri, 36, mother of six*

MOM'S THE WORD

"Discipline works best when it's paired with positive reinforcement. If the child is using his crayons to scribble on the wall and you take the crayons away, be sure to praise him the next day when you see him colouring on paper instead. Children love that sort of positive attention and will be motivated to try to get that kind of reaction from you again."

—*Lori, 31, mother of five*

---

this particular skill for the next 18 years and beyond! Here are a few important tips on using verbal methods of discipline with toddlers:

- Give your child a gentle reminder about a rule when she enters a situation that could lead to trouble: "Remember that beds are for sleeping in." If that reminder doesn't get the desired response, you may decide to progress to a gentle reprimand. "Please stop jumping on the bed. You could fall and bang your head. If you don't stop, you'll have to get off the bed."

- Once you state your behavioural expectation, be prepared to follow through. "Too many parents make idle, meaningless threats and then wonder why their kids won't listen to them," says Kristina, a 31-year-old mother of two. "My kids have learned that I mean what I say. As my 10-year-old daughter explained to her four-year-old brother the other day, 'You might as well stop whining. It's not going to work.'"

- Use words to explain what's going on if you have to take a toy or book away from your child. If, for example, your child is ripping a book and won't listen to your reminder about being gentle with books, take the book away from her and calmly state, "You've decided you want Mommy to put the book away."

- You can also use verbal prompting to give your child a warning that she's about to lose a particular privilege. "When my son is doing something inappropriate and redirection is not an option, I'll sometimes count to three to get him to stop what he's doing," says Julie, a 30-year-old mother of one. "By the time I reach 'two,' he has usually decided to listen to what I've asked him to do." Not all parents are big fans of this particular parenting technique, however. "When I hear parents doing the 1-2-3 counting thing, it makes me cringe," says Lise, a 35-year-old mother of two. "After all, in real life you don't get 10 seconds to learn a lesson."

- Keep in mind that words can hurt, so make sure that your verbal discipline techniques are positive in nature. That means avoiding insults or name calling, yelling at your child, shaming your child, lecturing your child, or describing your child (as opposed to the behaviour) as "bad." Not only are these methods of disciplining a toddler ineffective; they can actually be downright harmful. "I always make sure my kids understand that it's the behaviour I don't like, not them," says Anita, a 38-year-old mother of four. "I make a conscious effort to say 'You did a bad thing' rather than 'You're a bad girl.'"

MOM'S THE WORD

"I find that asking an active child to 'sit still' and think about the consequences of his actions just doesn't work. Active children require active parenting. You need to be constantly aware of where they are and what they're doing in order to prevent mishaps from happening. I find that if you're constantly aware of what your child is doing, the only thing you have to worry about is redirection."

—*Loree, 31, mother of three*

MOM'S THE WORD

"You have to believe in the discipline method you're using in order to be able to properly enforce it. If you don't believe in time outs, don't try to use that method."

—*Sharon, 29, mother of three*

---

10. **Give your child a time out.** Time outs tend to work best with older children, but they can also be used with older toddlers. They're not your best bet with a very young toddler, however, because a child under 18 months of age will have a difficult time figuring out what a time out is all about. Just in case you're not too clear on the concept either, let me explain how it works: A time out forces a child to remove herself from a situation so that she has a chance to reconsider her behaviour. If your toddler is throwing blocks at another child at playgroup, for example, you might remove her from the situation for a minute or two or until she seems ready to start playing again. Here are some important points to keep in mind if you decide to go the time-out route:

   • Avoid using the time-out technique until your child is at least 18 months of age. Younger toddlers will find it difficult to make the connection between their actions (throwing blocks) and the consequence (a time out).

   • Choose a time-out location that's free of distractions so that your child can focus on her behaviour. When you're dealing with very young toddlers, a time out is best served on your lap or in a chair in the same room (in which case it may be referred to as a "time away" or a "time-in" with you rather than a "time out"). Older toddlers can be sent to a boring (but safe) spot away from all the action. Note: It's best to avoid using your child's bedroom as a time-out location because you don't want her to consider being in her room as some sort of punishment. You'll also want to avoid using the kitchen, bathroom, basement, or any other part of the house that isn't 100% toddler safe.

- Stay calm when you're administering a time out. Getting a reaction from you will only serve to entertain her and may actually encourage her to act up enough to "earn" another time out!

- Consider the duration of the time out. One minute for each year of age is a good rule for older children, but two minutes may be far too long for a two-year-old. You may find it works best to simply wait until your child has had a chance to calm down.

- Don't talk to or cuddle your child during the time out. Getting all this attention from you may encourage her to

---

MOTHER WISDOM

Don't be afraid to give yourself a time out if your toddler is pushing your buttons and you feel as if you're going to explode. No one wants to consider the possibility that they could abuse their child, but it can happen. If you feel that you're about to lose your cool, place your toddler in a crib or playpen or other safe place and stay away from her until you're feeling calmer.

While most parents are aware of the dangers involved in shaking a baby, many don't realize that toddlers are also at risk. Like babies, toddlers are susceptible to shaken baby syndrome—a severe and potentially fatal form of head injury that occurs when a child is shaken, thrown vigorously into the air, or hit suddenly on the back. Because a toddler's neck muscles aren't fully developed and her brain tissue is still very fragile, the brain can end up being jostled around inside the skull if a toddler is suddenly jerked or shaken. This can result in brain swelling that can lead to permanent damage, including blindness or even death. The warning signs of shaken baby syndrome include a stunned, glassy-eyed look; an inability to lift the head; blood pooling in the eyes; dilated pupils that don't constrict when they're exposed to light; and unexplained vomiting.

repeat the behaviour that led to the time out in the first place.

- Let your child know when the time out is finished so that she'll understand that she's free to go play again. Some parents use this opportunity to remind the child about the rule they need to remember ("Blocks are for building with, not throwing"); others prefer to send their child off with a reassuring hug.
- Watch your child carefully for a couple of minutes after the time out is finished. With any luck, you'll have the opportunity to praise her newly improved behaviour!
- Don't overuse time outs. Most experts agree that they're most effective if they're reserved for a few specific situations rather than repeatedly administered over the course of a day.

Discipline techniques that don't work particularly well

NOT ALL DISCIPLINE methods are created equal. Here's the scoop on three that aren't very effective:

1. **Threatened abandonment:** The big problem with this so-called discipline technique is that it's based on a lie: you're not going to actually abandon your child in order to teach her a lesson. This technique can have one of two possible effects on your child, neither of which is particularly terrific: either she'll catch on to the fact that you're bluffing (shooting bullet holes in your credibility) or she'll secretly worry that you might actually abandon her after all.

MOM'S THE WORD

"I have never threatened abandonment with either of my kids. The love of a parent is supposed to be unconditional, and if you take that away by telling them you'll leave them behind you risk damaging the trust that the child has for you. It's also something that you're unlikely to carry out. You're unlikely to leave your screaming child in the shopping cart or standing in the driveway as you pull away, so don't threaten something you can't follow through with."

—*Maria, 32, mother of two*

2. **Bribery:** To bribe or not to bribe? That is the question. While bribing your child to behave may provide a temporary solution—she may stop misbehaving long enough in the grocery store to "earn" that package of Smarties,—you could end up creating a whole new set or problems for yourself. (Do you really want to have to buy your child a package of Smarties each and every time you hit the grocery store checkout in order to "buy" a half-hour of her good behaviour?) That's not to say that incentives are entirely taboo. Some parents swear that their toddler would never have been toilet-trained if it weren't for that box of Smarties or package of stickers! If you do decide to offer incentives to your child for behaving, make a point of using them judiciously. And remind yourself that the best reward of all that you can offer to your toddler is your time and attention.

MOM'S THE WORD

"I think offering rewards changes the focus of behaviour from something that's internal to something that's fairly random and external. It makes it hard for children to interpret their own behaviour and makes them look to others—particularly adults—to do the interpreting."

—*Lisa, 36, mother of two*

3. **Spanking:** I've saved the discussion about spanking until last—and it's certainly not because it's "the best"! In fact, most childrearing experts agree that it's the worst method of discipline to use on a toddler. Because spanking relies on negative reinforcement (you're telling your toddler what *not* to do rather than what *to* do), toddlers can find it difficult to make the connection between their actions and the spanking. And even when it does have an impact, that impact tends to be short-lived: Research has shown that spanking is not helpful in changing children's behaviour over the long term. But even worse than that is the fact that spanking can be harmful to your child. Not only does it teach your child that it's okay to hit other people (particularly those who are smaller and weaker than you), but that so-called "harmless" spanking may cross the line into child abuse territory over time. Studies have shown that spankings tend to escalate in intensity if they don't get the desired results right away. Note: By sheer coincidence, spanking ended up being the 13th method of discipline discussed in this chapter. My advice to you? Consider it "unlucky 13" and give it a pass. The other techniques are much more effective and—unlike spanking—will serve to build upon rather than break down the parent–child bond.

MOM'S THE WORD

"I don't find spanking effective at all in changing the behaviour and it leaves me feeling like a failure as a mother. I think resorting to spanking should be a warning sign to parents that maybe they need some time away from their children or some support from family, friends, or professionals. I think parents need to be more aware what their triggers are and to work on coming up with other methods of discipline that are more effective and that, in the end, help make a parent feel more in control and more satisfied with how they handled the situation."

—*Alyson, 33, mother of two*

Unfortunately, many parents find that the urge to spank is almost instinctive—a carry-over from their own growing-up experiences. "Spanking was the discipline method used in my home when I was growing up and I found it really difficult to break away from that method of dealing with frustrations," admits Diane, a 33-year-old mother of three. "I think it's easier to spank than to use other methods of disciplining a child, but in our family we choose not to act with violence."

In many ways, ours is a generation in transition. We're still struggling to find alternatives to spanking, the discipline main-stay of previous generations. "Many of us were raised by parents who spanked us and threatened us with wooden spoons," explains Kimberlee, a 28-year-old mother of two. "I didn't con-sider my parents to be abusive, but they certainly would have been considered so today. I've never used physical punishment in my parenting, and yet I think the few other resources avail-able can be limiting. That said, I love reading about creative dis-cipline and find myself constantly adapting to new concepts in childrearing."

Difficult as it may be to find alternatives to spanking, most parents feel that it's important to make the effort. "I don't believe in spanking," says Lisa, a 36-year-old mother of two. "I myself would not like to be physically punished for something I did

---

MOM'S THE WORD

"I don't think spanking is justified. Spanking is not a natural consequence; it is purely a punishment. When children are spanked, they begin to lie and/or to cover up when they do something wrong for fear of being punished; learn that physical violence solves problems; learn that winning is about being bigger and stronger; and behave out of fear, not because they have learned something."

—*Molly 37, mother of three*

wrong. I think spanking is a form of humiliation, not correction. I want my children to be confident thinkers and the only way to make that happen is to treat them with respect. Spanking is not a respectful way to treat people."

Coping with temper tantrums

IF THERE'S ONE element of toddler behaviour that most parents would gladly live without, this is it. After all, it's more than a little disconcerting to watch your sweet-faced toddler morph into a screaming, red-faced monster in a matter of seconds!

Temper tantrums tend to peak at around age two, gradually tapering off as a child's verbal skills and physical control improve and she learns more effective techniques for managing her frustration. Here are some tips to help you to stay sane in the meantime:

- Learn to identify and avoid your toddler's temper tantrum triggers. You'll probably find that she's more prone to have a tantrum if she's tired, bored, hungry, or sick, or if she's dealing with other types of stress in her life (e.g., she's determined to learn how to walk but tumbles every time she tries to take a step). Once you've clued into her trigger factors, you'll be able to come up with creative ways of handling the situation, such as postponing a less-than-urgent trip to the mall until a day when she's a little less volatile. (Hint: You'll find it easier to pinpoint your toddler's trigger factors if you keep a log of her tantrums over a week or two, noting the time of day, the type of situation she was in at the time the tantrum erupted, whether she was hungry or tired at the time, whether she might have benefited from a longer period of transition between activities, and so on.) Bottom line? It's a whole lot easier to learn to avoid the trigger than to have to deal with a full-blown temper tantrum.

- Be prepared to step in if you can tell that your toddler is becoming overly frustrated. "The toddler lives in a state of frequent frustration," says Jo-Anne, a 43-year-old mother of seven. "Learning to jump in before frustration sets in seems to be the key. I sit down and say, 'Hmmm … let's see what we can do here' before they fall apart with frustration. I think letting children become too frustrated before intervening creates a sense of incompetence."

- Try to distract her if it looks like she's about to lose it. (If you see her sucking in that telltale breath that heralds the imminent arrival of a huge scream, hand her something interesting to look at or ask her if she'd like you to read her a book.)

- Don't give in to tantrums or react strongly to your child's behaviour, or your child will quickly learn that she has the

MOTHER WISDOM

Is your child prone to throwing temper tantrums at the grocery store? Here are some tips on surviving this all-too-common toddler rite of passage:

- Plan your shopping trip so that it coincides with your child's most cooperative time of day—when she's well rested and well fed. There's no point trying to shop with a hungry or exhausted child in tow.
- Insist that your toddler sit in the grocery cart and then snap on the safety strap. Not only will this help to reduce the risk of injury (grocery cart mishaps result in a significant number of injuries to toddlers each year), but will also help to minimize the number of battles about what is—and isn't—going into the shopping cart. A toddler on the loose in a grocery store can't help but feel motivated to "help" Mom shop by loading all sorts of goodies into the cart.
- Find creative ways to keep your toddler entertained while you're making your way through the store. Tell her a story. Ask her to help you to spot various items on the grocery store shelves. Give her a coupon or two to hold onto for you. Or hand her a small toy or a snack that you tucked away in your purse before you left home.
- Let your toddler pick out one special item while you're shopping—perhaps a package of granola bars or a box of her favourite cereal. If she starts whining for a second item, let her know that she has a choice: she can have the second item if she agrees to let you put the first item back on the shelves.
- Make an effort to patronize grocery stores that feature candy-free checkout lanes. (Why give your business to the diabolical geniuses who place candy at your child's eye-level in the hope that she'll be able to badger you into buying her a treat?)

ultimate weapon at her disposal. Instead, ignore the tantrum and try to keep your cool no matter how frazzled and frustrated you may be feeling.

- Don't laugh at your toddler's tantrums or indicate that you find them "cute"—unless, of course, you'd like them to become an hourly occurrence.

- Move your toddler to a safer spot if there's any chance she could injure herself while she's throwing her tantrum.

- Give your child a reassuring hug once the tantrum has subsided. Chances are she found the intensity of her feelings a little frightening. She may be craving some reassurance from you.

- Don't be embarrassed if your child throws a tantrum in a public place. Any adult who has raised a child of their own has likely been in your shoes on at least one occasion; and any adult who hasn't served his or her time in the parenting trenches has absolutely no right to judge!

Whining, screaming, biting, and other hazards of toddlerhood

OF COURSE, temper tantrums aren't the only challenging type of behaviour you can expect to encounter during the toddler years. Here are some practical tips on coping with other common toddler behaviour problems.

Whining

Problem: Your toddler whines in order to get your attention or to blackmail you into giving in to her demands.
How to handle it:
- Avoid situations that tend to trigger major episodes of whining (e.g., visits to the toy store).
- Refuse to respond to your child's demands until she stops whining. Let her know that you're waiting for her "real voice" to return.

"When my daughter becomes demanding and whiny, we'll say, 'I'm sorry, I can't understand what you're saying. Could you use your real voice? This voice isn't clear.' Then she typically finds her 'real' voice."

—*Kimberlee, 28, mother of two*

- Don't give in. If you give in after 10 minutes of whining, you'll simply be teaching your child to whine longer the next time.
- Pay attention to your child when she stops whining so that she'll see the benefits of expressing her feelings by using other methods.

Screaming

Problem: Your toddler screams in order to get your attention or to blackmail you into giving in to her demands.

How to handle it:

- Avoid situations that tend to lead to screaming.
- Refuse to respond to your child's demands until she stops screaming. Let her know that it's impossible to understand what someone is trying to say when they're screaming at the top of their lungs.

"When my two-year-old twins start having a tantrum, I casually say, 'You're allowed to be angry. I understand why you're angry. But your screaming is really loud. Why don't I put you in your playpen so that you can be angry where it won't hurt Mommy's ears.' That usually stops them. I mean, what's the point in screaming if no one is there to pay attention to you?"

—*Catherine, 32, mother of four*

- Don't give in. If you give in to your child on the 10th scream, you'll simply be teaching her that it pays to be persistent.
- Pay attention to her when she stops screaming so that she'll see the benefits of expressing her feelings in other ways.

Biting

Problem: Your toddler chomps down on the nearest chunk of exposed flesh when she becomes really frustrated with a person or a toy. (Note: The techniques described in this section can also be used to deal with hitting and hair-pulling—two other common behaviours.)

How to handle it:

- Learn to watch for "pre-biting" behaviours. If your toddler is prone to biting and you see that her frustration level is starting to build, be prepared to intervene immediately to prevent the other person from being hurt.
- If your toddler manages to bite another child before you can jump in, make a big fuss over the bitee rather than the biter. You don't want to inadvertently reward your child for biting by giving her a lot of attention.
- Show your toddler the bite mark she left. Say, "That hurts. Joey is crying. Your teeth are for eating, not biting."
- Try to figure out what triggered the outburst. Biting tends to occur when a child is too upset to express her feelings in other ways or lacks the language skills to do so.
- Make sure that your toddler understands that biting is unacceptable. Encourage your child to use words or gestures or to find other ways of expressing her anger.
- Offer your child an alternative to biting a person: perhaps hitting a pillow or punching bag. (Note: Some childrearing experts recommend that you teach your child non-violent means of coping with her frustrations, as opposed to giving

TODDLER TALK

Approximately one in five toddlers engages in head banging—an activity that is soothing to some children but highly alarming to their parents. Some toddlers engage in head banging because they find it helps to relax and comfort them. Others do it because they find that it helps them to cope with the pain associated with teething or an ear infection. And still others engage in head banging when they're having temper tantrums. (It becomes their way of making it painfully obvious to others around them that they're just plain not happy!)

Head banging is four times as common in boys as in girls and typically lasts from age six months until a child is approximately two to four years of age. The best way to deal with head banging behaviour is to either attempt to substitute other soothing routines and comforting techniques or ignore the behaviour entirely.

Try not to worry that your child will end up with a severe head injury as a result of all that head banging; this activity is what the experts refer to as a "self-regulating behaviour." In other words, if it hurts too much, your child will stop doing it.

And here's another reassuring bit of information: Brain scans of individuals who were head bangers as children don't show evidence of any abnormalities, so there's no proof that this bizarre habit will affect your child's long-term development.

---

her the message that it's okay to pound things when you lose your cool. You'll have to be the judge on this one.)

- Don't bite your child back to "teach" her that biting hurts. You'll merely confuse and upset her: "Hey, if biting is bad, why did Mom just bite me?"

Running away

Problem: Your toddler likes to make a game of running away. She thinks it's hilariously funny to disappear from your sight momentarily, only to reappear a short time later.

How to handle it:

- Let your toddler know that while this is a fun game to play at home, it's not one you can play when you're at the shopping mall. If she doesn't seem to be able to grasp the distinction, you'll need to stop playing the game at home, or confine your toddler to her stroller, or keep a firm grasp on her hand when she's out in public.

- Give your toddler lots of opportunities to burn off some of her excess energy so that she'll be less inclined to want to run away. You might decide, for example, to make a quick pit stop at the park on your way to the bank. She'll be less likely to want to play hide-and-seek at the bank if she's spent the last half-hour running off steam.

Defiance and stubbornness

Problem: Your toddler consistently refuses to cooperate—a type of behaviour that the experts refer to as "toddler refusal." Typically, she'll respond to every request with the word "no."
How to handle it:

- Accept the fact that a certain amount of negativism is to be expected. It's part of the toddler turf. Try not to overreact when your toddler responds to every request with a heartfelt "no." It's not a personal attack on your authority. It's her new

---

MOTHER WISDOM

"We must remember when we speak of the 'negativism' of the toddler that this is also the child who is intoxicated with the discoveries of the second year, a joyful child who is fully bound to his parents and his new-found world through ties of love. The so-called negativism is one of the aspects of this development, but under ordinary circumstances, it does not become anarchy."

—*Selma H. Fraiberg,* **The Magic Years**

favourite word. (Sometimes she even blurts out "no" when you know she means "yes"!)

- Don't let on that her difficult behaviour is starting to get under your skin. Otherwise, she may continue being difficult because she knows it will get a great reaction out of you.
- When she's digging in her heels on a particular issue, try to find a creative way to offer her some choices. (See pages 183 and 184 for tips on offering choices.) If she refuses to choose from the options you've given her within a reasonable period of time, be prepared to make the decision for her.

Clinginess

Problem: You attempt to go to a family reunion or other social event only to find yourself with a toddler strapped to your leg. As much as you may enjoy the three-legged race, it can get a bit tiring after a while!

How to handle it:

- Accept the fact that a certain amount of clinginess is normal for toddlers—the flip side of their quest for independence.
- Be patient with your toddler. This phase tends to be relatively short-lived. Scolding her or pushing her away won't help her to pass through this stage any more quickly; if anything, it may actually prolong it by causing her to feel less secure.

Bossiness

Problem: Your toddler is determined to boss anyone and everyone around.

How to handle it:

- Realize that a certain amount of bossiness is normal, even healthy. It's an indication that your toddler is becoming more confident and independent.

- Don't tolerate rude behaviour, but don't expect your toddler to outgrow her bossiness overnight. It simply hasn't occurred to her that she's not the centre of the universe.
- Don't be a control freak yourself. The more you allow your toddler to make some decisions on her own, the less need she'll have to assert her authority.

Irrational fears

Problem: Your toddler suddenly develops a series of irrational fears that cause her a great deal of distress.

How to handle it:

- Realize that this is a normal stage of toddler development. Toddlers tend to find anything new frightening and they have highly vivid imaginations. Add to that the fact that they have difficulty distinguishing between fantasy and reality and a greater ability than ever before to remember past episodes in which they were frightened, and you can see why fears tend to be so common.
- Don't nag or belittle your child for being afraid or dismiss or laugh at her fears. No matter how ludicrous they may seem to you, those fears are very real to your child.
- Look for storybooks that deal with whatever type of issue your child happens to be struggling with, whether it's a fear of the dark, a fear of getting lost, or something else entirely. If you can't find a book because your child's fear is a little off the wall—one of my children was deathly afraid of toilet plungers and one of my nieces has an equally deep-rooted fear of pine cones!—you may have to make up a suitable story for your child. You can also encourage your child to work through her fears through art or dramatic play.
- Teach her how to take a slow, deep breath when she's afraid: this will help her to manage the physical manifestations of

fear. Holding her hand will also help her to feel more secure.

- Limit your child's exposure to scary TV shows or movies that other people in the household may be watching. Otherwise, you may be giving her an entirely new set of things to fear.
- Try to avoid passing along any of your own fears to your toddler. If you're petrified of dogs, try not to overreact if one walks by you when you and your toddler are out for a walk. Simply stand your ground and try to remain calm.
- Praise your child when she confronts some of her fears, but don't force her to do so before she's ready.
- Encourage your child to come up with ways of comforting herself when she's feeling scared. She might want to make like Anna in *The King and I* and whistle a happy tune. (Hey, it's a strategy that's worked for Kimberlee's kids: "My children seem to comfort themselves by singing," says the 29-year-old mother of two. "Sometimes I feel like I'm living in a musical!")

Interrupting

Problem: Your toddler interrupts you constantly when you're trying to carry on a conversation in person or over the phone.

How to handle it:

- Put together a box of toys that can be played with only when you're on the phone. Hand her the box when you need to make a phone call and don't want to be interrupted. (Note: Make sure they aren't toys that require any assistance from you or you'll defeat the whole purpose.)
- Set an egg timer for two minutes and let her know that she can have her turn to talk with you as soon as the timer rings. (You'll note that I suggest two minutes. It's unreasonable to expect a toddler to wait much longer than that. So rather than frustrating yourself and your toddler to no end, it's probably

best to postpone that 45-minute yak with your best friend until your toddler is in bed.)

- Hold your toddler and/or make faces at her so that she knows she still has some—if not all—of your attention. And make a point of talking on a cordless phone, since it'll be easier to find things for your toddler to do to keep her entertained.
- Apologize if you have to interrupt your toddler when she's speaking with someone else. Over time, she'll get the message that interrupting is not acceptable behaviour.

Dawdling

Problem: You're in a hurry, but your toddler insists on taking her sweet time about everything.

How to handle it:

- Factor some extra time into your schedule. If you know that your toddler is likely to dawdle over that bowl of cereal for a full 30 minutes, make sure to allow that much time for her breakfast.
- Try to negotiate with your toddler to see if you can speed the process along a little. Perhaps she might forgo her usual policy of insisting on doing everything herself and allow you to put her shoes and socks on while she's sitting at the breakfast table.
- Let your toddler know what's going to happen next if that knowledge is likely to motivate her. Your toddler may be a bit

---

MOM'S THE WORD

"I think we sometimes prevent toddlers from trying things, not because they shouldn't do them, but because it's easier or faster if we do them."

—*Lisa, 36, mother of two*

more inclined to finish her bowl of cereal in a hurry if she knows she's heading off to playgroup this morning.

- Praise your child when she manages to stick with a particular task until it's finished (e.g., eating her breakfast rather than hopping down from the table every 30 seconds).

Regression

Problem: Your toddler suddenly starts acting like a baby again.
How to handle it:

- Try to figure out what's triggered the behaviour. Regressive behaviour is most likely to occur after the birth of a new baby, but it can happen in any stressful situation. It's your toddler's way of letting you know that she's craving the same type of attention she received during her baby days.
- Resist the temptation to scold your child or insist that she "act her age." It's not unusual for a toddler to take these minor detours on the path to growing up. The less of a big deal you make of her behaviour, the sooner she'll pass through this stage and start acting like a "big kid" again.
- Gently sell your child on the benefits of being a big kid, while making it sound like being a baby is *boring*. Point out that babies can't ride bikes, play in the backyard, or eat ice cream cones. Make it sound like babies miss out on all the fun!

Throwing things

Problem: Your toddler develops a new passion for throwing things.
How to handle it:

- Don't assume your toddler is deliberately misbehaving. Chances are she's simply having fun learning about one of the basic rules of physics: what happens to an object if you throw it.

- Rather than attempting to discourage throwing altogether, let her know that certain types of throwing are acceptable (e.g., it's okay to throw balls and other objects that are meant to be thrown). You might also want to find some "helpful" ways for her to put her new-found fascination with throwing to good use. Perhaps she could make a point of scouting around for stray socks and then throwing them in the laundry basket.

Swearing

Problem: Your toddler has learned a swear word and is determined to work it into conversation at every opportunity.

How to handle it:

- Ignore the word in the hope that she won't be encouraged to repeat it. Chances are she heard it somewhere and picked up on the fact that it tends to get a reaction. If you don't provide her with that reaction, she'll have less of an incentive to continue using the word.
- Offer her an alternative expression that's equally appealing— perhaps a highly enthusiastic "Oh my gosh!" or "Oh, shoot!"

TODDLER TALK

Try not to hit the panic button if your toddler holds her breath until she faints or turns blue. As frightening as these breath-holding episodes may be to witness, your toddler's body will "reset" itself as soon as she loses consciousness. She'll start breathing again and recover quickly and completely from her breath-holding episode.

Breath-holding episodes occur in 0.1% to 4.6% of healthy children. They are most common in boys between the ages of 13 and 18 months and girls between the ages of 19 and 24 months. Most children will outgrow these episodes by age 37 to 42 months.

combined with a roll of the eyes and some other over-the-top body language. (Remember, you've got to make this new word even more appealing than the word you want it to replace!)

- Try not to be too embarrassed if your toddler ends up saying her new favourite word in public. Because much of what a toddler says is intelligible only to her parents, other people within earshot may fail to pick up on what she's saying. And even if the swear word ends up coming out crystal clear (odds are, your toddler will manage to utter it during that millisecond when the busy restaurant where you're dining becomes dead silent), most people will assume that she was trying to say something else. (Surely that sweet-faced little two-year-old wouldn't be saying a bad word like that!)
- If your toddler continues to insist on swearing like a trooper or engaging in a lot of "potty talk" (another delightful phase that tends to set in at around age three), you'll have to find ways of letting her know that such language is unacceptable—perhaps sending her for a time out to let her know that you don't want to hear any talk like that. (One mom I know sends children who want to engage in "potty talk" to the bathroom.)

Lying

Problem: You confront your child about a problem and she tells you a bald-faced lie.

How to handle it:
- Realize that children under the age of three or four don't fully grasp the concept of telling the truth. Lying may be caused by forgetfulness, an active imagination, or just plain wishful thinking. (She *wishes* she hadn't spilled the chocolate milk on the carpet, so she tries to convince you—and herself—it didn't happen.)

- Avoid putting your toddler on the spot when something happens or you may encourage her to lie. Instead of asking, "Did you paint on your sister's wall?" when you've managed to catch her red-handed (literally!), simply suggest that she help you scrub the paint off the wall.
- Don't set overly high standards for your toddler. Otherwise, she may be encouraged to lie in order to cover up any perceived shortcomings.
- Praise your toddler when she tells the truth about difficult situations.

Coming to terms with being a less-than-perfect parent

As YOU CAN SEE, your child's toddler years will be full of exciting challenges. (Just think of it as the ultimate personal growth experience for you as well as your toddler!) And because you're learning the ropes as you go, there are bound to be days when you blow things as a parent. Hey, you're only human.

Instead of beating yourself up for being a less-than-perfect parent, simply resolve to learn from your mistakes and move on. The great thing about being a parent is that history tends to repeat itself, so you'll probably find yourself faced with a similar

---

MOM'S THE WORD

"Parents are not perfect. There are going to be times when you overreact and times when things don't work out the way you'd planned. It's at these times that the lesson learned is by the parent rather than the child."

—*Lori, 31, mother of five*

type of parenting challenge again. When that happens, you'll have the confidence that comes from knowing that you already have the hands-on training necessary to come through that biting episode or grocery store meltdown with flying colours.

And as you handle your toddler's misbehaviour in a manner that would do Dr. Spock, Dr. Sears, and even Dr. Phil proud, I'd be willing to bet that you'll be able to hear the theme from *Rocky* playing in your head. (Well, either that or the theme from *Malcolm in the Middle.*)

CHAPTER 5

The Maintenance Manual

ANY THOUSANDS OF years of human evolution have
yet to produce anything even vaguely resembling a
self-cleaning toddler. Consequently, as a parent of one
of these invariably sticky creatures, you can expect to spend a fair
bit of your time in clean-up mode. (It's been my experience that
no sooner do you get the toast crumbs and milk moustache
wiped off your toddler's face at breakfast than it's time to start
doing battle with grass stains, mud puddles, and paint splatters.
And if you're really lucky, you get to cap off the day with my all-
time favourite toddler-related mess: spaghetti sauce that's been
massaged into the hair!) Fortunately, a little soap and water is
generally all that's required to remove the latest layer of grime and
goo. Thank goodness Mother Nature at least had the foresight to
make toddlers fully washable!

In this chapter, we're going to talk about what's involved in
keeping a toddler clean from head to toe. We'll start out with
ways of making bathtime fun rather than an exercise in torture
for your toddler (e.g., from-the-trenches advice on avoiding the
usual hair-washing hysteria). Then we'll talk about dental care,
hair care, and dressing your toddler (e.g., how to put together a

toddler-friendly wardrobe made up of clothing that's easy for your toddler to put on and take off and easy for you to keep clean). Along the way, we'll talk about masturbation, nose picking, and nudity—fairly routine rites of passage for toddlers. We'll wrap up the chapter by zeroing in on one of the most controversial issues that you'll face during the toddler years: toilet training. (Yes, ladies and gentlemen, it's potty time!)

Making a splash: Bathtime basics

IT'S HARD TO FIND a toddler who's ambivalent about bathtime. Most have pretty strong opinions either way. Some toddlers have so much fun during bathtime that they insist on staying in the tub until the water is ice-cold, seemingly oblivious to the fact that their teeth are chattering, while other toddlers are as petrified of water as is the Wicked Witch in *The Wizard of Oz*. (Remember what happened to her when she got wet? She melted!)

It's pretty easy to get along with a toddler who positively lives for bathtime—who hops down from the dinner table and sprints to the bathroom because he's so eager to get on with the show. If you happen to have been blessed with a toddler like this, count your lucky stars and skip to the next section of the chapter. The rest of the material in this section isn't for you!

It's much more difficult to get along with a toddler who makes it painfully clear that he doesn't want anything to do with the bathtub—not today, not tomorrow, *not ever*. While you can humour him for a day or two to see if the bathtub-refusal problem will go away on its own, at some point you'll have to force the issue a little. After all, you can get a toddler only so clean if the sole tools at your disposal are a face cloth, a sink full of water, and a bar of soap. Here are some tips on helping your toddler overcome his fear and/or loathing of all things bathtub related:

- Try to figure out what's fuelling your toddler's bathtub refusal. Is he actually afraid of the tub or does he simply consider bathtime to be the least interesting part of his day? Once you've identified the root cause of the problem, you can put your parenting skills to good use and start brainstorming some creative solutions.

- If your toddler appears to be genuinely afraid of the bathtub—this despite the fact that a fear of water hasn't been a problem for him in the past—try to figure out what may have happened to cause him to suddenly become so fearful. Perhaps he got soap in his eyes, slipped in the tub, or swallowed a mouthful of water the last time he had a bath—experiences that could (understandably) have dampened his enthusiasm for bathtime. Of course, it's also possible that he's developed some strange sort of bathtub-related fear, since toddlers are notorious for this kind of thing. While a fear of going down the drain is fairly common, toddlers can come up with all kinds of strange fears that may not make any sense at all to you. (My three-year-old developed a huge phobia about black plastic shower heads. Go figure.)

- If your toddler doesn't seem to have any particular fears about getting in the tub, perhaps there's something else about bathtime that's bothering him. Maybe he dislikes the temperature of the water, the temperature of the bathroom, or the sensa-

---

MOTHER WISDOM

If your toddler hates the feel of cold shampoo on his head, warm up the shampoo a little. Simply float the shampoo bottle in the bathtub for a couple of minutes to get rid of the chill. Take the same approach with the lotion that you slather on his skin after bathtime: float it in the tub for a minute or two before you remove your toddler from the tub.

MOTHER WISDOM

Store your child's bath toys in a plastic colander placed on the bottom of the tub or in a mesh-style lingerie bag that's hung from the shower head. The toys will have a chance to drip dry, which will help to keep them clean. You'll still need to wash your child's toys every now and again, but you won't have to do it quite so often.

When the moment of truth arrives and it's finally time to do serious battle with soap scum and mildew, here are two quick and easy solutions: either fill the bathtub with hot water and a bit of bleach and let the toys soak for a couple of minutes or run the toys through the dishwasher. (Just be careful what setting you use on the dishwasher: You don't want to accidentally melt or warp your toddler's toys.)

---

tion of being wet. It's also possible that he simply finds bathtime boring. After all, when you've got places to go and people to see, who has *time* for bathtime?

- Once you've identified the problem, try to come up with a possible solution: e.g., putting a non-slip bath mat in the bottom of the bathtub so that the tub isn't quite so slippery; getting in the tub with your toddler to help him feel more secure; putting a small space heater in the bathroom so that the room doesn't feel quite so chilly when he's wet; or making a deal with your toddler that you'll lift him out of the bath *before* you pull the plug.

- Load up on some really fun bath toys and reserve them for bathtime only. That way, your toddler will have a solid incentive to make peace with the tub. The following make terrific bath toys: pails, boats, ducks, water wheels, baby dolls that "wet," beach toys (hey, it's a great way to get year-round mileage out of these despite the Canadian climate!), vinyl books, measuring cups, squeeze bottles, plastic containers of various shapes and sizes, sponges (cut into shapes if you're particularly ambitious and/or having a Martha Stewart moment), and puppet-style washcloths. Note: For additional inspiration in the bath toy department, check out the list of water toys in Chapter 3.

• Find other creative ways to make bathtime fun for your toddler, like making hair sculptures while his hair is full of shampoo (hold up a mirror so that your toddler can admire his wacky 'do' for himself), washing him with animal-shaped or crayon-shaped soap, or treating him to a bubble bath. Note: Bubble baths should be an occasional treat because they can be tough on a toddler's tender skin and have been linked to recurrent urinary tract infections in little girls.

TODDLER TALK

Don't be surprised if you notice your toddler playing with his penis in the bathtub. Toddlers are naturally curious about anything and everything in their world, including their genitals. They may even try to insert objects into their anuses or vaginas—another part of bodily exploration. Some toddlers fondle their genitals for comfort and others hold their genitals as a way to stop themselves from urinating. Some may even masturbate to the point of orgasm, complete with heavy breathing and moaning and groaning. Needless to say, even the most liberal-minded parent can find this a little disconcerting.

While you're best to ignore his behaviour while he's still quite young, as your toddler gets older you'll want to start talking to him about privacy issues, e.g., "There are some things we do in public and some things we do in private." Obviously, you'll want to choose your words carefully so that you don't make your toddler feel that what he is doing is bad or dirty. It's not. It's perfectly natural.

One last thing: Try not to become unduly concerned that your toddler's new-found interest in his genitals may be a sign that he's been sexually abused. Toddlers who have been sexually abused are more likely to become withdrawn or to develop sleep problems than to masturbate excessively. So that's one worry you can probably strike off your list.

Hair washing 101

If there's one thing that toddlers hate, it's having their hair washed, whether it's due to the feel of the bubbles on their head or their fear of having soap and water end up in their eyes. Unfortunately, those all-too-frequent spaghetti-sauce scalp massages make hair washing *de rigueur*. Here are some tips on making the process a whole lot less stressful for you and your toddler:

- Provide your toddler with a snorkelling mask, a set of swim goggles, or a shampoo visor. All three products will help to keep the soap out of his eyes.

- Sit him in the bathtub and wet his hair using a washcloth or (if he'll let you!) a squirt bottle or child-sized watering can.

- Wash his hair with shampoo, making sure to keep the bubbles away from his eyes.

- Rinse his hair thoroughly by either leaning him back in the tub with your hand under his neck while you rinse the shampoo out of his hair or rinsing his hair while he sits in the tub (tilt his head back slightly and hold a face cloth over his eyes while you pour water down the back of his head). Note: You can encourage your child to bend his head back for rinsing if you hang some eye-catching pictures on the ceiling above the tub—perhaps a special "bathtime collage" that the two of you made together for this purpose.

- Keep your child amused by singing to him while you wash his hair. (If you're into old musicals like *South Pacific*, you might want to ham it up with a powerful rendition of "I'm Gonna Wash That Man Right Out of My Hair!" adapting the lyrics slightly to make them more suited to a toddler audience—something along the lines of "I'm Gonna Wash That Lunch Right Out of My Hair!")

TODDLER TALK

Don't worry about trying to clean out the orangey waxy buildup inside your toddler's ears. This waxy buildup helps to keep his ears free of dirt. While it's okay to wipe his outer ear with a washcloth to chase away all the day-to-day grime, resist the temptation to start poking around inside his ear with a Q-tip—something that could lead to damage to his ear drum.

If, however, your toddler seems to have a lot of excess ear wax, you'll want to point out the problem to his doctor. A clogged ear canal can lead to temporary hearing loss, which can interfere with language acquisition in toddlers.

Toddlers and dental care

DON'T MAKE THE mistake of assuming that you can afford to cut corners in caring for your toddler's teeth simply because he still has his baby teeth. Unrepaired decay in a child's "baby teeth" (a.k.a. "milk teeth" or "primary teeth") can lead to decay in his permanent teeth as well as to orthodontic problems. This is because your child's baby teeth have an important role to play in guiding the adult teeth into their correct position: They act as space holders for the permanent teeth.

TODDLER TALK

Most children can hold off on visiting the dentist until they're three years of age, but with some you'll need to schedule that first appointment a little sooner. You should plan to take your toddler to the dentist before his third birthday if

- he already has all 20 of his primary teeth;
- one of his teeth has become sensitive to hot, cold, or sweets;
- you notice a brown spot on one of your toddler's teeth;
- your toddler's teeth are misaligned; or
- one or more of his teeth are discoloured.

Your toddler's first molars (the second-to-last set of teeth at the back of the mouth) tend to disappear around the time of his first birthday. His second molars tend to appear roughly a year later, just in time for him to blow out the birthday candles again. By age three, a child should have all 20 of his baby teeth. (See Table 5.1 to find out when you can expect each of your toddler's baby teeth to come in.) He'll hold onto his baby teeth until around age six, at which point his adult or permanent teeth will start to come through.

The truth about teething

Some toddlers become miserable while they're teething, while others aren't the least bit fazed. If your toddler seems to be bothered by teething pain, try offering him a rubber teething ring (ideally the water-filled kind that can be put in the fridge or freezer to soothe his tender gums), a cold washcloth, or a frozen bagel to gnaw on. Note: According to the Canadian Paediatric Society, most children who are teething do not require any sort of pain relief, so you won't want to reach for that bottle of acetaminophen too quickly.

The basics of brushing

Chances are you're already in the habit of brushing your toddler's teeth. If you're not, you should be: The Canadian Dental

---

TODDLER TALK

If your toddler develops a fever, don't blame it on teething. According to the Canadian Paediatric Society, there's no link between teething and fever.

TABLE 5.1

Tooth Eruption Timeline

Teeth	Location	When They Come In
Central incisors (lower)	Front of mouth on lower jaw	6 to 10 months of age
Lateral incisors (lower)	Directly beside central incisors on lower jaw	7 to 16 months
Central incisors (upper)	Front of mouth on upper jaw	7 to 12 months
Lateral incisors (upper)	Directly beside central incisors on upper jaw	9 to 13 months
First molars (lower)	Second-last tooth at the back of the mouth on either side of the lower jaw	12 to 18 months
First molars (upper)	Second-last tooth at the back of the mouth on either side of the upper jaw	13 to 19 months
Canines (cuspids, upper)	Between the lateral incisors and the molars on the lower jaw	16 to 22 months
Canines (cuspids) (lower)	Between the lateral incisors and the molars on the lower jaw	16 to 23 months
Second molars (lower)	Very back of the mouth on the lower jaw	20 to 31 months
Second molars (upper)	Very back of the mouth on the upper jaw	25 to 33 months

Source: Canadian Dental Association Web site

MOM'S THE WORD

"During my son's first visit to the dentist, the dentist told him that he was to brush his teeth in the morning, and Mommy was to brush his teeth and floss at night. That's the way it is at our house because 'the dentist said so.'"

—Sandi, 31, mother of two

Association recommends that parents start brushing their children's teeth as soon as they erupt through the gum, starting with a pea-sized amount of fluoride toothpaste on a soft-bristled baby toothbrush. You should make a point of brushing your toddler's teeth at least twice a day—ideally after the first and last meals of the day—to help minimize tooth decay.

Here are some other important points to keep in mind when you're brushing your child's teeth:

- If your toddler has a tendency to want to wriggle away while you're trying to brush his teeth, try standing behind him and leaning his head back against your stomach. Not only will this position make it more difficult for him to run away, it'll also feel more natural to you because it's similar to the position that you use when you're brushing your own teeth.

- Here's another position that works well when you're trying to brush the teeth of a human jumping bean: in the bathtub. He'll be less likely to manage to get away with his teeth half cleaned if he's temporarily corralled in the tub.

- Give your child a flashlight and ask him to aim the light beam in his mouth while you're brushing his teeth. Not only will it give him something to do other than trying to wrestle the toothbrush away from you, it'll make it easier for you to see what you're doing.

MOM'S THE WORD

"We sing songs while my son is brushing his teeth. My husband taught him to say 'aaaahhhh' to brush his back teeth and 'eeeehhhh' to brush his front teeth."

—*Jennifer, 27, mother of two*

- To teach your toddler about the importance of thorough brushing, use a timer, a stopwatch, or a song on your child's tape recorder to "time" each toothbrushing session. Ideally, you should be spending two minutes or more brushing his teeth.

- If your toddler insists on brushing his own teeth, make a point of taking turns. It's great to encourage his toothbrushing skills, but you don't want him to go solo until he's at least six. "What works for us is using two toothbrushes: one for him and one for me," says Julie, a 30-year-old mother of one. Hint: You can sweeten the turn-taking bargain by allowing him to help you brush your teeth, too. It may seem a bit weird at first, but you'll actually be giving your toddler valuable toothbrushing practice because he'll be able to see what he's doing.

- If your child starts kicking up a fuss whenever you pull out the toothbrush and the toothpaste, try giving him some choices. While you can't let him get away without brushing his teeth, you can allow him to decide
  - which colour of toothbrush he wants to use tonight (it's always a good idea to have a spare toothbrush on hand for this very reason, especially one of those inexpensive battery-operated ones: kids go crazy for them!)
  - which flavour of toothpaste he'd like to use (some kids hate "adult" mint toothpaste but adore bubble gum or

MOM'S THE WORD

"When I'm brushing my son's teeth, I talk about all the things he's eaten that day: 'Oh, let's brush away that toast. There's some chicken. I have to get that broccoli.' It helps to distract him."

—*Julie, 30, mother of one*

---

berry-flavoured toothpaste). "Our son has a virtual arsenal of toothbrushes and several types of toothpastes, too," confesses Annie, a 44-year-old mother of one.

- whether he'd like to brush his teeth before or after his bedtime story (all that matters is that they're clean by the time his head hits the pillow). Don't allow your toddler to eat toothpaste or swallow the mouthful of toothpaste that builds up while you're brushing his teeth. Swallowing too much toothpaste can cause a condition called fluorosis, which can result in white spots forming on your child's teeth. (You'll find more information on fluorosis elsewhere in this chapter.)

- To minimize bacteria growth, rinse your child's toothbrush thoroughly before putting it away. And make a point of replacing the toothbrush at least twice a year, more often than that if the bristles start to look flattened and worn.

- Don't allow your toddler to run around while he's carrying his toothbrush. A child can be seriously injured as a result of falling with a toothbrush in his mouth.

- Try to introduce flossing early. Ideally, you should try to floss your child's teeth at least once a day. And try to give your toddler's tongue a scrub as often as he'll let you in order to remove some of the bacteria that lives on the tongue.

The baby bottle blues

If your toddler drinks from a bottle, it's important to switch him to a cup as soon as possible. The Canadian Dental Association recommends that parents introduce a cup by a child's first birthday to reduce the risk of tooth decay. (Drinking from a cup doesn't cause liquid to collect around the teeth in quite the same way as drinking from a bottle does, and is consequently less likely to contribute to tooth decay.)

Drinking from a bottle at night or nursing frequently throughout the night can lead to other serious problems with tooth decay. Baby bottle syndrome (taking a bottle to bed and drinking frequently throughout the night) and nursing caries (a similar problem that's caused by nursing at the breast almost continuously) can lead to toothaches, tooth decay, feeding difficulties, and the premature loss of the baby teeth (which can, in turn, result in speech problems, jaw development problems, and the need for orthodontic work).

The most severe tooth damage tends to occur in the areas where liquid can build up in the mouth: around the front and back of the upper front teeth. The earliest warning sign that there could be a problem is the presence of tiny white spots on the upper front teeth. Note: These spots are sometimes so small that they can only be detected by a dentist.

TODDLER TALK

You already know about the perils of baby bottle syndrome (a.k.a. nursing caries: tooth decay caused by constantly drinking from a bottle filled with anything other than water, especially during naps and at night). What you might not realize is that constant sipping from a juice box, bottle, or sippy cup during the day can also be harmful to a child's teeth. Fruit juice, pop, and milk all contain sugars that can cause tooth decay if left in contact with child's teeth for lengthy periods of time.

If your toddler absolutely insists on having a bottle within grabbing distance at any time of day or night, fill it with water. At least that way it won't be damaging to his teeth.

The facts on fluoride

Something else you need to think about is whether or not your toddler needs a fluoride supplement. Fluoride helps to strengthen tooth enamel to make it more resistant to acids and harmful bacteria—something that helps to stop tooth decay. If your community has fluoridated water, your toddler's fluoride needs are already being fully met, but if your water supply doesn't contain fluoride, your doctor may recommend that your toddler receive some sort of fluoride treatment or supplement (e.g., tablets or drops).

The issue of fluoride treatment is yet another hot topic in the field of pediatric medicine. While the Canadian Paediatric Society says that babies should start receiving fluoride treatments at six months of age if there's less than 0.3 parts per million of fluoride in the municipal drinking water, the Canadian Dental Association takes a slightly different stand on this issue, advising that fluoride supplementation be postponed until age three. It's important to discuss this issue with your toddler's doctor or dentist. The last thing you want to do is to give your toddler an unnecessary fluoride supplement. As I mentioned earlier, too much fluoride can cause a condition called fluorosis that will cause white spots to appear on his baby and/or adult teeth, permanently damaging those beautiful pearly whites.

Putting the bite on tooth decay

Here are some other important dental health tips:

- Ensure that your toddler is eating a balanced diet made up of a variety of healthy foods. (See Chapter 6 for practical tips on

TODDLER TALK

Approximately 30% of children grind their teeth when they're sleeping and, for whatever reason, teeth grinding is more common in toddlers than in older children. It's most likely to occur when a child is in a very deep sleep or under a lot of stress. Teeth grinding (bruxism) doesn't generally do any lasting damage to a toddler's teeth (his baby teeth have to last only for a couple of years), but if he continues grinding his teeth as he gets older, your dentist may wish to fit him for a mouthguard to prevent any damage to his jaw or his permanent teeth.

---

getting toddlers to eat the right kinds of foods.) This will help to promote good dental health.

- Offer alternatives to sticky, sugary-sweet snacks, since sugar promotes tooth decay. Note: Sugary and sticky foods (including raisins and other dried fruits) won't do quite as much harm to your toddler's teeth if they're eaten as part of a meal rather than on their own, so if you choose to include these foods in his diet, make sure they're served along with other foods.

- Don't allow your child to snack nonstop from morning until night. Try to structure his eating into three meals plus one or two snacks. Not only is this better for his teeth, but you'll be promoting healthy eating habits at the same time.

Thumbs and pacifiers

Most toddlers naturally give up their thumb-sucking or pacifier habit by the time they're two years of age. If your toddler hasn't kicked the habit by then, you'll want to encourage him to do so as soon as possible in order to prevent orthodontic problems down the road. A recent study at the University of Iowa College of Dentistry and the Tokyo Dental College found that sucking a thumb, finger, or pacifier beyond age two increases the likelihood that a child will develop protruding front teeth or a cross-bite (a narrowing of the upper jaw relative to the lower jaw).

To discourage your toddler from sucking his thumb, try to come up with creative ways of keeping his hands busy at those times of day when his thumb tends to find its way into his mouth. If, for example, your toddler is in the habit of sucking his thumb while you read him a bedtime story, give him two small toys to hold onto—one for each hand. This approach tends to be more effective than putting a bandage or a bitter substance on your child's thumb or constantly nagging him about his behaviour—strategies that can actually backfire by reinforcing the thumbsucking behaviour.

To discourage your toddler from turning to his pacifier each time he's upset (which, by the way, prevents him from learning other methods of managing his emotions), make an effort to keep the pacifier out of sight and your toddler's mind on other things. Some parents keep the pacifier in their toddler's room so that he has to go and retrieve it if he wants it. Others limit pacifier use to nighttime only.

You'll probably find that your toddler's pacifier use will decrease as he starts to develop other ways of comforting himself when he's upset, when he's able to communicate more effectively, and when he notices that other children his age no longer have pacifiers.

A gradual process of weaning a child off his pacifier generally works best. Forcing a child to give up his pacifier before he's ready can actually cause him to become more dependent on it than ever.

Here's another other important point to consider: Excessive pacifier use can interfere with your toddler's speech. Not only will he have fewer opportunities to practise his speech, but overuse of a pacifier can also interfere with his articulation skills. He may tend to replace his "t" and "d" sounds (which require that the front of the tongue brush up against the back of the front teeth)

TODDLER TALK

Many toddlers get in the habit of picking their nose, either because they're curious about what's inside the nasal cavity, they're looking for relief from cold or allergy symptoms, or their nasal passages are dry and itchy.

The best way to handle the problem is to try to get at the root cause.

- If you suspect that an overly dry home environment is making your toddler's nasal passages dry and itchy, you might want to run a room humidifier or squirt a blast or two of saline nasal spray up each of your toddler's nostrils.

- If you suspect that your toddler is bothered by a runny nose, let him pick out a box of tissues at the grocery store and then encourage him to use them to wipe or blow his nose.

- If you suspect that your toddler is picking his nose as a result of either curiosity or boredom, you might want to give him something else to do with his hands.

- Don't get into a power struggle with your toddler over nose picking, or you could make the problem worse. Rather than trying to kick him of this annoying bad habit right now, simply remind yourself that it's unlikely you'll catch him picking his nose 20 years from now as he marches across the stage to pick up his university diploma. Chances are he'll abandon the habit as soon as he starts getting social pressure to stop. (This is one of those times when peer pressure can actually work in a parent's favour!)

---

with "k" and "g" sounds (sounds produced at the back of the throat). The solution? Let your toddler know that you can't understand what he's saying when he tries talking with his pacifier in his mouth. Over time, he'll learn to take the pacifier out of his mouth while he's speaking.

Hair care

HAVING A HARD TIME convincing your toddler to allow you to run a comb through his hair? You're certainly in good company.

A lot of toddlers make it painfully obvious to anyone within earshot that they hate having their hair combed.

In many cases, this is because a toddler's hair is tangled and matted, which can make it painful to pass a fine-toothed comb through it. Using conditioner on a regular basis can help to detangle your child's hair, and temporarily switching to a wider-toothed comb will make hair-combing easier for him and for you. It's also wise to stick with shorter haircuts during the toddler years. Any parent who lets her toddler go for the long-haired Lady Godiva look is pretty much asking for trouble! (But then again, given the enjoyment most toddlers get out of being buck naked, the hairstyle may actually be kind of apropos.)

Cutting to the chase

Of course, it's one thing to want your child to have short hair. It's quite another to get his hair cut. That first haircut can be a rather hair-raising experience for both you and your toddler.

The first thing you have to do is decide if you'd like to cut your toddler's hair at home or whether it might be wiser to let the pros handle it. If your child is going through a real battle of wills with you at the moment, he might be more cooperative for a complete stranger. But if he's got a major problem with stranger anxiety, being greeted by a scissor-wielding stranger isn't going to make him feel terribly comfortable. Only you can decide what will work best for your toddler.

Here are some tips on making that first haircut less stressful, whether it happens at home or the salon:

At home:

- If you decide to cut your toddler's hair at home, put him in his high chair. You'll find it easier to keep him from wiggling around. Note: Some parents recommend planting the high chair in front of a mirror so that your toddler will be able to watch while you cut his hair, but obviously you'll want to go this route only if you're positive your toddler won't be unduly freaked out by the sight of those scissors approaching his head!

• Dampen your child's hair using a plant mister filled with water and a squirt of hair conditioner. (It'll help to detangle his hair.)

• Cut your toddler's hair with blunt-ended scissors to prevent any accidental nicks and scratches if he suddenly goes into wiggle mode. Be prepared to do the haircut in stages over the course of a day or two if he's at an exceptionally active stage.

• If your toddler is nervous about having his hair cut, try giving someone else a haircut at the same time: perhaps an older sibling or your partner!

• If you think your toddler may be scared silly by the blow dryer, allow his hair to air dry instead. You don't want to cap off a successful first haircut by traumatizing him with a noisy appliance!

At the hairdresser's:

• When you talk with your toddler about his upcoming trip to the local hair salon, use the word "trim" rather than "cut" to describe what's going to happen to his hair. He'll be less inclined to feel totally freaked out.

• Choose your child's hairdresser wisely. You want someone who's comfortable working with toddlers and who will have a whole bunch of creative strategies for getting your toddler to cooperate while his hair is being cut.

• Recognize the fact that the first haircut may be a little traumatic for your child. Not only is he confronted with a strange environment, but there are all kinds of scissors flashing and clippers buzzing! Your toddler may be petrified he's going to get cut.

- If you can swing it, let the hairdresser cut your hair or another family member's hair first. That way, your toddler will have a better idea of what's involved in getting a haircut and may be less fearful as a result.

- Change your child's shirt when the hairdresser is finished cutting his hair. That will help to minimize some of the post-haircut itchiness.

- Last but not least, remember to scoop up a lock of your child's hair—an important memento for his baby book.

Head lice

What chapter on hair care would be complete without a couple of paragraphs on every parent's least favourite topic, head lice?

As you've no doubt gathered from following the news, head lice (pediculosis) is becoming a major problem. According to the Canadian Paediatric Society, between 1 and 10% of elementary schoolchildren are infested with head lice at any given time.

Head lice are tiny insects that live on the scalp. Their eggs are called nits. Head lice tends to be spread through direct contact between children. According to the Canadian Paediatric Society, there isn't much hard evidence to support the widespread belief that head lice is spread via objects such as hats, combs, and brushes, so you don't have to go totally crazy if you catch your toddler trying on another child's hat!

Children don't always become itchy when they contract head lice, so it's a good idea to do periodic spot checks, particularly if you know your child has been in contact with someone with head lice. Be sure to focus on the area close to the scalp, behind the ears, toward the back of the neck, and on the top of the head. Mature insects (one millimetre–long, dark-coloured insects) are harder to spot than nits (greyish-white ovals that resemble dandruff).

To get rid of head lice, you will need to treat your child with an insecticide that kills lice. According to the Canadian Paediatric Society, this is the only effective method of treating head lice. Because products designed to treat head lice contain highly toxic chemicals, you should use one of these products if you're certain that your child has head lice. Once you've finished treating the nits, you can remove any remaining nits by either

- applying a damp towel to your toddler's scalp for 30 to 60 minutes;

- soaking his hair with a solution made up of equal parts of water and vinegar and then applying a towel soaked in the same solution for 15 minutes; or

- washing your child's hair and applying cream rinse containing 8% formic acid (a substance that helps to dissolve the "glue" that binds the nit to the hair shaft).

At this point, you can then back-comb the nits off your child's hair by using a fine-toothed nit comb or scrape the nits off your child's hair using your thumbnail. (Note: You're removing the

---

TODDLER TALK

Some daycare centres have "no nit" policies that prevent toddlers from returning to daycare until their heads are entirely nit-free. According to the Canadian Paediatric Society, these policies aren't based on any hard evidence that this is effective in controlling head lice. Their position is that once a child has been treated for head lice, he should be allowed to return to daycare with the understanding that a follow-up treatment will be done seven to ten days later.

MOTHER WISDOM

If your child becomes infected with head lice, you'll want to wash his bed linens and stuffed animals in hot water or place them in plastic bags in the freezer for at least 24 hours. Any stuffed animals that aren't fully washable should be placed in "quarantine" for ten days. Combs and brushes should be soaked in hot water for 10 minutes or washed with a pediculicide shampoo.

You may also want to treat any siblings who share the same bed as the affected child, whether or not you've actually spotted any nits on their heads. Note: Other family members will need to be treated only if they actually become infected.

---

nits only for cosmetic reasons, so don't feel that you need to remove every single one.)

All head-lice treatment products require a second treatment seven to ten days after the first treatment, so make a point of doing this important bit of follow-up. Otherwise, your child's head may end up playing host to head lice again. (Nits that were not killed by the first round of treatment can hatch and start the infestation cycle all over again.)

Clothes calls

YOU CAN'T EXPECT your toddler to learn how to dress himself if every item of clothing he owns is tricky to put on and take off. After all, we're talking about a toddler here, not Harry Houdini! Here are some tips to keep in mind the next time you hit the children's department of your local department store:

- Look for clothing that is comfortable and loose-fitting so that your child will be able to bend, jump, and otherwise go about the business of being a toddler.

- Steer clear of dresses or loose jumpsuits when your toddler is learning how to walk. They may cause her to trip.

- Choose garments that will be easy for your toddler to put on and take off. That means avoiding shirts with overly tight necklines like turtlenecks; clothes with zippers, buckles, and snaps that may be tricky for his little fingers to manoeuvre; and one-piece garments like overalls and jumpsuits. Instead, look for pants with elastic waistbands, shirts with oversized necklines that stretch as your toddler pulls the shirt over his head, and Velcro closure shoes that are easy for your toddler to put on and take off.

- There are some added advantages to going with two-piece rather than one-piece outfits: you won't have to do as much laundry (you'll have to wash only the half of the outfit that's actually dirty), and your toddler will have a much easier time getting his pants down in time when he needs to use the potty.

- Steer clear of one-piece sleepers. It's a rare two-year-old indeed who's got the skills and patience necessary to take a sleeper on and off each time he needs to use the potty in the middle of the night.

- For safety reasons, you'll want to look for skid-proof socks and slippers. These will help reduce the number of times your toddler slips and falls.

- If your child is easily irritated by the feel of his clothing, look for garments with oversewn seams (they're less irritating) and

---

MOTHER WISDOM

Here's another good reason to "just say no" to pants with zippers until your toddler is a little older: It's quite common for little boys to accidentally catch their penises in the zippers of their pants.

remove any labels that could end up scratching your child. Then wash the garment a few times to break it in, making a point of using fabric softener in the rinse cycle. Or save yourself all the bother of trying to break a garment in by buying second-hand clothing for your child.

Dollars and sense

While comfort and functionality are obviously the key considerations when you're putting together a wardrobe for your child, you'll also want to consider the bottom line. Here are some tips on getting maximum bang for your clothing buck:

- Don't overshop for your toddler. He'll be having fewer diaper blowouts than he did as an infant, and as his ability to feed himself improves, he'll be less likely to wear each meal. He probably won't go through more than two outfits in a day, so assuming you're willing to do laundry twice a week, you can probably get away with having eight to ten outfits in his size for each season. Since many of his outfits will end up being splattered with paint, mud, and whatever else happens to catch his interest these days, you'll be better off loading up on clothing at garage sales and second-hand stores or accepting offers of hand-me-downs from family members and friends rather than shopping for designer kids' clothes at high-priced boutiques.

- Clean out your toddler's closet and drawers at the start of each season. That way, you'll have a clearer idea of what types of clothing he needs before you hit the stores. If you're planning to visit the consignment stores in search of quality second-hand clothing for your child, bring along some of the garments that your child has outgrown so that you can put them on consignment at the same time.

- Organize a neighbourhood clothing swap each spring and fall. You can then donate any leftovers to a charity that collects used clothing for children in need.

- Shop for seconds at manufacturers' retail outlets. Often the flaw in the clothing is virtually unnoticeable or is something that you can repair easily at home with a needle and thread.

- When you're shopping for new clothing, try to give your business to stores that offer some sort of wear guarantee (e.g., they'll replace the item if the outfit wears out before your child outgrows it). And while you're at the checkout, find out if they offer any customer loyalty programs that reward you for your ongoing patronage. If they do and it seems like a good deal, sign up.

- Try not to fixate on the price tag. An expensive pair of jeans that makes it through the toddlerhoods of two or more kids may actually be cheaper than a poor-quality pair that doesn't even survive the toddlerhood of kid number one.

- Stick to a few basic colours of clothing so that you'll have more mix-and-match possibilities—something that will help to stretch your clothing dollars and reduce the odds that your child will look like a tacky tourist every time he dresses himself.

- Make a point of buying patterns rather than solids. Patterns help to hide stains. And for goodness sake, steer clear of anything white unless you want to make stain patrol part of your daily routine. (Actually, steer clear of any light colour, particularly if the fabric is unbleachable.) Note: You can find hands-on instructions for doing battle with the most common types of toddler-related stains in Table 5.2.

- Invest in durable, easy-care clothing that's designed to grow with your child (e.g., pants and shirts with "grow cuffs" that can be unrolled to add a bit more length to each pant leg or sleeve). While it's a good idea to buy garments that are slightly oversized so that your toddler can get a bit more wear out of them, don't go too crazy: you don't want him to trip because his pants are six inches longer than his legs.

- Learn to sew. You can save a tremendous amount of money on children's clothing if you sew even a handful of garments in your child's wardrobe.

Stain removal

The key to removing stains from your toddler's clothing is to act quickly, starting with the least powerful stain-removing ingredient. If that doesn't do the trick, you may have to up the ante. Be sure to test the stain remover on an inconspicuous part of the garment first if you're not sure how a particular fabric will react to it. It's best to treat the stain from the opposite side of the fabric, placing a paper towel under the stain as you work, and to blot—not rub—the stain. Then pre-treat the stain with a commercial stain remover and launder the garment promptly.

Note: Because heat will set a stain, it's important to treat stains before clothes go through the washer and dryer. They can be almost impossible to remove once the heat from the dryer has "baked" the stain in.

TABLE 5.2

The Mother of All Stain Removal Charts: Doing Battle with Toddler Stains from A to Z

Type of Stain	How to Treat It
Berries (strawberries, blueberries, etc.)	Apply red wine stain remover to the stain.
Blood	Soak garment in salt water or flush with club soda. If that doesn't work, try making a paste out of meat tenderizer and applying it to the stain or pouring hydrogen peroxide directly on the stain and then flushing with cold water.
Butter or margarine	Remove any blobs of butter or margarine and then work undiluted dish detergent into the stain. If the stain is old, you can reactivate the grease by spraying the spot with WD-40 lubricant and then working in undiluted dish detergent.
Chocolate	Soak garment in an enzyme prewash solution for 30 minutes and then rub liquid detergent into any remaining stain. Rinse well in cold water.
Crayon and coloured pencil	Place the stained area of the garment on a pile of paper towels and spray with WD-40. Turn the garment over and spray the other side of the spot. Allow the garment to sit for 10 minutes and then rub dish detergent into the stain. Launder in hot water.
Crayon, melted	Place the stained area of the garment on a pile of paper towels. Cover with an additional layer of paper towels. Using a hot iron, press the stained area until the crayon has lifted into the paper towels.

Stain	Treatment
Food dye (dyes from flavoured fruit drinks, Popsicles, gelatins, cough syrup, etc.)	Treat with cold water and ammonia (approximately 25 mL/1 tbsp of ammonia to 250 mL/1 cup of cold water) and then rub salt into the stain. Repeat if necessary. Red, orange, and purple stains can also be treated with red wine stain remover.
Formula, infant	White clothing: Apply lemon juice and lay garment in the sun or make a paste out of meat tenderizer and apply it to the stain. Coloured fabrics: Make a paste out of meat tenderizer and apply it to the stain.
Fruit and fruit juice	Treat the spot with club soda or cold water immediately. Rub in liquid detergent, then flush with hot water. If the stain still remains after this treatment, make a paste out of borax and apply to the stain. Allow the borax to dry and then brush it off. If you discover an old fruit or fruit juice stain try reactivating the stain with glycerin (available at the drugstore) and then following the same steps for treating fresh fruit or fruit juice stains.
Glue	Soak the garment in warm to hot water and then wash as usual.
Grass stains	Sponge grass stains with rubbing alcohol. If that's not effective at removing the stains, try sponging with vinegar instead or rubbing some non-gel toothpaste into the stains. Rub laundry detergent into the stained areas and launder as usual.
Ice cream	Sponge the garment with cold water, club soda, or seltzer and then treat any remaining stain with a paste made of cold water and meat tenderizer. (Leave the paste on for 30 minutes or so and then flush with cold water.)

continued on p. 240

Ink	Sponge a bit of rubbing alcohol onto ink stains. Or try soaking the ink-stained garment in milk. If that doesn't work, try scrubbing the spot with some non-gel toothpaste.
Markers, washable	Believe it or not, washable markers aren't always fully washable. The key is to get to the stain right away and flush the affected area with cold water. Then place the garment on paper towels and saturate the back of the stain with rubbing alcohol, using a cotton ball to blot away the stain. Finally, rub some liquid laundry detergent into the spot and launder as usual.
Milk	Rinse thoroughly and then treat with a paste of meat tenderizer and cold water. Leave the paste on for 30 minutes and then flush with cold water.
Mud	Allow the mud to dry and then brush or vacuum it off. Treat any remaining stains by rubbing them with the cut side of a potato or sponging them with a 50/50 solution of water and rubbing alcohol.
Mustard	Coloured clothing: Scrape off as much of the mustard as possible using a dull knife and then apply glycerin to the stain. Allow the glycerin to sit on the stain for at least an hour before laundering. White clothing: Saturate the stain with hydrogen peroxide or a denture-cleaning tablet dissolved in cold water and allow the solution to soak into the stain for 30 minutes.
Paint, acrylic	Wash the paint out before it has a chance to dry to maximize your chances of getting the stain out. Note: Some acrylic paints are permanent.
Pencil	Use a clean eraser to "erase" pencil marks from your toddler's clothing.
Rust	Saturate the affected area with lemon juice, sprinkle with salt, and then lay the garment out in the sun. If that doesn't do the trick, apply more lemon juice and salt and pour boiling water over the stain. Or make a paste out of water and cream of tartar and apply to the affected area.

Stickers	Apply undiluted heated white vinegar to the stained area, allowing it to soak until the sticker can be peeled away easily.
Tomato (including ketchup, barbecue sauce, tomato sauces, etc.)	Flush the stained area with cold water as soon as possible. Then sprinkle on some white vinegar and flush with cold water. If that doesn't work, try using some red wine stain remover to get rid of any remaining stains.
Zinc oxide (a common ingredient in diaper creams)	Treat the stain as you would a butter or margarine stain (see above) and then soak the garment in white vinegar for 30 minutes.

 MOTHER WISDOM

Don't throw that faded or stained T-shirt away. Your toddler can get some additional mileage out of it if you tie-dye it, dye it, or allow him to decorate it with fabric paints.

"Me do it": Encouraging self-care

If you haven't yet been greeted by an ear-piercing shriek of "Me do it!" you're living on borrowed time. Most toddlers become fiercely independent creatures at some point along the way and insist on doing everything for themselves, whether they've actually managed to master the necessary skills or not.

If you've made a point of shopping for toddler-friendly clothing, your toddler will have a less difficult time trying to dress himself, but he's still going to need a lot of practice. Your job is to act as his cheerleader. Encourage him to try dressing himself, be generous with your praise, and be willing to lend a hand if he becomes overly frustrated (assuming, of course, that he's actually open to offers of assistance). But don't fall into the trap of trying to do everything for him before he has a chance to try to figure things out on his own. The feeling of victory he'll experience when he manages to do up the Velcros on his shoes by himself will be 10 times as great if he made that discovery with a lot of hands-on help from you.

Of course, not every toddler seizes the opportunity to learn how to dress himself. Some are much happier to simply stand by and let you do all the work for them! If you find yourself dealing with a toddler like this, you may have to get creative in order to encourage cooperation, like partially removing a particular garment and then letting your toddler finish taking it off, or giving him some old Halloween costumes to play with. (He'll have a lot more fun dressing and undressing himself if he gets to be a fire-

---

MOM'S THE WORD

"It takes longer to let Morgan do things herself, but it's worth it to see the look of great pride on her face when she has successfully put her shirt on all by herself!"

—Kelli, 32, mother of one

TODDLER TALK

Convinced that your toddler is a prime candidate for a nudist colony? Relax. Chances are he will have kicked his streaking habit long before he leaves home.

Most toddlers go through a phase—albeit short-lived—where they enjoy taking their clothes off and running around nude.

Some toddlers enjoy being naked because they love the feel of the air against their skin. Others are simply eager to put one of their newest talents to good use: the ability to undress themselves. Since they have yet to pick up on any of the social norms governing nudity, they don't see anything wrong with taking their clothes off in the middle of the grocery store.

As with anything else toddler-related, the best way to handle the situation is to remain calm. You don't want to let your toddler know that you were more than a little freaked out by his streak through the produce department, or else he'll be encouraged to do it again! Simply explain to him that while it's okay to enjoy being naked before, during, and after your bath, it's important to keep your clothes on when you're in public.

If that's not enough to convince your in-house nudist to stay dressed, you may have to resort to more desperate measures, like dressing him in clothes that are a little more difficult to take off (e.g., overalls or playsuits with a zipper up the back) and—if he's not yet toilet trained—putting his diaper on backwards so that it's a little trickier to remove. You'll also want to make sure that his clothes are comfortable so that he'll have less of an incentive to disrobe. (How often have you ditched your pantyhose the moment you walked through the front door?)

---

man or a turtle!) If he's reluctant to put on any clothes at all, try warming up his clothes in the dryer for five minutes on a cold winter day. The warm, cozy feel of his clothing may be enough to convince him to try dressing himself.

Mix and match mania

Your toddler insists on wearing his rubber boots on a hot, summer day. Should you force him to put on his shoes?

MOTHER WISDOM

One hundred years ago, parents were warned about the dangers of allowing children to slide down banisters, wear ill-fitting garments, retain urine, or become constipated. The concern? Engaging in such behaviours was thought to encourage young children to start thinking about sex!

Not if you're smart! This is one of those battles you can definitely afford to walk away from. Chances are your toddler's newfound love of boots stems from the fact that he finds it easier to step into them than fiddle with the straps on his sandals. So what if your toddler looks like some strange holdover from the go-go boot era!

Of course, if your toddler is determined to try the reverse manoeuvre—insisting on wearing his beach flops in the middle of a winter blizzard—you'll have to come up with a creative compromise: perhaps allowing him to carry his flip-flops in a knapsack on his back while trudging through the snow in his boots or giving him permission to wear his bathing suit under his tracksuit if he's really-and-truly determined to rebel against the Canadian winter.

Perhaps there are some items of clothing in your child's closet that you'd prefer he steer clear of entirely: clothes that are too small, badly stained, or out of season, for example. Simply pack those garments away so that they won't even be an option for him. (Remember, out of sight, out of mind.)

Don't become too much of a control freak insofar as your child's clothing choices are concerned. How can you expect your in-house tacky tourist to learn what does—and doesn't—constitute an appropriately coordinated outfit if you're not prepared to let him learn some of these lessons for himself? Besides, parents who make a point of hanging perfectly coordinated items in their

MOTHER WISDOM

Here are some clothing tricks-of-the-trade that every parent needs to know about:

- You can firmly anchor buttons that refuse to stay on your toddler's clothing by sewing them on with dental floss rather than thread.
- You can "unstick" a zipper that's hard to zip and unzip by running a bar of soap up and down both sides of the zipper.
- The easiest way to re-thread a drawstring that's come out of the hood of a jacket is by taping the drawstring to a chopstick or knitting needle and then threading it through the drawstring pocket. (Obviously, you'll want to double-check that the drawstring doesn't pose a strangulation hazard to your toddler; the drawstring should extend no more than 12 to 15 centimetres on either side of the hood.)
- When the plastic tips on your toddler's shoelaces wear off, try dipping the ends in nail polish or wrapping them tightly with tape. And if your toddler's shoelaces have a tendency to come undone easily, wet them before you tie them up. This will help them to stay tied up.
- Speaking of shoes, if your toddler kicks up a fuss whenever it's time to put something on his feet, try putting his shoes on while he's sitting in his high chair. He'll have a harder time making a great escape!

---

toddler's closets—or, even scarier, packaging these picture-perfect ensembles in zip-lock bags and stacking them neatly in their toddler's drawer—scare me. What are they hoping to do—land themselves starring roles in the sequel to *The Stepford Wives*?

MOM'S THE WORD

"I make a point of packing up unseasonable clothing. That way, I don't have to explain to two three-year-olds why they can't wear shorts in the snow!"

—*Kelly, 31, mother of three*

Favourite outfit syndrome

Of course, if you think we've covered all the possible clothing-related battles by now, you're dreaming in technicolour! Here's the scoop on another perennial troublespot for parents and toddlers: favourite outfit syndrome.

If you've dealt with this particular hang-up, you know all too well how it plays out. Your toddler has one favourite outfit and one favourite outfit only. He's determined to wear it day after day: He'd even sleep in it if you'd let him.

The solution? Let him wear the outfit as often as he likes, provided that it's clean. Meanwhile, save yourself some wear-and-tear on your washing machine by tracking down a duplicate outfit or two so that you don't feel compelled to do laundry every single night. (I'm not sure those Maytag repairman ads apply to parents of toddlers.)

It's potty time!

GIVEN ALL THE time and energy some parents put into obsessing about toilet training, you'd think researchers had uncovered a link between the age at which a toddler is fully trained and his law school entrance exam scores two decades later. But since no study to date has been able to demonstrate that kind of connection, I'd urge you to do yourself and your toddler a favour and chill out about the whole potty training business!

Of course, that's easier said than done if all the other parents you hang out with are potty-mad—and chances are they are! A

MOTHER WISDOM

In 93% of Canadian and American families, it's Mom—not Dad—who is responsible for toilet training.

MOM'S THE WORD

"I absolutely hate it when mothers want to compare kids, but people do it all the time. The big thing, right now, is potty training. I've got aunts, sisters, friends, acquaintances, and people on the street breathing down my neck because Norah is still wearing diapers. Sheesh. I say give the kid a break. She's got enough to worry about right now with all the new things she's learning, and when she's ready, it will click for her. Thank goodness we have my mother on our side."

—*Myrna, 34, mother of one*

---

recent study found that 65% of moms felt pressured to toilet train their toddlers: 32% because of their child's age, 26% because of pressure from relatives or mothers with toilet-trained children, and 15% because a particular daycare or preschool program required that children be toilet-trained prior to enrolling.

So what's behind this potty mania? A lack of confidence on the part of parents, says Joan, a 35-year-old mother of five: "I think that parents who become competitive about things like toilet training are less confident in their parenting and need to have something measurable to reassure them that their child is on track developmentally and that they're okay parents."

Just don't make the mistake of assuming that your toddler is ready just because you are! Otherwise you could find yourself embroiled in The Mother of All Power Struggles. And if your child gets wind of the fact that you want him to "perform" on the potty, you could be in for a bit of a battle, says Judy, a 33-year-old mother of one: "Toddlers can only control a few things in their lives, and one of them is what and when stuff comes out of their bodies."

A lot of parents rush into toilet training in the mistaken belief that life will be a thousand times easier once their child is out of diapers. Any experienced parent can tell you that quite the opposite is true: It's a lot more work to mop up puddles and to sprint to public washrooms every 15 minutes than to change a diaper every now and again. Of course, you can't leave your toddler in diapers forever, just because it's a little more convenient for you. One of your jobs as a parent is to teach him the basics of self-care.

How soon is too soon?

Back in 1961, 90% of children were trained by the time they celebrated their second birthday. Today, only 22% of children can make the same claim. So does this mean that we're waiting too long to toilet-train the current generation of toddlers? Not in my opinion. In fact, I would argue quite the opposite: The previous generation of parents were a little too eager to get their toddlers out of diapers.

Consider this advice from the 1942 edition of *The Canadian Mother and Child*—the childrearing bible for many generations of Canadian parents. The message is clear—if you don't start the toilet-training process by the time your child is one month of age, you're kind of missing the boat: "If properly trained, it is surprising how easily a child may be made to acquire clean habits. Usually a child, when a month old, will go to stool at a definite time of the day, or it may be trained to this by the use of soap suppositories or a rubber catheter which will act as a

---

MOM'S THE WORD

"My daughter ended up being in diapers until she was four. She didn't mind being wet or dirty and—at one point as I rushed madly through a stop to get her to the bathroom in time—she calmly pointed out that it was easier if she wore diapers, then we didn't have to hurry so much!"

—*Lisa, 36, mother of two*

TODDLER TALK

Wondering when you can expect your toddler to be fully trained? A study conducted at the University of Pennsylvania found that 4% of children are trained by age two, 22% by age two-and-a-half, 60% by age three, 88% by age three-and-a-half, and 98% by age four. There's a bit of a gender gap when it comes to toilet training: While 70% of girls are trained by age three, just 50% of boys can make the same claim.

Here are a few final stats to consider while you're taking this crash course at Potty U: The average age at which children show an interest in toilet training is 24 months for girls and 26 months for boys; and the average age at which a toddler is able to stay dry during the day is 32.5 months for girls and 35 months for boys

stimulant to bowel action…. Later, at about the fifth or sixth month, the child may be made to sit on a specially constructed toilet chair. You will be amazed to find that around that age the child will express (by forcing) a desire to go stool, when without training, you would not expect this before the twelfth or thirteenth month."

Do you have anything to lose by trying to jump-start the process a little early? Yes, according to the experts. One study found that children whose parents started trying to train them at age 18 months typically weren't trained until four years of age, whereas children whose parents started training them at two years of age were typically trained by their third birthday.

The signs of readiness

So, given that it's not a great idea to rush the process, how can you tell when the moment of truth has arrived and it's actually time to start toilet training? The experts advise that you look for the following signs of physical and emotional readiness rather than become fixated on your child's age:

Physical readiness:

- Your toddler is able to recognize the physical sensations that tell her that she needs to pee or poop. He may pause while he's playing and then squat, grunt, or hold onto his genitals.

- Your toddler is aware when he's wet or dirty and is starting to show signs that he finds it unpleasant to be wearing a wet or dirty diaper.

- Your toddler is able to stay dry for several hours at a time and is capable of emptying his bladder fully rather than just passing a small amount of urine at a time—the typical pattern for younger toddlers.

- Your toddler is capable of controlling the sphincter muscles in the anus that hold in stool.

- Your toddler is able to pull down his own pants and get himself on and off the potty or toilet.

Emotional readiness:

- Your toddler is showing an interest in the potty or toilet.

- Your toddler is willing to sit on the potty or toilet instead of wearing a diaper.

- Your toddler understands what a toilet is for and how to use it.

MOM'S THE WORD

"If you start training too early, then it's the parents who get 'trained,' not the child. For example, if you know that your toddler poops every day after lunch but before naptime, then it's fairly easy to get him to poop in the toilet if you put him on the toilet right after lunch."

—*Maria, 33, mother of two*

FRIDGE NOTES

Andrea Wayne-Von-Konigslow's book *Toilet Tales* can be invaluable in giving toddlers the inside scoop on what potties are for. And, unlike most potty books, it's actually got a sense of humour! (Hey, what can I say? It's Canadian!) Along with *The Bare Naked Book* by Kathy Stinson—a fabulous book that teaches the names of all the major body parts in a matter-of-fact way—*Toilet Tales* should be required reading for every Canadian toddler.

- Your toddler is able to communicate effectively with words and gestures—something that makes it easier for you to pick up on the fact that he needs the potty now.

- Your toddler is able to tell you when he needs to urinate or have a bowel movement.

- Your toddler likes to please you. (Note: This desire to please you tends to rise and fall during the toddler years, so try to time toilet training to coincide with one of your child's more cooperative phases.)

The right stuff

Once you've determined that the time is right, you'll want to make sure you have all the necessary toilet-training paraphernalia on hand.

The first decision you'll have to make is whether to train your child on the potty or the big toilet. Here's a quick rundown of the pros and cons:

- **The potty:** A potty tends to be less intimidating to a child. Because it's child-sized, his feet can touch the floor and he'll be less afraid of falling off or falling in. You can also move the potty around so that it's easier for your toddler to get to during the early days of potty training when his bladder doesn't give him a lot of advance warning. On the other hand, it takes up extra space in the bathroom, it requires additional work on your part (you have to clean and disinfect it), and you may have to take it everywhere with you if your child refuses to use regular toilets at other people's houses. And then there's the fact that it's only a temporary solution; your child will have to start using the toilet eventually, since it would be cumbersome to have to tote his potty back and forth to high school each day!

- **The toilet:** If you're going to train your child on the big toilet, you'll need to purchase a toilet seat ring to help prevent him from falling in. The advantages of going this route are that it's easier to tote around (and clean) a toilet seat ring than a whole potty, and a toilet seat ring tends to be much less expensive than a potty. On the other hand, some toddlers have fears about using the big toilet because it tends to be a little more difficult to manoeuvre—something that could derail the whole toilet-training process before it begins. You also have to take the seat on and off so that other people can use the toilet, which can be a bit of a hassle if you have a large family.

Once you've weighed the pros and cons of potty versus toilet training, you'll have another decision to make: whether to use cloth or disposable training pants while you're training your child or simply leave him in diapers until he's managing to stay dry most of the time. Personally, I find the diaper method a bit

---

MOM'S THE WORD

"We use a potty because we live in a townhouse with one bathroom and that bathroom is upstairs. It isn't reasonable to expect a child to go that far when they're learning."

—*Lisa, 36, mother of two*

cumbersome, particularly when your toddler is at the stage of training where there are a lot of false alarms. (Despite what the diaper companies claim, those "reusable" plastic tabs on the diapers aren't nearly as reusable as you might think, so you can end up wasting bags and bags of disposable diapers while you're training your toddler. And even if he's wearing cloth diapers, he'll need your help in taking his diaper on and off.) So other than allowing your toddler to run around naked while he's learning to use the potty (a method that works well for a lot of parents, incidentally), you're left with two basic choices in toilet training wear: disposable training pants and cloth training pants or underwear.

- **Disposable training pants:** Disposable training pants are basically training pants made out of disposable diapers. They're designed to go up and down with ease as your child uses the potty. While they're highly convenient and can be a lifesaver if you're dining out in a restaurant with a semi-trained toddler, they have two key drawbacks: the price (they're more expensive than disposable diapers) and the fact that they're highly absorbent (your toddler will have a harder time figuring out if his diaper is actually wet). "I think disposable training pants are a bad idea," says Lisa, a 36-year-old mother of two. "They leave kids feeling dry when they're wet. Instead of paying attention to their bodies, they have to depend on disappearing pictures in a diaper to figure out whether or not they've wet themselves." Alyson, a 33-year-old mother of two, has another beef with disposable training pants: "They make such a mess when a child has a bowel movement in them that sometimes I prefer using plain old diapers."

- **Cloth training pants or underwear:** Cloth training pants (those super-thick cotton pants with ultra-tight leg holes) and regular underwear for toddlers are less expensive alternatives to disposable training pants, but they have one key drawback:

MOM'S THE WORD

"Some people say that it's easier to train a child who's in cloth diapers. I disagree. Because my daughter was used to feeling wet all the time, it didn't bother her when she peed in her underwear. I actually considered putting her in disposables for a month or two before we started toilet training to see if I could 'teach' her what it felt like to be dry!"

—*Maria, 32, mother of two*

they aren't great at containing accidents. So if you stick with cloth training pants and underwear, expect to spend a fair bit of time on puddle patrol! Note: When you're shopping for cloth training pants, make sure the pairs you buy are at least a size larger than your child's regular clothes. They tend to shrink a lot in the wash and get very tight around the legs, which makes them difficult and frustrating for toddlers to pull up and down.

And now that we've run through the list of must-have items (some sort of potty or toilet and some sort of training pants), let's talk about the things that you don't need. Believe it or not, there's a whole industry devoted to helping parents with potty training. Some of the goofy products that you can take a pass on include musical potties, talking potties, potties that change colour when they're peed in, and potty training videos. (Okay, buy the blasted video if you absolutely must, but I can tell you from personal experience that it will be years before you get that annoying "Potty Song" out of your head!)

If you're into potty-training gimmicks, at least go with items that can be had on the cheap: a handful of Cheerios for your son to use for "target practice" when he's mastering the art of the stand-up pee and food colouring to tint the toilet water all kinds of colourful shades. (The rationale for dyeing your toilet water? The colour changes after your child pees.)

Getting started

Wondering how to get started with potty training? Here's what you need to know to make this particular rite-of-passage as stress-free as possible for you and your toddler:

- Start changing your toddler's diaper in the bathroom so that he can start to make the link between diapers and the potty. Try emptying the contents of his diaper into the toilet and giving him a chance to flush. (If he's got a major toilet phobia, give him the option of leaving the room before you flush. The aim here is to lay the groundwork for toilet training, not to traumatize him for life!)

- When you're changing your child's diaper, don't make negative comments about its contents. Otherwise he may feel embarrassed or ashamed.

- Decide which words you intend to use to refer to body fluids, body functions, and body parts. You'll want to consider which words are used by friends and relatives or at daycare and which words are used in potty training books you've read to your child. Most experts suggest that you stick with the words "penis" and "vagina" for body parts, but that you use other less formal terms for defecation and urination since they don't tend to be used in everyday speech. (Unless, of course, you happen to be attending a convention of urologists!)

- Make sure that you have the correct potty-training equipment on hand: either a free-standing potty or a toilet seat ring and a stool. (Even if you lift your toddler on and off, he'll still need the stool to push against when he's having a bowel movement.) Note: If the potty or seat comes with a splash guard, take it off. While these splash guards help to contain the odd spray of urine, your son may end up bumping his penis against it, which could hurt him and considerably diminish his enthusiasm for potty training.

- Put the potty in the bathroom a few weeks or months before you start the toilet training process so that your toddler can get used to having it around before he's expected to start using it.

- Make sure that your toddler is ready. This is one situation in which you *don't* want to mess with Mother Nature. The moment you try to pressure your child into toilet training, you're setting yourself up for a battle. "Don't push the toilet training," says Marguerite, a 38-year-old mother of two. "It's so stressful if you're ready and they aren't. Most toddlers are physically ready, but some just don't want to train. We had so many tears—both mine and my son's—over this."

- Make sure that you're ready, too. Ideally, you want to choose a time when you're going to be home a fair bit. It's not reasonable to expect a toddler who is just starting to learn how to use the potty to stay dry while you run errands all over town. You might want to consider the time of year, too: Some parents swear that the secret to success is to toilet-train your child during the summer months, because there are fewer clothes to fumble with when the moment of truth arrives and your toddler needs to make a mad dash for the potty. You might even consider allowing your toddler to run around

---

MOM'S THE WORD

"When my twins started showing interest in training, I mistook it for readiness, something that led to frustration all around. We experienced many moments of sadness, anger, impatience, and anxiety, and all this was compounded and complicated by trying to train two toddlers at once. I feel a lot of regret, shame, and guilt about the way I handled potty training, so I'm planning to do things very differently this time around; there will be no pressure on my two-and-a-half-year-old at all."

—*Anita, mother of four*

MOTHER WISDOM

While it's a good idea to stay close to home during the early days of toilet training, you can't stay home forever. Here are some tips on surviving your toddler's first few trips to the public washroom:

- Keep a spare outfit in the trunk of your car or in your purse in case you can't sprint to the washroom quickly enough or—horror of horrors!—there's a lineup when you get there.
- Be patient. It may take your toddler longer to relax and "let go" if he's using a strange toilet. You might even want to get into the habit of carrying one of your toddler's favourite books in your purse to help him relax.
- Don't be surprised if your toddler has the odd hang-up about using a public washroom. Some children refuse to use toilets that look "different" from the ones at home. "Sarah used to refuse to use any toilet with rust in it," recalls Jennifer, a 33-year-old mother of one. "She insisted that it was dirty. Sometimes we were able to find another toilet; other times we had to just grin and bear it."
- Carry baby wipes and tissues with you in case the washroom is short of toilet paper.

---

nude or semi-nude while he's learning the potty-training ropes, something which is much easier to do on a warm summer day than on the coldest day of winter!

- Ask yourself if there's anything else going on in your child's life that would make toilet training a bad idea right now. If you're about to move, start your child in daycare, or welcome a new baby into your family, you might want to hold off on toilet training your toddler for a while.

- Make sure that you have the other key adults in your child's life psyched up for toilet training, too—especially his daycare provider. Training should happen at home and daycare at the same time, and you'll want to make a point of using the same toilet-training language and routines.

- Give your child the opportunity to watch a same-sex person use the toilet so that he or she will have a clear idea of how the process works. (Chances are your child's been following you and/or your partner to the bathroom for months, so this shouldn't be too hard to arrange!) While some parents suggest having a doll or teddy bear act as a toilet or potty model, this doesn't work nearly as well, unless you happen to own one of those old-fashioned plastic dolls that can really-and-truly pee on demand.

- Get your toddler involved in the planning process. Allow him to pick out his training pants and his potty and give him some say about where the potty ends up being stationed in your home. Hint: You'll want to encourage him to keep the potty on an easy-care floor to minimize the hassle of cleaning up the inevitable potty training "near misses."

- Encourage your child to sit on the potty with his clothes on. When he's ready, he can try sitting on it with his pants pulled down. Get him used to making a trip to the potty at certain times of day: after he gets up in the morning, after meals and snacks, before his nap, and before bedtime.

- Teach your son to pee in the sitting-down position first rather than the standing position. That way, he can focus on learning only one new skill at a time. Remind him that he'll have to point his penis downward while he's peeing to avoid spraying everywhere. Once you teach your son how to use the standing-up position, you'll want to establish some clear ground rules: It's okay to pee in the potty or the toilet, but it's not okay to pee in the potted plant in the living room.

- Resist the temptation to micromanage your child, e.g., nagging him every five minutes to see if he needs to use the toilet or trying to get him to sit on the toilet for extended

MOM'S THE WORD

"I let Joey pee outside when we were playing outdoors and he thought this was great. I found out, however, that doing this can backfire. One day when he was three we were at a public park and he decided to have a bowel movement on the grass—despite the fact that this had never been our practice at home! It was very embarrassing."

—*Alyson, 33, mother of two*

---

periods of time in the hope that he'll be successful. You'll only manage to drive him—and yourself—crazy.

- Teach your daughter to wipe from the front to the back after she's used the bathroom to avoid introducing bacteria or feces from the anus into her vaginal area. If she finds this too confusing, teach her to pat the area dry rather than wiping. Note: Little girls can be quite susceptible to bladder infections when they're first learning how to use the potty, so you'll want to be on the lookout for the following tell-tale signs of infection: a more frequent need to urinate, a sudden urge to urinate, pain while urinating, abdominal pain, and/or suddenly having a lot of accidents again after weeks or months of staying dry.

- Use baby wipes rather than toilet paper for cleaning up bowel movements until your toddler becomes a pro at wiping. Just make sure that the wipes find their way into the garbage can, not the toilet, or you'll be dealing with a major plumbing nightmare.

- Teach your toddler good hygiene habits like hand washing right from day one so that they'll become second nature to him.

- Don't scold your toddler for having accidents. They're inevitable. Instead of getting angry with your child if he has an accident en route to the toilet, praise him for trying to get there on time. And if he has an accident because he didn't clue into his body's signals or was too preoccupied playing with a toy, reassure him that he'll have better luck another time.

- If you're worried about the effects of all those accidents on your living room rug, put towels or drop cloths down to catch the mess. Or borrow a couple of extra baby gates so that you can block off the living room until your toddler is having fewer accidents.

- Be generous with your praise, but don't overdo it. Otherwise, your toddler may develop a bad case of performance anxiety. And if you overdo the "big boy" thing, your toddler may decide he wants the security of being a baby again—something that could have him back in diapers before you know it.

MOM'S THE WORD

"We recorded some party music on a tape and left the tape in the bathroom in Meagan's portable tape recorder. Whenever she peed or pooped in the potty, we'd turn on the party music and throw a few toilet paper streamers in the air and have a 'potty party.' It sounds silly, I know, but within three days, she was trained."

—Judy, 33, mother of one

TODDLER TALK

Think today's generation of parents tends to get a little carried away when celebrating their toddler's toilet-training successes? It's nothing compared with what went on in generations past! In her 1955 It's Fun Raising a Family guide, Canadian childrearing expert Kate Aitken told mothers to go a little crazy the first time their child managed to sleep through the night without wetting his bed: "Give him the same treatment you would a hero home from the wars."

MOTHER WISDOM

Putting a lot of miles on your toddler's potty because he refuses to have anything to do with any other toilet on the planet? Here's the secret to disposing of all those messes while you're on the road: simply line the potty with a large zip-lock bag. That way, when your toddler is finished using the potty, you can simply seal up the bag and deal with the mess when you get home.

MOM'S THE WORD

"My third child had a potty fetish. Every time we went someplace new, she would ask if there was a toilet. If there was, she said she had to go. We figured this out quickly. However, the 'helpful' sales staff would hear her and tell us where the toilet was and so off we would go to check out another bathroom. She was really excited the day we went shopping for a new toilet: oh boy, a whole room full of toilets!"

—*Kerri, 36, mother of six*

- Decide what you want to do about incentives. If you're not comfortable going the Smarties or stickers route because you think it smacks of bribery, you might want to try to find other creative ways to mark that momentous occasion when your toddler uses the potty for the very first time. (True confession: We used a Bundt cake tin to make a "potty cake" when our youngest child peed in the potty for the first time. We had every reason to celebrate. That moment was a long time coming!)

- Never underestimate the power of peer pressure. "When my daughter was 22 months old she moved from the toddler room to the junior room at daycare," recalls Christy, a 38-year-old mother of two. "On her first day, the daycare worker told her that all the big girls in the junior room were wearing underwear. Well, that was it!"

- Once daytime training is complete, start checking your child's diapers to see if he's staying dry at night or during naps. If he's consistently staying dry, he can probably give up his nighttime and naptime diapers. Note: It will likely be at least a few more months—perhaps even years—until he's reliably able to stay dry all night. Thirty percent of four-year-olds and 10% of six-year-olds still wet their beds at night. In the meantime, you can minimize the hassle of those middle-of-the-night sheet changes by making your child's bed in layers (waterproof mattress pad, fitted sheet, waterproof mattress pad, fitted sheet). This will save you from having to strip the bed and then remake it in the middle of the night. You'll also want to limit your toddler's fluid intake before bedtime and encourage him to use the bathroom right before bed—two other strategies that can help to minimize the number of nighttime accidents.

- Be patient with your toddler. According to the Canadian Paediatric Society, it typically takes three to six months to train a toddler, and it may take several attempts before a child is out of diapers for good.

TODDLER TALK

Previous generations of parents were a little obsessive about dealing with bedwetting. Consider this advice from the 1942 edition of *The Canadian Mother and Child:* "After two years of age, bedwetting is abnormal.... Do not give any fluids after five o'clock in the afternoon. For a few successive nights lift the baby out of bed at one o'clock, and place it on the toilet or chamber; then for a few other nights, get the baby up at two o'clock; and on succeeding nights at three, four and five o'clock. This routine must be followed closely and regularly to be effective. (An alarm clock is useful to indicate the time to lift the baby.) Eventually you will find that the baby can be made to go through the whole night without mishap."

- If your child asks to go back to diapers, let him. Chances are it'll be a temporary phase. Besides, if you refuse his request, you may find yourself embroiled in a huge power struggle with him—something that won't do either of you any good.

Stool toileting refusal

Approximately 20% of toddlers between the ages of 18 and 30 months experience an episode of "stool toileting refusal"—a refusal to have a bowel movement on the toilet. The problem usually arises if a child has been splashed while having a bowel movement on the toilet, if he recently had some problems with constipation and has now learned to associate the pain of passing a hard stool with using the toilet, or if he is afraid of allowing part of "himself" to disappear down the toilet.

Here are some tips on dealing with this common but distressing problem:

- If the problem is being caused by a fear of being splashed while having a bowel movement on the big toilet, allow him to switch to a potty until he regains his confidence in using the big toilet.

- If the problem is being caused by constipation, up his fibre intake, ensure that he's getting plenty of liquids, and be careful not to give him too many dairy products because they can be constipating. You might also want to talk to your child's doctor about ways of treating constipation. If a large, hard stool has accumulated in the rectum, suppositories or an enema may be required to encourage a bowel movement. Stool softeners or laxatives may also be recommended. Note: Leakage of stool can occur if a large hard mass forms in bowel. This can be an indication that your child is having problems with constipation.

- If the problem is caused by a fear of parting with his stool, try to explain to your toddler that it's not a part of his body that's disappearing down the toilet forever; it's the part of the food that his body doesn't need.

- Whatever the cause of your child's stool toileting refusal, be patient. According to Catherine, a 32-year-old mother of four, sometimes your best bet is to back off entirely. "Be prepared to compromise. My daughter could pee in the potty with no problem, but she couldn't bring herself to poop in it. I told her it was her poop and she could do whatever she wanted with it: poop in the potty or poop in a diaper. If she wanted to poop in a diaper, she could ask me to put one on and then I'd change her afterwards. We did that for maybe a week or two, and then she decided to try pooping on the potty. What a celebration we had then!"

So there you have it: a crash course in potty training and other topics related to the care and maintenance of toddlers. Now it's time to tackle another perennial hot topic: feeding a toddler.

CHAPTER 6

What's for Dinner?

"The food pyramid needs to be revised to fit the whims of
toddlers. The four basic food groups would be the never-fail
group, the if-I'm-in-the-mood-for-this-right-at-this-second
group, the this-would-look-good-in-my-hair group, and the
watch-how-fast-it-will-hit-the-floor group. The food
pyramid would just have to be left blank and a dry-erase
pen supplied for parents to fill out periodically."
—BARB HUFF, "THE TODDLER FOOD PYRAMID,"
PARENTINGHUMOR.COM

UNTIL YOU'VE LIVED through it, you cannot possibly
comprehend the frustration of having each and every
meal you so lovingly prepare given the thumbs down by
a two-foot-tall food critic—the same person, I might add, who's
been known to eat lint-covered Cheerios from inside the couch!
While some toddlers are enthusiastic eaters who eagerly
devour anything and everything that's placed in front of them,
these happy-go-lucky tots tend to be the exception rather than
the rule. In this chapter, we're mainly going to be focusing on the
other type of toddler—the not-so-silent majority who are only
too happy to boo any new food that dares to show up on the dinner table. We'll start out by talking about the key developmental

reasons that explain why feeding a toddler can be such a challenge. Next, we'll zero in on some proven strategies for taking the whining out of whining and dining. Then we'll cover the basics of toddler nutrition. (The key take-away message? It's not what goes into a toddler's mouth at any single meal that matters; it's what makes it in on a day-to-day or week-to-week basis that counts.) Then we'll swap some mom-proven strategies for coping with a fussy eater and with weaning from breast or bottle. We'll wrap up the chapter by considering some important health and safety issues: choking, food-borne illness, and food allergies and food intolerances. (I know: I'm giving you plenty of "food for thought"!)

Why feeding a toddler can be such a challenge

WE'VE ALREADY TALKED about how challenging toddlers can be when it comes to discipline and toilet training. It should therefore hardly come as a surprise that they tend to be more than a little difficult when it comes to eating, too! While there may be times when you'll swear that your toddler is turning her nose up at the meal you so lovingly prepared just for the sake of being ornery, try to give her the benefit of the doubt. There are a number of key developmental factors that help to explain why she's suddenly become such a discriminating gourmet. Here's what you need to know:

- **Your toddler's appetite is on the wane.** Because your toddler is no longer growing at the same rapid pace, she no longer needs the same amount of food. While she managed to double or even triple her birthweight during her first year of life, she will gain only about 30% of her bodyweight per year during each of the two toddler years.

- **Your toddler knows what she wants—and when and how she wants it.** As you've no doubt gathered by now, toddlers are big on routine, and—as you might expect—those routines carry over into the world of food. Your toddler may insist on having the same food served the same way on the same plate day after day. You'll quickly discover just how much ritual matters to your toddler if you dare to break any of her non-negotiable culinary "rules" (e.g., committing a mortal sin like allowing her peas to touch her potatoes). Of course, this doesn't mean that toddlers hold themselves to the same standards of consistency; heck, they reserve the right to change their food preferences every day!

- **Your toddler is able to communicate her food preferences much more clearly than she could when she was younger.** Your toddler no longer has to rely on making disgusted-looking faces or pushing her food out with her tongue to let you know that she's not a fan of broccoli; now she's able to communicate with words. While it can be helpful to know exactly

---

MOTHER WISDOM

Trying to come up with meal and snack ideas for a young toddler who insists on feeding herself, but who has not yet learned how to use a spoon? Simply offer your toddler a variety of healthy finger foods that can be easily navigated to her mouth: cooked pasta, grated cheese, cubed meatloaf, slices of hard-boiled eggs, miniature pancakes, grilled cheese sandwich "fingers," steamed vegetables, shredded vegetables, fruit slices, and so on. (Note: If you serve her fruit as a finger food, you'll want to make sure that the fruit is soft enough that it won't pose a choking hazard. If you serve fruits like apples or pears, you'll want to slice the fruit into ultra-thin, bite-sized pieces. And grapes, of course, should be cut in half length-wise.)

where she stands on particular issues, there may be days when you wish she didn't say "Yuck!" quite so emphatically.

- **Your toddler is still a rookie when it comes to feeding herself.** It takes time for a toddler to learn how to coordinate the muscles involved in chewing and swallowing and to figure out how to pick up food with her spoon and then navigate that spoon to her mouth. (Hey, remember how awkward you felt the first time you tried to use a pair of chopsticks?) She may also be highly distracted by the taste, texture, sight, and smell of her food—something that gives whole new meaning to the concept of leisurely dining!

- **Your toddler may be fiercely independent about feeding herself—even if she still lacks the necessary skills.** "My daughter went through a frustrating stage around 12 months of age when she would not let me feed her with a spoon," recalls Christina, a 26-year-old mother of three. "She would only eat foods that she could feed herself—very frustrating because she wasn't able to feed herself baby cereal or yogourt. We had to serve her finger foods and let her feed herself. I ended up offering her cheese, cooked chicken cut into cubes, bread, baked or mashed potatoes, cooked pasta, and any vegetable that could

---

MOTHER WISDOM

Wondering why your toddler is compelled to dissect any new food before she agrees to put it in her mouth? It's that powerful toddler curiosity at work again! She wants to know everything about a new food before she agrees to eat it. And if you're brave or foolhardy enough to serve her food like a casserole that's all mixed together, you may discover that she vetoes the meal entirely. If she can't separate the veggies in the casserole into neat little piles, she may not want to have anything to do with the casserole at all.

be boiled and then chopped into small pieces." Note: See Table 6.1 for some additional details on how your child's self-feeding skills will evolve during the toddler years.

TABLE 6.1

Eating-related Milestones

Here are some of the key eating-related milestones that you can expect your toddler to achieve during her second and third years of life.

Your 12- to 18-month-old

→ is fascinated by what other people are eating;
→ eats a variety of nutritious foods;
→ enjoys eating food with her hands;
→ is capable of drinking from a sippy cup (a spill-free cup);
→ is learning how to use a spoon;
→ loves hamming it up at the dinner table and throwing food to see how others will react.

Your 18- to 24-month-old

→ enjoys eating food with her hands, but is becoming more skilled at using a spoon and possibly a fork, too;
→ enjoys experimenting with different food textures;
→ has increasingly distinct food preferences (she likes what she likes and she hates the rest!);
→ is easily distracted while she's eating;
→ doesn't have as much of an appetite as she did a few months earlier.

Your Two- to Three-year-old

→ insists on feeding herself;
→ is becoming more skilled at guiding the spoon to her mouth, but still tends to make a bit of a mess;
→ has clear rules and rituals when it comes to foods (e.g., certain types of foods aren't allowed to touch one another);
→ may tend to become fixated on one or two favourite foods over an extended period of time—something that's known as a food jag;
→ is less prone to choking, although choking is still a major cause for concern;
→ tends to dawdle while she's eating.

Equipment 101

WONDERING WHAT feeding-related paraphernalia is essential and what's a complete waste of money? Here's what you need to know:

- **High chairs and booster seats:** Chances are you've been using a high chair (either a free-standing high chair or one of those smart new contraptions that either straps to the seat of a kitchen chair or hangs off the kitchen table) to feed your baby since she started indulging in the messier types of solid foods. While you'll probably get a few more months out of that high chair, you can expect your toddler to make the switch to a booster seat sometime between age one-and-a-half and two. When you're shopping for a booster seat, look for a model that's easy to clean and that features a secure strapping system to keep the booster seat in place. You don't want to buy an el cheapo booster seat that slides off the chair the moment your toddler stands up in it. Note: If your child is sitting in a booster seat, make sure that there is somewhere for her feet to rest—either on the chair itself or on a stool that you've provided for this purpose.

- **Toddler-sized cutlery sets:** Toddler-sized cutlery sets can be very useful provided that you don't expect much from the

---

MOM'S THE WORD

"If I didn't have the high chair from my older kids, I would buy one of those toddler seat/high chair combos that straps to a regular kitchen chair. Not only are they portable for when your child is eating somewhere else other than home, they don't take up space in your kitchen. And some of them can even fit into the dishwasher for a really heavy-duty cleaning."

—*Lori, 31, mother of five*

MOM'S THE WORD

"People are amazed that I don't 'teach' my children how to use utensils. I provide them with a fork and a spoon, and they learn how to use them by watching the rest of us and imitating us. I'll occasionally tell them 'other way' if they have the spoon upside down and can't figure out why the food keeps falling down on the tray, but most of the time I just give them their fork and spoon and let them go to it."

—*Kerri, 36, mother of six*

fork. Toddler-sized forks—plastic forks in particular—tend to have ultra-dull prongs that render them completely useless. So you'll probably be further ahead if you simply purchase a couple of toddler-sized spoons and give the forks a pass until your toddler is ready to move on to regular cutlery. If you want to introduce all three pieces of cutlery right from day one, however, you'll want to purchase spoons with short handles, blunt tips, and rounded bowls; forks with short handles and short, blunt tines; and knives that are small with rounded tips.

- **Splat mats:** This is one of those products that the baby world really didn't need, but that got invented nonetheless. While the idea is noble—the splat mat fits under your child's high chair and catches spills, thereby eliminating the need to mop the floor underneath—it's really not necessary in this age of easy-care flooring. Of course, if you were insane enough to put white plush broadloom in your kitchen, you might benefit from one of these products—but, then again, a plastic shower curtain will do the exact same thing for a fraction of the money, and will be a whole lot easier to clean. Instead of trying to mop or wipe down your splat mat, you can simply toss the spaghetti-coated shower curtain straight into the washing machine.

- **Bowls:** Look for toddler-sized dishes made of non-breakable materials. Plates with curved sides and small cups with broad bases generally work best. While bowls with suction cups on the bottom have been on the market since the beginning of time, I've yet to encounter a parent who thinks they're actually worth purchasing. "Those suction bowls don't stick to anything—and I tried about five different brands," insists Cindy, a 27-year-old mother of two. Jennifer, a 33-year-old mother of one, agrees: "Suction-cup bowls that stick on the high chair tray are a complete waste of money. Sarah would pull at them until they came loose, sending their contents flying across the room." And as for suction-style bowls with the compartment for hot water in the bottom, don't even go there. One of my sisters was notorious during our growing up years for removing the plastic screw covering the hot water fill-up hole and dropping her vegetables into the water compartment when no one was looking. The result? A super stinky dish that was almost impossible to clean

- **Bibs:** When you're shopping for a bib, think functionality, not fashion. Yes, those frilly little white bibs are adorable, but they don't provide much in the way of protection when a really serious stain comes calling. In those types of situations, you're far better off going with the heavy-duty artillery: a hard plastic bib with a scoop in the bottom. "I found that these were the best type of bib," says Lise, a 35-year-old mother of two. "They really cut down on the mess and you can wash

---

MOTHER WISDOM

Avoid bibs with strings. The strings get gummy and stained, and they tend to get tangled up in your toddler's hair. Velcro and snap fasteners are a much better bet for toddlers.

them in the sink along with your dishes." Other moms swear by children's paint smocks (not only are they waterproof, but they also cover a lot of square inches of toddler!) or T-shirt-style bibs made out of terrycloth (they're easy to get over your toddler's head). Finally, avoid plastic bibs with pockets, says Lori, a 31-year-old mother of five: "Food gets down inside the pocket and it can be a real pain to get out."

Mess patrol

Don't make the mistake of assuming that buying the right bib will allow you to avoid those infamous toddler-related food messes. You're unlikely to get off scot-free in that department, after all! There are, however, some things you can do to make that after-dinner cleanup a little less arduous. Here are a few mom proven strategies for minimizing the mealtime mess:

- Have plenty of bibs and washcloths on hand. That way, if your toddler's bib is totally saturated with food by the time she's halfway through her meal, you can yank off the messy one and give her a quick wipe-down before setting her loose for round two.

- If your toddler's cheeks tend to become sore or stained after she indulges in lasagna or other tomato-based foods, apply a thin layer of baby lotion to her cheeks before she dives into her meal (literally!). Not only will it make the after-dinner wipe-down a whole lot easier for the two of you, it will also help to protect her ultra-sensitive skin from the acidic bite of the tomato sauce.

- Learn how to anticipate and prevent toddler-related messes before they occur. If you're serving spaghetti and you have visions of the sauce being ground into your daughter's blonde

MOM'S THE WORD

"Toddlers love to make a mess, from throwing their food on the floor to squishing it between their fingers. I always have lots of bibs on hand and keep a pile of wash clothes in a cupboard in my kitchen. I sometimes use T-shirts that are already stained instead of bibs. And in warm weather, I strip my kids down to their diapers for meals."

—*Christina, 26, mother of three*

ringlets, see if she'll let you put something on her head during dinner time—perhaps a rain hat, a shower cap, or a bandana. And if you know from past experience that there's nothing in this world that your toddler loves more than the feeling of chocolate pudding squishing through her fingers, you might want to change her into an old T-shirt or strip her down to the buff before you place that bowl of pudding in front of her.

• Some parents go to rather extraordinary measures to keep meal-related messes under control. Kimberlee, a 29-year-old mother of two, feeds her kids spaghetti in the bathtub: "That way, I avoid the mess altogether. However, I'm a little concerned about what kind of therapy they may require in later years regarding pasta!" Other parents prefer that the actual eating take place in the kitchen, but then make an immediate pit stop in the bathroom once their toddlers are finished eating. "Sometimes we go straight from the table to the shower," admits Anita, a 38-year-old mother of four.

• Not every parent ends up singing the after-meal cleanup blues, however. Annie, a 44-year-old mother of one, is amazed by what a neat freak her son Tomas has turned out to be: "Our three-year-old will ask to have his hands and face washed midway through a meal because he can't stand being dirty. He also loves to use napkins. And when we're entertaining friends, he sets out drink coasters for our guests and makes a point of reminding them to use them. He's almost innately anal. And, trust me, we haven't worked on this, nor have we had the time to instill these habits in him!"

Whining and dining

DINING OUT WITH a toddler doesn't have to be a recipe for disaster—not if you know how to avoid some of the most pitfalls. Here's some from-the-trenches advice from parents who have taken their toddlers to restaurants and lived to tell:

- Choose the restaurant with care. You'll have plenty of time to hit the five-star restaurants after your kids are grown. For now, stick to spots that are 100% kid-friendly. According to Tanya, a 30-year-old mother of two, that means a restaurant with high chairs, booster seats, a good kids' menu, crayons and colouring books, and plenty of background noise! ("Noise is good because it's not so noticeable if your toddler ends up crying or making a lot of noise," she explains.) A special menu for kids is helpful, since there's no point spending $10 on an entrée for your toddler if he's likely to manage to eat only a mouthful or two. (Hint: If the restaurant you've chosen doesn't have a kids' menu, see if there's a suitable side dish or appetizer that could serve as your toddler's dinner. Or plan to share a few bites of your own dinner rather than ordering a separate dinner for your toddler.)

- Call ahead. If you have a large family or a toddler with a very limited attention span, call the restaurant ahead of time to see if they'll start preparing your order before you arrive, suggests Kerri, a 36-year-old mother of six. There's nothing worse than having your toddler run out of patience before your food has even arrived.

- Plan to hit the restaurant early. Not only will you beat the crowds, you'll also ensure that your toddler's dinner arrives before her blood sugar has a chance to hit rock bottom, triggering a major meltdown. "Plan to get to the restaurant at least half an hour before your toddler's regular mealtime, just in case it's busy and you have to wait," suggests Sue, a 35-year-old mother of three.

- Ask for a booth in a less crowded part of the restaurant so that you'll have more room for your toddler and her paraphernalia and won't feel quite as self-conscious about disturbing other diners. It's hard to enjoy your meal if every childless patron in the restaurant is shooting daggers your way.

- Let your server know that you're operating on "kid time." You may not have the luxury of waiting 20 minutes to place your

---

MOM'S THE WORD

"I usually bring a sippy cup full of milk to restaurants. It's cheaper to bring your own milk than to order a glass of milk there and it's much less messy to have your toddler drink from a sippy cup than a regular restaurant cup."

—*Maria, 33, mother of two*

MOM'S THE WORD

Buffet-style restaurants are a good bet because kids can start eating right away: there's no need to wait."

—*Lori, 31, mom of five*

order or for your bill to arrive! Anita, a 38-year-old mother of four, makes a point of asking for the bill as soon as she and her family have ordered. "That way, we can leave the restaurant quickly if we have to."

• When you order your toddler's dinner, hand the waitress your toddler's sippy cup and ask that the kitchen staff pour the drink directly into her cup. It'll save you the inevitable mess associated with trying to transfer liquids from cup to cup at the dinner table.

• Be sure to tote along everything you could possibly need: a bib for your child (restaurant bibs are always useless); baby wipes and/or a slightly soapy wet washcloth that you've sealed in a zip-lock bag (dry napkins won't do much when it comes time to clean up a ketchup-smeared toddler); a fully-stocked diaper bag (make sure you've got at least one spare outfit); a sippy cup (a more toddler-friendly alternative to breakable restaurant glasses); a non-breakable plate (to prevent a similar crisis if your toddler decides to use the restaurant plate as a Frisbee); a small snack, such as a box of raisins (to take the edge off your toddler's hunger in case her dinner is a little slow in showing up); and a couple of toys and activities to keep your toddler entertained until her dinner arrives (e.g., crayons, colouring books, and an assortment of small toys and household items such as measuring spoons that you reserve for such occasions). "Take playdough with you," adds Alyson, a 33-year-old mother of two. "It can be a real lifesaver when you're dining out in a restaurant with a toddler."

- Come up with fun ways of keeping your child entertained after you run through the bag of tricks you brought from home. "We take all the sugar packets out of the dish and let Sarah divide them into pink, white, and brown piles," says Jennifer, a 33-year-old mother of one. "Then we count them. Then we make them into patterns. This kills a lot of time while we're waiting for the food to arrive, and it helps with her counting skills."

- Don't be afraid to get up and walk around while you're waiting for your dinner to arrive. "We order and then we take our toddler for a walk around the restaurant," says Kerri, a 36-year old mother of six. "We go to the bathroom and wash our hands, and sometimes we'll even go out into the parking lot for a bit of a break."

Serving toddler-friendly meals and snacks

KNOW WHAT THEY call those poor misguided souls who spend hours and hours in the kitchen trying to whip up nutritionally balanced, toddler-pleasing gourmet meals? Masochists, that's what! (Besides, as any experienced parent will tell you, there's no such thing as a toddler-pleasing meal—at least, not a meal that's toddler-pleasing from one day to the next!)

Unless you're genetically wired to want to play chef, you can probably let the gourmet cooking bit go. Toddlers are notorious for preferring plain and simple foods, so your attempts to get your toddler to acquire a taste for pesto sauce at the tender age of two are pretty much an exercise in futility anyway!

TODDLER TALK

The amount of food that toddlers need varies tremendously from toddler to toddler. Some are surprisingly hearty eaters, while others eat like birds. Your toddler's age, body size, activity level, growth rate, and mood will determine how much food she actually needs and wants. Your job is to ensure that she's provided with a variety of foods daily, and her job is to decide what does—and doesn't—make it in her mouth.

Still, while you're unlikely to attract rave reviews from your in-house restaurant critic at each and every meal, it's important to make a point of serving your toddler nutritionally balanced meals and snacks. That's what the next section of the chapter is all about.

One-year-olds

The Canadian Paediatric Society, Dietitians of Canada, and Health Canada recommend that feeding times reflect the food requirements of one-year-olds. Here's what they have to say on this issue in *Nutrition for Healthy Term Infants: Statement of the Joint Working Group: Canadian Paediatric Society, Dietitians of Canada, and Health Canada:* "Small and frequent, nutritious, energy-dense feedings are important for meeting the nutrient and energy requirements of infants during the second year. The term 'feedings' is used rather than 'meals and snacks,' because it better reflects toddlers' need for food when they are hungry or willing to eat rather than at conventional meal and snack times."

According to these three leading Canadian health authorities, most one-year-olds require four to six small feedings per day. Ideally, you'll want to make sure that your one-year-old is consuming 500 millilitres (16 ounces) of milk plus the recommended number of servings from each of the food groups in *Canada's Food Guide to Healthy Eating* (see Table 6.2). Note: The portion size for a one-year-old can range from one-quarter to

TODDLER TALK

Don't make the mistake of eliminating a particular food group from your child's diet just because your one-year-old seems to be determined to avoid it. It's important that you continue to offer her a wide variety of foods. Studies have shown that most young children will consume adequate amounts of nutrients and obtain adequate calories from their diet if they are provided with foods from each of the food groups on a regular basis. If they don't have access to a variety of healthy foods from all the food groups, they don't have the same opportunity to obtain these nutrients.

---

one-third that of a portion size for an adult, while the portion size for a two-year-old can range anywhere from one-half the portion size for an adult to a full, adult-sized serving size.

Two-year-olds

By age two, most toddlers should be ready to start following the guidelines spelled out in *Canada's Food Guide to Healthy Eating*. Just don't expect your toddler to be able to consume as much food as the adults in her life. The guide provides a range of recommended servings for each food group. Most toddlers will stick to the lower end of the range when deciding how many servings to consume from each of the various food groups, and the portions that they eat will be toddler-sized. (Note: Servings for a two-year-old are anywhere from one-half to the full size of the corresponding adult-sized portion.)

Winning at food group roulette

It's one thing to see *Canada's Food Guide to Healthy Eating* neatly mapped out on a piece of paper. It's quite another to get your

TABLE 6.2

Canada's Food Guide to Healthy Eating: What Toddlers Need

The number of food servings that a toddler requires varies from toddler to toddler and from day to day. One-year-olds may not even be able to manage to eat the minimum number of servings recommended for each food group. As long as a toddler is full of energy, continuing to grow at a healthy rate, and eating a variety of healthy foods from each of the different food groups, however, you can feel confident that her food intake is adequate.

Food Group	Why Your Toddler Needs Them	Number of Servings	What Constitutes a Typical Serving
Grain products	Grain products are critical for converting food to energy and for maintaining a healthy nervous system. They're also an excellent source of B vitamins, minerals (especially iron), and fibre (if whole-grain products are served).	5 to 12 servings/day	**Bread** For a one-year-old: less than ½ a slice of bread For a two-year-old: ½ to 1 slice of bread **Roll/muffin** For a one-year-old: less than ¼ of a roll or muffin For a two-year-old: ¼ to ½ of a roll or muffin **Hamburger/hot dog bun** For a one-year-old: less than ⅓ of a hamburger or hot dog bun For a two-year-old: ⅓ to ½ of a hamburger or hot dog bun **Cooked cereal** For a one-year-old: less than 75 mL (⅓ cup) For a two-year-old: 75 to 125 mL (⅓ to ½ cup)

continued on p. 282

Food Group	Why Your Toddler Needs Them	Number of Servings	What Constitutes a Typical Serving
Grain products *continued*			**Dry cereal** For a one-year-old: less than 75 mL (1/3 cup) of flaked cereal or less than 125 mL (1/2 cup) of puffed cereal or less than 15 mL (1 tbsp.) of granola For a two-year-old: 125 mL to 250 mL (1/2 to 1 cup) of flaked cereal or 250 mL to 500 mL (1 to 2 cups) of puffed cereal or 30 mL to 80 mL (2 tbsp. to 1/3 cup) of granola **Pasta (noodles)** For a one-year-old: less than 1/4 cup (50 mL) For a two-year-old: 50 to 175 mL (1/4 to 3/4 cup) **Rice** For a one-year-old: less than 1/4 cup (50 mL) For a two-year-old: 50 to 125 mL (1/4 to 1/2 cup)
Vegetables and fruits	Vegetables and fruits are a good source of fibre and an excellent source of vitamin C as well as hundreds of disease-fighting compounds called phytochemicals.	5 to 10 servings/day	**Fresh fruit (whole)** For a one-year-old: 1/4 to 1/2 piece of fruit For a two-year-old: 1/2 to 1 piece of fruit **Cooked fruit** For a one-year-old: less than 50 mL (1/4 cup) For a two-year-old: 50 to 125 mL (1/4 to 1/2 cup)

	Vegetables are also an excellent source of vitamin A, folacin, and iron.	**Juice** For a one-year-old: less than 50 mL (¼ cup) For a two-year-old: 50 to 125 mL (¼ to ½ cup) **Potatoes** For a one-year-old: less than 50 mL (¼ cup) For a two-year-old: 50 to 125 mL (¼ to ½ cup) **Cooked vegetables** For a one-year-old: less than 50 mL (¼ cup) For a two-year-old: 50 to 125 mL (¼ to ½ cup) **Raw vegetables** For a one-year-old: less than 50 mL (¼ cup) For a two-year-old: 50 to 125 mL (¼ to ½ cup)
Milk products	Milk products are an excellent source of protein, calcium (the mineral responsible for keeping bones healthy and strong), and vitamins D, A, and B12.	2–3 servings/day	**Milk** For a one-year-old: less than 125 mL (½ cup) For a two-year-old: 125 to 175 mL (½ to ¾ cup) **Cheese** For a one-year-old: less than 25 g (¾ of an ounce) For a two-year-old: 25 to 50 g (¾ to 1½ ounce) **Cottage cheese** For a one-year-old: less than 50 mL (¼ cup) For a two-year-old: 50 to 125 mL (¼ to ½ cup)

continued on p. 284

Food Group	Why Your Toddler Needs Them	Number of Servings	What Constitutes a Typical Serving
Milk products continued			**Yogourt** For a one-year-old: less than 75 mL (⅓ cup) For a two-year-old: 75 to 175 mL (⅓ to ¾ cup)

Note: Toddlers should consume 500 mL (2 cups) of milk each day because it is their main dietary source of vitamin D. This can be counted as two servings. Toddlers under the age of two should drink only homogenized milk. (Note: Some pediatricians recommend 2% milk starting at age 15 months.) In addition, you may also choose to include a child-sized serving of other milk products such as cheese and yogourt in one of your toddler's meals or snacks. If your toddler is lactose intolerant, you will want to serve her lactose-reduced milk. If your toddler can't drink milk because of a milk protein allergy, you may need to supplement her diet with calcium and vitamin D. Not all dairy-free milk substitutes are fortified with supplemental calcium and vitamin D. Toddlers who can't tolerate cow's milk often have difficulty tolerating goat's milk, too. Soy beverages are not recommended for toddlers under the age of two, even if they are fortified with supplemental calcium and vitamin D, but soy formula is acceptable if the toddler is able to tolerate it.

Food Group	Why Your Toddler Needs Them	Number of Servings	What Constitutes a Typical Serving
Meat and alternatives	Meat and alternatives are an important source of proteins and B-vitamins and minerals (particularly iron). Protein helps to build and repair body tissues, including muscle, bone, and blood, and to manufacture the antibodies needed to fight infection.	2–3 servings/day	**Cooked lean meat/fish/poultry** For a one-year-old: 20 to 30 g (⅔ to 1 oz.) For a two-year-old: 25 to 50 g (¾ to 1¾ oz.) **Peanut butter** (avoid if allergies are a concern) For a one-year-old: less than 15 g (1 tbsp.) For a two-year-old: 15 to 30 g (1 to 2 tbsp.) **Legumes** For a one-year-old: less than 50 mL (¼ cup) For a two-year-old: 50 to 125 mL (¼ to ½ cup)

Egg

For a one-year-old: less than ½ an egg

For a two-year-old: ½ to 1 egg

Tofu

For a one-year-old: less than 50 mL (¼ cup)

For a two-year-old: 50-75 mL (¼ to ⅓ cup)

Note: You should aim to provide at least one serving from each of the four food groups during each meal. Ideally, snacks should provide servings from at least two of the four food groups. But don't be panicked if your child ignores some food groups entirely for a day or two. Rather than analyzing her nutrient intake over a single meal, look at her food choices over the course of a week or two. Chances are she's managed to squeeze in at least a few servings from each food group.

Canada's Food Guide to Healthy Eating also makes mention of "other foods"—foods and beverages that aren't part of any other food group. They include foods that are mostly fats and oils, such as butter, margarine, cooking oil, and lard; foods that are mostly sugar, such as jams, honey, syrup, and candy; high-fat and or high-salt snack foods such as chips and pretzels; beverages such as soft drinks; and herbs, spices, and condiments such as pickles, mustard, and ketchup. Some of these foods, like water, should be enjoyed often. Others, like snack foods, should be consumed in moderation.

Eager to learn more about toddler nutrition? The following two publications are available free of charge from Health Canada: *Nutrition for Healthy Term Infants: Statement of the Joint Working Group: Canadian Paediatric Society, Dietitians of Canada, Health Canada* (for babies and toddlers up to age two) and *Canada's Food Guide to Healthy Eating: Focus on Preschoolers* (for toddlers and preschoolers age two to five years). To request your copies, either visit the nutrition publications order page on the Health Canada Web site (www.hc-sc.gc.ca/hppb/nutrition/order.html), call 613-954-5995, or write to Publications, Health Canada, Ottawa, Ontario, K1A 0K9.

toddler to actually follow it. Here are some practical tips on getting nutrient-rich foods from each food group into your toddler:

Grain products

- Continue to serve your toddler iron-fortified cereals for as
  long as she'll eat them. Infant cereals are an important source
  of iron for young toddlers—especially those who turn their
  nose up at anything that even remotely resembles meat! And
  because you can increase the amount of iron that is absorbed
  from infant cereal by serving foods that are high in vitamin
  C, you might want to get in the habit of topping off your
  child's bowl of cereal with a few sliced strawberries or offering her a glass of orange juice on the side. Note: You can get
  a detailed rundown on the roles played by vitamin C and
  other important nutrients by consulting Table 6.3.

- You'll get more bang for your nutritional buck if you get in
  the habit of serving your toddler whole-grain breads and cereals, brown rice, and whole wheat pasta. Why settle for plain
  old white bread when there are so many tasty and healthy
  alternatives?

TODDLER TALK

Researchers at the Mount Sinai School of Medicine in New York
City and the Stanford Center for Disease Prevention in Palo Alto, California,
have discovered that children as young as two years of age may be influ-
enced by food advertisements on TV. They found that children who had
seen television commercials promoting certain food products were more
likely to choose those products than other children who had not viewed the
commercials. And what's more, they only had to see the commercial once
or twice to develop this food preference. So there you have it: yet another
reason to keep the television turned off!

TABLE 6.3

Vitamin Watch: The Key Vitamins and Minerals Your Toddler Needs

A well-balanced diet will provide most toddlers with the nutrients needed to thrive. Here's a quick rundown of the key vitamins and minerals that your toddler needs, along with an explanation of how each nutrient helps to keep your toddler healthy.

Nutrient	Food Sources	What It Does
FAT-SOLUBLE VITAMINS		
Vitamin A	Liver, eggs, whole milk, dark green leafy vegetables such as spinach, yellow/orange fruits and vegetables	Promotes healthy eyes, skin, hair, nails, teeth, and gums; assists in growth and bone development, and promotes resistance against infection
Vitamin D	Liver, butter, milk (fluid, evaporated, or powdered), fatty fish, and exposure to the sun	Plays an important role in the formation and maintenance of healthy bones and teeth as well as overall growth and development
Vitamin E	Vegetable and fish oils, nuts and seeds, egg yolk, whole grains	Protects red blood cells that are required for healthy muscles and assists with neurological functioning
WATER-SOLUBLE VITAMINS		
Thiamin (Vitamin B1)	Oatmeal enriched breads and cereals, grains, rice, dairy products, fish, pork, pork liver sesame seeds, legumes	Assists in the release of energy from carbohydrates; allows for the growth and repair of tissues, especially nerve and muscle tissues; and plays a role in appetite regulation

continued on p. 288

Nutrient	Food Sources	What It Does
WATER-SOLUBLE VITAMINS (continued)		
Riboflavin (Vitamin B2)	Dairy products, eggs, organ meats, enriched breads and cereals, green leafy vegetables	Assists in the metabolism of foods and aids in overall growth, essential for healthy skin, mucuous membranes, and cornea
Niacin (Vitamin B3)	Organ meats, peanuts, brewers yeast, enriched breads and grains, meats, poultry, fish, and nuts	Involved in tissue repair and the metabolism of nutrients
Pyridoxine (Vitamin B6)	Brewer's yeast, wheat germ, pork, liver, whole grain cereals, potatoes, milk, and fruits and vegetables	Assists in the metabolism of nutrients
Folacin (Folic Acid)	Liver, lima and kidney beans, dark green leafy vegetables, beef, potatoes, whole wheat bread, eggs, yogourt, orange juice, oranges	Plays a role in growth and enzyme activity and in the formation of red blood cells
Vitamin B12	Liver, kidneys, meat, fish, dairy products, and eggs	Involved in the metabolism of nutrients; helps to prevent anemia; essential for the formation of red blood cells and nerve fibres
Vitamin C	Citrus fruits, leafy vegetables, green and red pepper, tomatoes, and strawberries	Promotes healthy teeth and skin; aids in tissue repair; assists in the absorption of iron

MINERALS

Calcium	Milk and milk products, salmon and sardines with bones, dark green leafy vegetables, broccoli, fortified soya milk, and fortified tofu	Helps to build and maintain strong bones and teeth; promotes normal blood clotting; promotes the healthy functioning of the nervous system
Phosphorus	Meat, fish, poultry, eggs, milk and milk products, soya milk, tofu, whole grain breads, and cereals	Aids in the formation and maintenance of strong bones and teeth; assists in the transportation of nutrients; helps to regulate the body's energy balance; helps to maintain the body's acid balance
Magnesium	Dark leafy green vegetables, legumes, almonds, peanut butter, seafood, milk and milk products, and cereals	Assists with the formation and maintenance of strong bones and teeth as well as the transmission of nerve impulses and the release of energy
Iron	Meat, fish, and poultry; whole grain or enriched breads, cereals, and pastas; iron-fortified infant cereals; dark green leafy vegetables; and dried fruits such as raisins	Prevents anemia and helps red blood cells to deliver oxygen throughout the body
Fluoride	Municipal water supplies with water added; toothpastes containing fluoride (although, of course, your toddler should not be swallowing large quantities of toothpaste to meet her fluoride needs!)	Promotes healthy, decay-resistant teeth

continued on p. 290

Nutrient	Food Sources	What It Does
MINERALS (continued)		
Zinc	Meat, poultry, eggs, dairy products	Promotes healthy growth and development and gives the immune system a boost
Iodine	Table salt, seafood, and vegetables (depending on iodine content of soil and water supply in locations where the vegetables were grown)	Plays a role in the production of thyroid hormones, which help to regulate both the metabolism and the growth rate

Note: According to Health Canada, vitamin and mineral supplements are rarely necessary if a child is eating a variety of foods, is growing well, and is in good health. If you do decide to give your child a pediatric vitamin supplement, make sure that you keep the vitamin jar well out of her reach. Ingesting large quantities of vitamins can be harmful to a toddler.

TODDLER TALK

Iron-fortified infant cereals are the primary source of iron from solid foods for toddlers. A ½ cup serving of infant cereal delivers 6.7 mg of iron—slightly more than the 6 mg/iron a toddler needs over the course of a day. A 100-gram (3.5 oz.) serving of beef, on the other hand, delivers just 2.35 mg of iron. (Not that your toddler is likely to be a steak fan any time soon!)

Toddlers between 12 and 18 months are vulnerable to iron-deficiency anemia because

- they are growing rapidly and have a high need for iron;
- they have long since run through the iron reserves that they were born with;
- they have not yet started eating a lot of iron-rich foods.

If your toddler exhibits such symptoms as paleness, a lack of energy, irritability, and a decreased appetite, she could be suffering from iron-deficiency anemia. Oral iron supplements may be prescribed until your toddler's iron level returns to normal and she's able to obtain adequate amounts of iron from food sources.

- When you're baking, get in the habit of using a mixture of whole wheat flour and white flour. The baked goods you put on the table will be tastier and more nutritious.

- When you're shopping for pasta, look for whole wheat varieties and zero in on shapes that are both fun to eat and easy to chew. Miniature wagon wheels, miniature rotini, and plain-Jane macaroni are usually your best bets. (While spaghetti noodles are easy to chew, they can be very challenging for a toddler to get on her fork or spoon unless you cut them into bite-sized pieces.)

- Add fresh or dried fruits to cereals, pancakes, and muffins rather than sweetening these foods with syrups or sugars.

- Try cutting back on the amount of sugar in muffin recipes where sugar is required. Note: You'll find practical tips on reducing the sugar and fat content in favourite family recipes by reading *Tailoring Your Tastes* by Linda Omichinski and Heather Wiebe Hildebrand.

Vegetables and fruits

- Offer your toddler a variety of different vegetables and fruit rather than getting stuck in a rut. You want to expose her to as many different tastes as possible. Who knows? She may be the first member of your family in three generations to actually *like* Brussels sprouts.

- Prepare fruits and vegetables in a variety of different ways: raw, cooked, au naturel, or sprinkled with cheese or herbs and spices. (Go easy with the spices for now; you don't want to scare your toddler off vegetables for life because you went a little too crazy with the garlic during her formative years!)

- Don't be surprised if your toddler prefers raw veggies to cooked ones. Most vegetables acquire a stronger, more bitter taste when they're cooked—something that turns toddlers (and some adults!) off.

- Find fun ways to serve vegetables to your toddler. You might want to make face shapes on a plate using vegetable pieces, for example, or use vegetable pieces to spell out the first letter in your child's name. (Forget flash cards—let vegetable sticks give your budding genius that educational edge!)

MOTHER WISDOM

It's unusual for a toddler to hate all vegetables. Your mission as a parent is to try to uncover the ones she likes. Your best bets? Corn, peas, carrots, beans, and sweet potatoes. According to the experts, these are the vegetables that toddlers like best.

TODDLER TALK

Not all fruits are created equal. *The Nutrition Action Health-letter* scored 47 fruits on such nutrients as vitamin C, carotenoids, folate, potassium, and fibre. The big winners were guava, watermelon, pink or red grapefruit, kiwi, papaya, cantaloupe, dried apricots, oranges, strawberries, and fresh apricots.

While you'll want to include as many servings of these "superfruits" in your toddler's diet as possible, don't feel obligated to steer clear of toddler favourites such as apples, pears, and bananas just because they didn't walk away with top honours. As the editors of the newsletter noted, "Even the lowest-scoring fruit beats a low-fat Twinkie hands down."

- You'll probably find that your toddler is more receptive to gnawing her way through a plate of vegetables if you offer them as a snack while you're making dinner. To make that veggie platter even more enticing, include a yummy dip made from plain yogourt or puréed cottage cheese. Not only will your toddler be more likely to munch her way through that plate of veggies if she's got some dip to play around with, but the fat in the dip will also make it easier for her body to absorb the vitamin A and beta carotene in the veggies.

- When you're planning your toddler's meals, try to zero in on fruits and vegetables that are rich in vitamin A (carrots, spinach, cantaloupe, and apricots) and vitamin C (tomatoes, green peppers, oranges, and strawberries). Fruits and vegetables are important sources of these two vital vitamins.

- Get in the habit of serving a vitamin C–rich vegetable along with iron-rich foods such as red meats, dark green vegetables, breads and cereals, dried beans, peas, and lentils. Vitamin C aids in iron absorption, and iron deficiency can be a problem for toddlers.

- If your toddler is a card-carrying veggie-o-phobe, you may have to find creative ways to sneak vegetables into foods she already likes. Try puréeing vegetables and including them in spaghetti sauces, soups, or stews; sneaking finely chopped spinach, mushroom, or green pepper into omelettes; cooking vegetable lasagna, pizza with vegetable toppings, or meatloaf with lots of built-in veggies; or whipping up a batch of pumpkin, carrot, or zucchini muffins. If all else fails, up her fruit intake instead. That will help to make up for some of the nutrients she's missing on the veggie front.

Milk products

Milk is an excellent source of vitamin D and calcium—the nutrients needed to build healthy bones and strong teeth. If your toddler doesn't drink milk, you may need to supplement her diet with vitamin D. (While milk is fortified with vitamin D, other dairy products such as cheese, yogourt, and ice cream are not.) Toddlers should consume 500 millilitres of milk each day, either by drinking milk on its own, adding it to cereal or fruit, or consuming it in puddings or soups made with milk. If your child doesn't drink milk, you'll need to consult with her doctor or your local public health nutritionist to come up with ways of ensuring that she gets adequate quantities of vitamin D and calcium. Note: Vitamin D is added to all cow's milk sold in stores, including powdered skim milk. Goat's milk may or may not have vitamin

---

TODDLER TALK

While vitamin D can be obtained through sun exposure, increased use of sunscreens limits the amount of vitamin D that can be obtained from the sun. Consequently, it's more important than ever to ensure that your toddler's diet contains vitamin D–rich foods, especially milk.

D added, so be sure to check the label carefully if your toddler drinks goat's milk rather than cow's milk.

- While it's okay to offer your toddler chocolate milk on occasion, don't let it replace the regular milk in her diet. Chocolate milk is much higher in sugar than regular milk. If your toddler really enjoys her chocolate milk, dilute it with regular milk so that she's not getting quite as much sugar. Note: Chocolate milk is much more nutritious than soda pop, however, so if you want to give her the choice of ordering something other than regular milk at a fast-food restaurant, chocolate milk is a healthy choice.

- Limit your toddler's use of processed cheese slices and spreads, as these products are much higher in salt than natural cheeses. And don't get in the habit of serving ice cream and frozen yogourt on a regular basis because they tend to contain a lot of fat and sugar.

- Don't go crazy with flavoured yogourts, as they tend to be quite high in sugar. You can get a lot of mileage out of a small serving of flavoured yogourt by letting your toddler use it as dip for fruit slices. Or, if you prefer, buy plain yogourt and add your own flavouring, e.g. fruit, vanilla, and so on.

Meat and alternatives

If your toddler rejects any meat that is "chewy," stick to softer meats and alternatives instead: lean ground beef, meatballs, boneless fish, eggs, tofu, baked beans or other legumes, and peanut butter. Note: You can also make a piece of meat more tender and moist by stewing it or cooking it slowly in a covered dish so that it's able to retain its natural juices. And, of course, you can always moisten up meat after the fact by topping it with broth, natural juices, or tomato sauce before serving it to your toddler.

MOTHER WISDOM

Sandwiches are a toddler's best friend. (Well, most toddlers at least. There's no food that scores points with every toddler!) Because sandwiches tend to be so popular with the toddler crowd, you'll want to use them as a nutrient transport vehicle, packing them with maximum nutritional punch! Try puréeing together turkey, finely chopped celery, and plain yogourt; tuna, apple or pineapple, and a mild salad dressing; or peanut butter and mashed bananas. Of course, if your toddler turns her nose up at these gourmet concoctions, you can always fall back on such old favourites as egg salad or tuna salad sandwiches (made with yogourt or mayonnaise), grilled cheese sandwiches, and— of course—peanut butter (unless allergies are a concern) and jam. (Note: Be sure to spread the peanut butter thinly to reduce the risk of choking.)

- Get in the habit of trimming visible fat from meats before cooking and removing skin from poultry before you serve it to your child. It's a good habit to introduce your toddler to at an early age.

- If you serve luncheon meats to your child, stick with lower-sodium, lower-fat varieties. And try to find alternatives to frying and deep-frying meat, fish, and poultry, like barbecuing or grilling instead.

- Make a point of working lean organ meats (liver and kidney) into your toddler's diet occasionally. These foods may not be your all-time favourites, but they may be perfectly palatable to your toddler. And no matter what her final verdict might be on these two organ meats, it's certainly worth *trying* to get her hooked on liver and kidney: Both of these organ meats are rich in iron. Just one word of caution on the liver front: Because the liver is the organ responsible for filtering pollutants and toxins, it's best to limit your toddler's liver intake to no more than one serving every two weeks. This is one of those situations when you can get too much of a good thing.

TODDLER TALK

Meat is an important source of iron in a toddler's diet. It's absorbed two to three times more efficiently than the type of iron found in vegetables and grains. It may be difficult for a toddler on a vegan diet (a diet made up of only non-animal foods) to obtain enough calories, protein, iron, calcium, vitamin D, vitamin B12, and riboflavin. That's why most nutritionists recommend that very young children have at least some animal sources of protein (e.g., eggs).

Here are some important points to keep in mind if your toddler is following a meat-free diet:

- To ensure that your toddler is consuming an adequate amount of protein, make a point of including eggs and legumes (dried peas, dried beans, and lentils) in her diet every day. When she's older and less likely to choke, you can add nuts and seeds to her diet, too.
- If you're not feeding your toddler cow's milk, serve her soy formula rather than other soy or nut beverages. These other beverages do not contain as much calcium as cow's milk and they aren't fortified with vitamin D.
- Offer your toddler foods that are high in vitamin C at two of her meals each day. This will allow her body to more readily absorb iron from plant sources of food. The following are excellent sources of vitamin C: broccoli, Brussels sprouts, cabbage, cauliflower, kohlrabi, cantaloupe, grapefruit, mango, papaya, oranges, peppers, spinach, and strawberries.
- Make sure that your toddler is getting enough fat in her diet, since she won't be obtaining fat from meat. You might want to add butter or margarine to her vegetables and to work sauces or gravies into your meals on occasion.
- To prevent the bulk in whole grains from filling your toddler up before she can consume all the nutrients she needs, alternate between whole grains and enriched refined grains. Consuming excessive quantities of fibre can interfere with the absorption of iron, copper, and zinc.

MOM'S THE WORD

"My son is only eating meat for dinner right now. I try not to get too stressed about it. I simply make sure he gets some fruit for lunch and milk and cereal at breakfast. I know he'll eventually grow out of this."

—*Cindy, 27, mother of two*

Snack attack

Because toddlers have small stomachs and relatively high energy needs, most need to eat every two to three hours. Consequently, you'll probably want to schedule snacks for midway between breakfast and lunch, midway between lunch and dinner, and at bedtime.

Snacks served to toddlers should be "mini-meals" that are packed with important nutrients. While the sky is the limit when it comes to drumming up ideas for toddler-friendly snacks, it never hurts to have a few ideas on hand for those days when your creativity is running on empty. Here are a few ideas:

- a toddler-sized muffin (you can buy tins with extra-small muffin cups) and a few slices of banana

- whole-grain crackers or rice cakes spread with puréed cottage cheese or mashed avocado

- carrot or pumpkin bread with cream cheese

- dry cereal (e.g., Cheerios) mixed with bite-sized crackers and raisins (a healthier alternative to ultra high-fat and high-salt "snack mixes")

- mini-pitas topped with melted cheese and accompanied by a small serving of raisins

- half an English muffin topped with melted cheese, hummus, peanut butter (spread thinly), tuna salad, or egg salad

- oatmeal cookies (ideally homemade cookies made with a mixture of whole wheat flour and all-purpose flour)

- sliced strawberries and kiwi with a spoonful of yogourt

- a smoothie made with milk, yogourt, and puréed fruit

- yogourt topped with fruit and a sprinkle of cinnamon

MOM'S THE WORD

"I always have two non-perishable snacks in Maddie's diaper bag. It helps to keep her filled up so that she's less cranky, and it keeps her busy when we're out and about."

—*Christina, 26, mother of three*

- apple slices sprinkled with cinnamon and heated in the microwave

- raw vegetables and dip

- half a hard-boiled egg

Sweets and treats

While there's no hard evidence to back up all those claims about sugar causing hyperactivity, there are still plenty of good reasons to limit the number of sweets and treats that find their way into your toddler's diet. Children who develop a sweet tooth may be less inclined to reach for vegetables and other less-sweet foods at mealtime, and, what's more, sugar is often teamed up with artery-clogging saturated fat. Add to that the fact that sugar helps to promote tooth decay, and you've got a laundry list of excellent reasons to limit your toddler's sugar intake. That means limiting the number of sugary foods that find their way into your home and offering fruit at the end of a meal as opposed to a sugary dessert. That's not to say that your toddler needs to lead an entirely sugar-free existence, of course. Everything in moderation.

The truth about juice

Contrary to popular belief, juice is not a necessity in a toddler's diet. It's definitely a frill.

While fruit juices are an excellent source of vitamin C and may also provide a variety of other important nutrients including folate, potassium, vitamin A, and calcium, they shouldn't become a mainstay of your toddler's diet. Here's why:

- Fruit juices can take the edge off your toddler's appetite at mealtime and make it less likely that she'll consume a variety of other types of foods.

- Unlike the fruit that it was originally derived from, fruit juice doesn't contain fibre.

- Too much fruit juice can interfere with the absorption of nutrients and add empty calories to your child's diet. It can also trigger *toddler's diarrhea*—a condition that is caused by excessive quantities of sorbitol and fructose in the digestive tract—and make diarrhea triggered by garden-variety gastro-intestinal infections a whole lot worse.

If you decide to include juice in your toddler's diet, you'll want to

- limit the number of servings of juice your toddler is allowed to consume over the course of a day ("I allow juice only at breakfast," says Stephanie, a 29-year-old mother of one. "I've always had that as a rule for my daughter so that she won't have the chance to develop a juice habit");

- offer your child unsweetened juice as opposed to fruit "drinks," "punches," or "cocktails"—beverages that tend to contain large quantities of sugar, but little in the way of real juice;

- avoid unpasteurized apple cider and fruit juices—a potential source of deadly E. coli bacteria;

- make a point of selecting juices like orange juice that are rich in vitamin C;

- ensure that your toddler's juice intake doesn't exceed the 125 millilitre (four ounce) daily maximum for toddlers under 18 months of age or the 250 millilitre (eight ounce) daily maximum for toddlers over 18 months of age;

- dilute your child's juice with water (e.g., one part juice to two or three parts water) to reduce its sweetness and limit your toddler's juice intake.

The facts on fat

While it's not advisable to limit a child's intake of dietary fat during the first two years of life, most experts agree that it's a good idea to gradually wean a child off high-fat foods after age two so that she can start to acquire a taste for lower-fat foods. That means

- using high-fat sauces, salad dressings, margarine, butter, and other spreads in moderation;

- trimming visible fat from meat;

- limiting the amount of processed meat (hot dog wieners, luncheon meats, sausages, etc.) that you serve your toddler

---

TODDLER TALK

While you're encouraging your two-year-old to go easy on the butter, you might want to start teaching her to go light on the salt, too. A preference for salty foods is acquired rather than inherited, so it's important to limit your child's intake of salty foods such as snack foods, canned soups, condiments, and salted crackers. It's also a good idea to keep salt shakers out of reach of children. (And adults, too!)

TODDLER TALK

"The transition from the high-fat diet of infancy to the lower-fat diet of adults should occur slowly from age two until adolescence.... During this transition, it is important to provide children with sufficient calories to promote normal growth and development. But this [is] also the critical period for developing healthy eating habits and a positive attitude towards food. This includes consuming a variety of foods from the four food groups, including complex carbohydrates and lower-fat foods, as well as participating in a physically active lifestyle."

—*Diana Kalnins and Joanne Saab,* The Hospital for Sick Children Better Baby Food: Your Essential Guide to Nutrition, Feeding, and Cooking for All Babies and Toddlers

---

and looking for lower-fat choices when you're shopping for processed meats;

• limiting the amount of fried food that your child consumes;

• offering fruits or vegetables at snack-time rather than higher-fat foods.

No more food fights!

YOU'VE NO DOUBT heard all sorts of rumours about those infamous parent–toddler face-offs over food. They are, after all, the stuff of which legends are made: a frustrated parent and a stubborn toddler glaring at each other over an untouched serving of casserole du jour.

But contrary to popular belief, feeding a toddler doesn't have to be this way—not if you're clear about who does what at the dinner table. Fortunately, we're not talking brain surgery here. In fact, here's everything you need to know: It's your job to decide what type of food to serve and when to serve it, and it's your toddler's job to decide whether she wants to eat and, if so, how much she wants to eat. If you stick to these basic rules of engagement, you'll find mealtimes a whole lot less stressful.

That's not to say that your in-house food critic will magically expand her repertoire of foods overnight or that she'll start applauding the moment you place her dinner plate in front of her. If only it were that easy! But if you're like most parents, you'll gradually learn how to work around her many food-related idiosyncrasies—something that will help to dramatically reduce the number of battles over broccoli and Brussels sprouts.

Here are some important points to keep in mind:

- Toddlers need plenty of transition time. They need time to wind down from playtime before you drag them off to the dinner table. After all, it's pretty hard to settle down to eat your meal if you were in the middle of building the very best sandcastle ever! (Imagine how you'd feel if you were dragged to the dinner table just before your favourite steamy scene in *Bridges of Madison County* or—if you're a big hockey fan— during the final minutes of the Stanley Cup final.)

- Plan a quiet activity for your toddler for the half-hour leading up to dinnertime. Your toddler will find it easier to make

---

TODDLER TALK

Your toddler isn't being picky when she turns her nose up at the mystery vegetable du jour; she's putting Darwinian theory into action. Scientists believe that being skeptical toward new foods actually makes a lot of sense from an evolutionary standpoint. A small amount of something poisonous might not kill you, but an entire meal of it might. It's therefore much more prudent to nibble at a new food tentatively and wait to see if you keel over than it is to down an entire dinner plateful with great gusto. (Psst ... This lesson in "survival of the fittest" was brought to you by your toddler!)

MOTHER WISDOM

Your toddler isn't trying to drive you crazy by dumping her spaghetti on the floor. She just wants to see if the same laws of physics that apply to toys also apply to food. (And, if truth be told, she's also eager to find out if you'll react the same way when she dumps her spaghetti as you do when she dumps her blocks on the floor!)

The best way to deal with this annoying—and messy—habit is to play it cool. Calmly remind her that food belongs in the bowl, not on the floor. And if you get the sense that your toddler is performing for an audience—e.g., her older brother who finds it gut-splittingly funny to see the spaghetti flung all over the floor—you might want to convey the message to your older child that he who laughs hardest gets to mop up the floor.

Of course, physics experiments involving food don't tend to happen until a toddler gets restless and bored, so you'll also want to learn to spot the warning signs that she's finished eating and ready to give anything in grabbing distance the old heave-ho. At this point, you'll simply want to remove her food and lift her down from her high chair or booster seat.

One other quick tip: It's easier to dump food that's on a plate than food that's on a high chair tray, so you might want to try packing away her dinner plate for now. Just be sure to keep your toddler's high chair tray meticulously clean to prevent it from becoming a breeding ground for bacteria.

---

the transition from the playroom to the dinner table if she's been quietly working on a puzzle as opposed to playing tickle monster with her older brother. You can't expect her to go from a high-energy activity (particularly one that's big on goofiness!) to a quiet activity in the blink of an eye.

- Keep mealtime distractions to a minimum. Toddlers tend to have difficulty settling down to eat if they're too excited or distracted, so turn off the telephone and the TV. You'll also want to keep the mood at dinnertime light and upbeat. (Hint: This is no time to discuss the unexpectedly high credit card bill with your partner!)

- Get in the habit of feeding your toddler when she's hungry. This will encourage her to tap into her body's natural hunger signals. If she happens to get hungry an hour before dinner is ready, give her a healthy snack and don't fret if she doesn't finish all of her dinner. If she's hungry a half-hour after dinner, however, this means she's not eating enough at mealtime and may be relying too much on snacks. You may want to discourage her grazing habit by trying to hold off on giving her more food until the next scheduled snack or mealtime. Note: If you find that your toddler doesn't have much appetite at dinnertime, it may be because she's still full from her afternoon snack. If this continues to be a problem, you might want to try cutting back on the size of the snack in the future or offering it to your toddler a little earlier in the afternoon.

- Offer your toddler a variety of different types of foods. Some parents find that toddlers respond well to "buffet-style" meals where they can pick and choose from an assortment of foods

---

MOM'S THE WORD

"My toddlers seem to prefer the simplest meals—meals where they can identify what they're eating and choose what they want."

—*Kerri, 36, mom of six*

MOM'S THE WORD

"We have always allowed the girls to pick one toy from the kitchen box (a small box with a few trinkets that they're only allowed to play with at the dinner table). They are allowed to pick one toy and play with it between bites while they are swallowing. It works for us because it keeps them eating and sitting."

—*Sharon, 29, mother of three*

on the dinner table. You don't have to hire a short-order cook to pull this off, by the way: simply offer your toddler small servings of whatever you're having for dinner that night plus any leftovers that happen to be hanging out in your refrigerator at any given time. (Obviously, anything that's well on its way to becoming a science experiment should find its way into the trash, not the toddler.)

- Try to make your toddler's meals as appealing as possible by making an effort to include foods of different colours, flavours, and textures. If you're a culinary whiz kid who really likes to go to town with these sorts of things, you could use metal cookie cutters to cut your child's grilled cheese sandwiches into interesting shapes.

- Make a point of offering foods that are easy for a toddler to eat: foods that are soft, moist, and easy to chew. You might also want to bear in mind that toddlers don't like foods that are too hot or too cold. Room temperature is their food temperature of choice.

- If your toddler tends to freak out if her potatoes end up touching her peas or her meatballs, try to work around this

---

TODDLER TALK

Don't be surprised if your toddler refuses to have anything to do with a broken cracker or bruised banana. The appearance of these foods conflicts with her ideas about what a cracker or banana is supposed to look like. As frustrating as it can be to deal with these types of food idiosyncrasies, it's important to remind yourself that they're actually evidence a good thing— proof positive that your toddler is getting more and more tuned into her world. In the meantime, be prepared to compromise with your toddler: "Give her a whole cookie and a piece of banana without a bruise," advises Anita, a 38-year-old mother of four. "It's cheaper than therapy!"

strange little toddlerism by either keeping her foods far apart on a single plate, serving the foods in separate dishes, or using a dinner plate that features divided sections. Save your energy for the battles that really count!

- Trust your child to eat the right amount of food. She's the best judge of how much food she needs. You'll probably notice that your toddler eats more at some meals than others, and that she may pick at her food one day and then eat everything in sight the next. She's simply adjusting her food intake to match her energy needs—a skill many adults have lost along the way.

- Don't encourage your toddler to overeat by insisting that she "clean her plate" or by trying to shove a few extra spoonfuls into her when she clearly doesn't want any more food. You'll only be teaching her to ignore her body's natural signals of hunger and fullness—something that could lead to weight problems down the road.

- Remind yourself that it's unrealistic to expect a toddler to eat adult-sized portions. If you present her with too much food, she may feel so overwhelmed by the amount of food on her plate that she loses her appetite entirely. Stick to toddler-sized portions and make a point of having extra servings of food on hand in case your toddler happens to be feeling particularly hungry. If she's been running around the backyard all afternoon, she may come back for seconds or thirds.

- Allow adequate time for your toddler to eat so she doesn't have to feel rushed. Some toddlers aren't necessarily picky eaters— they're leisurely diners. It takes them a while to pick up their spoons and get down to the business of eating.

- Give some thought to how you go about introducing new foods. Toddlers are more likely to accept a new food if
  - they're asked to try only one new food at a time;
  - the new food is accompanied by other foods that the toddler likes;
  - the new food is presented in an appealing way;
  - the toddler sees other family members eating it (watching your toddler eat Brussels sprouts shouldn't be a spectator sport!);
  - the toddler's parents aren't putting undue pressure on her to try the new food.

- Try not to become overly discouraged if you follow all these rules and your toddler still refuses to have anything to do with the new food. It can take time for a toddler to warm up to a new food. If at first you don't succeed, try, try again. And then

MOTHER WISDOM

Having a hard time deciding what to feed your picky eater for dinner? Here's an online tool you'll want to know about: the Picky Eater Problem Solver at the FamilyFun Web site: http://family.go.com/recipes/kids/tool/pickyeater_tlp.This interactive recipe database allows you to search for recipes by ingredient. (You can either search by ingredients that you wish to include or ingredients that you wish to exclude!) Just type in the most recent list of your toddler's 10—or 100!—least wanted foods and hit return. Who knows? You may even end up with a match or two!

---

try a dozen more times! If you offer the new food again in a few weeks' time (and perhaps cook it in a slightly different manner), you may find that she's much more willing to try it. Studies have shown that some toddlers have to be exposed to a new food on as many as 15 different occasions before they'll actually eat it. (And, no, making the broccoli magically disappear and reappear 15 different times during the same meal isn't going to do the trick, moms and dads!)

- Don't get into battles with your child over food. This—like toilet training—is a battle you simply can't win. Dietitian and author Ellyn Satter suggests that parents avoid introducing any sort of family rule that states that toddlers must at least try any new food. According to Satter, this strategy can backfire. In her book *Child of Mine: Feeding with Love and Good Sense*, she makes this important point: "If a food is presented over and over in a neutral fashion, sooner or later a child will taste it, and in most cases after she tastes it lots of times, she will like it. If you try to speed up the process, you will in fact slow it down. In a child's mind, the response is something like this, 'If they have to make me eat that, then it must not be so good.'" Not all parents agree with Satter's take on the situation, however. "We have a 'must try it' rule at our house," says

MOM'S THE WORD

"I rarely make separate meals for the toddlers. Most of the time, they eat what the rest of us eat. I may slightly modify the food, however, serving them the chunky parts of the soup rather than the broth or cutting back the amount of sauce on their pasta."

—*Kerri, 36, mother of six, including 17-month-old twins*

Lori, a 31-year-old mother of five. "Even if they don't like something, they have to take one big mouthful before they can decide that they don't want to eat it. Sometimes they surprise themselves and actually like something!"

- Try to win over your picky eater by involving her in various aspects of food preparation: everything from shopping for groceries to growing your own vegetables and herbs to whipping up meals and snacks in the kitchen. She'll be more inclined to try a new food if she played a role in getting it to the dinner table.

- Don't bribe your toddler to eat her veggies by promising her an exciting dessert. You'll simply be teaching her to value dessert over vegetables—not exactly the kind of message you want to convey to your child!

- Don't turn sweets and other treats into "forbidden foods" or your toddler may develop a heightened interest in them. It's better to allow her to have the occasional ice cream cone than to ban desserts from her diet entirely.

- Respect your toddler's likes and dislikes, but don't become a slave to her food preferences. Remember, you're a mother—not a short-order cook! Besides, as Ellyn Satter puts it: "Letting what the child will readily accept dictate the family menu is like letting the child drive the family car." Trust me, you don't want to go there!

Coping with food jags

It's not unusual for toddlers to develop a temporary fixation with a particular food and to insist on eating that food morning, noon, and night. (Fish sticks for breakfast, lunch, and dinner? Yum!)

Fortunately, food jags tend to be relatively short-lived—something that Catherine, a 32-year-old mother of four, discovered for herself: "My son wanted Kraft Macaroni and Cheese with wieners every day for a month. I gave in, but I still had the upper hand. I only allowed him to have his favourite meal at lunchtime and I served vegetables as well as a piece of whole wheat bread on the side. Now he's back to eating just about anything."

Brandy had a similar experience and, like Catherine, found that it was easier to simply go along with the food jag rather than trying to fight it: "My son wanted pizza all the time, so I made dough out of whole wheat flour and topped it with lots of veggies, meat, and cheese," the 24-year-old mother of two recalls. "That way, he got foods from all four food groups and actually ate his meal—something he might not have done if I had tried to serve him something else entirely."

So try not to get too worked up if your toddler decides that the only food on the planet worth eating is cheese. It won't be long before she agrees to negotiate some sort of peace accord with representatives from the other food groups!

TODDLER TALK

Some toddlers develop a strange craving for non-edible substances such as dirt, paint, string, cloth, or hair. This condition—which is known as pica—is most common in children between the ages of 18 months and two years. Contrary to what nutritionists used to believe, it's not triggered by any clearly identifiable nutritional deficiency.

Pica generally only lasts for a couple months, but until your toddler outgrows it, you'll have to monitor her closely to make sure she's not dining on driveway dirt or other potentially harmful substances.

Weaning your breastfed baby

ACCORDING TO Statistics Canada, only 3% of Canadian babies are breastfed for more than 12 months—this despite the fact that the Canadian Paediatric Society, Dietitians of Canada, Health Canada, and the World Health Organization all recommend that babies be breastfed for at least two years.

Unfortunately, mothers who choose to breastfeed their babies into the toddler years are sometimes made to feel that they're doing something wrong. "My daughter was breastfed until she was three years old and that was a huge issue with my husband's family," says Stephanie, a 29-year-old mother of one. "I received a lot of advice and negative comments about the length of time I was allowing my child to nurse."

What many people fail to realize is that there are tremendous benefits to breastfeeding a toddler. In addition to continuing to confer a smorgasbord of health benefits, breastfeeding helps to cement the bond between mother and child.

"Breastfeeding a toddler makes life so much more pleasant and enjoying his or her company so much easier," says Joanne, a 43-year-old mother of seven. "So many challenging behaviours, frustrations, and wounded spirits are soothed and healed by the familiar comfort of breastfeeding."

MOM'S THE WORD

"The ancient art of a birthing circle has been lost. Women today know more about mutual funds and IPOs than breastfeeding. A whole generation or two has lost precious knowledge that has been handed down by the birthing support circle of matriarchs that has nurtured us since the beginning of time. Too many of us are foraging alone and unprepared into parenthood."

—*Debbie, 37, mother of two*

MOTHER WISDOM

Here's a statistic to share with those people who aren't exactly supportive of prolonged breastfeeding: pilot whales nurse their babies for up to 17 years!

Stephanie agrees. "I found it a joy to be able to extend our nursing relationship for so long—until right before Isabel's third birthday," the 29-year-old mother of one recalls. "It is a joy that she still remembers it and that she'll still talk about when she used to nurse—this despite the fact that it has now been over a year since she was weaned."

Not every mother finds breastfeeding a toddler to be totally hassle-free, but most, like Joan, agree that the benefits far outweigh the challenges. "Breastfeeding a toddler is a whole different ballgame than breastfeeding a baby, but I'm so glad I did it," says the 35-year-old mother of five. "I didn't love toddler nursing as I did nursing a baby; they were heavy, squirmy, and awkward to hold, particularly when there were two of them nursing. They got more acrobatic in their nursing, which was often uncomfortable and required correction. However, it was a fabulous way to reconnect with my children when I returned from work, and it was an excellent tool to use when the child was getting frustrated, was hurt, or was sick."

TODDLER TALK

As your toddler becomes more mobile—something that typically happens around one year of age—her nursing patterns may vary. Some days your toddler may be too busy to nurse; on other days—particularly on days when she's in need of a little extra comfort—she may want to nurse more frequently.

But as wonderful as breastfeeding is, it doesn't last forever. At some point you or your baby will decide that it's time to leave your breastfeeding days behind. Here are some tips on making the weaning process as gentle as possible for both you and your toddler:

- Don't let anyone else pressure you into weaning your toddler before you're ready just because your toddler has reached a particular age or has passed the point at which you had originally planned to wean her. Remind anyone who dares to express an opinion on this all-important issue that you're the one who owns the breasts and consequently you'll be making all the breast-feeding-related decisions! Allowing someone else to convince you to wean your toddler before you or your toddler are ready could lead to painful feelings of regret down the road.

- Pay careful attention to your timing. You don't want to try to wean your toddler at the same time that she's dealing with an ear infection, making the transition from crib to bed, or trying to adjust to your return to work or the birth of a new sibling.

- If you choose to go with a mother-led style of weaning, try to eliminate one feeding at a time, starting with the feeding that your toddler cares about least—typically the ones that fall in the middle of the day. Most mothers find it works best to

---

MOM'S THE WORD

"Weaning was child-led one time and mother-led the other time. Both times I was profoundly saddened by it and sorry it was ending so soon. (Yes, I cried.) I really enjoy breastfeeding. It's an act of love between a mother and her baby."

—*Anita, mom of four*

MOM'S THE WORD

"Because nursing is a relationship that includes both the toddler and the parent, I feel that the decision to wean should be a mutual one. There were times when I just couldn't nurse, and there were times when I nursed simply because it was important to my child. I usually practised a 'don't offer, don't refuse' style of nursing and gradually met my own comfort level with toddler nursing by setting limits on the length of nursings ('How about a 'count to ten' drink this time?'), the frequency of nursings ('Can you wait until I finish doing this?'), or where we nursed (we nursed less and less in public as they got older). Of course, if my toddler was hurt or sick, then they got to nurse as they needed."

—*Joan, 35, mother of five*

---

eliminate one feeding per week (or every couple of weeks)— something that allows weaning to become a slow, gradual process. Just don't feel obliged to stick to your pre-determined "schedule" if you or your toddler find that you want to hang onto breast-feeding a little longer. Remember, you're the ones calling the shots.

- If your child indicates that she'd like to nurse, try interesting her in an activity or offering a snack instead. "As my toddlers got older, I stopped offering to nurse, but if they asked, I nursed them," says Kerri, a 36-year-old mother of six. "Then I started offering alternatives: 'Are you thirsty? Would you like a drink of water from your cup? Are you hungry? Would you like a slice of apple? Do you want Mommy time? Would you like to cuddle and read a book or would you like Mommy to play with you?' I found that this helped to teach them the difference between being thirsty, being hungry, wanting snuggles, wanting someone to play with them, or wanting to nurse. If they truly wanted to nurse, I would let them. Eventually, they all weaned themselves."

- Steer clear of "the nursing chair" during the day and keep your toddler busy so she'll have her mind on something other than breastfeeding.

- Offer milk in a cup during mealtimes. If your toddler still wants to nurse after the meal, you can offer the breast, but you'll probably find that she'll either skip her nursing session entirely or just nurse for a minute or two.

- Find other ways to show your love for your child to help ease the transition for her. Read stories together or have some quiet cuddling time at the end of the day. You don't want your toddler to miss out on the special together time that you enjoyed while she was nursing just because you'll no longer be breastfeeding her.

- Don't be surprised if you find yourself grieving the loss of your breastfeeding relationship, even if both you and your toddler are ready to wean. "No matter now much you want to wean your baby or how gradually you might do it, it's only natural to have mixed emotions about it," says Lori, a 31-year-old

---

 MOM'S THE WORD

"I let Christopher decide when he was ready to wean, but I felt so sad the last night he nursed. I cried actually. I can tell you what day it was and what time it was. Nursing was something only he and I shared. I didn't feel a refreshing sense of freedom; I just felt sad."

—*Brandy, 26, mother of one*

 MOM'S THE WORD

"I never knew the end of breastfeeding could be so heartbreaking."

—*Catherine, 32, mother of four*

mother of five. "You gain 'freedom,' but you lose cuddle sessions." If you're feeling totally heartbroken about weaning
your toddler, you might want to give in to your feelings and
decide to postpone the weaning process for a little longer
(assuming, of course, that your toddler is still interested in
breastfeeding). After all, what difference is a few extra weeks
or months going to make in the big picture of things?

While you might assume that your milk will dry up and disappear overnight once you've weaned your toddler, it may take
several months for you to lose the bulk of your milk, even though
you might not notice much, if any, leaking after your last nursing session. Some women, in fact, are able to express a drop or
two of milk from their breasts for up to several years after weaning. The only time you're likely to be troubled by a lot of leaking and pressure is if you wean your toddler overnight— or, of

---

MOTHER WISDOM

Don't feel that you have to wean your toddler just because
there's another baby on the way. According to pediatrician Jack Newman of
Toronto's Hospital for Sick Children, breastfeeding during pregnancy poses
little risk to the developing baby provided that your previous pregnancies
have been relatively complication-free (i.e., you don't have a history of premature labour) and your current pregnancy is medically low-risk. Breast tenderness during pregnancy may make nursing uncomfortable for you,
however, so you may wish to limit the duration of nursing sessions and to
ensure that your toddler is latching on properly. And toward the end of pregnancy, nursing may trigger painful Braxton-Hicks contractions that may
cause you to want to end the feeding as soon as possible.

Because your milk supply diminishes significantly during early pregnancy and the milk being produced changes to colostrum (the "first food"
for infants) as pregnancy progresses, many toddlers wean themselves during their mother's pregnancies. Not all do, however, so you may find yourself "tandem nursing": nursing more than one baby a time.

course, if your toddler weans *you* cold turkey. In this case, you'll want to wear a bra that provides plenty of support and express just enough milk to relieve your discomfort. (If you express too much milk, you'll continue producing milk.) You may also find that applying ice packs to your breasts several times a day helps to relieve any breast pain you're experiencing.

It may take several months for your breasts to return to their pre-pregnancy size, at which point you may be surprised to discover that they're a little less firm than when you set out on this adventure called motherhood. (Breastfeeding isn't to blame for these breast changes, by the way; they're an inevitable side effect of child-bearing whether you breastfeed or not. Like the stretch marks that may now adorn your belly, they're souvenirs of your childbearing years.)

From bottle to cup

While there's no great rush to wean your baby from the breast, most doctors recommend that bottle-fed babies make the switch to a cup around their first birthday. Toddlers who drink from bottles can develop an overdependence on liquids (which may discourage them from trying a variety of nutrient-rich solid foods) and, if they're in the habit of sipping from a bottle all day long, they may also develop tooth decay.

Here are some tips on weaning your toddler to a cup:

• Start by introducing a two-handled sippy cup (ideally one with a weighted bottom that will tend to right itself if your toddler accidentally knocks it over).

• As your toddler starts to understand how cups work and what they're for, you can gradually start eliminating bottle feedings. (Of course, if she takes to the cup with great gusto right from day one, you can pack the bottles away immediately.)

- If your child is reluctant to give up her bottle, you might want to make it a rule that she has to sit in the high chair or booster seat rather than wander around and play while she's having her bottle. This will considerably reduce the appeal of her bottle.

- If your child is particularly stubborn about giving up her bottle (and, frankly, some toddlers are incredibly stubborn about saying goodbye to their beloved bottle), you might want to get in the habit of offering her a choice of water in her bottle or milk in a cup. Again, your goal is to make the bottle a much less appealing option.

- Speaking of milk, here's the scoop on infant formula and toddlers. While most toddlers can get the nutrients they need by drinking cow's milk and eating a balanced diet, toddlers whose diets contain minimal iron or who have been slow to gain weight may be better off sticking with infant formula for a while longer.

Avoiding choking and food-borne illness

IT'S IMPORTANT to give some thought to two important food-safety issues while you're raising a toddler: choking and food-borne illness.

Choking

Choking is one of the leading causes of death among children under five years of age. It can happen if toddlers are eating too quickly; not chewing their food properly; laughing, crying, or running around with food in their mouths; or eating chunks of food that are too large for them to handle.

Toddlers are at particular risk of choking because they have sharp teeth at the front of the mouth that allow them to bite off chunks of food, but do not yet have all the back teeth that are responsible for the grinding and crushing of food.

Here are some important tips on preventing a choking tragedy:

- Supervise your toddler closely while she's eating. If she starts to choke, you'll want to be able to react quickly. (Note: You'll find some step-by-step instructions on coping with a choking emergency in Chapter 8.)

- Assess your toddler's chewing and swallowing abilities and make food choices on that basis. Some children are more prone to choking than others.

- When you're serving peanut butter to a toddler, make sure that you spread it thinly. Otherwise, the food may become stuck in her throat when she tries to swallow.

- Don't allow your toddler to eat with single-use disposable plastic utensils. It's too easy for her to bite off and swallow the prongs. (Note: Durable plastic utensils that are designed to be used by toddlers don't pose the same risk.)

- Hold off on giving your toddler Popsicles until she's a little older. A piece of the Popsicle could break off and become lodged in her throat.

- Insist that your toddler sit in an upright position while she's eating. Don't allow her to eat anything while she's laughing, crying, or running around.

- Don't allow your toddler to eat while she's in the car. Sudden starts and stops can cause a child to choke, and if your toddler starts choking while you're on a busy highway, you may not be able to pull over quickly enough to deal with it.

- Steer clear of foods that are known to pose a choking hazard for toddlers: cough drops, fish with bones, gum, hard candy, nuts, popcorn, raisins, snacks with toothpicks, and sunflower seeds. And offer wieners only if they've been chopped lengthwise in quarters, grapes if they've been chopped in half lengthwise, and hard fruits and vegetables if they've been grated or chipped into small pieces.

Food-borne illness

Food-borne illness (a.k.a. poisoning) can result in stomach pain, diarrhea, or vomiting, and in some cases can lead to kidney failure, blood infection, and even paralysis. Because toddlers are more susceptible to food-borne illnesses than older children, you'll want to take extra care when you're preparing your toddler's foods. Here are some important points to keep in mind:

- Wash your hands thoroughly in hot, soapy water both before and after handling food.

- Steer clear of unpasteurized milk and fruit juices. The risk of food poisoning is greater with these types of products because they haven't been through the germ-killing pasteurization process.

- Rinse fruits and vegetables thoroughly under tap water before serving them to your toddler.

- Refrigerate or freeze meat after purchase. And when it's time to thaw meat, thaw it in the refrigerator rather than at room temperature.

- Ensure that raw meat and poultry is kept away from other foods and that all surfaces that come into contact with raw meat and poultry are decontaminated after use.

- Cook meat and poultry thoroughly. Ground meat and rolled roasts should be cooked until the meat is brown and the juices are clear, and poultry should be cooked until there is no pink left near the bone. Avoid sushi and other raw fish.

- Avoid serving your toddler products that contain raw eggs (e.g., uncooked cookie dough).

- Serve cooked foods promptly and make sure that any leftovers are placed in the refrigerator as soon as possible. And when you reheat leftovers, ensure that foods are reheated all the way through.

Allergy alert

APPROXIMATELY 10 to 12% of children between the ages of 12 and 18 months have food allergies. By age three, this number drops to 8%.

While people tend to use the terms "food allergy" and "food intolerance" interchangeably, they refer to two entirely different medical conditions. Here's what you need to know about each.

Food allergies

The term "food allergy" is used to describe an immune system reaction (an allergic reaction) that is triggered by eating a particular food or food additive. Food allergy symptoms may include wheezing, hives, eczema, vomiting, and diarrhea, and can be

---

TODDLER TALK

Don't try to diagnose food allergies on your own or you may place unnecessary restrictions on your child's diet—something that could deprive her of much-needed nutrients.

FRIDGE NOTES

If your toddler suffers from a life-threatening allergy, you'll want to download a copy of the B.C. Ministry of Health Services brochure entitled *Life-Threatening Food Allergies in School and Child Care Settings: A Practical Resource for Parents, Care Providers, and Staff.* It's available for download at www.healthservices.gov.bc.ca/cpa/publications/food_allergies.pdf.

triggered by a small amount of food. These symptoms can be serious or even life-threatening. (In this case, a child is said to be experiencing anaphylactic shock or anaphylaxis.)

Children under the age of five are most susceptible to food allergies because their digestive systems are not yet mature. Common trigger foods include cow's milk, nuts, eggs, peanut butter, fish, and shellfish. While children tend to outgrow most food allergies, some—including nut and fish allergies—are usually permanent.

If your toddler is diagnosed with a food allergy, you'll need to take steps to avoid the offending food. This may be relatively easy when you're cooking meals from scratch at home, but it can be a lot more challenging when you're buying packaged foods or eating out. You'll probably want to ask your doctor or public health nutritionist for a list of ingredients that could cause problems for your toddler; for example, not every product that contains wheat identifies it as such (wheat is sometimes identified as gluten). Note: If your toddler has a serious allergy such as a peanut allergy, you'll need to ensure that she carries injectable epinephrine. It could literally save her life in the event of an allergic reaction.

Food intolerances

A food intolerance is an adverse reaction to food that does not involve the immune system. If your toddler experiences such

FRIDGE NOTES

If you'd like to do some additional reading on food allergies and intolerances, you'll want to check out the Food and Nutrition Information Center's Resource List on Food Allergies and Intolerances. You can find it online at www.nal.usda.gov/fnic/pubs/bibs/gen/allergy.htm.

symptoms as bloating, loose stools, and gas after eating a particular food, she may have a food intolerance. Because it's easy to mistake some of the symptoms of a food intolerance with those of a food allergy, it's important to have food intolerances properly diagnosed.

Lactose intolerance is a common example of a food intolerance. A person with lactose intolerance lacks an enzyme needed to digest milk sugar. When she eats milk products, symptoms such as gas, bloating, and abdominal pain may occur.

We've covered a lot of material in this chapter: everything from coping with toddler-related food hang-ups to putting together toddler-friendly menus. If you've still got a ton of questions left, you'll want to hit some of the Web sites listed in Appendix C.

And now that we've wrapped up our discussion of toddlers and food, it's time to tackle another perennial hot topic: toddlers and sleep.

CHAPTER 7

Will the Sandman
Ever Come?

*"Kids need sleep and it's up to parents to help them
get it. Most parents wouldn't give in if their child
wanted to have potato chips for dinner each night, but
I know so many parents who let their children sleep
with them even though no one is getting much sleep."*
—LESLIE, 37, MOTHER OF TWO

*"People still have to parent their children at night;
it isn't a daytime-only thing. You can't close the
door and forget you have kids."*
—STEPHANIE, 30, MOTHER OF THREE

SLEEP DEPRIVATION MAY be a rite of passage for most parents, but that doesn't necessarily mean that we all see eye-to-eye on the subject of nighttime parenting. Some parents argue that parents should be every bit as responsive to their toddler's needs in the middle of the night as they are during the day, while others make the case that it's up to parents to help their toddlers develop healthy sleep habits, even if that means practising a little after-hours "tough love."

TODDLER TALK

While a typical newborn spends about 15.5 hours each day sleeping, by the time that baby celebrates his first birthday he'll be able to get by on about 14 hours of sleep each day—a full hour and a half less than he needed a year earlier.

In this chapter, we're going to tackle an issue that may be causing you to lose sleep—literally! We'll start out by looking at what's normal and what's not when it comes to toddler sleep patterns. Then we'll talk about naps, bedtime routines, and a range of different sleep challenges—everything from night waking to nightmares to night terrors. Finally, we'll talk about the art of moving a toddler from a crib to a bed or from the family bed to his own bed. (And, trust me, it truly can be an art.)

Toddlers and sleep

As WITH ANYTHING else toddler-related, there's no such thing as a "one size fits all" sleep pattern. Some toddlers need consid-

MOTHER WISDOM

Your toddler's need for sleep may be less than your own need for a break from the round-the-clock demands of parenting. While *you* may need your toddler to take a nap or head for bed early in the evening so that you can enjoy a brief time out, he may not necessarily need that much sleep. As Penelope Leach notes in her book *Babyhood*, "Sleep is ... a simple biological necessity and, like food, human beings will take it, in varying amounts which are adequate for them, if they are left to 'help themselves.'"

Now if only you could convince your toddler to hit the "sleep buffet" a little more often!

MOTHER WISDOM

Wondering if your toddler is getting the sleep he needs? As a rule of thumb, you can assume that your toddler is getting enough sleep if

- he wakes up on his own in the morning and after naptime;
- he tends to be in a good mood when he wakes up;
- he doesn't have any trouble staying awake in the car or the stroller when you're running short errands around town;
- he's alert and in good spirits in the late afternoon;
- he's calm and happy rather than grumpy and overtired when bedtime rolls around.

erably more sleep than the 12 to 14 hours that a "typical" toddler requires (see Table 7.1), while others seem to be able to survive on a whole lot less.

If your sleep schedule tends to correspond with your toddler's, the amount of time he spends sleeping may be a total non-issue for you. If, on the other hand, your toddler tends to catch up on his sleep at a time of day when you're not able to do the same, you may find yourself becoming positively obsessed by when he is—and isn't—sleeping. (Hey, it's hard to keep your cool when your sleep deficit is increasing by the day!)

TABLE 7.1

Average Sleep Needs of Toddlers

Age	Daytime Hours	Nighttime Hours	Total Hours of Sleep
1 year	2.5	11.5	14
1.5 years	2	11.5	13.5
2 years	1.25	11.75	13
3 years	1	11	12

To nap or not to nap?

IF YOU RELY ON your child's naps to catch up on your sleep or to attend to other responsibilities, I've got some bad news for you. Some really bad news, in fact! At some point during your toddler's second year of life, he'll go from taking two naps a day to one; and at some point during his third year of life, he'll give up that nap, too.

While your child is still taking naps, you'll want to encourage him to nap in his bed or in his crib so that he's able to make the connection between naptime and sleep. It's not a good idea to allow him to nap on the run (e.g., to simply fall asleep in the middle of the floor while he's playing with his blocks). He'll find it easier to wind down if you take him to the room in the house that he's learned to associate with sleep.

Most toddlers go through a difficult period each time they're ready to give up one of their naps. They may be wide awake at naptime, but extremely sleepy—and grumpy!—by late afternoon. You may find it helpful to encourage your toddler to enjoy a quiet activity around the time when he used to take his nap, and to schedule a more active activity for late afternoon so that he'll be less inclined to fall asleep on the spot. (Note: You'll want to steer clear of activities that require a trip by car, as that will almost certainly cause an overtired toddler to doze off.)

MOM'S THE WORD

"My husband and I have put a lot of energy into making sure that Lucy gets her regular naps. It makes a huge difference. If she gets her naps, she's always in a great mood. And it's good for us, too, because we get a little break."

—*Debbie, 33, mom of one*

MOM'S THE WORD

"If Talia fell asleep in the car when she was a toddler, she'd wake up and refuse to go to sleep when we got home. As a result, I'd end up driving home singing at the top of my lungs with the windows rolled down, trying to shake her foot from the front seat—all in an effort to keep her awake until we got home. I've never figured out how five minutes in the car could replace a two-and-a-half-hour nap, but that's how it seemed to work with her."

—*Maria, 32, mother of two*

Sometimes it's the parent rather than the toddler who decides the time has come to get rid of that afternoon nap. If you find that your toddler's daytime nap is interfering with the length of time he spends sleeping at night, you might want to pull the plug on that nap sooner rather than later. (Of course, some parents find quite the opposite to be true: A daytime nap helps to keep their child calm and happy, something that may help to promote better sleep at night. You may have to experiment a little to find out what works best for your toddler. To nap or not to nap? That is the question!)

Avoiding bedtime battles

BEDTIME BATTLES ARE a common problem for parents of toddlers. Studies have shown that approximately 50% of children between the ages of one and two regularly kick up a fuss at bedtime (something the sleep gurus euphemistically refer to as "bedtime refusal").

Unfortunately, these battles get played out at the time of day when you're most likely to be running low on energy, patience, and creativity. So what's an exhausted—and frustrated—parent to do? Why, pull out the ultimate parenting ace card, of course: your toddler's love of routine.

Bedtime routines

We've already talked about how much toddlers thrive on routine—and how freaked out they can be by even the most minute deviation from that routine. (Just try reading your toddler his bedtime story *before* rather than *after* his bath and you'll find out first-hand what I'm talking about!) Given that toddlers are such creatures of habit, it only makes sense to put that love of routine to work for you at bedtime. Here are a few tips:

- Come up with a standard bedtime routine that will signal to your toddler that it's almost time to go to bed. Toddlers are so excited about the world around them that they need time to make the transition between play time and sleep time. You should aim for a gradual wind-down that consists of some sort of predictable series of events—perhaps a snack followed by tooth-brushing, a quiet bath, soothing music, a story, and a quick cuddle. (Don't feel obligated to devote hours of your evening to carrying out this bedtime routine, by the way; sleep experts have found that a half-hour wind-down will do the trick for most toddlers.)

- When you're trying to decide what sort of snack to serve your toddler at bedtime, zero in on something light that includes both protein and carbohydrates. Cheese and crackers is one option: The carbohydrates will help to make him sleepy, and the protein will keep him from feeling hungry in the middle of the night. Don't go overboard with the bedtime snack, however, or your toddler may have trouble sleeping. If you give him a huge, heaping serving of spaghetti and meatballs, his digestive system may kick into overdrive, preventing him from getting the shut-eye that he (and you!) so desperately need.

- If your toddler finds his bath stimulating rather than soothing, you'll want to do his bath at another time of day. The last thing you want to end up with at bedtime is a toddler who's wide awake and ready for another hour or two of play! (Groan....)

- Try to work as many choices as possible into your toddler's bedtime routine. This will help to elicit his cooperation. While you won't want to flirt with disaster by giving him the choice of whether or not to go to bed, you're probably perfectly okay with letting him decide what toys he'd like to take in the tub, what pyjamas he'd like to wear to bed, and what bedtime stories he'd like you to read to him while you enjoy your pre-bedtime cuddle.

- Give your toddler the chance to get himself to sleep. Don't rock him to sleep or lay down beside him until he dozes off or he may awaken in a panic in the middle of the night when he realizes that you're not there. (Note: If you're already in the habit of rocking your toddler to sleep or laying down with him while he's getting to sleep, you'll want to wean him off this habit sooner rather than later. Toddlers who aren't able to get themselves to sleep are more prone to night waking than other toddlers.)

- Accept the fact that your toddler may need a period of quiet play before he's able to settle down for the night. You may hear him babbling to himself or quietly playing with his toys for a half-hour or even longer. Instead of sweating the fact that he didn't go to sleep right away, applaud the fact that he's mastering the art of getting himself to sleep—a skill that will reap tremendous dividends for him and for you.

MOTHER WISDOM

Don't be so rigid with your toddler's bedtime routine that you're afraid to move his bedtime up by a half-hour or so if he's showing signs of being sleepy. If he's yawning, rubbing his eyes or ears, playing with his hair, sucking his thumb, acting bored, or seems a bit clumsier than usual, he may need sleep.

Note: It's best to respond to these early warning signals of tiredness rather than allow your toddler to become extremely sleepy. If you wait too long before trying to put him to bed, he may end up getting his second wind—which can make it extremely challenging to get him to wind down for the evening. You'll also want to start teaching him to recognize these signs of tiredness for himself; that way, as he gets older, he'll be able to train his body to succumb to sleep as soon as the sandman comes calling.

- If you find that your toddler is having a great deal of difficulty settling down for the night, it could be because he isn't tired quite yet. You may want to try moving his bedtime back by an hour or two or to think about eliminating one or both of his naps.

- If your toddler seems panicked at the thought of being away from you, promise him that you'll come back if he needs you, and then make a point of responding to him right away when he calls. (Note: You may find yourself making a lot of treks to his room at first, but, over time, he'll feel less of a need to test your willingness to deliver on your promise. Or at least that's the theory!) You can also let him know that you'll be back to check on him in a few minutes' time and then again before you go to bed—something that may make it easier for him to go to sleep without you in the room.

Comfort objects

No chapter on toddlers and sleep would be complete without a mention of comfort objects (the term child development experts use to describe teddy bears, blankets, and other "lovies" that, along with mom and dad, may serve as an anchor in a toddler's world). Of course, not all experts use the exact same terminology here; others prefer the term "transitional object" or "security object." But whatever you call them, we're all talking about the same thing: inanimate objects to which a toddler forms an exceptionally strong attachment.

While most parents recognize that bonding with a comfort object is a sign of healthy emotional development, they may worry that their child's dependence on a teddy bear or other object may discourage him from becoming more independent. Actually, quite the opposite is true. Allowing your toddler to turn to his comfort object for reassurance whenever he needs it actually encourages great independence. After all, it's a whole lot easier to go to sleep by yourself if you've got your best friend (a.k.a. "Bunny") tucked under your arm.

Just one quick word of warning with regard to comfort objects. If your toddler needs a special stuffed animal or blanket in order to get to sleep at night, you may want to confine that object to your home. After all, if your child becomes distraught waiting for his special blanket to make it through the washer and dryer every now and again, imagine how much worse it would be if that blanket were to be lost forever. Christy has made it a rule that her toddler's special blanket never leave the house for any reason: "My son needs to have his blue blanket put over him in a particular way before he'll go to sleep," the 38-year-old mother of two explains. "There have been many nights when we've had to turn the house upside down looking for this blanket. At least I always know it's in the house, however, since

MOM'S THE WORD

"Sarah has a bunny that was given to her when she was a new-born. He's almost furless now (he wears a sweater), but I can't even imagine what would happen if he were lost. There has been the occasional night where he's been forgotten at daycare, the dentist, or at a friend's house. Bunny has even been transported by courier on occasion. Oh, the tears we've had about Bunny!"

—*Jennifer, 33, mother of one*

we don't allow him to take it anywhere. That would be too risky; we might lose it!"

By the way, you needn't worry that your toddler will want to take his prized bunny off to university with him or insist that it accompany him down the aisle on his wedding day. The vast majority of children outgrow their dependence on comfort objects long before they start school. So don't feel a need to take matters into your own hands by following the advice of well-meaning but misguided relatives who recommend that you "accidentally" drop Bunny over Niagara Falls or otherwise "lose" your child's comfort objects. Not only will you be prolonging his dependence on his beloved Bunny, but you could end up ringing up some rather hefty child therapy bills to boot! Or—even worse—you could find yourself confessing your sins to Dr. Phil on some future episode of *Oprah*!

Night waking

WHILE YOU MAY feel like the only parent on your street who's up in the middle of the night tending to the needs of a toddler, chances are you're in pretty good company. Approximately 30%

of parents with children between the ages of one and four report that their toddlers and preschoolers wake them up in the middle of the night at least three times each week, and 10% of parents with children in this age bracket report being awakened from their sleep at least twice each night. (No wonder so many parents with young children feel as if they're a shoo-in for a part in the next remake of *The Night of the Living Dead!*)

Chronic sleep deprivation can really take its toll on your energy and patience levels, to say nothing of your sex life, so if you're contending with an in-house night owl, you'll want to come up with creative strategies for catching up on your sleep. That might mean trading "night shifts" with your partner or lining up friends or relatives to come to your house so that you can squeeze in a late-afternoon or after-dinner siesta. It can also help to understand what causes toddlers to disrupt their parents' sleep night after night.

The causes of night waking

There are almost as many reasons for night waking as there are night-waking toddlers. Here's a quick run-through of some of the most common reasons for night waking:

- **Physical discomfort:** The physical discomfort associated with such medical conditions as teething, ear infections, allergies, pinworms, urinary tract infections, colds, and fevers can cause a toddler who was previously sleeping through the night to start waking in the night again.

- **Environmental factors:** If your toddler wets his bed or becomes uncomfortably hot or cold while he's sleeping, he's more likely to wake up in the middle of the night. Since toddlers are notorious for kicking off the covers midway through the night, you'll want to make sure your toddler gets tucked into bed in suitably warm pyjamas.

- **Developmental issues:** It's not unusual for a toddler to experience difficulty sleeping when he's just achieved a new developmental milestone like walking. He may be so excited about mastering this new skill that he finds it difficult to wind down at the end of the day, or he may be feeling frustrated if he's unable to immediately achieve a related skill—like climbing! Another developmental issue that can wreak havoc on his— and your—ability to sleep is separation anxiety. If your toddler can't bear being away from you for even 15 seconds during the daytime, he's bound to find it difficult to get through an entire night without you.

- **Emotional issues:** A toddler's sleep patterns can be thrown off track by a stressful event like a move to a new house, the birth of a new baby, or a recent hospital stay. The more sensitive your toddler, the more likely he is to have his sleep patterns disrupted by this sort of event.

- **Sleep problems:** If your child has not yet learned how to soothe himself back to sleep if he awakens in the night, he's likely to call for you. He's also likely to call out in the night if

---

TODDLER TALK

Approximately 60 to 70% of one-year-olds are capable of soothing themselves back to sleep if they wake up in the night.

---

he suffers from nightmares or night terrors. (We'll be talking more about these two sleep problems later in this chapter.)

Of course, it's one thing to understand what's causing your toddler to get up in the night, and quite another to devise strategies for coping with the situation. After all, It's pretty hard to come up with all kinds of creative solutions when you're suffering from chronic sleep deprivation! Here are a few tips on dealing with toddlers and night waking:

- Stop feeding your toddler in the night. If he's still waking up to eat or drink, it's time to get rid of that nighttime feeding. Most healthy toddlers should be able to obtain the nutrition they need during the daytime If you're still bottlefeeding, cut the feeding size back by an ounce a day or start offering water only in the middle of the night. If you're breastfeeding, try to cut back on the duration of feedings. Until you've eliminated the nighttime feeding, it's almost impossible to deal with the underlying sleep problem.

- Give your toddler a chance to settle himself if he wakes up in the night. If he's tossing and turning and muttering in his sleep, he may still be half-asleep and— if left undisturbed— may actually manage to get back to sleep on his own. Rushing to his room and picking him up may only add to your nighttime woes: instead of having a half-awake toddler, you'll have a wide-awake toddler on your hands. Of course, if he's crying or screaming, you'll want to check in on him right away to see if there's some sort of underlying problem. "As a parent, you know the difference between an 'I want attention' cry and a cry that comes out of a real need," says Stephanie, a 30-year-old mother of three. "The latter cries need to be attended to."

- Remind yourself that sleeping through the night is a skill that needs to be learned. Expecting your toddler to master this skill overnight will lead to endless frustration for you and for him. "Don't get into a power struggle with your kids about sleep," warns Karen, a 33-year-old mother of three. "It will only make them more determined not to go to sleep. Calmness and patience are definitely required."

- Don't feel pressured to try a sleep training method that flies in the face of your basic parenting values. If, for example, you feel quite strongly that it's important to be as responsive as possible to a toddler by day, the "cry it out" method of sleep training may feel very uncomfortable to you. "When my oldest was 18 months, we tried a modified crying-it-out method that consisted of responding after two minutes—the longest period of time she had ever cried without being responded to in her life," recalls Joan, a 35-year-old mother of five. "It worked in just three nights, but it felt wrong, like I was abandoning her and teaching her that she couldn't rely on my being there when she needed me. I decided against taking that

---

MOM'S THE WORD

"At one point, my husband was in the habit of tossing his bath towel up on the corner of the bathroom door so that it could dry after bathtime. This scared our son. He thought it was a monster when he got up to use the bathroom."

—Annie, 44, mother of one

MOM'S THE WORD

"Most adults I know don't sleep through the night, so I decided it was unreasonable of me to expect my children to sleep through. Besides, I remember what it was like when I was a child: how scary it was to wake up in the dark alone, hungry, thirsty, needing to pee, whatever, and I decided that just as an infant awakes with a need, a toddler likely does, too. Just because I don't fully understand what that need is doesn't make it any less important."

—*Joan, 35, mother of five*

approach with my other children." Maria had a similar experience with sleep training: "Ferber didn't work for us," the 32-year-old mother of two explains. "I would just end up sitting outside Talia's door crying while she sat on the other side of the door crying!"

- As your toddler gets a little older, try talking to him about the problem to see if you can negotiate some sort of sleep treaty. Hey, you've got nothing to lose but those bags under your eyes! "I sat down with Sophie and told her flat-out that I loved her, but I wouldn't be coming into her room when she called me in the middle of the night any more: I needed my sleep and so did she. It was that easy. She stopped calling out in the night, and we all slept," recalls Leslie, a 37-year-old mother of two.

- Come up with an incentive program to reward your child for staying in his bed all night. "We went through a phase when Sarah was about two and a half where she would crawl into our bed every night," recalls Jennifer, a 33-year-old mother of one. "It didn't bother me, but my husband couldn't sleep. He struggled with it for months. Then we decided to offer her a sticker to put on the calendar every night that she stayed in

TODDLER TALK

Some toddlers have a tendency to get up at the crack of dawn—sometimes even earlier than that! If you've got an early riser in your house, you might try to buy yourself a bit more sleep by pulling down the blind in her room so that it stays dark a little longer, encouraging her to crawl into bed with you for an early-morning snuggle, leaving a couple of special "morning-only toys" in her room for her to play with before she starts calling for you, and/or adjusting your own sleep schedule so that it more closely corresponds with hers.

---

her bed all night. And if she got seven stickers in a row, she got a toy on the weekend. Her patterns changed immediately! Eventually, she started staying in her bed without any stickers. I wish all parenting issues could be resolved this easily!"

- Remind yourself that this too shall pass—eventually. "We tried all kinds of things to get Talia to stay in her room when she woke in the night," recalls Maria, a 32-year-old mother of two. "We put a gate on her doorway so she could see out, but couldn't get out. We tried playing a radio, we tried running a fan for background noise, we moved her from a crib to a double mattress on the floor, we put on two layers of pyjamas rather than one so that she'd be warmer at night, we gave her a sippy cup of water in her room in case she was waking up because she was thirsty, we gave her a toy flashlight, we stopped letting her drink water at bedtime in case she was waking in order to empty her bladder. We even tried changing the settings on the thermostat so the furnace wouldn't kick in so frequently, in case that was what was waking her up! In the end, I think she just started sleeping through the night on her own."

Night terrors, sleepwalking, and sleep apnea

NOW THAT WE'VE covered most of the garden-variety sleep problems, it's time to zero in on a few of the more exotic types of sleep problems: night terrors, sleep walking, and sleep apnea.

Night terrors

While some parents use the terms "night terrors" and "nightmares" interchangeably, they're actually two entirely different things.

Nightmares occur during a period of light sleep (dream sleep). When a toddler is having a nightmare, he may be crying and screaming, but he can be easily woken up. All that may be required to get him back to sleep is a cuddle and a bit of reassurance that what happened in his dream wasn't real.

Night terrors, on the other hand, occur when a child is moving from a deep stage of sleep to a lighter stage of sleep. A toddler who is experiencing night terrors may let out a blood-curdling scream and then sit bolt upright in bed with his heart pounding, his body dripping with sweat, and his eyes wide open in a zombie-like state. He is completely unaware of his surroundings and—despite the fact that the episode may last as long as half an hour—he will have no memory of it in the morning. It's impossible to wake a toddler who is experiencing night terrors—nor would you want to: waking your child will only serve to prolong the episode. One thing you will want to do, however, is to stay with your child to prevent him from accidentally injuring himself.

Most children outgrow night terrors after about four years. During this period, the night terrors will tend to come and go, appearing most often when a child is overtired or agitated and when the child is between the ages of three and six.

MOM'S THE WORD

"Sarah is a sleepwalker. As near as we can tell, she's getting up to go to the bathroom, but because she's still asleep, she just wanders aimlessly. We keep an ear open and try to grab her and direct her to the right room before an accident happens."

—*Jennifer, 33, mother of one*

Sleepwalking

While sleepwalking is much more common during the pre-teen years (peaking at ages 10 to 12), it can also be a problem for toddlers. They may get out of bed, wander around aimlessly, and talk incoherently. Because sleepwalkers are totally unaware of danger, you'll want to ensure that you keep your doors and windows locked if you have a toddler who sleepwalks.

Note: Sleepwalking is more common in boys than in girls and is more likely to occur if a child tends to have problems with bedwetting. Studies have shown that sleepwalking can be avoided if parents get in the habit of waking their child up approximately 15 minutes before the time of night when sleepwalking tends to occur and then keeping their child awake for five minutes. This will prevent sleepwalking 80% of the time.

Sleep apnea

Approximately 1 to 3% of children suffer from obstructive sleep apnea syndrome, a condition that causes them to stop breathing for short periods of time. If left untreated, this condition can lead to neurological or behavioural problems, poor growth, and—in the most severe cases—heart damage. The symptoms of obstructive sleep apnea syndrome include snoring, difficulty breathing during sleep, mouth breathing during sleep, sleeping in unusual positions, a change in colour while sleeping, and chronic sleepiness or tiredness during the day. The condition can be treated with continuous positive airway pressure (a mask worn at night to deliver air through the nasal passages) or through the surgical removal of the tonsils and adenoids (a treatment method that cures 95% of cases of sleep apnea).

From crib to bed: When and how to do it

As ATTACHED AS your toddler may be to his crib, at some point he's going to outgrow it. Here are some tips that will help you to decide when and how to move your toddler from his crib to a bed:

- Be on the lookout for signs that your toddler may be physically ready to make the move from a crib to a bed—a move that most toddlers make around the time of their second birthday. As a rule of thumb, you should plan to make the switch before your toddler gets too tall for his crib. Ideally, the crib's side rails should fall below your toddler's mid-chest level—something that typically occurs when a toddler reaches approximately 90 centimetres (35 inches) in height. Something else to consider is how easy it is for your toddler to roll around in his crib. If he bumps into the sides of the crib each time he changes position, he may end up waking up quite frequently in the night—which can prevent the entire family from getting much sleep.

- Consider your timing carefully. You don't want to boot your toddler out of his crib the same week that you move to a new house or introduce a new sibling. Doing so would simply be asking for trouble! Instead, pick a time in his life that's relatively stress-free so that he won't have to focus on any other changes while he's busy getting used to his new bed.

- Decide what type of bed you intend to switch him to: a toddler bed (a miniature bed designed to hold a crib-sized mattress), a twin bed, or a mattress or futon on the floor. Note: A toddler bed can be used only for a short period of time, so most parents consider it to be an unnecessary frill, preferring to go with a twin bed or a mattress or futon on the floor instead.

- Give your toddler the opportunity to participate in the process of shopping for his new bed. You might encourage him to pick out some new sheets or ask him to help you put the new bed together.

- Make sure that you use a bed rail if you're moving your toddler to a twin bed. Otherwise he may be badly frightened if he tumbles out of bed in the middle of the night. And choose a safe location for your toddler's new bed—a spot that's away from windows, heating units, wall laps, drapery and blind cords, and other hazards. (Note: You'll find these and other important safety tips in Chapter 9.)

- Don't rush to take down the crib. "We moved Talia from her crib to her bed at 22 months," recalls Maria, a 32-year-old

---

MOM'S THE WORD

"I don't recommend buying a toddler bed. I find that a double mattress on the floor works better. That way, there's plenty of room for an adult to snuggle and read at bedtime or to actually sleep with the child if the child needs comfort."

—*Maria, 32, mother of two*

"We're expecting another baby in the summer and have decided to buy another bed for Brandon and put it beside our bed, making a giant bed. We didn't want to kick him out of our bed when the baby arrived, possibly causing jealousy. We're going to get him some special sheets and make a big deal out of him having his own bed, but we're still going to keep his bed next to ours until he's ready to move into his own room."

—*Julie, 30, mother of one*

mother of two. "The bed was in her room for about three weeks while she was still sleeping in her crib. At night, we would read in the bed and then put her to sleep in the crib. One night, we asked her if she wanted to sleep in the bed or in the crib, and she said 'bed.' There was no pressure for her to stay in the bed. If she had wanted to go back into the crib, we would have let her."

Getting out of bed

Once you move your toddler from a crib to a bed, you may find yourself with another major challenge on your hands—a toddler who refuses to stay in bed.

"My son started to climb out of his crib at about 20 months of age, so we moved him to a toddler bed," recalls Christy, a 38-year-old mother of two. "This just opened a new can of worms. For about three months, he would not stay in his bed. I'd sit in the hallway at the top of the stairs and keep putting him back to bed. I thought it would never end."

The best way to deal with a toddler who refuses to stay in bed is to nip the problem in the bud the moment it starts to occur; you need to let your toddler know kindly but firmly that it's

MOM'S THE WORD

"I've told my children that it's fine if they don't want to go to sleep, but they must stay in their beds. That way, they don't feel like they're being forced to go to sleep. This really helps to ease the tension."

—*Karen, 33, mother of three*

bedtime and he needs to stay in his room, and that if he can't manage to keep himself in his room, you'll have to close the door or put up the baby gate. (Of course, if your child is toilet trained and may legitimately need to come out of his room to use the bathroom, you'll have to find other creative ways of handling the problem—like camping out in the hall outside his room for a couple of hours each night until he realizes that you're serious about keeping him in his room for all but bathroom breaks.)

No matter what plan of attack you come up with for dealing with this common and frustrating problem, it's important to be consistent in your response from night to night. After all, your toddler won't know where you stand on the whole getting-out-of-bed issue if you enforce the rules only on nights when you can muster up the energy to play hall monitor!

MOM'S THE WORD

"I use what's called a 'bedtime pass' to keep my children in bed. Each child has a wallet with an old credit card of mine. It serves as 'credit' for a trip out of bed should they need one after lights out. They know it's only good for one outing on a particular night. Bathroom breaks aren't considered an outing, but other than that they have to hand over the pass if they get out of bed."

—*Loree, 31, mother of three*

Co-sleeping revisited

Many parents who enjoy co-sleeping with a baby aren't quite so keen about sharing their bed with a toddler—particularly if that particular toddler is prone to noctural gymnastics. Others are quite happy to continue to share their bed with their child through the toddler years and beyond. It's a very personal decision—one that each family needs to make for itself.

If you feel that the time has come for your toddler to make the move to his own bed, you'll want to plan for a gradual transition. You might try moving him to a mattress or futon in your room before you move him to his own room or into a room with a sibling. Obviously, you'll want to pay careful attention to your timing before you begin the process of "weaning" your toddler from the family bed to his new bed. You won't want to initiate the process at a time in his life when he's already dealing with a lot of other stress. As with anything else toddler-related, it's best to proceed gently and with love.

And now we come to the most important thing to remember about toddlers and sleep: this particular form of sleep deprivation is a limited-time offer. It won't be long before you have to tell your child to stop napping on the couch and get on with his chores—or face his wrath when you drag him out of bed before noon on a Saturday morning.

Yes, Virginia, you will sleep again....

CHAPTER 8

The Health Department

HILE YOU WON'T be trekking off to the doctor's office quite as often now that your child is a toddler, you can still expect to spend a fair bit of time sitting in waiting rooms reading year-old magazines. (Hey, it's one way to catch up on all the news stories you missed out on around the time of your baby's birth!)

In this chapter, we're going to be talking about toddlers and health. We'll discuss the importance of "well child" visits to the doctor, consider where Canadian health authorities stand on the immunization issue, talk about ways to tell if your toddler is sick, swap strategies for getting medication inside of (as opposed to merely in the general vicinity of) a toddler, look at the causes and treatments of the most common types of pediatric illnesses, swap some "insider tips" on dealing with a toddler's hospital stay, and much more. Here we go....

What's up, doc?

YOUR TODDLER'S DOCTOR will probably want to see her at 12 months, 18 months, two years, and three years, and—of course—

whenever any sort of health problem warrants an extra visit. These regular doctor visits play a critical role in helping to keep your toddler healthy by allowing the doctor to keep tabs on your her overall health and to quickly identify any conditions requiring treatment.

At each visit, your doctor will check your toddler's height and weight; give her a head-to-toe examination to ensure that she's continuing to develop normally; provide immunizations at the appropriate intervals (see the material on immunizations below); and ask you questions about her overall health. It's a fabulous opportunity to obtain answers to all your pediatric health questions, so you'll want to make sure to bring a list of them with you to each appointment.

Of course, while you may look forward to your visits with your child's doctor, she may be somewhat less enthusiastic about the whole process. Here are some tips on dealing with a toddler who seems well on her way to developing a full-blown case of white coat syndrome!

TODDLER TALK

While your toddler's doctor will make a point of screening her for eye problems during checkups, it's important to be on the lookout for evidence of any such problems yourself. You'll want to let the doctor know if her eyes wander in or out, her pupils are different sizes, her eyes don't seem to work together (e.g., she tilts or turns her head to one side so that she only has to use one eye or closes one eye entirely), she doesn't seem to be able to recognize distant objects or people, she squints frequently or seems to be particularly sensitive to light, or she has droopy eyelids.

Note: It's important to follow up on eye problems right away if you suspect there could be a problem. Certain types of vision problems—including crossed eyes and lazy eye—can lead to permanent vision loss if they aren't detected and treated early enough. That's why the Canadian Paediatric Society recommends that all children be screened for vision problems at or before age three to four years.

TODDLER TALK

Approximately 1 out of every 500 babies born in Canada is born with autism—a developmental disorder that is characterized by motor, sensory, cognitive, and behavioural dysfunctions. Autism is four times more common in boys than in girls and can be diagnosed during toddlerhood. The warning signs of autism include not speaking by age two; not maintaining eye contact; repeating and ritualizing certain words or movements; reacting intensely to certain sights, sounds, and feelings; not wanting to be swung or bounced; not wanting to climb; having limited interest in playing with toys or with other children; and not engaging in imaginative play.

A recent study at the University of Washington in Seattle indicated that autistic children may lack the ability to decode facial signals and pick up on other people's emotions. Researchers found that the brain activity of three- and four-year olds with autism did not change when they were shown photographs of faces depicting various emotions. Behavioural interventions that teach autistic children how to pay attention to facial cues are therefore very important in managing autism, according to the researchers involved in the study.

For more information on the diagnosis and treatment of autism, contact the Autism Society Canada at 1-866-874-3334 or info@autismsocietycanada.ca.

- Do a bit of prep work before your toddler's next doctor's visit. Talk to her about the important role that the doctor plays in helping to keep her healthy. You might find it helpful to pick up one of the many excellent children's books that talk about visits to the doctor's office. Or you might pick up a toy doctor's kit so that you and your toddler can talk about what each piece of equipment does. (Who knows? Maybe she'll allow you to flake out on the couch while she takes your temperature and checks your blood pressure!)

- Schedule your toddler's doctor appointments at her most cooperative time of day (assuming, of course, that she has one!) Some parents find that it's best to go first thing in the morning. Not only is your toddler likely to be well rested and well fed, but you may actually manage to avoid the midday "rush hour" at the doctor's office.

- Let your toddler know ahead of time what's on the agenda for a particular doctor's visit. It's not fair to spring an unexpected immunization on her at the last minute—or to try to convince her that the needle won't hurt. Instead, take the time to prepare her for the shot. Let her know that it's going to hurt for a minute, but that she'll be able to hold onto her favourite stuffed animal or special blanket while the doctor is giving her the needle.

- If your toddler is a bit skittish because she finds the doctor's office scary, try to find out what's at the root of the problem. It could be that she's put off by the idea of lying on the paper on the examining table—a problem you can easily solve by bringing a blanket or a towel from home. (Some toddlers become frightened by the noise the paper makes as they wriggle around.)

- Let the doctor know that your toddler is feeling a little nervous. She may want to go slow with her examination and involve you as much as possible in an effort to make it less scary.

- Praise your child for cooperating, even if you have to do a fair bit of spin doctoring to come up with anything positive to

---

TODDLER TALK

Toddlers start looking taller and thinner as they head into the preschool years, but this doesn't happen overnight. Most toddlers don't lose their sway-backed stance and pot-belly until sometime after their third birthday.

A typical toddler grows five inches and gains four to five pounds between ages one and two, and grows two to three inches and gains five pounds between ages two and three.

say about the visit. With any luck, she may be encouraged to try a little harder the next time around!

The facts on immunizations

WHILE THEY'VE BEEN the subject of much controversy over the years, immunizations continue to play a vital role in helping to protect children against disease—so vital, in fact, that both the Canadian Paediatric Society and the National Advisory Committee on Immunization have spoken out strongly in favour of the current practice of routinely immunizing Canadian children against a number of potentially life-threatening diseases.

How immunizations work

Immunizations help the body produce antibodies against a particular disease. Depending on the type of immunization, it may be injected or given orally. Still, as much as they've revolutionized pediatric health, they aren't always 100% effective. Studies have shown that up to 15% of children will fail to build up antibodies to a particular disease after receiving the appropriate immunization.

Here's what you need to know about the immunizations given to Canadian children. (See Table 8.1 for a schedule outlining when these immunizations typically occur.)

TODDLER TALK

Over 80% of Canadian children are immunized against diphtheria, pertussis, and tetanus, and over 95% are immunized against measles, mumps, and rubella. Approximately 1% of Canadian children cannot be immunized for specific medical reasons (e.g., a compromised immune system).

TABLE 8.1

Immunization Schedule for Canadian Toddlers

Toddler's Age	Diphtheria, Tetanus, Pertussis (Acellular) Vaccine	Inactivated Polio Vaccine	Haemophilus Influenzae Type B Conjugate Vaccine	Measles, Mumps, Rubella Vaccine	Tetanus and Diphtheria
two months	X	X	X		
four months	X	X	X		
six months	X	X	X		
12 months				X	
18 months	X	X	X	X (or at age four to six years)	
four to six years	X	X		X (or at age 18 months)	
14 to 16 years					X

Note: In some parts of Canada, infants are given three doses of the Hepatitis B vaccine. In other parts of the country, this vaccine isn't administered until early adolescence (ages nine to 13). There may be other slight variations to this schedule depending on where you live (e.g., in Ontario, there's a follow-up dose of inactivated polio at age 15 included with the tetanus and diphtheria shot).

TODDLER TALK

If the polio vaccine is administered orally rather than via injection, there is a slight risk (one out of every 2.4 million doses of the vaccine) that your child or another family member could develop polio. If you're concerned about this possibility, ask your doctor if it's possible to have your child receive an injection rather than an oral dose of the vaccine.

DTP-Polio-Hib

The DTP-Polio-Hib immunization provides protection against five different diseases:

- diphtheria (a disease that attacks the throat and heart and that can lead to heart failure or death);

- pertussis or whooping cough (a disease characterized by a severe cough that makes it difficult to breathe, eat, or drink and that can lead to pneumonia, convulsions, brain damage, and death);

- tetanus (a disease that can lead to muscle spasms and death);

- polio (a disease that can result in muscle pain and paralysis and death); and

- haemophilus influenzae type b (Hib) (a disease that can lead to meningitis, pneumonia, and a severe throat infection [epiglottis] that can cause choking).

While seizures occasionally occur after a child is given a DTP-Polio-Hib shot, the vast majority of children who experience some sort of reaction to the needle don't experience anything more serious than a fever that lasts for a day or two and increased fussiness or sleepiness.

Measles, mumps, rubella (MMR) vaccine

This vaccine provides protection against three diseases:

- measles (a disease that involves fever, rash, cough, runny nose, and watery eyes and that can cause ear infections, pneumonia, brain swelling, and even death);

- mumps (a disease that can result in meningitis—the swelling of the coverings of the brain and spinal cord—and, in rare cases, testicular damage that may result in sterility);

- rubella (a disease that can result in severe injury to or even the death of the fetus if it's contracted by a pregnant woman).

While most children who have the MMR vaccine experience few, if any, side effects (e.g., when such reactions occur, they tend to be limited to a rash or fever that develops six to ten days after the immunization or a swelling of the glands in the neck), some children react to the vaccine by developing a high fever that may lead to convulsions. This type of reaction is more common in

---

TODDLER TALK
Your toddler should not receive the MMR vaccine if she
- has a disease or is taking a medication that affects the immune system;
- has had a gamma globulin shot within the previous three months; or
- is allergic to an antibiotic called neomycin.

TODDLER TALK
While there have been some reports in the media about a possible link between the MMR vaccine and autism, there's no hard evidence to back up this theory. So this is one worry you can strike off your immunization worry list right away.

children who have reacted to a previous immunization or whose parents or siblings have experienced convulsions following an immunization. In rare cases, a child may develop meningitis (an infection of the fluid lining covering the brain and the spinal cord) or swelling of the testicles in response to the mumps portion of the vaccine.

Note: While the measles, mumps, and rubella vaccines are typically packaged together in a single injection, they can also be given separately—something to bear in mind if, for whatever reason, your child is not a good candidate for one of the individual vaccines.

About the chicken pox vaccine (Varivax)

Canadian parents now have the option of having their children immunized against chicken pox—a generally mild and non-life-threatening disease that can, in some cases, lead to a number of potentially serious complications, including pneumonia (an infection of the lungs) and encephalitis (an infection of the brain). Approximately 1,900 Canadian children are hospitalized each year as a result of such complications, and a few even die.

The chicken pox vaccine can be given to your toddler shortly after her first birthday (at the same time that the MMR vaccine is administered, but using a separate syringe and a different injection side). If you don't have the chicken pox vaccine given to your child at the same time, you'll have to wait for at least four more weeks before having the vaccine administered.

MOM'S THE WORD

"My oldest barely batted an eye when she got a needle. But with my youngest, it's murder each and every time."

—*Karen, 33, mother of three*

The chicken pox vaccine is not recommended for toddlers who are allergic to any of the vaccine compounds (including gelatin and neomycin); who have a blood disorder or any type of cancer that affects the immune system; who are taking medications to suppress the immune system; who have active, untreated tuberculosis; or who have a fever.

The chicken pox vaccine is 98% effective against the severe forms of chicken pox and has only minor side effects: redness, stiffness, soreness, and/or swelling at the immunization site; fatigue; fussiness; fever; nausea; and, in 7 to 8% of cases, a temporary outbreak of small bumps or pimples at the immunization site approximately one month after the child has been immunized. Some toddlers will develop a mild case of chicken pox (typically 50 spots or fewer as compared with the up-to-500 spots that can accompany a full-blown case of the chicken pox) one to two weeks after having the vaccine.

Note: While the cost of the vaccine is not covered by any provincial or territorial health plans, many private health insurance companies cover it.

About the Meningococcal-C vaccine (Menjugate)

The Meningococcal-C vaccine (Menjugate) is one of the newest vaccines. It was first approved for use in Canada in June of 2001. It protects children against the Neisseria meningitidis bacteria— a bacteria that can cause meningitis and blood infection and that is fatal in 10% of cases. Infants, toddlers, and individuals with certain types of health problems (e.g., immunodeficiencies such as HIV, sickle-cell disease, and those without a spleen) are particularly vulnerable to meningoccocal disease.

The recommended schedule for immunization with Menjugate is as follows:

Age at First Dose	Number of Doses	Schedule
2 to 4 months	3 doses	3 doses, one to two months apart
4 to 11 months	2 doses	2 doses, one to two months apart
12 months and older	1 dose	

Up to 50% of people receiving this vaccine will experience some mild pain and redness at the injection site or a fever, but no serious side effects have been reported. It can be given at the same time as other childhood vaccines as long as a separate incision site is used.

There is a fee for having this vaccine administered to your child— approximately $110 per dose.

About the Pneumococcal vaccine for children (Prevnar)

The Pneumococcal vaccine for children (Prevnar) is another brand new vaccine. It was first approved for use in Canada in June of 2001. It provides protection against Pneumoccocal disease—a disease caused by the Streptococcus pneumoniae bacterium. This bacterium is the most frequent cause of pneumonia, blood infection, sinusitis, and ear infection in children under the age of five.

Canada's National Advisory Committee on Immunization recommends Prevnar for all children age 23 months or less and all children ages 24 to 59 months of age with the following health conditions: sickle-cell anemia, no spleen or a malfunctioning spleen, HIV infection, chronic disease, immunodeficiencies. It is also recommended for children ages 24 to 59 months who spend four or more hours per week with at least two unrelated children (e.g., in a group daycare setting).

Prevnar can be administered along with all other childhood vaccines. The recommended schedule for dosage follows:

Age at First Dose	Number of Doses	Schedule
Birth to six months	4 doses	3 doses spaced two months apart and a booster at 12 to 15 months (must be given at least two months after the third dose)
Seven to eleven months	3 doses	2 doses spaced two months apart and a booster at 12 to 15 months (must be given at least two months after the third dose)
12 to 23 months	2 doses	2 doses two months apart
24 months to 59 months or older	1 dose	

The side effects of the Prevnar vaccine are relatively minor: 10 to 20% of infants under one year of age will experience pain and redness at the injection site as well as a fever; in children ages seven months to five years, up to 50% will experience pain and redness at the injection site and between 10% and 40% will experience a fever.

The approximate cost of this vaccine is $95 per dose.

How will I know if my child is sick?

Most first-time parents live in fear that they'll mistakenly assume their child's runny nose is caused by nothing more sinister than the common cold when, in fact, it's actually a symptom of some life-threatening disease. Just in case this is one of those

FRIDGE NOTES

Looking for a way to keep track of your toddler's medical information? Health Canada has produced a cheque register–sized Child Health Record that allows you to record a variety of information related to your toddler's health: the dates of her vaccinations and any medical tests she's had, details about any childhood illnesses and/or hospitalizations, important facts about allergies or other health concerns, and so on. You can request a copy for each child in your family by e-mailing Health Canada at childhealthrecord@hc-sc.gc.ca or by phoning your nearest Health Canada regional office.

---

things that has you tossing and turning in the middle of the night, allow me to reassure you.

As you've no doubt discovered over the past year, your "parent radar" is more highly developed than you might previously have believed. Mother Nature has "programmed" your toddler with a series of symptoms that are designed to tell you if she's developed some sort of illness. (They're not unlike the error messages that show up on your computer screen from time to time, alerting you to the fact that your computer is anything but happy. But unlike that nice, neat little text box, toddler-related "error messages" tend to be a whole lot messier.) You can expect your toddler to experience one or more of the following symptoms if she's doing battle with an illness:

Respiratory symptoms

- **Runny nose:** Your toddler's nose starts secreting clear, colourless mucus that may become thick and yellowish or greenish within a day or two. A runny nose is usually caused by a viral infection such as the common cold, but it can also be caused by environmental or food allergies or chemical irritations. Note: Your toddler should be checked by a doctor if the runny nose continues for longer than 10 days in order to rule out these causes and to check for the presence of a sinus infection.

- **Coughing:** Your toddler starts coughing because there's some sort of inflammation in the respiratory tract—anywhere from the nose to the lungs. Common causes of coughing include the common cold, allergies, chemical irritations (e.g., exposure to cigarette smoke), chronic lung diseases that may trigger coughing, or because she has inhaled an object that's causing her to cough.

- **Wheezing:** Your toddler makes wheezing sounds that are particularly noticeable when she's breathing out. Wheezing is caused by both the narrowing of the air passages in the lungs and the presence of excess mucus in those major airways (bronchi) or in the lungs, most often triggered by a viral infection. (The more rapid and laboured your child's breathing, the more serious the infection.) Note: There's no link between wheezing during early childhood and asthma later in life.

- **Croup:** Your toddler's breathing becomes very noisy (some toddlers become very hoarse and develop a cough that sounds like a seal's bark) and, in severe cases, her windpipe may

---

TODDLER TALK

Believe it or not, your child's endlessly runny nose may actually bode well for her future health. A recent German study indicated that children who have a series of minor infections early in life are less likely to develop asthma in later years. The researchers found that children who had two or more head colds before age one were only half as likely as their "healthier" counterparts to go on to develop asthma and, what's more, they were less likely to develop allergies.

actually become obstructed. (The more laboured and noisy your toddler's breathing, the more serious the airway obstruction.) Croup is caused by an inflammation of the windpipe below the vocal cords. See the section on treating croup later in this chapter.

Gastrointestinal symptoms

• **Diarrhea:** Your toddler's bowel movements become more frequent and/or their texture changes dramatically (e.g., they become watery or unformed). Diarrhea is often accompanied by abdominal cramps or a stomach ache and is triggered when the bowel is stimulated or irritated (often by the presence of an infection). It can lead to dehydration if it's severe or continues for an extended period of time, so you'll want to monitor your toddler for any possible signs of dehydration. Note: See the section on treating diarrhea later in this chapter.

• **Dehydration:** Your toddler has a dry mouth, isn't drinking as much as usual, is urinating less often than usual, and doesn't shed any tears when she cries. She may also be experiencing vomiting and/or diarrhea. Dehydration is triggered by the loss of body fluids and results in reduced circulating blood volume. It can occur quite rapidly in children with diarrhea, so you'll want to watch your toddler carefully if she's suffering from this problem—especially if she's also experiencing some vomiting. Signs that your toddler's dehydration may be severe include a weight loss of more than 5% of her weight; lethargic or irritable behaviour; sunken eyes; a dry mouth; an absence of tears; pale, wrinkled skin; highly concentrated urine (urine that is dark yellow rather than pale in colour); and infrequent urination. Note: See the section on dealing with dehydration later in this chapter.

- **Vomiting:** Your toddler begins vomiting. Vomiting is more common in children than in adults and tends to be less bothersome to children than adults (except, of course, the adults on clean-up patrol!). It can be caused by specific irritation to the stomach or, more commonly, is simply a side effect of another illness. It's generally only worrisome if your child vomits often enough to become dehydrated or if she chokes and inhales vomit. Note: See the section on managing vomiting later in this chapter.

Skin changes

- **Change in skin colour:** Your toddler suddenly becomes pale or flushed, or the whites of her eyes take on a yellowish or pinkish hue. She may have developed some sort of an infection, whether it be a systemic infection (e.g., stomach flu or jaundice) or a more localized variety (pink eye).

- **Rashes:** Your toddler develops some sort of skin rash. It could be the result of a viral or bacterial infection, or an allergic reaction to a food, medication, or other substance. Note: See the section on skin rashes later in this chapter.

Other symptoms

- **Behavioural changes:** Your toddler becomes uncharacteristically fussy and irritable, or sleepy and lethargic. It's possible that some sort of illness or infection is responsible for these changes to her usual behaviour.

- **Fever:** Your toddler's temperature is higher than normal, which often indicates the presence of an infection but that can also be caused by a reaction to an immunization or over-dressing your toddler. Note: See the discussion of fever below.

MOTHER WISDOM

Mother knows best—well, at least 75% of the time. Studies have shown that mothers who put a hand on their child's forehead can determine whether or not their child has a fever approximately three out of four times.

More about fever

BEFORE WE MOVE on to our discussion of the most common types of childhood illnesses, let's take a moment to talk about toddlers and fevers—a perennial cause of concern to parents.

Fever isn't the bad guy; the illness is

The first thing you need to know about fevers is that in and of itself it's rarely dangerous. Contrary to popular belief, brain damage due to a high temperature is extremely rare. In order for brain damage to occur, your toddler's temperature would have to shoot to about 107.6 degrees Fahrenheit (42 degrees Celsius) for an extended period of time. Fevers that are caused by an infection rarely manage to climb above 105 degrees Fahrenheit (40.5 degrees Celsius) unless a child is overdressed or in an extremely hot environment. So that's one fever-related worry you can strike off your list relatively easily.

Fever can, in fact, be a *good* thing, even though it can make your toddler (and consequently you) feel downright miserable for a while. The presence of a fever is usually a sign that your

TODDLER TALK

Fever can also be a sign of heat stroke—an important point to keep in mind on a hot day.

toddler's body is hard at work fighting off an infection (typically a common illness such as a cold, a sore throat, or an ear infection, but possibly something more serious). According to pediatrician Alan Greene, M.D., of DrGreene.com, most of the bacteria and viruses that cause infections in humans thrive at our normal body temperature, so one of the body's key strategies for defending itself is to elevate its temperature by a couple of degrees. Add the fact that fever helps to activate the immune system, boosting the production of white blood cells, antibodies, and many other infection-fighting agents, and you'll see that there's no need to sweat it when your child gets a fever. (Sorry, I couldn't resist that particular pun!)

This does not compute

Something else you need to know is that the height of the fever is not necessarily directly related to the severity of your child's illness. In other words, even though your child may have a relatively high fever, it's possible that she's only mildly ill. On the other hand, a child with a relatively low fever can, in fact, be quite ill, which is why it's important to pay attention to her other symptoms. Instead of getting hung up on the number on the thermometer—an easy trap to fall into, by the way—concentrate on how sick your child is acting and look for symptoms of any underlying infection. (See Table 8.2.)

What type of thermometer to use

If you've checked out the thermometer aisle at your local drugstore lately, you already know that there are dozens of different models on the market today—everything from old-fashioned glass thermometers (the Chevys of the thermometer world) to state-of-the-art ear thermometers (the undisputed Cadillacs—at least

TABLE 8.2

Common Illnesses That Can Cause a Fever

Symptoms	What Could Be Causing These Symptoms
Fever, cough, runny nose, trouble breathing, sore throat, sore muscles	Common cold, influenza, other respiratory infections
Fever, rash, sore throat, and/or swollen glands	Chicken pox or viral illness such as stomach flu
Fever, earache, discharge from ears, dizziness from pain	Ear infection
Fever, swollen glands, sore throat	Tonsillitis, streptococcal or viral infection, mononucleosis
Fever, nausea, vomiting, diarrhea, and/or cramps	Infectious gastroenteritis (viral or bacterial)

when it comes to price!). Fortunately, the decision about which thermometer to buy is relatively simple: The Canadian Paediatric Society recommends that parents of toddlers stick to using digital rather than glass thermometers, due to the risk of breakage.

How to take your toddler's temperature

You have two basic choices when it comes to taking the temperature of a young toddler: taking it rectally or taking an axillary temperature (under the armpit). Temperatures of children under four years of age should not be taken orally.

MOTHER WISDOM

If you decide to use a glass thermometer, make sure to either shake it or run it under cold water to bring its temperature down below 36°C (96.8°F). Otherwise, the reading may be inaccurate.

MOTHER WISDOM

Today's digital thermometers are every bit as accurate as the glass thermometers of yesteryear (the traditional gold standard). And, what's more, they offer a few additional advantages: they're faster to use; they beep when the maximum temperature has been reached; they're easier to read; and the same thermometer can be used for both oral and rectal temperatures.

Rectal temperatures tend to be the most accurate, but they aren't exactly the temperature-taking method of choice for either parents or toddlers. Here's what's involved in taking your toddler's temperature rectally:

- Place your child on her back with her knees bent over her abdomen.

- Coat the tip of the thermometer with water-soluble jelly and insert it about 2.5 centimetres (one inch) into your toddler's rectum.

- Hold the thermometer in place until the digital thermometer beeps to indicate that the final temperature reading has been obtained—something that typically takes about two minutes.

- Clean the thermometer thoroughly using soap and warm water.

- Keep in mind that rectal temperature readings tend to be about 0.5°C higher than temperatures taken orally: A "normal" range for a rectal temperature is 36.6 to 38°C (97.9 to 101°F).

Axillary temperatures (temperatures that are taken under the armpit) tend to be slightly less accurate, but they're much easier to take. Here's what's involved:

- Place the bulb of the thermometer under your toddler's arm so that it's nestled in her armpit, and then hold her arm against her body so that the bulb is thoroughly covered.

MOTHER WISDOM

Avoid using fever strips (strips that are placed on a child's forehead to take her temperature). According to the College of Family Physicians of Canada, they aren't sufficiently accurate. You'll also want to hold off on using a tympanic (ear) thermometer on your toddler until after her second birthday. These types of thermometers are only recommended for use with children over the age of two due to concerns about the quality of the readings they produce when they're used on younger toddlers.

- Hold the thermometer in place until it beeps to indicate that the final temperature reading has been obtained—something that typically takes about two minutes.

- Clean the thermometer thoroughly using soap and warm water.

- Keep in mind that axillary temperature readings tend to be about 0.3°C lower than temperatures taken orally: A "normal" range for an axillary temperature is 34.7 to 37.3°C (94.5 to 99.1°F).

What you need to know about febrile convulsions

Febrile convulsions (seizures) tend to occur when a toddler's temperature shoots up very suddenly. They are more common in infants than in older children, and are more likely to occur in families with a history of febrile convulsions. They occur in approximately 4% of children.

While febrile convulsions are relatively common and generally quite harmless, they can be extremely frightening to watch. If your toddler has a febrile convulsion, she may breathe heavily, drool, turn blue, roll her eyes back in her head, and/or shake her arms and legs uncontrollably.

If your toddler has a febrile convulsion, you should lie her on her back or side (ensuring that she's far away from anything she could hurt herself on) and then gently turn her head to one side so that any vomit or saliva can drain easily. You should note how long the convulsion lasts—anywhere from ten seconds to three to four minutes—and then try to prevent a recurrence by taking steps to bring down your toddler's temperature. (See the tips on managing your child's fever later in this chapter.)

When to call the doctor

While most fevers are harmless, you should plan to get in touch with your toddler's doctor if

- your toddler's fever is very high for a child her age (your one-year-old has a temperature above 38°C or 101°F and your two-year-old has a temperature above 39°C or 102.2°F) regardless of whether or not she actually appears to be very ill (see Table 8.2);

- your toddler has had a fever for a couple of days and her temperature is not coming down;

- she's crying inconsolably or seems cranky or irritable, or she's whimpering and seems weak;

- she's having difficulty waking up or seems listless and confused;

- she's limp;

- she's having convulsions (if she turned blue during the seizure, had convulsions that lasted more than a few minutes, had difficulty breathing after the seizure passed, or still seems drowsy or lethargic an hour later, seek emergency medical assistance);

- the soft spot (fontanel) on her head is beginning to swell;

- she appears to have a stiff neck or a headache;

- she's acting as if she's experiencing stomach pain;

- she has purple (not red) spots on the skin or large purple blotches (possible signs of meningitis, an infection of the brain);

- she has developed a skin rash;

- she is noticeably pale or flushed;

- she's having difficulty breathing (a possible sign of asthma or pneumonia);

- she's looking or acting very sick;

- she's refusing to drink or nurse;

- she has constant vomiting or diarrhea;

- she's unable to swallow and is drooling excessively (a possible sign of epiglottitis, a life-threatening infection that causes swelling in the back of the throat);

- you know that she has a weakened immune system.

Treating a fever

Of course, it's not necessary to rush off to the emergency ward every time your toddler's temperature shoots up by a degree or two. The majority of fevers can be managed at home. Here's what you need to know:

TODDLER TALK

Don't expect your doctor to prescribe an antibiotic to ward off your child's fever unless there's a specific underlying infection that requires treatment. According to the Canadian Paediatric Society, the vast majority of children with fevers have non-bacterial (viral) upper respiratory infections that don't require antibiotics. That means your first-line of defence against fever is likely to be none other than acetaminophen.

TODDLER TALK

While American parents have the choice of using either acetaminophen or ibuprofen to treat fevers in young children, acetaminophen is
the drug of choice for Canadian children under the age of two. The Canadian
Paediatric Society does not routinely recommend the use of ibuprofen in
children under the age of two because there's less data available to demonstrate the safety of administering this drug to young children. Here's what
the Canadian Paediatric Society says in its April 2000 position paper on the
subject: "Given the substantially greater volume of safety data available for
[acetaminophen], it remains the first choice for therapy, while ibuprofen
should be reserved for more problematic cases."

- The best way to treat a fever—assuming, of course, that it
  actually needs to be treated at all—is by administering acetaminophen—an analgesic that helps to bring down your child's
  fever while relieving some of her discomfort. (Note: See Table
  8.3 for a complete list of items that should be in the family
  medicine chest during the toddler years.)

- It's dangerous to exceed the recommended dose of acetaminophen, so make sure that you use a medication syringe
  or dropper to measure your child's dose and that you stick to
  the recommended schedule for administering the medication
  (every four to six hours, but no more than five times in any
  24-hour period, according to the College of Family Physicians
  of Canada). You should also check to see if any of the other
  cough or cold medications that your child is taking contain
  acetaminophen.

- If your toddler spits up within minutes of taking her acetaminophen, ask your doctor if you should repeat the dose. It
  generally takes between 30 and 45 minutes for a medication to
  be absorbed by the intestines. But if the medication has been
  in your child's stomach for more than a few minutes, don't risk

TODDLER TALK

A study reported in the *Archives of Pediatrics and Adolescent Medicine* found that 43% of parents and caregivers gave the children in their care the wrong dose of acetaminophen.

Studies have shown that giving a child twice the recommended dose of acetaminophen over a period of days can be toxic. If your child becomes nauseated, starts vomiting, and experiences some abdominal pain, you should try to determine whether or not she might have been given too much acetaminophen.

TABLE 8.3

Medicine Chest Essentials

Keep the following items on hand at all times so that you'll have them in the event of illness or injury:

→ acetaminophen

→ adhesive tape

→ antibiotic ointment

→ antiseptic solution

→ bandages

→ cotton balls

→ flashlight

→ gauze

→ hydrogen peroxide

→ ice packs (the instant type that don't require refrigeration)

→ infant dropper or medicine syringe

→ ipecac syrup or activated charcoal (to induce vomiting in certain situations when a child has been poisoned)

→ nail clippers (toddler-safe type)

→ nasal aspirator

→ nose drops (saline)

→ oral electrolyte solution (to prevent dehydration)

→ poison control hotline phone number

→ Q-Tips

→ scissors (blunt ended)

→ thermometer (digital)

→ tongue depressors

→ tweezers

giving her a double dose. It's simply too difficult to determine how much of the original dose she managed to keep down.

- You can find some other helpful tips on administering medication to a toddler in Table 8.4.

- Give your toddler plenty of fluids in order to help bring her body temperature down and to help protect against dehydration.

- Avoid overdressing your child. Instead, dress her in loose, lightweight cotton clothing with only a sheet or light blanket for covering.

- Keep your toddler's room cool, but not cold. If she gets too cold her body will start shivering, which will cause her body temperature to rise.

- You can also try to lower your child's temperature by sponging her down with lukewarm water (a sponge bath) or giving her a lukewarm bath. (Don't use cold water or she'll start shivering.) Instead of drying her off, let the water evaporate from her skin. This will help to cool her down. Whatever you do, don't add alcohol to the water in the mistaken belief that this will somehow help to bring down your toddler's temperature. Doing so could lead to serious—even life-threatening—complications.

TABLE 8.4

Administering Medication to a Toddler

Forget about the spoonful of sugar; what it really takes to get the medicine down is proper technique. Here are tips on administering some of the types of medication that your doctor might prescribe for your toddler:

Oral medications:

→ Use a syringe or an oral dropper to administer medication. A spoon is too awkward to use; you and your toddler will both end up wearing the medication.

→ Slowly squirt the medication into the area between the toddler's tongue and the side of her mouth, pausing between squirts so that she has a chance to swallow. Otherwise, she'll start to gag and spit the medication out, and you'll be back at square one.

→ Avoid squirting the medication into the back of your toddler's throat or you'll trigger her gag reflex. And try to avoid hitting the taste buds at the front and centre of your toddler's tongue. (Should the medication not meet with her exacting standards for taste, she'll use her tongue to push it right back out!)

→ Avoid adding any sort of medication to a glass of milk or bowl of cereal. If your child wants only part of her milk or her cereal, she'll miss out on some of the medication. If you absolutely have to mix it with some sort of food because she refuses to take it any other way, make sure to use a very small amount of food or liquid—a quantity that you know your child will have no trouble eating or drinking.

→ Let your doctor know if your child vomits repeatedly after taking a particular medication or if she has a stomach flu that makes it impossible for her to keep anything down. Your doctor might decide to prescribe an injection or suppository instead.

→ If you miss a dose, administer the next dose as soon as you remember. Then add the missed dose to the end of the course of medication. Don't double up on doses unless your doctor specifically tells you to do so; and be sure to get in touch with your doctor if your child ends up missing an entire day's worth of medication.

Ear drops:

→ Lay your child down.

→ Remove any medication that may have built up on the outer ear as a result of past treatments before you administer the next dose.

→ Turn your toddler's head to one side and gently pull the middle of the outer ear back slightly. This will allow fluid to enter the ear canal more readily.

Eye drops/ointments:

→ Gently pull down the lower lid of your toddler's eye and apply the ointments or administer the drops. Don't allow the dropper or the tube to touch your toddler's eye or it may become contaminated. (Just to be on the safe side, wipe the dropper or the tube with a tissue once you're finished doing the treatment.)

Skin ointments or creams:

→ Apply some of the ointment or cream to a tissue.

→ Using the tissue, apply the ointment or cream to your child's skin. To reduce the chances of contaminating the ointment or cream, discard the used tissue and use a fresh one if more ointment or cream is required

MOTHER WISDOM

Don't rely on your memory when administering your toddler's medications. It's easy to make mistakes. That's why it's a good idea to get in the habit of writing down the time that the medication was given and the dose administered. (This is particularly important if more than one person will be responsible for administering the medication.) And if you're likely to forget to give your child her medication, set the alarm on your watch to go off the next time she's due for a dose.

Coping with common childhood illnesses and infections

WHILE THERE ARE literally hundreds of illnesses and conditions that can occur during early childhood, we aren't going to be able to touch on each and every one in this chapter. Due to space constraints, I had to limit myself to the more common ones—pediatric medicine's "greatest hits," so to speak! If you'd like to find out about an illness that isn't covered here, you might want to visit one of the many excellent pediatric health Web sites listed in Appendix C.

Respiratory and related conditions

Condition: Allergies

Cause: Allergies can be caused by pollens, animal dander, moulds, dust, and other substances.

Signs and symptoms: A clear runny nose and watery eyes, sneezing fits, constant sniffing, nosebleeds, dark circles under the eyes, frequent colds or ear infections, a cough that is bothersome at night, a stuffy nose in the morning, and/or noisy breathing at night.

What you can do:

- Eliminate or limit exposure to the substances that seem to trigger your toddler's allergies.
- "Allergy-proof" your toddler's room by using allergy-proof zippered covers, purchasing non-allergenic bedding, removing stuffed animals from your toddler's room, removing all room deodorizers, vacuuming the mattress and washing all of your toddler's bedding at least once every two weeks, avoiding plush carpet (if possible), keeping your toddler's windows closed during allergy season, investing in a high-efficiency particulate remover (HEPA) filter, and vacuuming your toddler's room only when she's away from it (since vacuuming tends to stir up

---

TODDLER TALK

According to the Canadian Institute of Child Health, approximately one-third of toddlers who are hospitalized during the first year of life are admitted as a result of respiratory problems.

MOTHER WISDOM

Here are some important questions to ask your doctor or pharmacist when she prescribes a medication for your child for the very first time:

- How will this medication help my child?
- What is the correct dosage?
- Do I need to shake the bottle before administering the medication?
- How often do I need to give my child the medication? Does it have to be administered at a particular time of day?
- How long does my child have to take the medication? Will the prescription be repeated or is this a one-shot deal?
- Should the medication be taken on a full or empty stomach?
- Are there any foods or drinks my child needs to avoid while taking this medication?
- Should the medication be stored in the refrigerator or at room temperature?
- Is it necessary to wake my toddler in the night to administer this medication?
- Are there any side effects to this medication that I need to know about?
- Is there any chance that my child could have an allergic reaction to this medication? If so, what warning signs should I watch out for?

---

dust). One final tip: If you haven't done so already, make your home smoke-free. The last thing a toddler with allergies needs is to be exposed to smoke on a regular basis.

- Keep your child comfortable by treating her symptoms (e.g., using a nasal aspirator to clear her nose). You might want to ask your doctor if your toddler would benefit from taking a decongestant or an antihistamine.

Condition: Asthma (a lung condition that affects the bronchial tubes)

Cause: Most commonly triggered after a viral respiratory infection inflames the lining of the bronchial tubes in the lungs. Asthma can also be caused by an irritant such as cigarette smoke or paint fumes; allergens such as pollens, mould spores, animal danders, house dust mites, and cockroaches; inhaling cold air; and certain cough medications. In some older children, exercise may also be a trigger for asthma.

Signs and symptoms: Coughing and/or high-pitched wheezing or whistling as your toddler breathes. The cough typically gets worse at night or if your toddler comes into contact with an irritant such as cigarette smoke. In cases of severe asthma, your toddler's breathing may become very rapid, her heart rate may increase, and she may vomit; or she may become very tired and slow-moving and cough all the time (in which case she requires immediate medical attention).

What you can do:

- Try to eliminate anything that could be triggering your toddler's asthma problems, including such irritants as cigarette smoke and any allergens.
- Work with your doctor to come up with a game plan for preventing and treating future asthma attacks through medication and/or lifestyle modifications.

Condition: Bronchiolitis (an infection of the small breathing tubes of the lungs; not to be confused with bronchitis, which is an infection of the larger, more central airways)

Cause: Caused by a virus that results in swelling of the small bronchial tubes. It is typically picked up as a result of being exposed to someone with an upper respiratory tract illness. Bronchiolitis is most common in children under the age of two and is most likely to occur during the winter months. Note: According to the American Academy of Pediatrics, almost half of toddlers who develop bronchiolitis will go on to develop asthma later in life.

Signs and symptoms: Triggered by a virus that results in swelling of the bronchioles, which in turn leads to reduced air flow through the lungs. It initially starts out like a normal cold with a runny

nose and sneezing, but after a couple of days, a toddler with bronchiolitis starts coughing, wheezing, and having trouble breathing.
Your toddler may also be irritable and may experience difficulty
eating due to the coughing and breathing problems.

What you can do:

- Keep your toddler comfortable by using a nasal aspirator or
  a vaporizer. (Just make sure that you clean the vaporizer on
  a regular basis—ideally once or twice a week—to prevent it
  from becoming a breeding ground for bacteria.)
- Watch for signs of dehydration, since toddlers with bronchiolitis can become dehydrated.
- Get in touch with your doctor to find out whether any additional treatment may be required. Some toddlers who have a
  lot of difficulty breathing may require medication to open the
  bronchial tubes. A few will also need to be hospitalized so that
  oxygen and fluids may be administered until the toddler's
  breathing improves.

Condition: Common cold
Cause: Spread from person to person via airborne droplets containing the cold virus or via contaminated hands and/or objects
(e.g., toys). It is most contagious from one day before to seven
days after the onset of symptoms, which helps to explain why
your toddler managed to pick up a cold at playgroup even
though every child in the room appeared to be the absolute picture of health!
Signs and symptoms: Runny nose, sore throat, cough, decreased
appetite. May be accompanied by a fever, in which case your
child may also experience muscle aches and/or a headache. While
a cold typically lasts for five to seven days in an adult, children's
colds tend to drag on a little longer—bad news, I know, if your
toddler is waking up every hour on the hour, enraged because her
nose is clogged up!

TODDLER TALK

According to the Canadian Paediatric Society, there are more than 200 viruses that cause colds. Unfortunately, being infected by a particular virus once doesn't provide you with any protection against getting that virus again—something that goes a long way toward explaining why the common cold is so, well, *common!*

What you can do:
- Keep your toddler comfortable. You might want to clear out her runny nose by using a nasal aspirator or—if her nose is really stuffed up—by placing a vaporizer in her room. (Note: Be sure to clean the vaporizer frequently to prevent it from becoming a breeding ground for bacteria.)
- Keep your toddler's face clean. Infections of the face can occur as a result of prolonged exposure to nasal secretions, and your toddler could end up with yellow pustules or wide, honey-coloured scabs (impetigo).
- Expect feedings to take a little longer when your toddler has a cold, and don't be surprised if she ends up drinking less than she normally does. She may have difficulty nursing or drinking from a bottle if her nose is really stuffed up, which can quickly result in a hungry, gassy, unhappy toddler.
- Get your doctor's go-ahead before administering any sort of cold medication to your toddler. According to the Canadian Paediatric Society, nose drops and sprays tend to be ineffective in children and can, in fact, make nasal congestion even worse. Oral decongestants also tend to be ineffective and can result in rapid heartbeat or insomnia. Antihistamines are not effective for colds. The only medication that may be worth administering is a cough syrup that contains dextromethorphan (DM) to treat a frequent, dry, hacking, non-productive cough—but before you go this route, check with your doctor

or pharmacist to ensure that the product you're intending to give your child is a suitable choice.

- Watch for signs that your child's cold could be developing into something more serious. You'll want to get in touch with your doctor if she develops an earache or a fever over 39°C (102.2°F); if she becomes exceptionally sleepy, cranky, or fussy; if she develops a skin rash; if her breathing becomes rapid or laboured, or if her cough becomes persistent or severe.

Condition: Croup, or laryngotracheitis (an inflammation of the voice box or larynx and windpipe or trachea)

Cause: Usually caused by a viral infection in or around the voice box. Children are most susceptible to croup between six months and three years of age. As children get older, their windpipe gets larger, so swelling to the larynx and trachea is less likely to result in breathing difficulties. There are two types of croup: spasmodic croup (which comes on suddenly and is caused by a mild upper respiratory infection or allergy) and viral croup (which results from a viral infection in the voice box and windpipe and which may be accompanied by noisy or laboured breathing—a condition known as "stridor").

Signs and symptoms: A cough that sounds similar to a seal-like bark and/or a fever.

What you can do:

- Keep your toddler comfortable by using a cool-mist vaporizer in her room; by filling your bathroom with hot steam from the shower and then letting her breathe in the moist vapours; or by taking her for a walk in the cool night air.
- Get in touch with your doctor if the croup seems to be particularly severe or if your toddler shows the following types of symptoms: fever higher than 39°C (102°F); rapid or difficult breathing; severe sore throat; increased drooling; refusal to swallow; and/or discomfort when lying down.

Condition: Ear infections (otitis media)

Cause: Caused by a virus and/or bacteria, and typically occur in the aftermath of a cold. Because a child's Eustachian tube (the tube that connects the middle ear to the back of the nose) is very short and very narrow, children are highly susceptible to ear infections. In fact, three-quarters of children will have at least one ear infection by the time they reach age three. Ear infections cannot be spread from one child to another.

Signs and symptoms: Fussiness and irritability, difficulty sleeping (because lying down tends to increase ear pain), difficulty nursing or drinking from a bottle (because sucking and swallowing can result in painful pressure changes in the middle ear), difficulty hearing (e.g., your toddler stops responding to certain types of sounds), fluid draining from your toddler's ear, and fever and cold symptoms. Note: If there is pus coming from your toddler's ear, this means that her eardrum has burst—something that will require treatment with antibiotic drops and/or oral antibiotics.

TODDLER TALK

Certain toddlers are more susceptible to ear infections than others. According to the College of Family Physicians of Canada, a toddler is more likely to develop an ear infection if she's exposed to cigarette smoke, has had one or more ear infections in the past (particularly if those infections occurred before her first birthday), is formula-fed rather than breast-fed, attends daycare, or was born prematurely or was a low-birth-weight toddler, and if the toddler is male. And, as if that weren't enough to wrap your head around, a recent study indicates that toddlers who use pacifiers face an increased risk of ear infections. Not only can pacifiers be breeding grounds for germs (trust me, you don't want to know where the average toddler's soother has been), some experts believe that the constant sucking motion associated with using a pacifier may cause fluid to be pulled from the nose and throat into the middle ear. (Yuck!)

TODDLER TALK

Not everyone agrees that antibiotics should be prescribed for children with uncomplicated ear infections. A recent study sponsored by the Agency for Healthcare Research and Quality (AHRQ) revealed that almost two-thirds of children with garden-variety ear infections recover from pain and fever within 24 hours of diagnosis without any treatment and that over 80% recover spontaneously within one to seven days. (When children are treated with antibiotics, 93% recover within the first week.)

What you can do:

- Keep your toddler comfortable by treating her fever and cold symptoms (see earlier sections of this chapter) and by offering her acetaminophen to treat her earache.
- Get in touch with your doctor to arrange for your toddler's ears to be checked. Your doctor may want to prescribe an antibiotic to clear up the infection. (Note: In most cases, there's no need to rush off to the emergency ward in the middle of the night to seek treatment for an ear infection. Simply treat your toddler's pain with acetaminophen during the night and then call your doctor's office in the morning to set up an appointment to have your toddler's ears checked.)
- Even if your toddler's ear infection has already been diagnosed by a doctor, you should call your doctor's office again if she develops one or more of the following symptoms: an earache that worsens even after she's on antibiotics, a fever that's greater than 39°C (102°F) after treatment begins or a fever that lasts more than three days, excessive sleepiness, excessive crankiness or fussiness, a skin rash, rapid or difficult breathing, or hearing loss.
- See that your child's ears are checked again after she's finished the antibiotic to ensure that there's no fluid remaining in her

ear. (Fluid in the ear can lead to further infections and/or hearing problems down the road.) Note: If your child has recurrent problems with ear infections, your doctor may recommend that she stay on antibiotics for a long period of time to prevent ear infections from developing. Or, he might recommend that myringotomy tubes be inserted in your child's ears to help balance the pressure between the middle ear and the ear canal and allow the fluid that accumulates in the middle ear to drain. These tubes are inserted while your child is under general anaesthetic and generally stay in place for six to nine months, at which point they typically fall out on their own. Some children need a second set of tubes.

Condition: Influenza
Cause: Caused by a respiratory virus that is spread from person to person via droplets or contaminated objects.
Signs and symptoms: Fever, chills, and shakes; extreme tiredness or fatigue; muscle aches and pains; and a dry, hacking cough. (It's different from the common cold in that a toddler with the common cold only has a fever, a runny nose, and a small amount of coughing.)

TODDLER TALK

Some toddlers develop a painful infection known as "swimmer's ear." It occurs in the delicate skin of the outer ear canal. The condition is caused when frequent exposure to water allows bacteria and fungi to grow. A toddler will typically experience itching followed by a swelling of the skin of the ear canal and then some drainage. A toddler with "swimmer's ear" will experience extreme pain when the ear lobe or other outside parts of the ear are touched. The condition is treated with eardrops containing antibiotics and/or corticosteroids to help fight infection and reduce the amount of swelling in the ear canal. Your child's doctor may also recommend that you give her an over-the-counter pain relief medication to help relieve her discomfort.

What you can do:
- Keep your toddler comfortable by treating her fever and cold symptoms (see relevant sections above).

Condition: Pink eye (conjunctivitis)
Cause: Spread from person to person as a result of direct contact with secretions from the eye. It can also be triggered by excessive eye rubbing, allergies, or by viruses or bacteria. Pink eye is contagious for the duration of the illness or until 24 hours after antibiotic treatment has been started.
Signs and symptoms: Redness, itching, pain, and discharge from the eye.
What you can do:
- Get in touch with your doctor to see if antibiotic eye drops should be prescribed (e.g., if your child's eye discharge is yellowish and thick).
- Keep your child away from other people until the antibiotic eye drops have been used for at least one full day.

Condition: Pneumonia (infection of the lung)
Cause: Spread from person to person via droplets or by touching contaminated objects. The infectious period varies according to the cause. Pneumonia can be caused by both viruses and bacterial infections.
Signs and symptoms: Rapid or noisy breathing, possibly accompanied by a cough and/or flaring of the nostrils, pale or bluish skin colour; shaking or chills; high fever; decreased appetite and energy.
What you can do:
- Get in touch with your doctor so that the cause of the pneumonia can be determined and an appropriate course of treatment can be mapped out. Viral pneumonias are typically treated with acetaminophen (for fever) and bronchodilators

(to minimize wheezing). Bacterial pneumonias, on the other hand, respond better to treatment that involves antibiotics, fluids, and humid air.

- Monitor your child's symptoms carefully if she's being cared for at home and report any changes in her condition to her doctor. Your child may require emergency assistance if she's having difficulty breathing.

Condition: Respiratory syncytial virus (RSV)
Cause: A virus with an incubation period of five to eight days.
Signs and symptoms: A raspy cough, rapid breathing, and wheezing.
What you can do:
- Keep your toddler comfortable by using a nasal aspirator or a vaporizer.
- Watch for any signs of dehydration.
- Get in touch with your doctor to talk about treatment options. Some toddlers who have a lot of difficulty breathing may require medication to open the bronchial tubes. A few will also need to be hospitalized so that oxygen and fluids can be administered until the toddler's breathing improves.

Condition: Strep throat
Cause: Strep throat is a bacterial infection. It is transmitted via droplets or by touching contaminated objects and is contagious until 24 to 36 hours after the start of antibiotic treatment. Fortunately, strep throat is more common in children over the age of three, so hopefully this is one infection your toddler won't have to deal with during her first year of life.
Signs and symptoms: Sore throat, fever, swollen glands in the neck. (Note: If a skin rash is also present, the condition is known as scarlet fever.)

TODDLER TALK

Antibiotics are powerful medications that can be used to treat life-threatening illnesses like meningitis as well as less serious infections such as impetigo. Because they're so effective, they tend to be used widely, which has unfortunately led to the emergence of antibiotic-resistant strains of bacteria. You can do your bit to prevent these strains of bacteria from becoming more of a problem by ensuring that you follow your doctor's instructions for antibiotic use carefully and that your child finishes taking any antibiotic she starts.

What you can do:

- Get in touch with your toddler's doctor to arrange to have a throat swab taken to determine whether or not she has strep throat. If she does, an antibiotic will be prescribed to help kill off the strep germ. If left untreated, strep throat can result in kidney disease or rheumatic fever (a serious condition that can cause heart damage and joint swelling). It can also lead to skin infections, bloodstream infections, ear infections, and pneumonia.
- Offer liquids and bland foods (if your toddler is old enough for solid foods) and watch for signs of dehydration.

Condition: Sinusitis (sinus infection)

Cause: The mucus in your child's sinuses becomes infected with bacteria, usually as the result of a lingering cold.

Signs and symptoms: Persistent nasal discharge, fever, a cough that gets worse at night, tenderness in the face, dark circles under the eyes, puffy lower eyelids, bad breath, fatigue.

What you can do:

- Get in touch with your toddler's doctor to talk about whether she should be on some sort of an antibiotic. (As a rule of thumb, most doctors will prescribe an antibiotic only if a

TODDLER TALK

Don't be surprised if your child's temperature remains high for the first day or two after she starts antibiotic treatment. It takes time for the antibiotics to start working their magic.

---

toddler is experiencing both a nasal discharge and a cough that hasn't shown any sign of improvement after more than 10 to 14 days.) But if your doctor does decide to prescribe an antibiotic, don't be surprised if she prescribes a four- to six-week supply! Sinus infections can be time-consuming to clear up.

- Keep your child comfortable. (See the tips on treating the common cold above.)

Condition: Tonsillitis
Cause: Can be bacterial or viral in origin.
Signs and symptoms: Fever, swollen glands under the jaw, a very sore throat, cold symptoms, and abdominal pain.
What you can do:
- Treat your toddler's fever and cold symptoms. (See above.)
- Have your toddler examined by your doctor to see if an antibiotic should be prescribed.

Condition: Whooping cough
Cause: Caused by a bacterial infection. The incubation period is seven to ten days.
Signs and symptoms: Cold-like symptoms that linger. About two weeks into the illness, the cough suddenly worsens. When the toddler coughs, thick mucus is dislodged, causing her to gasp for her next breath (the "whoop" in whooping cough). She turns red in the face during the cough and then vomits afterwards. Whooping cough typically lasts for three to six weeks and is considered to be a serious illness in a child under age one.

What you can do:
- Offer your toddler plenty of fluids.
- See if a cool-mist vaporizer will help with your toddler's cough.
- Check with your doctor or pharmacist to see if an expectorant cough syrup would help.
- Seek immediate medical attention if your child becomes exhausted or is having difficulty breathing. Most children under one year of age end up being hospitalized so that they can be treated with oxygen (and antibiotics in the hope of preventing the illness from spreading).

Skin and scalp conditions

Condition: Boils
Cause: Usually caused by staphylococcus bacteria from an infected pimple.
Signs and symptoms: Raised red, tender, warm swellings on the skin. Most commonly found on the buttocks.
What you can do:
- Apply hot compresses to the boils 10 times daily in order to bring them to a head, and then continue applying them for a few days after the boils pop and drain. Avoid picking at or squeezing at your toddler's boils, as this may result in scarring and spreading.
- Get in touch with your toddler's doctor. If the boils don't drain on their own, they may need to be incised and drained by your doctor. A topical antibiotic or systemic antibiotics may also be required.

Condition: Cellulitis
Cause: Usually caused by a bacterial infection such as staphylococcus or streptococcus.

Signs and symptoms: Swollen, red, tender, warm areas of skin that are usually found on the extremities or the buttocks. They often start out as a boil or a puncture wound but then become infected. They're typically accompanied by a fever and swollen and tender lymph glands.

What you can do:

- Apply hot compresses for a few minutes every two hours.
- Elevate the affected area.
- Give your toddler acetaminophen to help control the fever and pain.
- Contact your toddler's doctor. This condition will need to be treated with antibiotics (oral, injected, or intravenous, depending on the severity of the case).

Condition: Chicken pox

Cause: Caused by a viral infection that is spread from person to person. The incubation period is two to three weeks. It is very difficult to control the spread of chicken pox because it can be transmitted through direct contact with an infected person (usually via fluid from broken blisters), through the air when an infected person coughs or sneezes, and through direct contact with lesions (sores) from a person with shingles (a possible complication of chicken pox). Outbreaks are most common in winter and in early spring.

Signs and symptoms: A rash with small blisters that develops on the scalp and body and then spreads to the face, arms, and legs over a period of three to four days. A child can end up with anywhere from less than a dozen to more than 500 itchy blisters that dry up and turn into scabs two to four days later. Other symptoms of chicken pox include coughing, fussiness, loss of appetite, and headaches. Chicken pox is contagious from two days before to five days after the rash appears.

What you can do:

- Keep your toddler's nails trimmed so that she'll be less able to scratch at her chicken pox. If that doesn't seem to do the trick, you might want to consider providing her with a set of hand puppets or mittens to wear around the house.
- Try to minimize the amount of itching your toddler experiences by giving her oatmeal or baking soda baths or by dabbing calamine lotion on her spots. (Note: Don't apply calamine lotion to the spots in her mouth. Calamine lotion is for external use only.)
- Give your child acetaminophen to help bring down her fever and eliminate some of her discomfort. Note: Do not give children Aspirin or drugs containing salicylate at any time, since Aspirin use during certain illnesses, including chicken pox, has been linked to Reye's syndrome—a potentially fatal disease that affects the liver and the brain.
- Be sure to get in touch with your doctor if your child's fever lasts longer than four days; if it remains high after the third day after the spots appear; if your child shows signs of becoming dehydrated; or if your child's rash becomes warm, red, or tender. Note: Some doctors choose to prescribe an antiviral medicine to make the chicken pox less severe, but, in order to be effective, this medication must be administered within the first 24 hours of the onset of chicken pox.

TODDLER TALK

If your child has an immune system problem and you suspect that she may have been exposed to chicken pox, you'll want to get in touch with your doctor as soon as possible. The doctor may recommend that your child receive a dose of a special immune globulin (VZIG) that can help to prevent chicken pox.

Condition: Eczema

Cause: Unknown, but it tends to be worse in winter when your toddler's skin is driest. Eczema is no longer believed to be triggered by allergies. It is not contagious.

Signs and symptoms: Extreme itchiness that results in a rash in areas that are scratched.

What you can do:

- Keep your toddler's skin well moisturized by applying a non-allergenic moisturizing lotion a couple of times each day.
- Dress your child in cotton and other breathable fabrics.
- Keep your toddler's nails trimmed so that she'll be less likely to infect her skin through scratching.
- Give your toddler an oatmeal bath. (Don't open the cereal cupboard; you need colloidal oatmeal, a product that can be purchased in the drugstore.)
- Your doctor may prescribe a steroid cream if your toddler's eczema is particularly severe, but she'll recommend that you use it sparingly.

Condition: Fifth disease (erythema infectiosum)

Cause: Caused by a virus known as parvovirus B19. Once the rash appears, the disease is no longer likely to spread.

Signs and symptoms: A "slapped cheek" rash on the face accompanied by a red rash on the trunk and extremities. The child may also have a fever and sore joints. Fortunately, this illness is more common in school-aged children than in younger children.

What you can do:

- Get in touch with your toddler's doctor as soon as possible if your child has sickle-cell anemia or some other form of chronic anemia. Fifth disease may heighten anemia in children who are already anemic.
- There is no treatment for fifth disease, nor is there any vaccine available. This is one of those diseases that you simply have to "wait out."

Condition: Hand, foot, and mouth syndrome

Cause: Caused by the Coxsackie virus—a contagious virus with an incubation period of three to six days.

Signs and symptoms: Tiny blister like sores in the mouth, on the palms of the hands, and on the soles of the feet that are accompanied by a mild fever, a sore throat, and painful swallowing. Lasts approximately seven to ten days and is contagious from one day before until one day after the blisters appear.

What you can do:

- Give your toddler plenty of liquids and, if she's old enough, soft foods as well. Note: Popsicles can ease some of the discomfort of the sores in the mouth while ensuring that your child remains well hydrated.
- Keep your toddler comfortable by treating her with acetaminophen until her symptoms start to subside.

Condition: Herpangina (inflammation of the inside of the mouth)

Cause: Caused by the Coxsackie virus (the same virus responsible for hand, foot, and mouth syndrome), a contagious virus that has an incubation period of three to six days.

Signs and symptoms: Numerous painful greyish-white ulcers on the toddler's tongue and on the roof of the toddler's mouth toward the back, painful swallowing, a fever of 38.9 to 40°C (102 to 104°F), diarrhea, and a pink rash on the trunk. The symptoms last about seven days and the illness is highly contagious until the ulcers are gone.

What you can do:

- Take your toddler to the doctor to have the diagnosis confirmed.
- Give your toddler plenty of fluids, but avoid giving your toddler acidic juices that may make her mouth ulcers sting. If your toddler refuses to eat, offer soft food and liquids to prevent dehydration.

- Give your child acetaminophen to help bring down her fever and to help reduce the pain associated with the mouth ulcers.

Condition: Impetigo (an infection of the skin)
Cause: Caused by a bacterial infection.
Signs and symptoms: A rash featuring oozing, blister-like, honey-coloured crusts that may be as small as pimples or as large as coins. Outbreaks of impetigo typically occur below the nose or on the buttocks or at the site of an insect bite or scrape.
What you can do:
- Have your toddler seen by a doctor so that the rash can be diagnosed and an antibacterial ointment and/or an oral anti-biotic can be prescribed.
- Trim your toddler's nails to prevent her from scratching the rash, and keep the sores covered to minimize the chance that they'll spread to other parts of the body and other people.

Condition: Measles (rubeola)
Cause: Spread by a virus that has an incubation period of 8 to 12 days.
Signs and symptoms: Cold, high fever (40°C or 104°F), cough, bloodshot eyes that are sensitive to light. Around the fourth day of illness, a bright red rash erupts on the face and spreads all over the body. (Even the inner cheeks will have spots, which will be white in colour.) At around the time that the spots break out, the child starts feeling quite ill. The infectious period lasts from three to five days before the rash appears until after the rash disappears (typically four days after the rash appears).
What you can do:
- Have your toddler seen by your doctor so that the illness can be properly diagnosed and any complications (pneumonia, encephalitis, ear infections, etc.) can be treated.
- Give your child acetaminophen to manage her fever and plenty of fluids to keep her well hydrated.

Condition: Ringworm
Cause: Caused by a fungus that is spread from person to person through touch.
Signs and symptoms: An itchy and flaky rash that may be ring-shaped and have a raised edge. When the scalp is affected, a bald area may develop. Ringworm is highly contagious until treatment has commenced.
What you can do:
• Take your toddler to see the doctor so that oral medications and/or topical ointments or creams may be prescribed to treat the outbreak.

Condition: Roseola
Cause: Caused by a virus with an incubation period of five to ten days. Roseola is very common in 6- to 24-month-old toddlers.
Signs and symptoms: High fever that arises suddenly in a previously well toddler, and which may result in febrile convulsions. The fever breaks on the third day and is then followed by a faint pink rash that appears on the trunk and the extremities and lasts for one day.
What you can do:
• Treat your toddler's fever and give her plenty of fluids to prevent dehydration.

Condition: Rubella (German measles)
Cause: Caused by the rubella virus—a virus that has an incubation period of 14 to 21 days and that is contagious from a few days before until seven days after the rash appears.
Signs and symptoms: A low-grade fever, flu-like symptoms, a slight cold, and a pinkish red, spotted rash that starts on the face, spreads rapidly to the trunk, and disappears by the third day. Also accompanied by swollen glands behind the ears and in the nape of the neck.

What you can do:

- Have your child examined by a doctor to confirm that she has developed rubella. Sometimes only a blood test can confirm that the rash and other symptoms have been caused by rubella as opposed to some other illness.
- Keep your child away from women who are or could be pregnant. Rubella can be very dangerous to the developing fetus.

Condition: Scarlet fever

Cause: Caused by streptococcus bacteria. Has an incubation period of two to five days.

Signs and symptoms: Sunburn-like rash over face, trunk, and extremities, including a moustache-like gap of unaffected skin around the mouth; sandpaper-like skin; fever; tonsillitis; vomiting. The rash usually disappears in five days. Despite its scary name, it's usually no more serious than strep throat, but it's contagious until one to two days after antibiotic treatment has begun. It's more common in school-aged children than in infants.

What you can do:

- Have your toddler seen by your doctor so that antibiotic treatment can be started. (Note: Other members of your family may also be treated at the same time, even if they haven't actually developed the illness.)
- Offer liquids and bland foods (if your toddler is old enough for solid foods) and watch for signs of dehydration.

Condition: Shingles

Cause: Caused by the zoster virus—the same virus that is responsible for the chicken pox.

Signs and symptoms: A rash with small blisters that begin to crust over; intense itching. Shingles is very contagious while the rash is present; it's possible to spread the disease to anyone who has not had the chicken pox. They won't become infected with shingles, however: what you risk passing along is a case of the chicken pox.

What you can do:

- Follow the guidelines for treating the chicken pox. (See above.)

Gastrointestinal conditions

Condition: Campylobacter

Cause: Source of infection may be poultry, beef, unpasteurized milk, or other food. The germ that causes this condition is excreted in the stool, so your child is infectious while she has symptoms.

Signs and symptoms: Fever, diarrhea, blood in stool, cramps.

What you can do:

- Get in touch with your toddler's doctor to see if a stool sample is required in order to confirm that your toddler has been infected with campylobacter.
- Keep your toddler away from other children while you treat the illness.
- Give your child acetaminophen to reduce her discomfort and treat her fever. Also, see tips under diarrhea (below) for advice on managing your child's diarrhea.

Condition: Constipation

Cause: Too little water in the intestines and/or poor muscle tone in the lower intestines and rectum. The problem can be triggered by a change in diet (e.g., switching from breast milk to formula or from formula to cow's milk).

Signs and symptoms: Abdominal discomfort and hard, dry stools that may be painful for your toddler to pass (e.g., your toddler draws up her legs to her abdomen, grunts, and gets red faced) and that may be streaked with blood when they finally emerge.

What you can do:

- Up your toddler's intake of water, prune juice, prunes, pears, plums, and peaches—nature's stool softeners! If they aren't effective, ask your doctor about the pros and cons of using mineral oil, non-prescription stool softeners, or laxative suppositories.
- Limit the number and quantities of constipating foods that your toddler eats (e.g., white rice, rice cereal, bananas, apples, cooked carrots, milk, and cheese) while adding fibre to your toddler's diet. (Good sources of fibre for older toddlers include bran cereals, whole grain breads and crackers, and fibre-rich vegetables such as peas and beans).

Condition: Diarrhea

Cause: Caused by gastrointestinal infections (especially gastroenteritis), colds, food intolerances, and antibiotic treatments.

Signs and symptoms: Frequent watery, green, mucusy, foul-smelling, explosive, and occasionally blood-tinged stools. Diarrhea is frequently accompanied by a bright red rash around the anus. A toddler with diarrhea can also be expected to show other signs of a viral infection. Note: Because each child's pattern of bowel movements is different, what you're looking for is a change in the consistency of your toddler's bowel movements.

What you can do:

- Start tracking the frequency and quality of your toddler's stools and note whether she's vomiting or not, how much food and liquid she's been taking in, and how ill she seems. This information will help your doctor assess whether your toddler is at risk of becoming dehydrated.
- Try to figure out what has triggered the diarrhea: illness, a change in diet (e.g., too much fruit juice), or the result of antibiotic treatment for an ear infection, for example.
- If you're breastfeeding, continue to breastfeed on demand and

offer an oral electrolyte solution. If you're not breastfeeding, stop giving your toddler any food or drink and offer her oral electrolyte solution in the following quantities, as recommended by the Canadian Paediatric Society:

First 6 hours:

- If the toddler is 12 to 24 months of age: 90 to 125 millilitres (three to four ounces) every hour.
- If the toddler is over 24 months of age: 125 to 250 millilitres (four to eight ounces) every hour.

From 6 to 24 hours:

- Keep giving your child the oral electrolyte solution.
- Once the vomiting stops, reintroduce your toddler's usual formula or whole milk or offer small quantities of non-irritating foods throughout the day. (Do not offer fruit juices or sweetened desserts until the diarrhea has stopped, or it may worsen again.)
- Don't be alarmed if your toddler has more frequent bowel movements once you reintroduce these foods. It may take seven to ten days or even longer for her stools to go back to normal again. The bowel is relatively slow to heal.
- Don't give your toddler any diarrhea medication unless you're specifically advised to do so by your doctor. These medications—which slow down the action of the intestines—can actually worsen diarrhea by allowing the germs and infected fluid to stagnate in the gut.
- Assess the severity of the diarrhea and watch for any signs of dehydration, particularly if your toddler is also experiencing a lot of vomiting. Diarrhea can throw your toddler's balance of salts (called electrolytes) and water out of whack—something that can affect the functioning of her organs.
- Make sure that you apply a barrier cream at each diaper change to prevent your toddler's bottom from developing a diarrhea-related rash. (These can be incredibly painful.)

- Once the diarrhea subsides, start re-introducing other foods. Keeping your toddler on a clear fluid diet for too long may itself produce diarrhea (aptly named "starvation stools"). If your toddler is drinking cow's milk, your doctor may recommend that you use a non-lactose, soy-based formula since your toddler's intestines may have difficulty tolerating lactose for up to six weeks. Ditto for any potentially irritating foods. Your best bet is to stick to the so-called "brat" diet at first: bananas, rice, applesauce, and toast.

- If you notice the diarrhea starting up again, you might want to back off and stick to foods that you know she can tolerate well. If the diarrhea continues to be a problem, get in touch with your doctor: She may want to order stool cultures to see if there's a parasite such as giardia responsible for your toddler's misery.

- Call your toddler's doctor or go to the hospital immediately if your toddler is having bloody or black stools, has been

---

TODDLER TALK

While mothers a generation ago were told to treat diarrhea by giving their children ginger ale, juice, and sugar water, doctors no longer recommend that these beverages be given because their salt content is too low and their sugar content is too high—something that can actually aggravate the child's diarrhea. Add to this the fact that certain types of fruit juices can have a laxative effect—the last thing your toddler needs when she's battling diarrhea!—and that many types of soda pop contain caffeine (a diuretic that can cause your toddler to become dehydrated) and you can see why oral electrolyte solutions (also known as oral rehydration solutions) are becoming the first-line defence against diarrhea. Believe it or not, even plain water isn't recommended for a toddler who's becoming dehydrated because it can result in a lowering in the amount of salt or sugar in the blood. (Obviously, your toddler will be able to tolerate water once she's healthy again, so don't get rid of that water cooler yet!)

TODDLER TALK

According to The College of Family Physicians of Canada, you should call your doctor if your toddler

- has diarrhea and a fever of over 38.5°C (101.3°F);
- is exhibiting some of the signs of dehydration (irritability, decreased appetite, less frequent urination, more concentrated urine, weight loss, dry mouth, thirst, sunken eyes, lack of tears when crying, skin that isn't as "springy" as usual);
- has stools that are bloody and slimy or has blood in her vomit;
- is bloated, listless, and/or unusually sleepy;
- has had abdominal pain for more than two hours;
- hasn't passed urine in eight hours.

---

vomiting for more than four to six hours, has a fever of 38.5°C (101.3°F) or greater, or is showing some signs of dehydration. (See the section on dehydration earlier in this chapter.)

Condition: Escherichia coli (E. coli)
Cause: Can be picked up from poultry, beef, unpasteurized milk, or other food sources.
Signs and symptoms: Fever, diarrhea, blood in stool, cramps. The germ that causes this condition is excreted in the stool, so your child is infectious while she has symptoms.
What you can do:
- Get in touch with your toddler's doctor to see if a stool sample is required to attempt to confirm that your toddler has been infected with E. coli.
- Keep your toddler away from other children while you treat the illness.
- Give your child acetaminophen to reduce her discomfort and treat her fever. Also, see tips under diarrhea (above) for advice on how to manage your child's diarrhea.

Condition: Food poisoning
Cause: Caused by eating contaminated food.
Signs and symptoms: Nausea, vomiting, cramps, diarrhea. Not infectious, but symptoms may be shared by all members of the family who ate the same food.
What you can do:
* Contact your toddler's doctor if your child's symptoms are severe. Otherwise, offer plenty of fluids and follow the tips on treating vomiting and diarrhea.

Condition: Giardia (a parasite in the stool that causes bowel infections)
Cause: Spread from person to person.
Signs and symptoms: Most children have no symptoms, but some may experience loss of appetite, vomiting, cramps, diarrhea, very soft stools, and excessive gas. This condition is infectious until cured.
What you can do:
* Get in touch with your toddler's doctor to see if a stool sample is required to attempt to confirm that your toddler has been infected with giardia.
* Keep your toddler away from other children while you treat the illness.
* Give your child acetaminophen to reduce her discomfort and treat her fever. Also, see tips under diarrhea (above) for advice on how to manage your child's diarrhea.

Condition: Hepatitis A (a liver infection)
Cause: A virus in the stool that can be spread from person to person or via food or water.
Signs and symptoms: Most children exhibit few symptoms. Where symptoms are present, they include fever, reduced appetite, nausea, vomiting, and jaundice (a yellowish tinge to skin and

eyes). Hepatitis A is infectious from two weeks before to one week after the onset of jaundice.

What you can do:

- Get in touch with your toddler's doctor. She may want to order an immune globulin vaccine for all members of your family, including your toddler.

Condition: Norwalk virus

Cause: Spread from person to person via the air.

Signs and symptoms: Vomiting for one to two days. Contagious for the duration of the illness.

What you can do:

- Get in touch with your toddler's doctor to see if a stool sample is required to attempt to confirm that your toddler has been infected with Norwalk virus.
- Keep your toddler away from other children while you treat the illness.
- Give your child acetaminophen to reduce her discomfort and treat her fever. Also, see tips under diarrhea (above) for advice on how to manage your child's diarrhea.

Condition: Rotavirus

Cause: Caused by a virus in the stool that is spread through person-to-person contact. Rotavirus is the most common cause of diarrhea outbreaks in child-care centres.

Signs and symptoms: Fever and vomiting followed by watery diarrhea. Can lead to rapid dehydration in infants. Contagious for duration of illness.

What you can do:

- Get in touch with your toddler's doctor to see if a stool sample is required to attempt to confirm that your toddler has been infected with rotavirus.
- Keep your toddler away from other children while you treat the illness.

- Give your child acetaminophen to reduce her discomfort and treat her fever. Also, see diarrhea section (above) for managing your child's diarrhea.

Condition: Salmonella
Cause: Acquired mainly by eating food that has been contaminated with salmonella. Such foods typically include eggs, egg products, beef, poultry, and unpasteurized milk.
Signs and symptoms: Diarrhea, fever, blood in stool. Infectious while symptoms persist.
What you can do:
- Contact your toddler's doctor if your child's symptoms are severe. Otherwise, offer plenty of fluids and follow the tips on treating vomiting and diarrhea.

Condition: Shigella
Cause: Caused by a virus in the stool that can be spread from person to person.
Signs and symptoms: Diarrhea, fever, blood and/or mucus in stool, cramps. Highly contagious for the duration of the illness.
What you can do:
- Get in touch with your toddler's doctor to see if a stool sample is required to attempt to confirm that your toddler has been infected with shigella.
- Keep your toddler away from other children while you treat the illness.
- Give your child acetaminophen to reduce her discomfort and treat her fever. Also, see tips under diarrhea (above) for advice on how to manage your child's diarrhea.

Condition: Vomiting
Cause: Vomiting can be caused by a viral infection, food poisoning, or by a medical condition such as pyloric stenosis (projectile

vomiting caused by a partial or complete intestinal blockage that requires surgical correction) or gastroesophageal reflux (a condition in which stomach acids are regurgitated into the esophagus, frequently resulting in forceful regurgitation through the nose).

Signs and symptoms: Vomiting can be accompanied by diarrhea or other symptoms depending on the underlying cause.

What you can do:

- Offer small, frequent servings of fluid to prevent dehydration. If your toddler is old enough to eat a Popsicle, you might want to try making Popsicles out of the oral electrolyte solution to see if this makes it easier for her to keep the fluid down.

Other conditions

Condition: Meningitis

Cause: Can be bacterial or viral in origin. Meningitis can be fatal. The incubation period is usually 10 to 14 days. Fortunately, bacterial meningitis—the most deadly kind—is very rare in preschool children over the age of six weeks who have been fully immunized.

Signs and symptoms: Bacterial meningitis (spinal meningitis) may begin like a cold, flu, or ear infection, but the child becomes increasingly ill and very lethargic; develops a fever of 38.9 to 40°C (102 to 104°F). The toddler typically has a stiff neck. With viral meningitis, the toddler exhibits similar symptoms but isn't quite as ill.

What you can do:

- Contact your doctor immediately. She'll want to do a spinal tap to determine whether the meningitis is bacterial or viral in origin. The sooner the illness is diagnosed and treated, the better the outcome.
- If the meningitis turns out to be bacterial in origin, your doctor will want to treat the illness with intravenous antibiotics for at least seven days.

- If it turns out to be viral in origin, the illness will be treated like the flu.

Condition: Mumps
Cause: Spread by a virus that has an incubation period of seven to ten days.
Signs and symptoms: Flu-like symptoms and an upset stomach initially; then tender swollen glands beneath the ear lobes two or three days later. Your child may look as if she has "chipmunk cheeks" and may find it painful to open her jaw. She may also have a low-grade fever. Mumps typically last for seven to ten days, and the illness is contagious until the swelling is gone.
What you can do:
- Feed your child liquids and soft foods.
- Apply cool compresses to the neck.
- Administer acetaminophen to relieve discomfort and pain.
- Call your doctor's office immediately if your child becomes drowsy, starts vomiting repeatedly, becomes dehydrated, or develops a stiff neck.

Condition: Pinworms
Cause: Caused by a parasite (intestinal worms)
Signs and symptoms: Night waking and restlessness; intense itching around the anus or in the vagina; and the presence of thread-like, one-centimetre-long worms that travel out of the rectum to deposit eggs around the anus or the vagina.
What you can do:
- Use a flashlight at night to try to detect worms coming out of your toddler's anus (they're more visible in the dark) and/or place sticky tape around your toddler's anus so that you can capture some eggs and take them to your doctor's office for identification.
- Keep your toddler's fingernails trimmed short to discourage scratching.

- Each member of the family will have to be treated with a medication to eradicate the parasite.

Condition: Tetanus (lockjaw)
Cause: Caused by bacteria in a deeply contaminated wound. The incubation period can be anywhere from 3 to 21 days.
Signs and symptoms: Muscle spasms, particularly in the jaw muscles; convulsions.
What you can do:
- Contact your doctor immediately. Your toddler will need to be treated with antibiotics.

Condition: Urinary tract infections (UTIs)
Cause: Can be difficult to diagnose. If your child suffers from recurrent urinary tract infections, your doctor may order an ultrasound and X-ray or some other type of test to make sure that the kidneys are functioning properly and to see if there is a correctable reason for the infection.
Signs and symptoms: Fever, painful and frequent urination, vomiting, abdominal pain. In toddlers, a persistent fever with no obvious cause may be the only symptom of a urinary tract infection.
What you can do:
- Get in touch with your toddler's doctor so that the urinary tract infection can be diagnosed and antibiotic treatment begun.

Caring for a sick toddler

UNLESS YOUR GUARDIAN angel happens to offer round-the-clock care and a bullet-proof guarantee, you're bound to have to take your child to the hospital at some point in her life—assuming, of course, that you haven't already.

Whether you end up making a spur-of-the-moment trip to the emergency room with a sick or injured toddler or playing nursemaid at the bedside of a toddler who is scheduled for surgery, you're bound to find the experience stressful. Here are some tips on surviving your toddler's hospital trip.

Emergency room visits

- Make sure that you know where your toddler's health card is at all times. That way, you won't have to waste valuable time looking for it if you have to make an impromptu trip to the emergency room. And if you get in the habit of storing a phone card with your toddler's health card, you won't have to worry about fumbling for change if you have to make a phone call or two from the hospital payphone.

- Get in the habit of keeping a fully stocked change bag in the trunk of your car. In addition to including all the essentials— diapers, wipes, a spare outfit or two, and a change pad—you'll also want to ensure that it's equipped with enough drinks, snacks, and toys to keep your toddler entertained for a couple of hours, and enough cash to pay for parking at even the most overpriced of hospital parking lots.

- Don't forget to bring your stroller. It can serve as a portable storage bin (you can put your change bag and all your other stuff inside) or a bed or chair for your toddler.

MOM'S THE WORD

"I have an 'emergency room trip bag' packed at all times. In it, I have a few juice boxes, packages of cookies or crackers, Halloween goodies for a treat, and a few dollar-store items. It helps to pass the time if we end up with a lengthy wait."

—*Terri, 34, mother of three*

Overnight stays

- Find out what services are available to you while your child is staying in the hospital. Some hospitals provide meals to parents of patients. Others provide roll-up cots and access to shower facilities. (Gone are the days when parents were expected to restrict their visits to "visiting hours." Most hospitals today recognize that parents may wish to stay with their children 24 hours per day.)

- If you weren't able to pack a lot of your toddler's favourite things before she was checked into the hospital, ask a friend or relative to go home and scoop up her favourite blanket, her pillow, her booster seat, and some of her favourite bed-time stories. The more familiar objects she has around her, the more relaxed she'll feel. Just be sure to put her name on all of her personal possessions. It would be nothing short of disastrous to have her favourite blanket accidentally find itself in the hospital laundry!

- Even if you're not in the habit of allowing your toddler to watch television when she's at home, you might want to consider giving her—and yourself—a brief exemption from your family's no-TV rule by renting a TV set and a VCR to entertain her while she's in the hospital. It can, after all, be pretty challenging to find hours and hours' worth of activities to entertain a sick two year-old who may or may not feel well enough to do much more than lie there anyway.

- Don't be afraid to express your feelings about the situation. Depending on the circumstances and the nature of your child's illness, you may feel panicked, angry, and/or totally stressed. "I cried every day," confesses Christina, a 32-year-old mother of three whose 14 month-old daughter was recently hospitalized with pneumonia. "I needed to get my feelings out. I was tired, scared, and worried about my child. Sometimes I broke down in front of the nurses or our doctor, and I always broke down when my husband got there at the end of the day."

• If you're having difficulty understanding what the medical staff are telling you about your child's condition, ask a friend or family member to stay at the hospital with you so that they can help you to obtain the answers you need. You may find it difficult to process complex medical information if you're feeling frightened and exhausted.

Preparing your child for surgery

• If you know ahead of time that your toddler will be having surgery, you'll want to take steps to prepare her for what will happen before, during, and after her surgery. But because toddlers don't have a particularly clear concept of time, you'll probably want to hold off on having "the big talk" until a day or two before her operation.

• Make sure that you understand hospital policies about eating and drinking restrictions prior to surgery. Most hospitals will require that your toddler stop eating solid foods at midnight the night before surgery. She may be allowed to breastfeed up

---

TODDLER TALK

If your toddler is scheduled to undergo a general anaesthetic during surgery, it's important to notify the surgeon or the anaesthetist about any changes to your toddler's health condition during the days leading up to the scheduled surgery (e.g., if your toddler has been exposed to infectious diseases such as measles, mumps, or chicken pox or has developed such cold symptoms as a cough, runny nose, or fever).

until three hours before your scheduled arrival time or to consume clear liquids such as apple juice, Kool-Aid, and Jell-O up until two hours before her scheduled surgery, however, so make sure you're crystal clear about the rules.

- To give your toddler a bit of control over the situation, allow her to make some choices, where appropriate. For example, she might want to decide which pair of pyjamas or which stuffed animal gets to accompany her to the hospital.

- Expect some behavioural changes during and after your toddler's hospital stay. Most toddlers find it difficult to adjust to such dramatic changes to their normal routines. You may find that your toddler is extra-clingy, hyperactive, and/or that she's developed some new fears. The best way to handle the situation is to be patient and give your toddler plenty of extra reassurance and love.

Up until now, we've been focusing on keeping toddlers healthy. Now it's time to zero in on an even bigger challenge: keeping toddlers safe!

CHAPTER 9

The Safety Department

"Toddlers are curious by nature and have no inhibitions! I think that's the biggest challenge about keeping them safe. They just want to explore and haven't yet had the experience of hurting themselves or being faced with danger."
—JUDITH, 32, MOTHER OF ONE

"If the hospital awarded frequent flyer miles for each of my son's visits to the hospital, I would have been around the world by now."
—TERRI, 34, MOTHER OF THREE

WHILE IT'S A RARE toddler indeed who manages to get through the toddler years without ending up with at least a few bumps and bruises, one of your key responsibilities as a parent is to do as much as possible to keep your child safe. Of course, as any veteran parent will tell you, this is definitely one of those things that's easier said than done. At this stage of his development, your toddler is hungry to explore his world, but almost oblivious to the dangers that surround him.

Add to that the fact that he's still pretty clumsy—his balance is still imperfect and he may have difficulty slowing down, stopping, and turning when he's walking—and you can see why keeping a toddler safe is pretty much a full-time job!

And, of course, it practically goes without saying that certain toddlers will demand a little bit more vigilance from their parents than others. If, like Alyson, you've got a pint-sized daredevil on your hands, you could find yourself on safety patrol from dawn until dusk and beyond: "My daughter, Maggie, constantly has me on my toes," says the 33-year-old mother of two. "She loves to climb, has no fear of the water, and picks up on new things—like how to unscrew lids!—very quickly. I find her a real challenge, since I'm not really able to take my eyes off of her at all."

So if you're looking for some nitty-gritty information on what you can do to keep your toddler safe, this is the chapter for you. We're going to start by talking about what you can do to eliminate hundreds of the biggest dangers to be found in a typical home. Then we'll talk about how to make car travel as safe as possible for your toddler. We'll also discuss summer and winter safety—what you can do to keep your child safe throughout the year. Next we'll consider the generation gap with regard to child safety—something that can lead to heated discussions between you and your child's grandparents if they seem to pooh-pooh the importance of car seats and other child safety equipment. Finally, we'll run through the basics of emergency first aid: information that I hope you'll never need, but that every parent needs to know.

Babyproofing: The sequel

YOU'VE SPENT THE past year babyproofing your child's world. Now it's time to make sure that your home is toddlerproof as well. That means training yourself to see your home through the

MOM'S THE WORD

"We hired a babyproofing company to come into our home when the boys were about 10 months of age. For $35, they gave us a list of everything they recommended. We actually ended up hiring them to install all the babyproofing hardware because—with two babies to care for—we didn't have the time to run around and find all the items and then install everything on our own. It had taken us three weekends to hang up two strands of Christmas lights, so we knew better by this point!"

—*Jennie, 32, mother of two*

eyes of an ultra-curious, high-energy one- or two-year-old. (Trust me, you'll never look at a kitchen chair the same way again. Rather than a place to sit down, you'll see it as a launching pad to all sorts of incredible adventures!)

While it's unrealistic to think you can prevent every conceivable type of accident from occurring, there's plenty you can do to make your toddler's world a safe and secure place. Here's what you need to know to zero in on the biggest hazards that could be lurking in your very own home.

Every room

- Keep a set of emergency telephone numbers beside each telephone throughout your house—not just your main telephone. And be sure to include the phone number of the local poison control centre. The toddler years are the peak years for accidental poisonings.

- Keep curtain and blind cords out of your toddler's reach to reduce the risk of strangulation.

- Keep high chairs, cribs, and furniture away from windows, appliances, and other potential hazards. Note: If some of these pieces of furniture are portable (e.g., kitchen chairs or stepstools), you may have to store them in a closet or some inaccessible area to prevent your toddler from using them to climb up on things. One of the moms I interviewed for this book confessed to stashing her kitchen chairs in the bathroom! (Hey, Martha Stewart might not approve, but Elmer the Safety Elephant sure would.)

- Ensure that all windows in your house are lockable and that the screens in each of your windows are secure and backed with screen guards (safety devices designed to catch the screen and your toddler if he starts to fall out the window).

- Keep your toddler away from baseboards and portable heaters. If you have a tiny space heater, you'll want to ensure that you keep it well out of your toddler's reach so that he isn't tempted to touch it.

- Use plastic safety covers and cord locks on electrical outlets.

- Get in the habit of unplugging electrical appliances and extension cords when they're not in use.

- Install toddlerproof latches on drawers and cupboard doors.

- Place window guards on all second-storey windows.

TODDLER TALK

Toppling TV sets pose a significant threat to toddlers. According to a recent study reported in the *Archives of Pediatrics and Adolescent Medicine*, 2.7% of the 183 U.S. children age seven or younger who were injured by falling television sets between 1988 and 1999 died as a result of their injuries. And, what's more, the U.S. Consumer Product Safety Commission estimates that 2,300 children end up in emergency rooms each year as a result of injuries from falling TVs. Sadly, most of these children were age four or younger.

- Attach bookcases and tall dressers to the wall to prevent tipping, and avoid placing heavy items on top of these pieces of furniture. Many young children are injured—or even killed—each year as a result of these types of accidents.

- Keep a fire extinguisher near each exit to your home.

- Store lighters and matches out of your toddler's reach and insist that visitors do the same.

- Be careful what you do with loose change and keys. Toddlers can choke if they swallow coins or loose keys.

- Change the batteries in your smoke detector at least twice a year (whenever you move your clock forward or backward).

- Make sure that any space heaters and extension cords in use in your home are in good condition and meet current safety standards.

- Store medications and cleaners in their original containers so that you'll be able to identify which products your child has consumed in the event of a poisoning. (As you can see from Table 9.1, medications are responsible for a large percentage of the poisonings that occur in the home.)

TABLE 9.1

Type of Product Involved in Accidental Poisonings of Toddlers

	ONE-YEAR-OLDS	TWO-YEAR-OLDS
Medications	39.7%	68.8%
➜ Antihistamines	5.3%	17.2%
➜ Acetaminophen	7.7%	14.9%
➜ Barbituates, sedatives, tranquillizers, and other psychotropic agents	7.1%	6.0%
➜ Vitamins	4.0%	3.5%

➔ Acetylsalicylic acid (aspirin)	1.3%	2.4%
➔ Other	11.1%	21.8%
➔ Unspecified	3.2%	3.0%
Household Products	**26.7%**	**9.5%**
➔ General household products	11.6%	2.8%
➔ Bleach	5.5%	2.8%
➔ Oven cleaner	2.4%	2.4%
➔ Laundry detergent	1.9%	0.2%
➔ Toilet bowl cleaner	0.8%	0.4%
➔ Dishwasher detergent	1.9%	—
➔ Paint, varnish	0.5%	—
➔ Deodorizer, air freshener	0.5%	0.2%
➔ Unspecified	1.6%	0.7%
Beauty Products	**7.1%**	**4.3%**
➔ Perfume, aftershave lotion	1.8%	1.5%
➔ Nail polish, nail polish remover	1.6%	1.1%
➔ Other	3.7%	1.7%
Other	**26.5%**	**17.4%**
➔ Pesticides, insecticides	3.7%	3.0%
➔ Pharmaceutical products, liniments, rubbing compounds, ointments	3.4%	3.2%
➔ Berries, fungi	1.9%	1.7%
➔ Alcohol, illegal drugs	1.1%	—
➔ Chemical products, other products	16.4%	9.5%

Note: Figures do not total to 100 due to rounding.

Source: Canadian Hospitals Injury Reporting and Prevention Programme, 1993.

- Wipe up spills promptly and avoid area rugs, which can pose a tripping hazard.

- Avoid leaving your toddler and your pet alone in the same room. (Note: You'll find some additional information on toddlers and pets in Chapter 10.)

- Keep coins, marbles, pen or marker caps, button-sized batteries, and other small items safely out of your toddler's reach. This may mean clearing out the family junk drawer and/or locking the desk in your home office until your child is considerably older.

- Keep your cat's litter box in a part of the house that is off limits to your toddler.

- Make sure that every plant in your home is toddler-friendly. Call your local poison control centre if you're not sure which houseplants are and aren't dangerous if ingested.

Halls and stairways

- Hang a shelf near the front door so that Grandma can keep her purse (and her heart medication) out of your toddler's reach while she's visiting.

- Install wall-mounted baby gates at the top (and, if necessary, the bottom) of each set of stairs. Stairs are responsible for a large proportion of falls requiring hospitalization in children between the ages of one and four. (See Table 9.2.)

- Ensure that each set of stairs is equipped with a handrail that's firmly attached to the wall or the floor, and that the carpet on the stairs is tacked down securely to prevent tripping.

- Keep the stairs free of objects, including toys.

TABLE 9.2

**Most Common Types of Falls Requiring Hospitalization in Children
Between the Ages of One and Four**

→ Fall from one level to another	18.7%
→ Other and unspecified fall	16.8%
→ Fall from chair or bed	16.6%
→ Fall on or from stairs or steps	15.0%
→ Fall on same level from slipping, tripping, or tumbling, collision, pushing, or shoving	13.6%
→ Fall from playground equipment	12.2%
→ Fall from or out of building or other structure	4.7%
→ Fall on or from ladders or scaffolding	0.7%
→ Fall into hole or other opening in surface	0.4%
→ Fracture, cause unspecified	1.3%

Source: Statistics Canada, Health Statistics Division, unpublished data, 1990 to 1992.

- Get rid of your drycleaning bags as soon as you bring your drycleaning into the house. Tie them in knots and toss them in the trash.

- Install door alarms on all exterior doors.

Your toddler's room

- If your toddler is still sleeping in a crib, make sure that it's still in good condition. You'll want to tighten the screws and to ensure that the sides of the crib are still firmly locked in place. And you'll want to check that the crib mattress is still in good condition. Replace it immediately if it's too soft, too worn, or it doesn't fit the crib snugly.

- Make sure that your toddler's crib mattress has been dropped to the lowest setting to prevent him from tumbling out.

- Remove any large toys from your toddler's crib. He may use his toys as a stepstool to climb out of the crib.

- Pay attention to the warning signs that your toddler is ready to make the move from a crib to a big bed. You want to move him to a bed before he's old enough to start climbing out of the crib. See Chapter 7 for tips on helping your toddler make this important transition.

- Don't allow a child under the age of six to sleep on the top bunk of a bunk bed. The risk of falls and/or suffocation is simply too great.

- Make sure that your toddler wears fire-retardant sleepwear rather than regular clothing at bedtime. And contact your local fire department to see if they recommend that you put a special decal on the lower part of your child's door to indicate that there's a child sleeping in the room. (You can obtain these types of decals from child safety supply stores.)

- Remove any drawstrings or cords from your toddler's clothing in order to reduce the risk of strangulation.

- Keep the diaper pail out of reach of your toddler or purchase a model with a childproof latch.

- Avoid using decorative plug covers in your toddler's room. They'll only encourage him to touch the electrical outlets.

- Move rocking chairs and gliders to another part of the house. They can pinch fingers or otherwise injure a toddler.

- If your toddler is still using a pacifier, regularly inspect it for signs of deterioration. According to Health Canada, pacifiers should be changed at least every two months.

- If your toddler likes the security of having a night light in his room, choose a simple light that doesn't look like a toy. If it looks too much like a toy, your toddler may try to play with it and could end up with an electrical burn. Because night lights can pose a hazard to curious toddlers, some parents prefer to hook the main light in the room up to a dimmer switch instead.

- Tie a small parts tester (a.k.a. "choke tube") to your toddler's change table. That way, you'll know where it is whenever you want to find out whether a particular toy contains parts that are small enough to pose a choking hazard. (If you're away from home, you can use a toilet paper roll instead. It's slightly larger than a choke tube, but it's best to err on the side of caution anyway.)

Bathroom

- Check the temperature on your hot water heater. According to Safe Kids Canada, most water heaters are set at 60°C (140°F) or higher rather than the 49°C (120°F) that most safety experts recommend.

- Fill your toddler's bath with a few inches of cold water and then add hot water until the bath has reached the appropriate temperature.

- Use bath mats in the bathtub to reduce the risk of slipping.

- Place your toddler as far away as possible from the taps and faucet, both to prevent him from reaching for the taps and

---

TODDLER TALK

Each year, an estimated 9,000 Canadian children visit hospital emergency rooms for treatment for burns. In nearly half of these cases, they have suffered scalds from hot liquids.

accidentally scalding himself and to reduce the likelihood that he'll bang his head on the faucet.

- Never leave a toddler unattended in the bathtub. The peak risk period for drowning is age one through four.

- Empty the tub as soon as you're finished bathing your toddler to reduce the risk of an accidental drowning after the fact.

- Lock all medications (including vitamins and herbal remedies) in a lockable medicine cabinet or, even better, store them in a small cash box or medium-sized fishing-tackle box that can be locked and then stashed on the top shelf of your bedroom closet.

- Keep all medications in their original containers and ensure that the products you buy are equipped with child safety caps. Then, to reduce the number of products that are available to a toddler on the loose, weed out the out-of-date and obsolete medications on a regular basis.

- Keep mouthwash, shampoo, cosmetics, nail polish remover, and other toiletries out of your toddler's reach, along with scissors, razor blades, and other hazardous objects.

- Don't allow your toddler to run around with a toothbrush in his mouth; he could be seriously injured in the event of a fall.

- Keep electrical appliances like blow-dryers and curling irons out of your toddler's reach.

- Equip the toilet seat with a childproof latch.

TODDLER TALK

A child's skin burns four times as quickly and burns more deeply than the skin of an adult.

Kitchen

- Check that the base of your toddler's high chair is wide enough to be stable, and that the chair's safety harness is still functional. If your toddler has graduated to a booster seat, you'll want to ensure that it's firmly strapped to the chair so that it doesn't slide off when your toddler starts squirming around.

- Be mindful of where you place your toddler's high chair. You want to make sure that it's clear of walls or other objects that your toddler could push against, potentially tipping the high chair, and far away from hazards such as stoves.

- Use placemats rather than a tablecloth at your kitchen table. Otherwise, your toddler could tug on the tablecloth, causing everything on the table to come tumbling down on him.

- Don't hold your toddler when you're eating or drinking anything hot, and keep him safely out of the way when you're cooking meals. If he's determined to be part of the action, put him in his high chair. He'll be able to see what you're doing without injuring himself on hot pans or sharp knives.

- Keep stuffed animals and other flammable toys away from the cooking area. Not only is your child likely to be traumatized if Bunny goes up in smoke, but you could also end up with a house fire on your hands.

- Turn pot handles toward the back of the stove and cook only on the back burners.

- Be aware that oven doors can become hot enough to burn children. Be sure to supervise your toddler carefully the entire time he's in the kitchen and to turn off the oven immediately after you're finished using it to reduce the odds of his being burned.

- Keep knives, can openers, and other sharp items out of the reach of children.

- Organize your kitchen cupboards so that the items that are of the greatest interest to your child (e.g., cookies) are the farthest distance from the stove.

- Keep cords for kettles, toasters, and other electrical appliances out of the reach of children, and get in the habit of leaving appliances unplugged unless they're actually in use.

- Learn which foods (e.g., whole grapes, hot dog wieners, carrot sticks) pose a choking risk to toddlers, and either chop the foods into very small pieces or avoid them entirely until your child is older. (Note: You'll find some other valuable tips on preventing choking in Chapter 6.)

- Be careful if you heat your toddler's food in the microwave. Stir the food thoroughly and check the temperature carefully before serving it.

- Use cups with lids when you're drinking hot beverages like coffee or tea.

- Keep household cleaners—including dishwasher detergent—out of reach of children.

- Never leave your toddler unattended when he's eating. Choking is responsible for a significant number of infant deaths each year. (See Table 9.3.)

MOTHER WISDOM

Feeling overwhelmed by the round-the-clock demands of parenting? Afraid that you might snap and hurt your toddler? Support is only a phone call away. You can call the Parent Help Line (1-888-603-9100) at any time of day or night. Or, if you prefer, you can access the Parent Help Line's online library and message boards by visiting the Parent Help Line Web site at www.parentsinfo.sympatico.ca.

TABLE 9.3

The Leading Causes of Injury-Related Deaths in Children Between the Ages of One and Four (Canada 1990–1992)

→ Motor vehicles and other road vehicles	32%
→ Drownings	22.4%
→ Fires and burns	17.3%
→ Other causes	8.9%
→ Choking and suffocation	8.0%
→ Homicide	8.0%
→ Falls	2.2%
→ Unintentional poisonings	1.2%

Source: Statistics Canada, Health Statistics Division, Unpublished data.

- Since you're likely to be spending a lot of time in the kitchen, make sure that your toddler has a safe play area. When he starts exploring the cupboards, give him his own cupboard full of plastic containers, measuring spoons, and other "treasures" that he can dump on the floor. I can practically guarantee that these will soon become his favourite toys! And, of course, you might want to set up an art centre for him at the kitchen table. That way, he can play Picasso while you're busy playing chef!

Family room

- Make sure that the toys you buy for your child are age-appropriate. (See Chapter 3).

- Avoid buying toys that have sharp points or edges that could injure your toddler or that contain smaller pieces that could be removed and swallowed. And discard any broken toys that have developed sharp edges or that could present a choking hazard.

- Steer clear of toys that feature drawstrings and other dangling strings that are any longer than 20 centimetres. If your toddler inherits any such toys from an older cousin, take scissors to any offending strings.

- Ensure that the packaging that came with the toy is disposed of appropriately to avoid any choking or suffocation hazards.

- Ensure that any toys that require batteries have child-safe battery compartments (ones that can be opened only with a screwdriver).

- Teach your toddler to put his toys away when he's finished playing with them to prevent trips and falls.

- If you have a toy box, make sure that it's safe. The toy box should have a safety hinge to prevent the lid from closing too quickly and ventilation holes to ensure that your toddler will be able to breathe if he happens to get trapped inside. Note: You'll find all kinds of other suggestions for storing your child's toys in Chapter 3.

Living room

- Use a fireplace pad on your hearth and keep your child far away from the fireplace while it's being used. It's also important to keep children away from gas fireplaces. The glass doors on a gas fireplace can reach 200°C (400°F) while the fireplace

---

MOM'S THE WORD

"Childproofing for a toddler is difficult when you have an older child because the older child may leave toys around that a toddler shouldn't have."

—*Karen, 36, mother of three*

TODDLER TALK

Stick to Mylar rather than latex balloons when you're throwing a birthday party for your toddler. Latex balloons pose a significant choking risk to very young children.

---

is on, and it can take up to 45 minutes for the glass to cool to a safe temperature after the fireplace has been turned off. You can protect your toddler by installing a fireplace guard or simply decide not to use your fireplace while he's underfoot. What matters is that you find a way to ensure that he isn't exposed to dangerously hot fireplace doors.

- Put your vacuum cleaner away when it's not being used so that your child won't accidentally hurt his fingers or toes with the beater bar.

- Position floor lamps so that they're out of your toddler's reach or pack them away entirely.

- Place table lamps toward the back of the table and wrap the cord around the table leg for added stability.

Laundry room

- Store laundry products out of your toddler's reach.

- Never allow your toddler to play in or around the washer or dryer, and ensure that the washer and dryer doors are kept closed at all times.

Basement

- Store paint thinners and other harmful substances out of your toddler's reach.

MOM'S THE WORD

"We have to balance our desire to keep our toddlers safe against our desire to let them learn."

—*Anita, 38, mother of four*

- Ensure that woodworking tools are kept in a locked room or cabinet.

- Keep your toddler off unfinished basement stairs. Not only may the stairs be lacking a toddler-safe railing, but they may also lead down to a rock-hard cement floor—not exactly the type of surface you want your toddler to be landing on if he happens to take a tumble.

Garage

- Store your toddler's ride-on toys and other outdoor playthings somewhere other than the garage so that he learns the garage is off limits to children.

- Ensure that the garage door is equipped with a safety feature that will cause it to go back up if it comes into contact with a person or object.

- Store tools, pesticides, automotive parts, and other hazardous items out of your child's reach.

Backyard

- Keep the barbecue away from your child's play area.

- Get in the habit of putting your garden hose away when you're finished using it; otherwise, the water in the hose may become hot enough to scald a curious toddler.

- Ensure that your pool area is properly fenced (the fence should be at least 1.2 metres high and should surround the entire pool) and that the gate on the fence is both self-closing and self-locking. Eighty-two percent of people who drown in swimming pools are children between the ages of one and four.

- Check that any playground equipment is safe and well anchored. You can find a detailed playground safety checklist at the Safe Kids Canada Web site (see Appendix C). You'll find additional pointers on playground safety later in this chapter.

- Empty your toddler's wading pool whenever it's not in use.

- Ensure that your toddler's sandbox has a lid to keep neighbourhood cats out.

- Keep your toddler away from any poisonous plants or weeds that are growing in your yard—or, better yet, plant something else until your toddler is a little older.

- Don't even think about trying to mow the lawn or using any electrical garden tools while your toddler's underfoot. It's simply too risky.

- Ensure that your child's riding toys feature wheels that are spaced wide enough apart to promote maximum stability.

- Supervise your toddler closely when he's using a riding toy. Some children have been killed as a result of rolling down

---

MOTHER WISDOM

Remember to be extra-vigilant when you have friends and family members visiting. A friend or relative could leave her purse in reach of your toddler, forgetting about all the hazardous items it contains. The same thing applies when you're visiting other people: You have no way of knowing whether their house is toddlerproofed to the same degree as yours. (Unless they have a toddler the same age, chances are it's not.)

sloping driveways and into oncoming traffic; others have been run over by vehicles backing out of driveways.

Safety on the road

WHILE MOST PARENTS assume that they've done their bit for safety by buckling their child into his car seat, studies have shown that as many as 88% of car seats are installed incorrectly or improperly used. Here's what you need to know to prevent a needless tragedy.

Toddler car seats

Your toddler is ready to graduate to a forward-facing car seat when his weight reaches nine kilograms (20 pounds). He'll stay in his car seat until he reaches 20 kilograms (40 pounds), at which point he'll be ready for a booster seat. Here are some important safety tips to keep in mind:

- Make sure that the harness straps pass through the slots in the back of the car seat at the appropriate level (e.g., at or just above your child's shoulder height).

- Make sure that the seat is facing forward, not backwards.

TODDLER TALK

All forward-facing car seats in Canada are fitted with a tether strap designed to hold the seat in place in the event of a collision or sudden stop. The tether anchorage hardware must be securely attached to the frame of the vehicle. If you're not sure where to find your car's tether anchors, consult the owner's manual that came with your vehicle, call the dealership for further information, or visit the Transport Canada Web site at www.tc.gc.ca/roadsafety/childsafe/cindex_e.htm.

TODDLER TALK

Wondering how Canadians in various parts of the country measure up when it comes to car-seat safety? Transport Canada recently conducted a study to find out what percentage of parents were using car seats properly. Here's how parents of one- to two-year-olds ranked in various provinces. Note: The national average was 71.4%.

Newfoundland	83.2%	Alberta	66.6%
Saskatchewan	80.3%	Quebec	66.5%
Manitoba	70.9%	Ontario	65.6%
Nova Scotia	69.5%	Prince Edward Island	65.0%
British Columbia	67.1%	New Brunswick	41.3%

- Make sure that the tether strap is used to anchor the car seat in place.

- Make sure that a locking clip is used to hold the seat belt in place if you are using a shoulder belt/lap belt combination.

- Plan to replace your child's car seat if you're involved in an automobile accident, even if it was just a minor fender bender. Car seats are designed to withstand the impact of only a single car accident.

Note: If you're using a convertible car seat (which can be used from birth until a child weighs 18 kilograms, or 40 pounds), you'll want to make sure that you're using the seat in the proper position—backward-facing when your toddler is under nine kilograms (20 pounds) and forward-facing when he's over nine kilograms.

Other car safety tips

Here are some other important car safety tips:

- Always use a government-approved car seat (apparently our standards are a bit more rigorous than those of our neighbours to the south, so that means sticking to "homegrown" car seats rather than trying to bring one across the border). And don't attempt to use any other sort of juvenile product (e.g., a kitchen booster seat) as a substitute for a real car seat.

• Never allow your toddler to ride in your arms when the car is moving, no matter how unhappy he may be about being

---

MOTHER WISDOM

Travelling with a toddler doesn't have to be a total nightmare—not if you plan ahead. Here are some tips on making your next car trip as stress-free as possible for the entire family:

• Be realistic about the distance you can reasonably expect to cover in a day when you're travelling with a toddler. Gone are the days when you could drive all day and night in the hope of getting to your vacation destination a day sooner. Try that same manoeuvre with a toddler and you'll be looking for a psychiatric hospital with a drive-thru admitting department!

• Give some thought to the time of day when you'll be travelling. The last thing you want is to waste an hour or two battling rush-hour traffic. Otherwise, you could use up all of your toddler's patience before you've even clocked 20 kilometres on the odometer!

• Make sure that the straps on your toddler's car seat are tight enough to be safe but not so tight as to be uncomfortable. Otherwise, your toddler could be singing the blues before you even get out of the driveway. And remember to readjust the straps frequently as you add and subtract layers of outerwear.

• Come up with creative ways of keeping your toddler entertained while you're on the road. Stock the car with a variety of toys and games: books on tapes, music CDs, hand puppets, felt boards, a cookie sheet covered with magnetic letters, and so on. You might also want to create a special "no mess" travel art kit by gathering together such items as washable, nontoxic markers and crayons, stencils, lick-and-stick stickers, index cards, sticky notes, Scotch Tape, and a small pad of paper. Just watch out for heavy items that could become dangerous projectiles in the event of a collision.

strapped in his car seat. (Hint: You're likely to have a happier toddler if you're realistic about the length of the car trips you plan at this stage of his life. It's a rare toddler who can stand spending more than a couple of hours in the car at once.)

- Don't place groceries or other objects near your toddler, since they may end up becoming dangerous projectiles in the event

---

- If your toddler drops a toy while the car is moving, wait until you can safely pull over before retrieving it. Or—better yet—keep a bag of toys within grabbing distance so that you can hand him another toy instead.
- Attach a child-safe mirror to the back of the passenger or driver's seat so that your baby or toddler can enjoy looking in the mirror while you're on the go.
- Make sure your vehicle is also stocked with drinks, snacks, damp washcloths, and at least one full change of clothing for your toddler (two or more complete outfits if you're in the middle of toilet training).
- Don't just fuel up the car; fuel up your toddler, too. Make sure he's well fed before you leave home and pack an ample supply of snacks for the trip. Just one small but important caveat on the food front: be sure to go light on the liquids if your toddler is newly trained. Otherwise, you'll be stopping for bathroom breaks every half-hour or so. And speaking of bathroom breaks, you might want to bring your child's potty along for the ride. It could prove to be a lifesaver.
- Take advantage of points of interest along the way—parks and playgrounds, children's museums, and other kid-friendly attractions. If you're not familiar with the cities you'll be passing through, do your homework before you hit the highway. Frommer's publishes a line of *Frommer's with Kids* guidebooks that can be invaluable in planning your family's pit stops. Remember, getting there is half the fun (or at least that's the theory).
- Plan to arrive home a day or two before you have to return to work. Not only will you need to catch up on the family's laundry, but you may also need to catch up on your sleep! Travelling with a toddler is fun, but it can be exhausting, too.
- Last but not least, have fun. Family trips are the stuff of which memories are made. Be sure to make the most of this special time with your child.

MOM'S THE WORD

"My daughter was a monkey in the car. She would wiggle until she managed to work her way free from her five-point harness. One day when I once again had to pull over to the side of the highway to put her back into her car seat, I came up with a plan. I got Heaven out of the car and the two of us started walking. She quickly became tired and wanted to be carried. I simply informed her that, without a car, we would always get around this way. Needless to say, we returned to the car with no further incidents!"

—*Kimberlee, 29, mother of two*

---

of an accident. Store them in your trunk or luggage compartment instead. A soup can, flying at 100 kilometres an hour, can do a lot of damage to a toddler or young child.

- Don't forget to take your toddler's car seat along if you're planning to travel by air. While airlines currently allow parents to hold young children in their laps rather than buckling them into a car seat, doing so leaves them vulnerable to injury or even death in the event of severe turbulence or a crash. You can find some important information on using your toddler's car seat in an airplane by visiting the Safe Kids Canada Web site: www.safekidscanada.ca.

Summer safety

IT'S SUMMERTIME AND the living is easy—but that doesn't mean you can afford to give safety a vacation. If anything, parents need to be more vigilant about keeping their toddlers safe during the spring and summer months. According to Safe Kids Canada—the national injury prevention program of the Hospital for Sick Children in Toronto—the summer months are the peak time of year for injuries. Here are the key areas you'll want to focus on in order to keep your toddler safe:

- **Drowning:** According to the Canadian Red Cross, drowning is one of the leading causes of death for Canadian children between the ages of one and four, second only to motor vehicle accidents. Children can drown in less than four centimetres (one-and-a-half inches) of water—just enough water to cover the nose and mouth—and the majority of drownings occur when an adult's attention is momentarily distracted (e.g., someone runs in the house for a moment to answer the phone). Take appropriate precautions with your own backyard pool: Use pool alarms and ensure that the pool area is enclosed inside a 1.2-metre (four-foot-high) fence with a self-closing, self-latching gate, and turn wading pools upside down when they're not in use. You'll also want to give some thought to other water hazards near your home, such as ponds, your neighbour's backyard hot tub, and so on.

- **Sun safety:** It's also important to protect your children from the harmful effects of the sun. Children should wear sunhats and a sunscreen with a sun protection factor (SPF) of at least 30, and they should avoid the sun around midday, when the sun's rays are strongest. Be sure to reapply your child's sunscreen throughout the day to ensure maximum protection.

- **Playground safety:** More than 28,000 Canadian children are injured on playgrounds each year. The three biggest culprits are slides, monkey bars, and swings. Because the majority of

TODDLER TALK

Kids face a 96% greater risk of drowning during the summer months than at other times of the year.

injuries result from falls, it's a good idea to remember the rule of five (keep children under age five off any piece of equipment that's higher than 1.5 metres, or five feet). It's also important to choose age-appropriate equipment; to check playground equipment for signs of wear and tear; to ensure that the equipment conforms with current safety standards; and to provide a loose-fill surface that is at least 15 centimetres (six inches) deep under swings, climbers, and slides to cushion falls. You'll also want to be on the lookout for any related hazards that could result in injury or illness, like puddles of water that could pose a drowning hazard, animal feces, broken glass, and garbage. Note: You can find detailed information on playground safety on the Safe Kids Canada Web site: www.safekidscanada.ca.

- **Garage injuries:** Garages play host to some of the most hazardous items in our homes: gasoline, antifreeze, paints, solvents, pesticides, power tools, lawnmowers, and so on. That's why it's a good idea to designate them as kid-free zones and to store bicycles and other outdoor play equipment in a shed or other location. That way, your toddler will never have any reason to step foot in the garage.

- **Dog bites:** Dog bites are yet another hazard of the season. While nearly half of dog bites are caused by the child's own pet, it's important to teach your toddler how to behave around other people's dogs and to supervise him closely whenever he's around animals. Teach your child to stand still if he is approached or chased by a strange dog. Make sure that

TODDLER TALK

According to Safe Kids Canada, 20% of the 28,000 playground injuries that occur in Canada each year happen in backyard playgrounds.

TODDLER TALK

According to Health Canada, 40% of injuries on slides occur to children ages two through four; in one out of 10 cases, the injury is serious enough to warrant hospitalization.

---

he understands the importance of not running, kicking, or making threatening gestures toward the dog, no matter how frightened he may feel. (A better strategy is to face the dog and back away slowly until he's out of the dog's reach.) Note: You'll find some additional information on toddlers and pets in Chapter 10.

- **Travel safety:** If you'll be visiting out-of-town relatives or staying in hotels this summer, you'll want to keep in mind that hotel rooms and other people's homes may not have been adequately childproofed. You don't want to find out the hard way that medications and other hazardous products were left within your child's reach—perhaps in Grandma's purse. You should also give some thought to the types of items that may be stashed away in your own suitcase while you're travelling: pain relief medications, birth control pills, and so on. It's easy to slip up on safety while you're on the road.

Winter safety

OF COURSE, SAFETY is a year-round responsibility, so you'll also need to take steps to keep your toddler safe during the fall and winter months. Here are some important points to keep in mind:

- **Frostbite:** Skin that is exposed to extreme temperatures will freeze quickly if it's left exposed. That's why it's important to bundle up your toddler during cold weather, dressing him in several layers of warm clothing (e.g., a coat or snowsuit that is both water and wind resistant, mitts, boots that are neither too small nor too tight, a warm hat, and a scarf). Your toddler's cheeks, ears, nose, hands, and feet are most vulnerable to frostbite. Affected skin initially becomes red and swollen and feels as though it's stinging or burning. If the skin continues to be exposed to the cold, it will tingle and turn greyish, and then turn shiny and white and lose all sensation. If your toddler comes in from the cold complaining of a sore body part—the key warning symptom of frostbite—you should gently remove any clothing that's covering the frostbitten area and slowly rewarm the area using body heat. Do not massage or rub snow onto the frostbitten skin or use heat or warm water to warm the skin. Instead, call your child's doctor to discuss treatment.

- **Holiday safety:** If you're doing some entertaining during the holiday season and guests are smoking or drinking in your home, you'll want to make a point of scooping up leftover drinks and ashtrays full of cigarette butts before you call it a night. Otherwise your toddler could end up eating the butts and drinking the remnants of the drinks, something that could lead to poisoning. (Of course, it's best to prevent those cigarette butts and the smoke that comes with them from entering your house in the first place; kids and cigarette smoke don't make a particularly good mix.)

TODDLER TALK

Holly and mistletoe are poisonous plants, so you'll want to make a point of hanging them above the doorway out of the reach of children. You'll also want to keep breakable ornaments, candles, and strings of lights out of your toddler's reach to prevent cuts and burns.

The safety generation gap

WHILE SOME GRANDPARENTS do a terrific job of getting up to speed on modern child safety practices, some seem determined to stick with the practices that were in vogue a generation earlier.

While Kelli's parents respect her wishes when it comes to child safety, they make it clear that they think she's being overly protective of her child. "They find our use of technology (baby monitors) and fancy accoutrements (bouncy chairs and swings) superfluous," the 32-year-old mother of two explains. "When I ask my parents to do things for my child in a certain way, they say things like, 'How did we ever raise three children without you and your baby books?'"

This type of generation gap can be a real problem for families today. Here are some tips on getting Grandma on board without sacrificing the safety of your child:

- Educate your parents and your in-laws about safety-related issues. Either pass along a few safety pamphlets or point them in the direction of one of the many excellent child safety Web sites. (Note: You'll find leads on many such Web sites in Appendix C.) Once they find out how many children's lives are saved each year by "newfangled" inventions such as car seats, they may be a little bit more willing to respect your wishes with regard to your child's safety.

- Make sure that your parents and in-laws are walking the talk of child safety. Even if you think they've absorbed all the important safety information you've passed along, keep an eye on them when they're around your toddler. Your mother may accidentally slip up and hand your toddler a bowl full of popcorn, forgetting that popcorn poses a significant choking risk for a toddler. Or she may show up with latex balloons on his first birthday. If you notice a number of such slip-ups, you'll want to hold off on leaving your toddler in your mother's care. You'll feel much more comfortable—and your toddler will be much safer—if you're on hand to supervise their visits together.

• Show the older generation how it's done. Rather than talking to your parents or in-laws about the importance of using a car seat correctly, save them a lot of grief by installing your toddler's car seat for them. Not only will you eliminate the very real possibility that they'll install the seat incorrectly, but you'll also be making it as convenient as possible for them to be safety conscious. ("When my children go out in cars with relatives, I simply ask for their car keys so that I can go install the seats myself," explains Sandi, a 31-year-old mother of two.)

• Don't be afraid to take a hard line insofar as your child's safety is concerned. This is one of those situations where there's quite simply no room to compromise. "My mother-in-law purchased an old used car seat and set up an old crib that she'd used for both of her children," confides one mother of three. "Because she wouldn't listen to us when we tried to convince her that these items weren't safe, my daughter has never been allowed to drive in the car with my mother-in-law, nor has she ever slept overnight at my in-laws' house."

• Promise to be the most safety-conscious grandparent in the world when you get your own turn up at bat. (Hey, it's only fair to practise what you preach!)

First-aid essentials

EVERY PARENT SHOULD make a point of taking an infant and toddler first-aid and cardiopulmonary resuscitation (CPR) course.

But even if you have taken appropriate training in emergency first aid, it can be easy to draw a blank when your child starts choking or gets a bad burn. That's why I decided to include a quick reference chart outlining some basic infant first-aid procedures (see Table 9.4). Please note that I was barely able to scratch the surface here, due to space constraints, so don't make the mistake of considering this chart as a substitute for proper training in first aid and CPR or emergency medical assistance. You need hands-on training to perform chest compressions and other life-saving manoeuvres safety and effectively.

TABLE 9.4

Emergency First-Aid Procedures

Type of Emergency	What to Do
Allergic reaction	→ If your toddler is exhibiting the symptoms of an allergic reaction (e.g., swollen hands and eyelids, wheezing, and a hive-like rash), take him to your doctor's office or the hospital emergency ward immediately.
	→ Talk to your doctor about how to handle future allergic reactions, which, by the way, are likely to be more severe. You might want to carry a kit with injectable adrenalin in order to buy your toddler enough time to get to the hospital for emergency treatment.
Bleeding	→ If your child starts bleeding and the cut appears to be fairly deep, place a clean piece of gauze or cloth over the site of the bleeding and apply firm pressure for two minutes. If that stops the bleeding, you should attempt to clean the wound by running it under cold water. If the bleeding continues, apply more gauze and wrap tape around the cut to keep pressure on the bleeding.
	→ Position your toddler so that the area that is bleeding is above the level of his heart. This will help to reduce the amount of bleeding.

continued on p. 442

Type of Emergency	*What to Do*
Bleeding *continued*	➜ If the bleeding still won't stop, the wound is gaping, and the cut appears to be quite deep, you'll need to take your toddler to the hospital or your doctor's office for stitches. You'll also need to seek medical attention for your toddler if the cut has dirt in it that won't come out; the cut becomes inflamed; your child starts running a fever; the cut begins oozing a thick, creamy, greyish fluid; red streaks form near the wound; or the wound is caused by a human or animal bite.
Breathing, cessation of	➜ Try to figure out why your toddler isn't breathing if you discover that he's pale or turning blue. Look for any foreign objects in the mouth and clear out any vomit, mucus, or fluid that could be making it difficult for him to breathe by turning him on one side. If you suspect that he's choking, follow the steps outlined below on dealing with a choking emergency and call for help. If you're on your own, call for help as soon as it's practical—within a minute or two of starting CPR. ➜ Place your toddler on his back. Push down on the back of his head and up on his chin in order to clear the tongue away from the back of his throat. Don't push his head too far back, however, or you may end up obstructing the airway. If you roll a towel and slide it under your toddler's neck, he'll probably end up in the correct position. ➜ Give your toddler mouth-to-mouth resuscitation. Make a seal around your toddler's mouth and nose and give two quick breaths. If his chest rises with each breath, the airway is clear and you should continue administering mouth-to-mouth resuscitation until help arrives or your child starts breathing on his own. If he still isn't breathing, follow the procedures outlined below for dealing with choking. ➜ Check your toddler's pulse to see if his heart is beating. If it's not, you'll need to begin chest compressions (rhythmic thrusts of two to three fingers on your toddler's breastbone at a rate of at least 100 thrusts per minute), pausing to give

him a puff of air through mouth-to-mouth
resuscitation after every fifth heart compression.

Burns

➜ Assess the severity of the burn. First-degree burns
(such as sunburns) cause redness and minor
soreness and can be treated with cool water and
some soothing ointment. Second-degree burns
cause blistering, swelling, and peeling, are very
painful, and may require medical treatment.
Third-degree burns damage the underlying layers
of the skin and can lead to permanent damage;
medical treatment is a must.

➜ Submerge the burned area in cool water for at
least 20 minutes (or, in the case of a burn to the
face, apply a cool, water-soaked face cloth to the
burn). This will help to ease your toddler's pain
as well as lessen the amount of skin damage.
Note: Do not apply ice to a burn, as this can cause
damage to the tissues.

➜ If the skin becomes blistered, white, or charred,
apply an antiseptic ointment and cover the wound
before heading to your doctor's office or the
hospital. Note: You'll also want to give your toddler
a dose of acetaminophen to help control the pain.

➜ If your child gets a chemical burn as a result of
coming into contact with a caustic substance,
immerse the burned area under cool, running
water for 20 minutes. Gently wash the affected area
with soap. (Vigorous scrubbing will cause more of
the poison to be absorbed into the skin.) If the
substance was also inhaled or swallowed, get in
touch with your local poison control centre immediately. If a caustic substance was splashed into
your toddler's eyes, flush the area for 20 minutes.
(Swaddle your toddler in a towel to keep his arms
out of the way and lay him on his side. Then pour
water into his eye and onto a towel below. If your
toddler closes his eyes tightly, pull down on the
lower lid or put your index finger on the upper lid
just below the eyebrow and gently pry your
toddler's eyes open. Once you've finished flushing
your toddler's eyes, call for medical advice.)

continued on p. 444

Type of Emergency	What to Do
Choking	→ Quickly determine whether or not your toddler is able to breathe. If your toddler can cough, cry, or speak, the airway is not obstructed, and your toddler's built-in gag and cough reflex will help to dislodge the object. In this case, your best bet is to do nothing other than to reassure your toddler that he's going to be all right.
	→ If your toddler does not appear to be breathing, he will likely be gasping for air or turning blue, losing consciousness, and/or looking panicked (wide eyes and mouth wide open). In this case, you should straddle the toddler along your forearm so that his head is lower than his feet and his face is pointing toward the floor and then apply four quick, forceful blows between your toddler's shoulder blades using the heel of your hand. If you are in a public place, shout for help; if you're at home alone, run with the toddler to the phone and dial 911 while you attempt to resuscitate him.
	→ If the back blows don't dislodge the object and your toddler still isn't breathing, immediately flip your toddler over and deal four quick, forceful chest thrusts to the toddler's breastbone (about one finger's width below the level of the toddler's nipples, in the middle of the chest). To administer a chest thrust, you quickly depress the breastbone to a depth of 1.5 to 2.5 centimetres. You keep your fingers in the same position between thrusts but allow the breastbone to return to its normal position.
	→ If your toddler is still not breathing, hold his tongue down with your thumb and forefinger, lift the jaw open, and check if you can see the object that's causing the blockage. (The mere act of holding your toddler's tongue away from the back of his throat may relieve the obstruction.) If you see the object, carefully sweep it out. If you can't see it, don't poke your finger down your toddler's throat or you may accidentally cause an object that's

out of sight to become further lodged in your child's throat.

→ If the tongue-jaw lift doesn't work, begin mouth-to-mouth resuscitation on your toddler. Make a seal around his mouth and nose and give two quick breaths. If your toddler's chest rises with each breath and the airway is clear, you should continue administering mouth-to-mouth resuscitation until help arrives or your child starts breathing on his own.

→ If your toddler still isn't breathing, repeat all of these steps until help arrives.

Convulsions (seizures)	→ Assess the severity of the convulsion. Convulsions can range from localized muscle shakes to full-body shakes (grand mal seizures), which may involve falling and writhing on the ground, the rolling back of the eyes, frothing at the mouth, tongue biting, and a temporary loss of consciousness. → Take steps to ensure that your toddler's tongue or secretions do not block his airway. Place him safely on the floor, either face down or on his side to allow the tongue to come forward. This will also help to drain secretions from the mouth. → Keep your toddler away from furniture so that he won't injure himself during the convulsion. → Don't give your toddler any food or drink during or immediately after a convulsion. → If your toddler's lips start to turn blue or he stops breathing, clear his airway and give mouth-to-mouth resuscitation. Make a seal around his mouth and nose and give two quick breaths. If his chest rises with each breath, the airway is clear and you should continue administering mouth-to-mouth resuscitation until help arrives or your child starts breathing on his own. → If your toddler has a fever, treat the fever to try to prevent any subsequent seizures. (See Chapter 8 for how to treat a fever.) → Have your toddler seen by a doctor.

continued on p. 446

Type of Emergency	What to Do
Head injury	→ Try to assess the seriousness of the situation. If your toddler is unconscious but is still breathing and pinkish in colour rather than blue, lay him on a flat surface and call for emergency assistance. Note: Do not attempt to move him if you suspect that his neck may be injured.
	→ If he's not breathing, follow the steps outlined above on dealing with a child who isn't breathing.
	→ If he's having a convulsion, keep his airway clear by placing him on his back and pushing down on the back of his head and up on his chin in order to clear the tongue away from the back of his throat. Don't push his head too far back, however, or you may end up obstructing the airway. If you roll a towel and slide it under your toddler's neck, he'll probably end up in the correct position.
	→ If your toddler is acting like himself (e.g., he's alert and conscious and seems to be behaving normally), apply an ice pack (wrapped in a sock or face cloth) or a bag of frozen vegetables to the cut or bump and monitor your toddler closely over the next 24 hours—checking him every two hours around the clock to see if his colour is still normal (pink rather than pale or blue), that he's breathing normally (there may be cause for concern if your toddler's breathing becomes shallow, irregular, he's gasping for air, or he periodically stops breathing altogether), and to make sure that he's not twitching on one side (a sign of a possible brain injury). If he seems well, you can let him continue sleeping. If you're concerned that there could be a problem, sit or stand your toddler up and then lie him back down again. Normally this will cause the toddler to react. If you don't get a suitable reaction, seek medical attention immediately.
	→ You should seek medical attention immediately if you notice any signs of disorientation, crossed eyes, pupils that are unequal sizes, persistent vomiting (as opposed to just a one-time occurrence), oozing of blood or watery fluid from the ear canal,

convulsions, or any signs that your toddler's sense of balance has been thrown off by the fall.

Poisoning

→ Seek emergency medical attention if your toddler seems to be exhibiting any signs of severe poisoning-related distress (e.g., severe throat pain, excessive drooling, difficulty breathing, convulsions, and/or excessive drowsiness).

→ If the situation seems to be less urgent, call your local poison control centre for advice. The person handling the call will want to know the name of the product that was ingested and what its ingredients are, so be sure to have this information handy. You'll also be asked the time of the poisoning and approximately how much of the poison your toddler ingested, the age and weight of your toddler, and whether he's exhibiting any symptoms (e.g., vomiting, coughing, behavioural changes, and so on).

→ Do not attempt to induce vomiting unless the poison control centre staff member specifically instructs you to do so. Inducing vomiting under the wrong circumstances (e.g., if a caustic substance was ingested) could lead to severe tissue damage. In some cases, you'll be instructed to give your toddler a particular antidote—sometimes something as simple as a couple of glasses of water or a glass of milk.

→ If you're told to induce vomiting, give your toddler 15 millilitres (one tablespoon) of syrup of ipecac followed by 250 millilitres (one cup) of water or non-carbonated fruit juice. Then gently bounce him on your knee. Vomiting should occur within 20 minutes. If it does not, repeat the dose. When your toddler starts vomiting, hold him face down so that his head is lower than his body. Have your toddler vomit into a basin rather than the toilet so that the vomit can be analyzed to determine how much and what type(s) of poison he consumed. Be sure to observe your toddler closely for the next couple of hours and seek medical attention if warranted.

CHAPTER 10

All in the Family

D ESPITE WHAT SOME of the celebrity moms with their oh-so-perfect lives would have you believe, it's normal to have both up and down days as a parent. There are days when you feel unspeakably grateful to have a child in your life—and days when you wonder what on earth ever possessed you to sign up for this whole motherhood thing.

In this chapter, we're going to be talking about how having a toddler is likely to affect the rest of your life: your confidence in your parenting abilities, your relationship with your partner, your thoughts about having another baby, your decision to work outside the home (or not), and your relationship with your toddler's grandparents. Finally, we'll wrap up the book by talking about why the toddler years are the truly the stuff of which memories are made—a once-in-a-lifetime journey that's not to be missed.

MOM'S THE WORD

"My confidence in my parenting abilities has ebbed and flowed over the years. As a brand-new mother, I felt unsure with a new baby. As the baby grew, I gained more confidence. But then she moved into the toddler stage and I wasn't able to control her a lot of the time. That diminished my confidence again."

—*Karen, 36, mother of three*

MOM'S THE WORD
"I definitely felt more confident as Sarah got older. That first bump on the head, the first flu, the first unexplained rash—each milestone built my confidence as a parent."

—*Jennifer, 33, mother of one*

A good enough mom

IF YOU'RE LIKE most of us, you've probably set your sights on winning the Olympic gold medal for motherhood. Never mind the fact that they hand out only one gold medal every four years! Hey, why not shoot for the top?

I've got some good news for you, girlfriend. Motherhood has not yet become an Olympic sport—and, with any luck, it won't in our lifetimes. I mean, just imagine what the judging would be like! So rather than forcing yourself to measure up to some super-human standard of motherhood, why not take some advice from psychologist Bruno Bettelheim and settle for being a "good enough" mom.

Some women find that the toddler years are rocky years indeed when it comes to feeling confident as a parent. "My confidence goes up and down daily and sometimes hourly depending on the mood of my toddler," admits Jennifer, a 27-year-old mother of two.

Christy, on the other hand is finding it easier to cope with criticisms about her parenting abilities now that her children are moving into the preschool years: "I felt a strong need to measure up when my children were babies—more with my first child than with my second—but as my children moved into toddlerhood, I relaxed and stopped worrying about what everyone else thought," the 38-year-old mother of two explains.

Janie, however, finds it very difficult to cope with what she sees as unjust criticisms from friends and relatives. "Recently, a family member said that Rachel was 'spoiled,'" the 33-year-old mother of one recalls. "I took it as a great personal insult that anyone would say that. It's true that we don't battle Rachel on every little thing and we tend to turn a blind eye to many things, but if she's doing something that's either obnoxious or dangerous, we stop her immediately."

Maria believes that life would be a lot less stressful if mothers would learn to cut themselves—and other moms—a little bit more slack. "I don't want to be judged, so I try not to judge other parents," the 32-year-old mother of two explains. "Everyone has bad days. Just today, I had my children over to a girlfriend's house for a playdate. Her daughter—who is four—was very upset at her mother because she gave her a juice cup that she didn't want. She proceeded to cry and carry on for about 15 minutes. My friend removed her daughter from the situation and came back to apologize. I could tell she was embarrassed by her daughter's behaviour. I just looked at her and said, 'What? You think this doesn't happen at our house?' Parents have to learn to give other parents a break. There are enough other people out there putting pressure on us and our babies to 'measure up.' We need not eat our own."

Avoiding parent burnout

GIVEN HOW HIGH the standards are that we set for ourselves as mothers, it's hardly surprising that we sometimes find ourselves flirting with burnout. Kimberlee, a 29-year-old mother of two, has learned how to spot the warning signs in herself.

"I have experienced several episodes of pre-burnout, as I call it," she explains. "In each case, I felt a great fatigue that washed over me each morning as my children awoke....I found myself in

MOTHER WISDOM

"In the event of an oxygen shortage on airplanes, mothers of young children are always reminded to put on their own oxygen mask first, to better assist the children with theirs. The same tactic is necessary on terra firma. There's no way of sustaining our children if we don't first rescue ourselves. I don't call that selfish behaviour. I call it love."

—Joyce Maynard, "The Finishing Touches," *Parenting*, November 1992

a fog that followed me from morning until night. I also experienced racing thoughts, an overwhelming fear that I wasn't going to have it all, thoughts of making extreme changes to my career or personal life, a short temper, and avoidance symbolized by ever-larger laundry piles and unreturned phone calls."

Rather than ignoring the warning signs and progressing into full-blown burnout, Kimberlee has learned how to put on the brakes both personally and professionally: "What I do when I'm feeling this way is to schedule a 'Great Do Nothing Day' on the calendar. I plan for this by buying chips and ice cream, renting movies, cleaning my house, sorting mail, returning all those phone messages, and then I awake on the morning of Great Do Nothing Day and I do absolutely nothing. We all stay in our jammies all day and eat and play and make a big mess everywhere and cuddle and watch movies and sleep. It's marvellous!"

Not everyone can pull off a "Great Do Nothing Day" with quite the same style and finesse as Kimberlee, but there are a number of things you can do to recharge your parenting batteries. Here are a few ideas:

- Learn how to spot the early warning signs of parent burnout. If you find yourself becoming obsessed with the frustrations of parenting, second-guessing your parenting decisions most or all of the time, feeling trapped or hopeless, or starting to experience some of the physical symptoms of stress (e.g., headaches, heart palpitations, chronic colds or sinus problems, dizziness, nausea, and so on), you could be experiencing burnout.

- Make a point of keeping up some of your pre-baby interests so that you have something else to focus on than your role as a parent. "If I do something that I enjoy while my daughter is napping, I feel so much more contented when she gets up," says Debbie, a 33-year-old mother of one. Alyson, a 37-year-old mother of two, agrees that it's important to maintain interests outside the family: "Sometimes I feel like I'm being engulfed by family life and I need to remember that I'm not 'just' a mom."

- Designate part of your home as a toddler-free zone. That way, you'll have a small refuge to retreat to if you're feeling swallowed up by demands of motherhood. "My living room/dining room is a quiet, peaceful, child-toy-free zone that I use as my sanity saver," says Kimberlee.

- Make sure you take breaks from your toddler on a regular basis, even if you have to hire someone to buy yourself a little time away. "Who says a babysitter has to work in your house while you go out?" says Anita, a 39-year-old mother of four. "I hired a local teenager to take my kids for a one-hour walk three times a week just so I could put my feet up and either have a cup of tea or take a nap."

MOM'S THE WORD

"To recharge my batteries, I go snuggle the kids after they're asleep. I remind myself how much I love them and how much fun I have with them. Of course, sometimes a family-sized chocolate bar at midnight helps, too!"

—*Stephanie, 30, mother of three*

"Everything happens in doubles when you've got twins; while one is climbing on top of the piano, the other is ripping the plants apart! And while you're fixing the problem that kid number one created, you can bet your bottom dollar that kid number two knows you're busy and will take advantage of that moment to make some trouble of his own. Just be prepared, be patient, and know that you have been doubly blessed."

—*Catherine, 32, mother of four*

- Find creative ways to recharge your batteries. Alyson, a 37-year-old mother of two, has found that acting zany helps her to get through those less-than-wonderful days as a parent: "I was having a particularly difficult day with both Maggie and Joey recently. During lunch, one of my favourite dance songs came on the radio. I cranked up the volume and started to dance. Joey and Maggie joined in and we had a great time."

- Recognize that some parents face greater parenting challenges than others—and therefore face a greater risk of burnout. "When you're a single parent, it's a 24/7 job without someone at home helping to share the burden," says Jen, a 36-year-old mother of one. "I find that when the going gets tough, we both need to take a time out. Marisa goes to her crib and I go to my room. I take a deep breath and then—after a couple of minutes—go back to see her with a smile on my face."

Staying connected with your partner

Having a toddler underfoot can place a strain on your relationship with your partner. After all, it's pretty easy to fall out of touch when you've got a toddler competing for your attention day in and day out. "With a baby, we knew there would be time for us to be alone when the baby napped or slept at night," explains Sidney, a 33-year-old mother of one. "With a toddler, there isn't the same amount of time available."

Alyson, a 37-year-old mother of two, found that it was during the toddler years that parenting conflicts first came to the fore-front—something that led to extra friction between her and her husband. "No one ever seems to warn you about the strain that toddlers can put on a relationship. They only talk about the first year being difficult. But I can tell you that my husband and I have definitely had more disagreements during Joey and Maggie's toddler stages than we ever did when they were babies."

It's important to accept the fact that you may be in for a challenging period in your relationship. It's easy for tempers to flare and feelings to get hurt when you're in the parenting trenches. Fortunately, if the bond between the two of you is strong enough, you can expect to weather this particular relationship storm without too much difficulty: A study at the University of Washington revealed that couples who are good friends before they start their families are better able to adjust to the stresses of parenthood than couples who are less satisfied with their relationships.

With any luck, you'll find that your shared love for your child will help to forge a powerful bond between you over time. As one of the moms I interviewed for *The Mother of All Pregnancy Books* noted, "Having a baby made my relationship with my partner even stronger. Watching him take care of our son and seeing what a great dad he is made me love him even more."

MOTHER WISDOM

Finding that you've got less time and energy for sex than you did in your pre-baby days? You're in good company. Seventy-seven percent of the 2,500 parents who responded to *Today's Parent's* online sex survey admitted to having sex less often since they had kids than they did before, and 40% admitted to choosing sleep over sex on a regular basis.

MOM'S THE WORD

"I sometimes wonder if we approach parenting differently because our son was brought to us through the miracle of science—IVF. Do such children of grace and miracle—children born to parents who may have been through years of trial to get them—live in different parenting environments?"

—*Annie, 44, mom of one*

Dad's the word

REMEMBER THAT SCENE in *My Fair Lady* when an exasperated Professor Henry Higgins wonders aloud, "Why can't a woman be more like a man?" Well, we moms are sometimes guilty of indulging in a little bit of reverse sexism, insisting that dads would be much better parents if only they were more like moms!

Despite what many people believe, men are not biologically inferior when it comes to raising children; they simply have a different style. Here's what researchers have identified as the key differences between the two sexes in their interaction with children:

- **Type of play:** Mothers are more likely to introduce toys into play when they're playing with their children, while fathers are more likely to engage in rough-and-tumble play. (Now there's a newsflash for you!) The theory is that moms get enough body to body contact during pregnancy and breastfeeding, so they're less inclined to engage in this particular type of play than dads.

- **Frustration level:** Dads are more willing to allow toddlers to experience a greater amount of frustration than moms are when those toddlers are attempting to master a particular task.

- **Role of routine:** While mothers tend to be consistent and calm when handling children, dads prefer unpredictable, playful interactions—something that young children find highly stimulating.

Of course, it's important to bear in mind that mothers and fathers are actually more alike than different in caring for young children. A now-famous study conducted by Michael Lamb of the National Institute of Mental Health in the U.S. demonstrated that men and women's automatic nervous system responses to crying babies were virtually identical. In other words, moms don't have a monopoly on the hard-wiring that compels them to respond to their children's cries; dads are programmed to be nurturing, too.

Are you ready to have another baby?

A RECENT STUDY conducted by the U.S. Centers for Disease Control and Prevention concluded that the optimal gap between births is 18 to 23 months. According to the researchers, this results in the healthiest possible outcomes for both mothers and babies.

What this study—and others like it—fail to acknowledge, however, is the fact that there's no such thing as "one size fits all" family planning. While some women are ready to plunge into another pregnancy while they still have one or more children in

---

MOTHER WISDOM

"We can't nourish our children if we don't nourish ourselves.... Parents who manage to stay married, sane, and connected to one another share one basic characteristic: the ability to protect even small amounts of time together no matter what else is going on in their lives."

—*Ron Taffel*, Why Parents Disagree

diapers, others don't even want to think about seeing the pregnancy test come back positive again until their youngest child hops on the school bus for kindergarten!

Still, while there's no "perfect time" to have another baby, some times are definitely better than others. Here are some factors to consider when you're trying to decide whether you're ready to add another child to your family:

- How old is your youngest child? If you're still getting up two or three times a night with a young toddler, it may be hard to find the energy to cope with the physical demands of pregnancy.

- How much attention does your other child or children require? It's one thing to contemplate another pregnancy if your other children are all relatively self-sufficient, and quite another to think about becoming pregnant in the immediate future if you're busy caring for triplets or a child with complex medical needs.

- How does your partner feel about having another baby? While reproductive advances have made men almost obsolete in the reproductive process, most of us prefer to have them along for the ride! If your partner feels quite strongly that he's not ready for another baby, you might not want to toss the birth control pills in the trash just yet.

- Is your relationship on fairly solid ground right now? There's a myth that says having a baby can help to bring a couple closer together when actually the opposite is true. If you're already having difficulty communicating, having a colicky newborn on hand isn't going to help matters at all.

- How will having another child affect your family's financial situation? There's no denying it: kids cost money. If having another baby is going to stretch your budget to the breaking point, you might want to hold off on becoming pregnant until your financial situation is looking a little healthier. (Of course, if you wait until that wonderful day when your house is paid off, your RRSP contributions have been maximized, and you've got a healthy little nest egg stashed away in the bank, you may be well beyond your childbearing years!)

Pregnancy the second time around

Assuming you do decide to take the plunge and plan another pregnancy, you may wonder how your second pregnancy will compare to your first. While you'd need a crystal ball in order to predict exactly how your mind and body will react to this second stroll down Maternity Avenue—every pregnancy is different, after all!—it's possible to make a few educated guesses about how things will play out between now and delivery day. Here's what to expect:

- **You may find that you're less preoccupied with your pregnancy this time around.** It is, after all, a lot more difficult to find the time to luxuriate in the fact that you're pregnant again when you're busy chasing a toddler around the house. If you find yourself feeling guilty for letting the busyness of everyday life distract you from your excitement about being pregnant, try to cut yourself some slack; you'll have plenty of time to bond with your new baby after the birth.

- **You may find yourself worrying that you won't love the new baby as much as you love your toddler—or that you're ruining your older child's life by bringing a sibling into the picture.** While there may be a few rough patches during the early weeks and months of your new baby's life, you'll no doubt find that you're able to scratch these two items off your worry list relatively quickly. You'll adjust to the new baby's

arrival and so will baby number one—a.k.a. your toddler!
(Note: You'll find some practical tips on helping your toddler
prepare for the birth of a new baby later in this chapter.)

- **You're likely to feel extra-tired this time around.** Remember
  the good old days when you were able to succumb to the
  fatigue of early pregnancy by heading to bed at 7:00 p.m. or
  flopping out on the couch on Saturday and Sunday afternoons
  in order to catch up on your sleep? Well, that's all ancient history if you've got a toddler to look after. Even if your partner
  goes to truly heroic lengths to ensure that you get your rest,
  your mommy radar may make it difficult for you to relax and
  unwind if your toddler is playing in the next room. Add the
  fact that you're likely to be on nighttime parenting duty from
  time to time, and you can see why sleep may be nothing
  more than the stuff of which dreams are made at this point
  in your life.

- **You may start showing sooner.** Because your uterus has
  already been down this road before and your abdominal muscles might not be quite as taut as they were the first time
  around, you can expect to start showing sooner than you did
  during your first pregnancy. Some second-time moms find, in
  fact, that they're into their maternity clothes long before they
  reach their second trimester.

- **You may detect fetal movement sooner than you did the
  first time around.** Because you're already an old pro when it
  comes to detecting fetal movement, you can expect to start
  feeling your baby's flutters a few weeks earlier this time. First-
  time moms often have difficulty distinguishing between bona
  fide fetal movement and run-of-the-mill gastrointestinal sensations. Of course, as with anything else pregnancy-related,
  your mileage may vary on this front; if your baby decides to

camp out toward the back rather than the front of your uterus during this pregnancy, you may have difficulty detecting much fetal movement until you're well into the second half of your pregnancy.

- **Your second labour may be shorter—but there are no guarantees.** Just as there's no such thing as a one-size-fits-all pregnancy, there's no such thing as a one-size-fits-all labour. While most women find that their second labour progresses more quickly than their first (the average rate of cervical dilation is 1.2 centimetres per hour for a first baby and 1.5 centimetres an hour for subsequent deliveries, and the average length of the pushing stage drops from one to two hours for a first baby to less than an hour for subsequent babies), you won't know for certain if that's going to be the case for you until you're actually in the heat of labour.

- **The "afterpains" that you experience after giving birth are likely to be much more painful this time around.** While you may barely even remember experiencing afterpains after you gave birth to your first baby, you're unlikely to overlook these uterine contractions this time. Some second-time mothers find, in fact, that they require pain medication to deal with the painful uterine contractions they experience during the first few days after giving birth. While these afterpains are a sign that your uterus is doing exactly what it's supposed to be doing—morphing back to its pre-pregnancy state—some women find them to be every bit as painful as the contractions they experienced during labour.

Of course, it's not all gloom and doom on the second pregnancy front. Far from it! Many women who are pregnant for the second time find that they're able to relax and enjoy their second pregnancies much more than they did the first time. After all, they're old pros at this pregnancy thing now.

Preparing your toddler for the new baby

Wondering what you can do to encourage your toddler to welcome the new baby? Here are a few tips:

- Tap into your toddler's natural curiosity about babies. Take her to some of your prenatal checkups so that she'll have the opportunity to listen to the baby's heartbeat and watch the doctor or midwife measure your belly. Being involved in your pregnancy may help to make your pregnancy a little less abstract and the baby a little more real for her.

- Resist the temptation to oversell the new baby. Rather than focusing on how fun the baby will be in a year or two, let your child know what the baby will be like when she first arrives. Some toddlers are rather disappointed to find out that the new baby can't play with toys or run around the house, so it may be worthwhile to visit another family with a very young baby so that your toddler can see what newborns are all about.

- Sign your toddler up for sibling preparation classes. These types of classes are now being offered by a growing number of hospitals, childbirth associations, and adoption agencies, so you'll want to find out what's available in your community.

- Buy your toddler a small gift from the new baby—perhaps a new book or an activity that the two of you can enjoy together while the baby is eating or sleeping.

MOM'S THE WORD

"I gave birth to Silas at home in the night and Guthrie slept through all the excitement. Then, in the morning, my husband and I went downstairs, leaving Silas upstairs in bed. Guthrie woke up, found Silas, ran to the top of the stairs and yelled, 'Mommy, the baby came out.'"

—*Lynn, 36, mother of two*

- Take your toddler shopping with you when you're picking up items for the new baby. Encourage her to make as many purchasing decisions as possible—what colour of sleepers to buy, what brand of diapers to purchase, and so on. Being allowed to make some key decisions will help your toddler to feel a little more in control.

- Talk about what will happen to your toddler when you're in labour. She needs to know who will be taking care of her and when she'll get to see you again.

- If you're planning a home birth, you'll want to appoint someone to be totally responsible for your toddler's care while you're in labour. The last thing you want to have to do is to pour a glass of juice or run your toddler to the potty in the middle of a killer contraction! If you want your toddler to be present at the moment when her new brother or sister is born, you might want to hold off on bringing her in the room until your baby's head is starting to crown; some toddlers find it very stressful and upsetting to see their mothers in a great deal of pain and may be frightened by all the labour-related commotion.

- Don't expect the initial meeting between your toddler and the new baby to play out as the ultimate Kodak moment. Your toddler may be whiny or clingy because she misses you or because her world has just been rocked by the arrival of a new sibling.

- Make a point of spending time alone with your toddler. Find a few minutes each day to do something just with her, whether

---

MOTHER WISDOM

To minimize the risk of accidents, make sure that your baby is always securely strapped into her baby swing or car seat so that your toddler won't accidentally dump the baby out onto the floor.

MOM'S THE WORD

"My daughter gives the baby 'extreme hugs.' She sort of squeezes and kind of shakes when she does it. It's hard to describe, but it's hilarious!"

—*Karen, 36, mother of three*

it's reading a story, playing with playdough, or simply seizing the opportunity for a cuddle on the couch.

- Ask a friend or relative to do something special with your toddler shortly after the new baby's arrival. Some time alone with Grandma or Grandpa may help to reassure your toddler that she's still as special as ever, new baby or not!

- Encourage your toddler to help with the baby. She might want to pick out the baby's outfit for the day or to choose a toy to entertain her. You might even encourage your toddler to make a toy for the baby, like an eye-catching black-and-white mobile.

- Try not to hyperventilate each time your toddler gets close to the baby. Instead, show her how to move slowly and carefully and to be gentle with the baby. At the same time, you'll want to be prepared for aggression. Your toddler may get a sudden impulse to hit or bite the baby. (My sister found out the hard way that a jealous toddler can chomp down on the new baby's foot quicker than you can say "sibling rivalry"!)

- Look for subtle (and not-so-subtle!) indications that your toddler may be having a little bit of trouble accepting the new baby. One family was taken by surprise when their preschooler drew a picture of a baby surrounded by a red circle with a line through it—the international symbol for "no babies," I presume.

- When you pull out your camera to take dozens of shots of the new baby, be sure take at least one shot of your toddler. Otherwise, she'll be quite disappointed when the film comes back from the photo lab and there isn't a single picture of her.

- Don't despair if sibling love doesn't blossom overnight. It can take time for your older child to develop feelings for the new baby, but that special bond will emerge over time.

Toddlers and pets

PLANNING TO ADD another member to the family—one of the four-legged variety? You might want to give some thought to your timing. Toddlers and pets don't always make the best mix.

"While I think it's important for all children to learn about the value of life and the responsibility we have to care compassionately for other living things, I don't think it's a good idea for households with toddlers to introduce new pets into their homes," says Anita, a 39-year-old mother of four. "The friskiness of a new puppy or kitten doesn't mix well with the adventurousness of a toddler, in my opinion."

If you do decide to throw caution to the wind and introduce a pet to the family during your child's toddler years (something that practically guarantees, by the way, that you'll be training a puppy and a toddler at virtually the same time), you'll want to keep these important health and safety points in mind:

- Choose your pet with care. Some types of animals are completely unsuitable for families with young children. Ferrets and vicious dogs are a poor choice, due to the risk of the toddler being attacked; and reptiles are not recommended because they're a source of the potentially deadly bacteria salmonella—

FRIDGE NOTES

The Canadian Paediatric Society has prepared a helpful document that summarizes the diseases that various types of animals can spread to humans. You'll find it online at www.caringforkids.cps.ca/healthy/Pets.htm.

---

a bacteria that will contaminate the cage and any other surface the reptile comes into contact with, incidentally.

- If you're in the market for a dog, look for a puppy with an easygoing temperament. The Canadian Veterinary Medical Association recommends that you crouch down, clap your hands, and call to the puppy you're considering purchasing to see how the dog will react. If the dog is overly aggressive or seems antisocial, you'll want to look for another pet. If, however, the dog approaches you eagerly with his tail level or pointing down, he'll probably respond well to training. You should also note his response to petting and playing in deciding whether or not this is the dog for you.

- Make sure your toddler understands that the new pet is a living creature, not a toy. According to the Canadian Veterinary Medical Association, failing to teach your toddler how to handle pets properly could result in suffering on the part of the pet and—in some cases—injury to the child. To prevent such incidents, you'll want to supervise your toddler carefully. Teach her how to be gentle in handling or stroking the family pet and the importance of avoiding sudden movements and loud noises that could frighten or anger the pet.

- Teach your toddler to respect the pet's need for privacy. Provide the pet with a crate or specific corner in the house where it can retreat if it needs a bit of time away from your toddler.

FRIDGE NOTES

You can find additional information on choosing a toddler-friendly pet by reading *A Commonsense Guide to Selecting a Dog or a Cat*, available for download from the Canadian Veterinary Medical Association's pet health Web site: www.animalhealthcare.ca.

- Teach your toddler to respect strange animals, e.g., to never approach or pet someone else's dog or cat unless you or another trusted adult have given them permission to do so. In the majority of cases when people are bitten by pets, children are the victims. If your toddler is bitten by a dog or a cat, you'll need to clean the wound right away and call your toddler's doctor to see if she'll require medical attention. While dog bites generally look worse than cat bites, cat bites are more likely to lead to infection. If your toddler has been bitten by a cat, antibiotic treatment may be required.

The working mother's survival guide

TO RETURN TO work or not to return to work—that is the question many mothers struggle with as their maternity leave draws to a close. Should they kiss the working world goodbye for a couple of years and stay at home to raise a family, or should they try their hand at the ultimate of juggling acts—being a mother who works outside the home (a.k.a. a working mom)?

If the decision about whether to work outside the home or stay at home with your kids were entirely financial, you'd simply plug some numbers into a computer spreadsheet and—voilà!—you'd have your answer in a matter of seconds. Unfortunately, this decision is nowhere near that easy to make. You'll need to consider a number of additional factors, including the following:

TODDLER TALK

Stay-at-home moms like the June Cleaver of *Leave It to Beaver* fame have practically made their way onto the endangered species list. According to Statistics Canada, the dual-income family is now officially the norm: In 68% of families with young children, both parents work outside the home. It isn't difficult to figure out why we've evolved into a nation of two-income families. According to Statistics Canada, more than one-third of Canadian dual-income families would find themselves living below the poverty line if they had to survive on a single income alone.

- **How you feel about being home with a toddler.** Some women are cut out for being stay-at-home mothers; others aren't. Don't let anyone talk you into staying home with your toddler if the whole stay-at-home mom thing causes you to break out into a cold sweat. Likewise, don't let anyone pressure you into going back to work if you can't bear the thought of being away from your toddler for an hour, let alone an entire day, or if you simply can't imagine missing out on any of your child's amazing "firsts." This is definitely one of those issues that you have to sort through for yourself. Note: If it turns out that you have no choice but to go back to work even though your heart is telling you to do otherwise, be honest with yourself about how you're feeling and give yourself permission to grieve the loss of your dream of being at home with your child.

- **How you feel about being financially dependent upon your partner.** The moment you make the decision to stay home and raise a family, you lose your financial independence. For better or worse, you're dependent on your partner to bring home the bacon—something that can significantly alter the balance of power in your marriage and leave you more vulnerable to financial disaster. (If your marriage were to break up or your partner were to die or become disabled, you could find yourself trying to re-enter the workplace with few, if any, marketable skills.) The best way to deal with this particular concern is to have a frank discussion with your partner about how the two of you will handle money issues when you go from two incomes to one and to ensure that your partner carries enough insurance to provide for you and the children should something happen to him.

- **How much you enjoy your career.** If you were counting down the days until the start of your maternity leave so that you could get a break from the Job from Hell, chances are you won't mind taking a little time off to be at home with your child. If, on the other hand, you derive a great deal of satisfaction from your job and consider your co-workers to be among your best friends in the world, you may be more inclined to want to return to your job after your maternity leave ends. Just don't be surprised if you discover that your feelings about your career have shifted since your child was born. Your priorities may be significantly different from what they were in your pre-baby days.

- **How you feel about being a stay-at-home mother.** Believe it or not, there are still people in this world who look down

---

MOM'S THE WORD

"With my first child, I learned that I could love her more than anything and yet not want to be with her 24 hours a day. I really looked forward to going back to work. I suffered a great deal of guilt for wanting some time to myself. Very few people supported my belief that daycare was good for her and working was good for me. Most other mothers I met who worked just talked about how much they wanted to be at home and how they worried all day about their children. I didn't share that view and therefore felt very isolated."

—*Christy, 38, mother of two*

MOTHER WISDOM

"The child-rearing years are relatively short in our increased life span. It is hard for young women caught between diapers and formula to believe, but there are years and years of freedom ahead. I regret my impatience to get on with my career. I wish I'd relaxed, allowed myself the luxury of watching the world through my little girl's eyes."

—*Educator and author Eda Le Shan, quoted in* Mister Rogers Talks with Parents, *by Fred Rogers*

---

their noses at stay-at-home mothers, massively underestimating the commitment and energy that goes into caring for young children. If you're going to stay at home to raise a family, you need to feel that the job of stay-at-home mother is the most important job in the world. As Marni Jackson noted in an article entitled "Bringing Up Baby" in the December 1989 issue of *Saturday Night*, "The mother who stays home needs an ego of Kryptonite because her self-esteem will suffer in hard-to-pin-down ways." If you choose to become a stay-at-home mom, you may want to connect with other moms who are at home with their children by either joining a neighbourhood playgroup or frequenting parenting Web sites with discussion areas devoted to stay-at-home moms.

Choosing child care

If you do make the decision to return to work, one of the first things you'll have to do is find a suitable child-care arrangement for your toddler.

According to Statistics Canada, 40% of children under the age of five are cared for by someone other than their own parents while their parents work or go to school. The vast majority of these children (56%) are cared for in someone else's home. Just 20% are cared for in daycare centres and 22% in their own homes.

MOM'S THE WORD

"I muddle through pangs of guilt that plague me throughout my week. I see or hear of a great stay-at-home mom and I find myself asking myself the universal question, 'Am I doing this right?'"

—*Kimberlee, 29, mother of two*

Because there's no guarantee that a child-care space will become available at the exact time you need it, it's best to hedge your bets by getting on the waiting list for every child-care centre or home daycare in your community that meets your criteria. (Obviously, this will necessitate spending a fair bit of time checking out your various options, but, trust me, this will prove to be time well spent. You can find a list of the types of questions you'll want to ask in Table 10.1.)

The only thing you can't do months ahead of time is hire an in-home child-care provider such as a live-in or live-out nanny. If you choose to have someone come into your home to care for your toddler, you'll have to leave the hiring process until one to two months prior to your return to work. Note: If you decide to hire an in-home caregiver, make sure you understand your responsibilities as an employer. You'll want to get in touch with both the Canada Customs and Revenue Agency and your provincial or territorial ministry of labour to find out what's involved in hiring a child-care provider. The last thing you want to do is get your-

---

MOM'S THE WORD

"I sometimes get this nagging feeling that my daughter would have preferred to be at home with me and that daycare may not have been the best idea for her."

—*Kelli, 32, mother of one*

self in hot water with the federal or provincial government. And if you want to hire a nanny through an agency, you'll want to read the section on this topic later in this chapter.

However, don't make the mistake of assuming that your job is finished the moment you find a suitable child-care provider. In many ways, it's just beginning. You'll need to monitor your child's child-care arrangement on an ongoing basis to ensure that it's continuing to meet her needs, and you'll need to be in constant contact with your toddler's child-care provider to troubleshoot any problems that may arise. You'll also need to come up with an emergency backup plan so that you won't find yourself left in the lurch on days when your child is sick or the childcare provider has to deal with a family emergency. (Hint: The more bullet-proof your backup plan, the more peace of mind you'll enjoy as a working parent.)

TABLE 10.1

Child Care Checklist

The following are the points to consider when you're checking out a particular type of child-care arrangement:

If you're considering a daycare centre:

→ **The hours of operation:** What hours is the centre open? Is there any flexibility when it comes to pickup and drop-off times?

→ **The age range of children enrolled at the centre:** Are all the children under the age of five or are there school-aged children as well? What is the age range within your child's group?

→ **Fees:** What fees does the centre charge? Are there any additional fees you should know about (e.g., an application fee, late charges in the event that you're late picking up your child one day, and so on)?

→ **Staff training:** What types of training have staff members had (e.g., formal training in early childhood education, cardiopulmonary resuscitation, first aid, and so on)?

continued on p. 472

If you're considering a daycare centre (continued)

→ **Staff turnover:** Does the centre seem to be able to retain good staff or is there a high turnover rate?

→ **Caregiver suitability:** Who will be responsible for caring for your child? How long has that person been working with children? How does she relate to your child? Does she seem like someone with whom you and your child could build a relationship?

→ **Centre policies:** Are the centre's policies stated in writing? Do they make sense to you? Are the centre's discipline policies compatible with your parenting philosophies?

→ **Safety:** Have the centre staff managed to provide a safe environment (both indoors and outdoors) for young children? Have all potential hazards been dealt with appropriately? What are the centre's policies for handling accidents and other serious occurrences?

→ **Health and hygiene:** Is the room well ventilated and well lit? Is there enough open space for children to crawl around and explore their environment? Are toys disinfected on a regular basis? Is there a clearly stated policy for isolating and caring for children who become ill while they're in care? Under what circumstances are parents telephoned at work and asked to pick up sick children?

→ **Rest periods:** Is there a safe place for your toddler to sleep? Can she be seen and heard while she's sleeping?

→ **Mealtimes:** Are you responsible for providing any food that your toddler eats? If meals are provided, are they varied, nutritious, and age-appropriate?

→ **Diapering:** How often are diapers changed? Is the diaper change area sanitized after each diaper change? Are you expected to supply diapers, ointments, and baby wipes, or are these items supplied?

→ **Program:** How is the child-care day structured? Are there predictable routines? Are toddlers separated from older children during active indoor and outdoor play? Does the program appear to be both organized and busy and yet warm and welcoming?

→ **Parent involvement:** Are parents welcome to drop by the centre at any time? Are parents recognized as the true "experts" when it comes to caring for their own children? What policies does the centre have in place to promote ongoing communication between parents and centre staff?

➜ **References:** Is the centre willing to provide you with the names of parents whose children have used the centre? Are these references enthusiastic about their children's experiences at the centre?

➜ **Overall impression:** How does your child react to the centre? Does this seem like a place you'd be comfortable leaving your child?

If you're considering a home daycare (a child-care business operated out of someone's home):

➜ **The hours of operation:** What hours is the home daycare open? Is there any flexibility when it comes to pickup and drop-off times? Are there certain times of the year when the home daycare is closed?

➜ **The age range of children in the home daycare:** Are all the children under the age of five or are there school-aged children as well? Does the home daycare provider accept any additional children on a drop-in basis? If so, are provincial and territorial standards for caregiver–child ratios consistently being met? (See Table 10.2.)

➜ **Fees:** What fees does the home daycare provider charge? Are there any additional fees you should know about?

➜ **Caregiver training:** What types of training has the caregiver had (e.g., formal training in early childhood education, cardiopulmonary resuscitation, first aid, and so on)?

➜ **Caregiver suitability:** How long has the caregiver been working with children? How does she relate to your child? Does she seem like someone with whom you and your child could build a relationship?

➜ **Home daycare policies:** Are the home daycare provider's policies spelled out in writing? Do they make sense to you? Are the discipline policies compatible with your parenting philosophies? What equipment, if any, are you expected to supply?

➜ **Environment:** Are there any other businesses being run out of the same home? If so, are they compatible with a home daycare operation? Are other members of the caregiver's family supportive of her home daycare business, or do they appear to resent it? Does anyone in the household smoke? Are there any pets?

continued on p. 4

If you're considering a home daycare (continued)

→ **Safety:** Has the home daycare provider managed to provide a safe environment (both indoors and outdoors) for young children? Have all potential hazards been dealt with appropriately? What are the home daycare provider's policies for handling accidents and other serious occurrences?

→ **Health and hygiene:** Is the home daycare well ventilated and well lit? Is there enough open space for children to crawl around and explore their environment? Are toys disinfected on a regular basis? Is there a clearly stated policy for isolating and caring for children who become ill while they're in care? Under what circumstances are parents telephoned at work and asked to pick up sick children?

→ **Rest periods:** Is there a safe place for your toddler to sleep? Can she be seen and heard while she's sleeping?

→ **Mealtimes:** Are you responsible for providing any food that your toddler eats? If meals are provided, are they varied, nutritious, and age-appropriate?

→ **Diapering:** How often are diapers changed? Is the diaper change area sanitized after each diaper change? Are you expected to supply diapers, ointments, and baby wipes, or are these items supplied?

→ **Program:** How is the home daycare structured? Are there predictable routines? Are toddlers separated from older children during active indoor and outdoor play? Does the program appear to be both organized and busy and yet warm and welcoming?

→ **Parent involvement:** Are parents welcome to drop by the home daycare at any time? Are parents recognized as the true "experts" when it comes to caring for their own children? Does the home daycare provider make a point of communicating with parents on a regular basis?

→ **References:** Is the home daycare provider willing to provide you with the names of parents whose children have been cared for in her home? Are these references enthusiastic about their children's experiences with the home daycare provider?

→ **Overall impression:** How does your child react to the home daycare? Does this seem like a place you'd be comfortable leaving your child?

If you're thinking of hiring someone to come into your own home to care for your child:

→ **Hours:** What hours and days of the week is the caregiver available?

→ **Salary:** What are her salary expectations?

→ **Career goals:** How long does she intend to continue working in the child-care field? Is she prepared to make at least a one-year commitment to your family? Is she willing to sign a work agreement?

→ **Experience:** How much experience has she had in caring for young children? Has she ever worked in someone else's home before or has her previous work experience with young children been in a daycare setting? What was her most recent position and what was her reason for leaving this position?

→ **Suitability:** How does she relate to your child? Does she appear to have a genuine love of children? Is she experienced in working with babies? Could she recognize and deal with illness?

→ **Philosophies:** Are her philosophies about childrearing compatible with your own? How does she deal with crying? Would she support your decision to continue breastfeeding after you return to work (assuming, of course, that is your choice)?

→ **Training:** What types of training has the caregiver had (e.g., formal training in early childhood education, cardiopulmonary resuscitation, first aid, and so on)?

→ **Health:** Is she a smoker?

→ **Driving:** Does she have a valid driver's licence and/or her own vehicle?

→ **Background check:** Would she be willing to undergo a background check (e.g., police-record check) at your expense?

→ **References:** Is she willing to provide you with a list of references? Are those people enthusiastic about her abilities?

→ **Overall impression:** Is she someone you'd feel comfortable employing in your home and leaving your child with?

Note: For a more detailed child-care checklist, please see my book *The Unofficial Guide to Childcare* (Hungry Minds, 1998).

TABLE 10.2

Caregiver–Child Ratios for Infants and Toddlers in Canadian Provinces and Territories

Province or Territory	Age	Caregiver–Child Ratio
Alberta	0 to 12 months	1:3
	13 to 18 months	1.4
	19 to 35 months	1:6
British Columbia	0 to 3 years	1:4
Manitoba	Mixed Age Groups	
	12 weeks to 2 years	1:4
	Separate Age Groups	
	12 weeks to 2 years	1:3
New Brunswick	0 to 2 years	1:3
	2 to 3 years	1:5
Newfoundland	0 to 2 years	not covered in legislation
	2 to 3 years	1:6
Northwest Territories	0 to 12 months	1:3
	13 to 24 months	1:4
	25 to 35 months	1:6
Nova Scotia	0 to 17 months	1:4
	17 months to 5 years (full day)	1:7
	17 months to 5 years (part day)	1:12
Ontario	0 to 18 months	1:3
	18 months to 2 years	1:5
	2 to 5 years	1:8
Prince Edward Island	0 to 2 years	1:3
	2 to 3 years	1:5
Quebec	0 to 18 months	1:5
	18 months to 5 years	1:8
Saskatchewan	Infants	1:3
	Toddlers	1:5
	Preschool (30 months to 6 years)	1:10
Yukon	0 to 18 months	1:4
	18 months to 2 years	1:6

Doing business with a nanny agency

If you think hiring a nanny through an agency is no more complicated than shopping for a licensed child-care space in your
community, I've got news for you: Mary Poppins isn't that easy
to find. Not only do you have to search out a reputable agency;
you also have to find the right nanny. And if you're lucky enough
to find the caregiver of your dreams, there are still references to
check, fees to pay, and government red tape to wade through
before she's happily in your home caring for your kids.

If you deal with a nanny agency, you should expect to pay a
placement fee that's roughly equivalent to one month of the
nanny's salary. And, what's more, you might also have to pick up
the tab for the nanny's airfare if she's relocating in order to take
the job. For its part, the agency should do some initial prescreening, weed out unqualified candidates, run a criminal reference
check on the nanny, and provide some sort of placement guarantee. However, the onus is on you to ensure that the agency actually follows through and delivers what it promises. That means
making sure that you're provided with an agency agreement up-
front and that the agency lives up to the letter of that agreement.

Ensuring that the agency delivers on its promises is where the
key challenge lies. According to Martha Friendly of the Child
Care Research Unit at the University of Toronto, nanny agencies
are covered by the relatively lax laws governing employment agencies rather than the more rigorous standards that apply to licensed
child-care operations. In the absence of any regulatory body over-
seeing nanny agency operations, parents can find themselves
swinging in the wind if a problem happens to arise.

Unfortunately, you can run a nanny agency with little more
than an answering machine or a Web site these days. One of the
hottest trends in the nanny recruitment business is to charge
nannies and parents hefty fees for accessing online databases,
whether or not a placement actually occurs. Instead of getting the

face-to-face contact and handholding that occurs when you're dealing with a reputable agency, you can be left paying a sizable fee for what essentially amounts to a do-it-yourself service. (Some sites leave all the candidate prescreening up to you, although others are willing to provide this service for an additional fee.)

Here are some questions to ask when you're shopping around for a nanny agency:

- What services are included? No two nanny agencies have identical policies for screening applicants and conducting police and reference checks. Ideally, you should look for an agency that's willing to walk you through all the red tape associated with becoming an employer for the first time: registering as a business; obtaining a payroll remittance number from Canada Customs and Revenue Agency; arranging for your nanny's health plan; and meeting all immigration requirements if you're hiring someone from another country.

- What about backup? Let's say your nanny has to leave town in a hurry for a family funeral. Does the agency provide backup nannies? Unfortunately, this type of backup care tends to be the exception rather than the rule, so don't be surprised if you have to come up with your own backup care arrangements.

- How will you help the nanny settle in? Look for an agency that is genuinely interested in ensuring that both you and your caregiver are a good fit for one another. A good agency should also be willing to help her connect with other nannies in the community.

- Is there a placement guarantee? If the nanny doesn't work out for whatever reason during her first couple of months on the job, it can be helpful to know that the agency will help you to find a more suitable candidate.

- What about references? While the lack of industry standards means there's always an element of risk, you can increase your chances of winning at agency roulette by asking friends and relatives for recommendations. If you don't know anyone who's actually used a nanny agency, you'll have to settle for the next best thing: checking the agency's references.

- Can I see your business licence? Before you sign on the dotted line, make sure the agency in question is operating legally. The challenge is in finding out exactly what laws apply to nanny agencies in your province or territory. According to Suzanne Potvin, team leader of the Foreign Worker Program at Human Resources Development Canada, there's an absolute mish-mash of legislation and standards governing nanny agencies, with government policies varying from jurisdiction to jurisdiction. Your best bet? Get in touch with your provincial or territorial ministry of labour and find out the rules of the game before you decide whether or not you want to play ball with a particular agency.

The first week survival guide

After months of preparation, the moment of truth has finally arrived: You're about to go back to work. Here are some tips on weathering that challenging first week back on the job:

- Talk to your employer ahead of time to see what arrangements can be made to make your first week back at work as stress-free as possible. See if it's possible to work part-time hours (half days or every other day) or to work only half a week (e.g., start back to work on a Wednesday or Thursday so that you have to work for only two or three days before the weekend rolls around).

MOM'S THE WORD

"I don't beat myself up about having my son in daycare. I know he's getting terrific care. In fact, I think his child-care provider has a lot more patience and energy when it comes to keeping him happy and stimulated than I do. I found my maternity leave long and stressful, and I've since concluded that I don't have what it takes to be a stay-at-home mom."

—*Marie, 38, mother of four*

- Invite a co-worker to lunch the week before you return to work so that she can quickly bring you up to speed on what's been happening while you were on maternity leave. That way, you won't feel quite so overwhelmed during your first day on the job. (You can kill two birds with one stone if you take this opportunity to give your toddler a "dry run" with the child-care provider—a perfect example of the multi-tasking abilities that will serve you so well as a working mom.)

- Test-drive your child-care arrangements before you go back to work so that both you and your toddler can get used to the routine. And use this opportunity to give your toddler's child-care provider as much information as you can about your toddler: details about her routine, her likes and dislikes, her food preferences, her sleep rituals, and so on. Ideally, you should provide this information in writing so that the caregiver can refer back to it if she has any questions down the road.

- Establish a rapport with your toddler's child-care provider. The better you get to know her, the more comfortable you'll feel about leaving your child in her care, and the easier it will be to talk about any problems that happen to arise down the road.

- Look for ways to cut corners on the home front during your first week back on the job. If friends or family members ask what they can do to help, suggest that they show up on your doorstep bearing healthy, homemade meals—a much more appealing alternative to the takeout pizza or frozen leftovers that might otherwise find their way onto the dinner table that first week.

- Plan to keep any outside commitments to a minimum. Your two priorities at this stage of your life are your family and your job. This is no time to offer to chair the hospital fundraising committee! Keep your evenings and weekends free so that you can spend as much of your non-working time as possible with your toddler. You'll want to be with her every bit as much as she wants to be with you.

- Give some thought to the timing of your return to work. You can make the transition easier on both your toddler and yourself if you try to avoid settling her into a new child-care arrangement during the peak period of separation anxiety— when your child is 8 to 14 months of age. Of course, your odds of being able to sidestep separation anxiety entirely are pretty much slim to none; separation anxiety recurs sporadically during the first few years of life. As frustrating as it can be to deal with, it's your toddler's way of announcing to the world that you're utterly irreplaceable.

- If your toddler is having a hard time settling into her new child-care arrangement, send along a comfort object or two— perhaps her favourite blanket or stuffed toy or something that belongs to you.

- Factor in a generous amount of time for the morning drop-off schedule. You and your toddler will find it easier to part ways if your goodbyes don't have to be hurried.

- Resist the temptation to sneak out the door when your toddler isn't looking. You might get away with it this time, but you'll pay a pretty high price for that one-time escape: Your toddler will always be wondering if you're about to sneak away again, so she may insist on being in physical contact with you every minute when you're not at work.

- When it's time to leave for work, hand your child to the caregiver rather than having the caregiver take your toddler from you. This will be more reassuring to your toddler.

- Even if you're feeling weepy, make sure that your body language is reassuring and that your voice isn't quivering too much as you say your goodbyes. Otherwise, your toddler will pick up on how you're feeling and become frightened and upset herself. An Academy Award–winning performance may be required. Fortunately, you only have to hold it together long enough to get to the car!

- Don't drag out your goodbyes any longer than necessary. Prolonging the goodbye will only make things more difficult for all concerned. If you want to know how well your toddler settles for the caregiver, give the child-care provider a phone call once you get to work.

- Be prepared for some tears when you show up at the end of the day. Research has shown that children are fussier when their parents return to pick them up than they are when their parents are at work. This is because they feel most free to express their emotions when they're with the people they're most comfortable with—so consider it a compliment if your toddler bursts into tears at the mere sight of you!

- Acknowledge your feelings rather than burying them. Chances are you're experiencing a smorgasbord of different emotions right now: perhaps guilt about being a working mother, sadness about being away from your toddler, excitement about being back at a job that you love (assuming you

MOM'S THE WORD

"We sometimes have mornings when I feel like I've been through a war zone before I even get to work."

—*Annie, 44, mother of one*

---

wanted to return to work), or anger at being forced to go back to work (if you had little or no choice but to return to work). Regardless of how you're feeling, it's important to come to terms with your decision by talking to other people who will understand and who will reassure you that it's normal to miss your toddler when you return to work. Your emotions won't always be this raw, nor will you always miss your toddler this intensely. Things will get easier over time.

Coping with the stress of being a working parent

Feeling a little stressed? Struggling to keep all the balls in the air? You're certainly in good company. According to the most recent stress-related data from Statistics Canada, 85% of mothers who work outside the home report that they're chronically short of time; there simply aren't enough hours in the day to accomplish everything that needs to be done. And rather than getting better, the situation seems to be getting worse: While women who worked full-time could count on putting in an extra 31.4 hours on the home front each week back in 1992, by 1998 that number had risen to 36 hours per week. Here's what you need to know to master the ultimate of juggling acts, being a working mom:

- **Set reasonable working hours and stick to them.** Swim against the tide of our workaholic culture and insist on taking time for yourself and your family. Don't let anyone make you feel guilty for turning off your phone or walking away

MOTHER WISDOM

Wondering why you're feeling so stressed? Sometimes numbers speak louder than words. Here are the latest figures from Statistics Canada on women and stress:

While women who are employed outside the home spend an average of 6.1 hours per day with their children, men who are outside the home typically spend a half-hour a day less with their kids. Both men and women regret not having more time to spend with their children; fully one-third of parents between the ages of 25 and 44 say that they're dissatisfied with the balance between their working lives and their family lives. Women are more likely to experience stress than men. And women who describe themselves as "highly stressed" are more likely to develop such health problems such as arthritis, ulcers, asthma, back problems, chronic bronchitis, or chronic emphysema.

Eighty-six percent of Canadian working women return to work within one year of giving birth, and 93% are back on the job within two years.

---

from your computer for a while. Everyone has the right to a personal life, regardless of how much they get paid or which rung they're clinging to on the corporate ladder.

- **Find a job that you love.** If you're going to do something 2,000 or more hours a year (and, frankly, you'll be putting in many more hours than that if you're self-employed or on the career fast-track!), you might as well make sure that it's something you enjoy. If you're not crazy about your current job or your present career path, there's no time like the present to start planning your great escape. And when you're coming up with a list of criteria for your dream job, make sure you've put "family-friendly" right at the top of the list. You want to work for a company that considers its employees and their families to be one of its greatest assets.

- **Work with people you like and respect.** There's nothing more poisonous to a working environment than having to work with a jerk. If you're saddled with the boss-from-you-know-where or a co-worker who just plain gets on your nerves, you might want to think about exiting stage left at the first opportunity.

- **Put your support team in place.** Whether you turn to family members, friends, or co-workers for support is unimportant. What matters is that there's someone waiting to cheer you on when you find yourself having a certifiably horrible day. And don't be afraid to wave the white flag and ask family members to pitch in with household tasks at home; there's no reason on earth you should be simultaneously making dinner and folding laundry when the rest of the family is flopped out on the couch watching TV. (If they seem to think this is reasonable, they've clearly tuned into a few too many episodes of *Leave It to Beaver*.)

- **Learn to cut corners on things that don't matter—or give yourself permission to delegate them to someone else.** Despite what you might have heard, there's no law that says you have to make all your meals from scratch, clean your own house, and faithfully read every issue of *Martha Stewart Living* (so that you can come up with even more things to do with your "spare time"). Do enough housework to keep yourself from going crazy, but don't overdo it. Better yet, hire someone else to do your cleaning for you so that you'll have more time for the things that really matter to you—like spending time with family members and friends.

- **Take care of your own needs rather than counting on someone else to take care of them for you.** No matter how great your boss, your partner, and your kids may be, it's your job to take care of yourself. This is one job you simply can't delegate.

MOTHER WISDOM

Eager to encourage your toddler to pick up his toys so that you'll have one less thing to do at the end of the day? Here are some fun ways to get him to buy into the tidy-up habit:

- Make it a game. "I think it really helps to make a game out of tidying up," says Lori, a 31-year-old mother of five. "If you ask your child to pick up all the blue toys and then the red toys and then the yellow toys, and so on, not only are you helping him to learn his colours, but he'll also find it a lot of fun."
- Turn it into a race. "If you challenge your toddler to see how many toys he can pick up before the timer goes off, he'll get excited and his adrenalin will start pumping," Lori adds.
- Show him how to tackle the job. Sometimes the most difficult part of tidying up is figuring out how to get started. Here's the system that works for Brandy, a 26-year-old mother of one: "We start by gathering up all his books and putting them in the toy box. Then we move on to picking up his blocks, his stuffed animals, his push-button toys, and so on. It makes the toy box neat and tidy, and he learns to group his toys in separate categories."
- Be realistic about your expectations. "You cannot expect a toddler to clean up a room all by himself," says Lori. "More often than not, you will have to participate in the cleanup, too. Looking at a room covered in toys is too overwhelming for a toddler. He'll end up playing more than cleaning."

- **Keep your sense of humour.** It's the ultimate weapon against the craziness around you, and the one thing that will keep you sane.

The intergenerational tug of war

THERE'S NO DENYING IT: Parents and grandparents don't always see eye-to-eye on important issues like discipline, feeding, and—as we noted in the last chapter—safety either. Here's what you need to prevent minor disagreements from exploding into full-blown intergenerational warfare:

- Be prepared for an outpouring of advice—both good and bad. Most grandparents feel this powerful need to share all the wisdom they accumulated during their own time in the parenting trenches. Unfortunately, they may not recognize the fact that some of their ways of doing things have long since gone the way of the dodo bird (e.g., we no longer start toilet training when a baby is one month of age!). Rather than getting freaked out because the advice you're receiving is wacky or even downright weird, simply accept it in the spirit in which it was offered (with only the best of intentions) and then quietly ignore anything that no longer holds water today.

- Don't be afraid to stand your ground on the issues that really matter. You may need to gently remind your child's grandparents that you're the one in charge when it comes to making important parenting decisions. They've already had their starring roles in that long-running melodrama known as parenthood. Now you're the one at centre stage.

- Remind yourself that—like Rome—grandparents are not built in a day. It may take time for your parents or your partner's parents to grow into the grandparenting role, particularly if your child is the first grandchild (a.k.a., the guinea pig). Not everyone feels up to the challenge of coping with the cries of a colicky baby or the tantrums of a fiercely determined toddler. Your child's grandparents may not be comfortable playing anything more than a minor supporting role until your child becomes a tad more civilized.

- Recognize that your parents are a generation older than they were when they were raising you, and that consequently they may not be up to a lot of loud noise or rough-and-tumble play. I found out the hard way during one intergenerational *helliday* that my father's hearing aid went crazy each time my son shrieked. (By the end of the weekend, it wasn't just the hearing aid that was going crazy, let me tell you!)

- Count your blessings if you've been blessed with exceptionally supportive parents and in-laws. Having the support of the older generation can make parenting a whole lot easier. "Sometimes I just want 'mommy time,'" admits Brandy, a 26-year-old mother of one. "I feel I'm never on my own schedule but always on Caleb's schedule. That can be so frustrating. Fortunately, I have a very wonderful mother-in-law who comes over a couple of times a week to watch him while I clean the house or do something fun like play around on the computer or have a bubble bath. My mother-in-law is also great on weekends when my husband and I want some time for ourselves. We go out shopping or for coffee and take time for each other."

- Remind yourself that having a loving relationship with her grandparents can be a tremendous gift to a child—and vice versa. As Lois Wyse notes in her book *Funny, You Don't Look Like a Grandmother*, "Grandchildren are the dots that connect the lines from generation to generation."

MOTHER WISDOM

"Most of the time, experienced mothers aren't judging the new mom at all; they're just eager to pass on what they've learned by trial and error at the hardest task any woman undertakes. It's nothing more than an act of sharing. In fact, often their stories aren't meant to be advice. They're more like picture postcards sent from farther down the road."

—*Margaret Renkl, "Shared Wisdom: Why It's Such a Touchy Thing When A Veteran Mom Offers a New One Advice,"* Parenting, September 2001

MOTHER WISDOM

Stash some of your garage sale finds at the homes of your child's grandparents. That way, there will always be something fun and exciting for her to play with while she's visiting—something that may reduce the likelihood of her wanting to play "Barbies" with her grandmother's Royal Doulton figurines.

Celebrating milestones and capturing family memories

LIKE SPECIAL TIMES spent with a beloved grandparent, holidays and birthday parties are the stuff of which memories are made. Here's what you need to make them sensational rather than stressful for you and your toddler.

Holiday stressbusters

While partying until the wee hours of the morning and dragging yourself into the office the next morning was probably no big deal back in your pre-baby days, you may find that you want to limit the number of social engagements you say yes to between Thanksgiving and New Year's. After all, your parenting responsibilities don't disappear just because it's rum and eggnog season; you're still as likely as ever to get a 3:00 a.m. visit from a night-waking toddler! Here are some things you can do to make the holiday season as stress-free as possible for you and your toddler:

- Rather than attempting to do a lot of travelling with a young toddler—something that can be both stressful and exhausting—invite friends and family members to visit you over the holiday season. Just make sure that potential houseguests understand up-front that you're not in a position to wait on people hand and foot this year: After all, you're already playing servant to the most demanding of masters, a toddler!

- Accept the fact that visiting other people is likely to be stressful if you've got a toddler in tow, and limit the length of your visits accordingly. While you might be up to a one-hour visit at Great Aunt Mildred's, an entire afternoon of trying to keep her Royal Doulton figurines away from your increasingly determined toddler might be a bit much for all concerned. (Personally, I feel that people who refuse to babyproof their homes when they're playing host to a toddler deserve to lose the odd Royal Doulton figurine, but that's just a bit of mean-spiritedness on my part!)

- Don't expect your toddler to give up his picky eating patterns in honour of the holiday season. If the only thing he's willing to eat for lunch these days is a plain cheese sandwich, don't expect him to whoop with joy when whatever relative you're visiting plunks a turkey-and-stuffing sandwich down in front of him instead. You can avoid an intergenerational crisis by keeping a backup sandwich in a cooler in the trunk of the car; that way, if your toddler balks at the idea of eating whatever Grandma's dished up, you'll have an easy out. (Of course,

---

MOTHER WISDOM

Don't have unrealistic expectations of your toddler in the manners department—especially during the busy and stressful holiday season. While the toddler years are the perfect time to start laying the groundwork for good manners, it may be a little while yet before she starts using words like "please" and "thank you" without any prompting from you. But if you make a consistent effort to model the types of behaviours you'd like to see from her, those good manners will come in time.

Grandma will then be convinced that you're mercilessly spoiling the child, but that's a whole other issue.)

- Don't convince yourself that you'll be depriving your children of a happy childhood if you're not able to squeeze a million different opportunities for memory-making into a single holiday season. Yes, it's wonderful to take your toddler on a sleigh ride, decorate a gingerbread house together, and whip up a batch of positively mouth-watering Christmas cookies—but trying to accomplish all this in a single day is a guaranteed recipe for a meltdown. (Hey, I'm talking about you, not the toddler.)

- Schedule plenty of downtime in the midst of the holiday hustle and bustle. Put on some holiday music and curl up on the couch with your toddler. Who says that the holiday season has to be insanely busy to be fun? Sometimes the most extraordinary experiences you have as a parent happen when you're doing the most unextraordinary things: reading a child a bedtime story, giving him a bath, or curling up on the couch together watching *How the Grinch Stole Christmas* for the umpteen millionth time!

- Take time to pamper yourself at the end of the day. Toss some peppermint-scented essential oil into your bathwater and light some festive holiday candles. Then soak in the tub while you escape into a magazine or book. You owe it to yourself and your kids to pamper yourself on a regular basis. After all, a happy and relaxed parent is the best present of all.

- Remind yourself to stop and smell the poinsettias. Twenty years from now, it won't matter whether or not the gingerbread house collapsed the moment you tried to put on the roof, or whether your one-year-old managed to spill cranberry sauce on Grandma's living room rug. (Okay, so Grandma may remember that last bit.) What you'll remember are the special moments you shared as a family.

Birthday party basics

It's easy to go overboard with children's birthday parties—something that Kelli, a 32-year-old mother of one, discovered for herself: "For my daughter's first birthday, my husband rented a party room at a local restaurant and we fed about 40 people. We also hired a clown and had cake. It was very expensive and our daughter doesn't even remember it. This year when she turns two we're going to have a small party at home with just family and a few friends."

As a rule of thumb, simpler is better when it comes to toddlers and their birthdays. Too much cake and too much chaos can have even the most easygoing toddler singing the birthday party blues! Here are some tips on making your toddler's birthday party fun rather than overwhelming:

- Limit the number of guests. You're probably best keeping your guest list to a bare minimum—perhaps your immediate family plus a few other friends or relatives. If you're inviting other toddlers, plan to have their parents stick around, too; most toddlers aren't up to attending birthday parties sans mom or dad. And besides, you'll need as many sets of hands as possible if you've planned a special birthday party activity like cupcake decorating or mural making.

- Time the party to coincide with your toddler's best time of day—unless, of course, she's at her happiest before breakfast! Since most toddlers tend to get increasingly crabby as the day wears on, you may find that a brunch party is a better bet than a late-afternoon get-together.

- Keep the party short—an hour to an hour-and-a-half maximum. You don't want the birthday girl to be totally exhausted before you've even had a chance to bring out the cake.

- Don't be frustrated or embarrassed if your toddler ends up having a bit of a meltdown. It's pretty much par for the course for a toddler who is overexcited.

- Pass on the latex balloons. For safety reasons, Mylar balloons are a much better bet for the toddler crowd.

Memories unlimited

Looking for some ways to harvest memories—both on your toddler's birthday and throughout the year? Here are a few ideas:

- Start a "birthday book" for your toddler and encourage friends or family members to jot down a memory or two of their favourite moments with your child. Friends and relatives who aren't able to attend the birthday festivities in person can mail or e-mail their memories in instead.

- Create a time capsule for your toddler. Encourage each adult who's attending your child's birthday party to bring something unique that could be put into a time capsule to be opened on her 16th birthday. Something as simple as a daily newspaper can be quite a treasure when it's unearthed 15 years down the road.

MOM'S THE WORD

"Write down all the adorable things your toddler does. Then, when you're having a particularly challenging day as a parent, go back and reread everything that you've written. It will make you feel better."

—*Maria, 32, mother of two*

- Start keeping a journal for your toddler. Fill it with random thoughts about her new discoveries and funny sayings. Don't feel obligated to write an entry each and every day. Just write something when the mood strikes.

- Start a scrapbook so that you'll have a safe place to store such treasures as photographs, ticket stubs from family trips to the zoo, and selected pieces of your child's artwork.

- Keep a video diary of your toddler. If you get in the habit of videotaping her for a few minutes each month, you'll be astounded to see just how much she changes from month to month.

MOTHER WISDOM

Tired of having your toddler turning out red-eyed or fuzzy in each photograph you take? Here's what the experts recommend for photographing toddlers:

- Use all-purpose, high-speed film. It's more forgiving of moving objects. (And if a toddler doesn't meet the definition of a moving object, frankly, I don't know what does.)

- Go for the candid shots. Most toddlers don't have the patience to sit for carefully orchestrated studio shots, so don't even go there. While you might luck out and get a shot or two to send to Grandma, it'll likely be one of those dreadfully boring "toddler propped in front of blue background" types of shots. (Or, worse, one of those super-cutesy shots of your toddler dressed up like a mermaid or cowboy.) You'll get much more natural-looking photographs if you simply snap candid shots of your toddler while she's playing in your family room or at the park.

- Get down to your child's level and try to capture her attention as you're pushing the button. It will make for a more intimate, eye-catching photo.

- Experiment with different lenses if you're lucky enough to have more than one lens at your disposal. A 35 mm or 28 mm lens will allow you to capture more of the scene in the background. On the other hand, a zoom lens

- Leave disposable cameras in different parts of your home, and be sure to keep one in the car, too. That way, you'll always have one within grabbing distance when your toddler does something unspeakably cute. Using disposable cameras also helps to spare you the worry about having something happen to your "good camera" if you accidentally leave it within grabbing distance of your toddler one day—something that could instantly spell doomsday for that state-of-the-art digital camera!

Just one final word of warning before you go into memory catching mode. Don't get so caught up in harvesting memories for the future that you fail to savour them in the here and now.

---

of 70 to 200 mm will allow you to take the shot from a bit of a distance, something that's less likely to tip your toddler off to the fact that she's being photographed. (Some toddlers drop everything and try to grab the camera as soon as they notice that someone's trying to take their photo. It's not that they're camera shy: heck, no—they just want the camera!)

- Bear in mind that the standard distance for flash photography is two to four metres (six to ten feet). If you use your flash from too far away, your toddler's face will be underexposed in the photo, but if you get too close, her face will be all washed out.
- Don't get too close if you're using a point-and-shoot camera. Most cameras of this type require that you be at least 1.5 metres (five feet) back. If you get too close, your toddler will appear fuzzy and out of focus—not unlike how she looked when she crawled into your bed at 5:00 a.m. this morning.
- Keep in mind that brightly coloured clothing makes for a more dynamic photograph. Save your toddler's beige playsuit for a day when you're not quite so inclined to play children's photographer.
- Get in the habit of photographing your child against the same backdrop on a regular basis. That way, you'll have a visual record of just how much she grows from month to month and year to year.

You don't want to miss out on one of your toddler's many marvellous firsts because you were too busy changing the lens on your camera!

The toddler years are amazing, but they fly by all too quickly. It won't be long before that wriggly little toddler has morphed into a practically civilized preschooler. In the meantime, you'll want to seize the moment and savour it.

Consider these words of wisdom from Helena, a 33-year-old mother of one: "Living with a toddler can be compared to a rollercoaster ride. Not only do you have your ups and downs, but there are times of quiet anticipation and times when you cannot help yourself from screaming! But most of the time it's an exciting, ever-changing, and thrilling ride. Enjoy the ride."

MOTHER WISDOM

"If I get the forty additional years statisticians say are likely coming to me, I could fit in at least one, maybe two, new lifetimes. Sad that only one of those lifetimes can include being the mother of young children."

—*Anna Quindlen*, Living Out Loud

Glossary

Anaphylactic shock: The type of allergic reaction that occurs when a child experiences a severe—even life-threatening—reaction to a particular food such as peanuts.

Aphasia: The loss of speech and language abilities resulting from a head injury or a stroke.

Articulation impairments: A speech problem that occurs when a child cannot make a particular speech sound or sounds, either because of a structural problem in the mouth or nose or an abnormality in the functioning of the muscles and nerves involved in the production of speech.

Associative play: Very loosely organized play (e.g., a group of preschoolers are sharing a box of blocks, but each is making his own block tower).

Asthma: A lung disease that causes the air passages to become narrowed as a result of muscular spasms and swelling of the air-passage walls.

Auditory learning: Learning that is based on hearing. A child with an auditory learning style will have no trouble memorizing the words to stories and songs, following directions, and repeating phrases and comments she's overheard.

Authoritarian parenting: A parenting style that is based on parental control, that is, "I'm the one in charge." *See also* permissive parenting and authoritative parenting.

Authoritative parenting: A parenting style that is based on communication and flexibility. *See also* authoritarian parenting and permissive parenting.

Axillary temperature: A temperature reading that is taken by placing a thermometer in the armpit.

Boils: Raised, red, tender, warm swellings on the skin that are most often found on the buttocks.

Bronchiolitis: A viral infection of the small breathing tubes of the lungs.

Bronchitis: An infection of the central and larger airways of the lungs.

Bruxism: Teeth grinding.

Campylobacter: A common bacterial cause of intestinal infections.

Canada Child Tax Benefit (CCBT): A tax-free monthly payment that is designed to help eligible families offset some of the costs of raising children under the age of 18.

Canada Education Savings Grant program: A federal program that provides a 20% government-paid subsidy to your own Registered Educational Savings Plan contributions.

Cellulitis: Swollen, red, tender, warm areas of skin that are typically found on the extremities or the buttocks and that often start out as a boil or puncture wound prior to becoming infected.

Conjunctivitis: Pink eye.

Cooperative play: When preschoolers play together and have a common goal in mind (e.g., "Let's play house!").

Co-sleeping: Sleeping with your baby or toddler.

Croup: A respiratory condition in which your toddler's breathing becomes very noisy. In some cases, his windpipe may become obstructed.

Diphtheria: A disease that attacks the throat and heart and that can lead to heart failure or death.

Dyspraxia: A speech problem that is defined as an inability to produce the fast and skilled mouth and tongue movements required for speech when there are no other obvious causes for the problem (e.g., hearing or other perceptual problems, motor problems, and structural problems involving the mouth and/or the tongue).

E-coli: Escherichia coli: A dangerous and even life-threatening type of germ that can be picked up from poultry, beef, unpasteurized milk, or other food sources.

Eczema: Extreme itchiness that results in a rash in areas that are scratched.

Encephalitis: An infection of the brain.

Epiglottitis: A life-threatening infection that causes swelling in the back of the throat.

Erythema toxicum: Red splotches with yellowish white bumps in the centre.

Febrile convulsions: Seizures that may occur when a toddler's temperature shoots up very suddenly.

Ferberize: Teaching your baby or toddler to sleep through the night by following the controversial "sleep training" methods made popular by Richard Ferber, M.D.

Fifth disease: A common childhood disease that is characterized by a fever and a "slapped cheek" rash on the face plus a red rash on the trunk and extremities.

Fontanels: The two so-called "soft spots" that can be found in the centre and toward the back of a newborn baby's and toddler's head.

German measles: *See* rubella.

Giardi lamblia: A parasite in the stool that causes bowel infections.

Haemophilus influenzae type b (Hib): A disease that can lead to meningitis, pneumonia, and a severe throat infection that can cause choking (epiglottitis).

Hand, foot, and mouth disease: A common childhood disease that is characterized by tiny blister-like sores in the mouth, on the palms of the hands, and on the soles of the feet. The sores are accompanied by a mild fever, a sore throat, and painful swallowing.

Head lice: Tiny insects that live on the scalp and that are spread through direct contact between children.

Herpangina: An inflammation of the inside of the mouth.

Impetigo: An infection of the skin that is characterized by yellow pustules or wide, honey-coloured scabs.

Kinesthetic learning: Learning based on movement. A child with a kinesthetic learning style learns best through movement. Most young children are both kinesthetic and tactual learners. *See also* tactual learning.

Laryngotracheitis: An inflammation of the voice box or larynx and windpipe or trachea.

Learning style: How a child learns. *See also* auditory learning, kinesthetic learning, tactual learning, and visual learning.

Meningitis: An inflammation of the membranes covering the brain and the spinal cord.

Mumps: An illness that is characterized by flu-like symptoms and an upset stomach followed by tender swollen glands beneath the earlobes two or three days later.

Onlooker play: When young toddlers observe others at play rather than participate themselves.

Otitis media: An ear infection.

Parallel play: When two toddlers play side by side but without actually interacting.

Parentese: A form of speech that parents around the world use when communicating with their babies. It involves exaggerated speech and high-pitched voices.

Pediculosis: *See* head lice.

Permissive parenting: A parenting style that involves few rules for children. *See also* authoritarian parenting and authoritative parenting.

Pertussis: *See* whooping cough.

Phonological impairments: Speech problems that occur when a child leaves certain sounds off the starts or ends of words or incorrectly uses one sound in the place of another.

Pinworms: Intestinal worms.

Pneumonia: An infection of the lungs.

Polio: A disease that can result in muscle pain and paralysis and/or death.

Regressive behaviour: When a toddler starts acting like a much younger child, e.g., insists on being fed like a baby, wearing diapers, talking in "baby talk," and so on. It is most likely to occur after the birth of a new baby, but can happen in any stressful situation.

Renal disease: Kidney disease.

Respiratory syncytial virus (RSV): A respiratory infection that results in a raspy cough, rapid breathing, and wheezing.

Rheumatic fever: A serious disease that can result in heart damage and/or joint swelling.

Roseola: A common childhood illness that is characterized by a high fever followed by the appearance of a faint pink rash on the trunk and the extremities. Lasts for one day.

Rotavirus: A virus in the stool that is spread through person-to-person contact.

Rubella: A disease that is characterized by a low-grade fever, flu-like symptoms, a slight cold, and a pinkish red spotted rash that starts on the face, spreads rapidly to the trunk, and then disappears by the third day. Rubella can be harmful—even fatal—to a developing fetus. Also known as German measles.

Salmonella: An illness that is typically acquired by eating food such as eggs, egg products, beef, poultry or unpasteurized milk that has been contaminated with salmonella.

Scarlet fever: *See* strep throat.

Sensorimotor play: Sometimes called practice play or solitary play. A repetitive form of play that allows a baby or young toddler to learn about the world and to master new skills.

Separation anxiety: A baby or toddler's fear of being separated from the person or persons he cares most about.

Sepsis: A serious infection caused by bacteria that has entered a wound or body tissue. Commonly known as "blood poisoning."

Shigella: An illness that is caused by a virus in the stool that can be spread from person to person.

Shingles: A disease that is characterized by a rash with small blisters that begin to crust over, resulting in itching and intense and prolonged pain.

Sinusitis: A sinus infection.

Social referencing: When a baby or toddler looks to his parents for information and guidance.

Soft spot: *See* fontanels.

Solitary play: When a toddler plays by herself, but is still in close proximity to other children.

Stranger anxiety: A baby or toddler's fear of strangers.

Strep throat: A bacterial infection that is characterized by a very sore throat, fever, and swollen glands in the neck. If a skin rash is also present, the condition is known as scarlet fever.

Tactual learning: Learning based on touch. A child with a tactual learning style needs to touch objects in order to understand how they work. Most young children are both tactual and kinesthetic learners. *See* kinesthetic learning.

Tympanic temperature: A temperature reading that is taken using a tympanic (ear) thermometer.

Varicella zoster immune globulin: A type of immune globulin that is given to prevent or minimize the severity of the chicken pox.

Vascular disease: Heart disease.

Visual learning: Learning that is based on seeing. A child with a visual learning style learns best through seeing.

Whooping cough: A disease that is characterized by a severe cough that makes it difficult to breathe, eat, or drink. Whooping cough can lead to pneumonia, convulsions, brain damage, and death.

Directory of Canadian Organizations

Adoption

Adoption Council of Canada
Bronson Centre
211 Bronson Avenue, #210
Ottawa, Ontario K1R 6H5
Phone: 613-235-0344
1-888-54-ADOPT
Fax: 613-235-1728
Web site: www.adoption.ca
E-mail: jgrove@adoption.ca

Breastfeeding

The Breastfeeding Committee for Canada
P.O. Box 65114
Toronto, Ontario M4K 3Z2
Fax: 416-465-8265
Web site: www.geocities.com/
    HotSprings/Falls/1136
E-mail: bfc.can@sympatico.ca

INFACT Canada
(Infant Feeding Action Coalition)
6 Trinity Square
Toronto, Ontario M5G 1B1
Phone: 416-595-9819
Fax: 416-591-9355
Web site: www.infactcanada.ca
E-mail: info@infactcanada.ca

La Leche League Canada
18C Industrial Drive
Box 29
Chesterville, Ontario K0C 1H0
Phone: 613-448-1842
Breast-feeding Referral:
    1-800-665-4324
Fax: 613-448-1845
Web site:
    www.lalecheleaguecanada.ca
E-mail: laleche@igs.net

Local LLL Phone Numbers:

Halifax: 902-470-7029
Montreal (English): 514-842-4781
Montreal (French): 1-866-255-2483
Ottawa: 613-238-5919
Toronto: 416-483-3368
Hamilton: 905-381-1010
Winnipeg: 204-257-3509
Regina: 306-584-5600
Lethbridge: 403-381-7718
Calgary: 403-242-0277
Edmonton: 780-478-0507
Vancouver: 604-520-4623
Victoria: 250-727-4384

Caregivers

Canadian Medical Association
1867 Alta Vista Drive
Ottawa, Ontario K1G 3Y6
Phone: 1-800 267 9703
Fax: 613-236-8864
Web site: www.cma.ca/cpgs
E-mail: public_affairs@cma.ca

Canadian Nurses Association
50 Driveway
Ottawa, Ontario K2P 1E2
Phone: 613-237-2133
1-800-361-8404
Fax: 613-237-3520
Web site: www.cna-nurses.ca
E-mail: cna@cna-nurses.ca

Canadian Paediatric Society
2204 Walkley Road, Suite 100
Ottawa, Ontario K1G 4G8
Phone: 613-526-9397
Fax: 613-526-3332
Web site: www.cps.ca
E-mail: info@cps.ca

The College of Family Physicians of Canada
2630 Skymark Avenue
Mississauga, Ontario L4W 5A4
Phone: 905-629-0900
Fax: 905-629-0893
Web site: www.cfpc.ca
E-mail: info@cfpc.ca

Child care

Canadian Child Care Federation
383 Parkdale Avenue, Suite 201
Ottawa, Ontario K1Y 4R4
Phone: 613-729-5289
1-800-858-1412
Fax: 613-729-3159
Web site: www.cccf-fcsge.ca
E-mail: info@cccf-fcsge.ca

Centre for Families, Work and Well-Being
900 MacKinnon
University of Guelph, Ontario
N1G 2W1
Phone: 519-824-4120 ext.3829
Web site: www.worklifecanada.ca
E-mail: cfww@uoguelph.ca

Child Care Advocacy Association of Canada
323 Chapel Street
Ottawa, Ontario K1N 7Z2
Phone: 613-594-3196
Fax: 613-594-9375
Web site: www.childcareadvocacy.ca
E-mail: info@childcareadvocacy.ca

Childcare Resource and Research Unit
Centre for Urban and Community
    Studies
University of Toronto
455 Spadina Avenue, Room 305
Toronto, Ontario M5S 2G8
Phone: 416-978-6895
FAX: 416-971-2139
Web site:
    www.childcarecanada.org
E-mail: crru@chass.utoronto.ca

Ontario Coalition for Better Child Care
726 Bloor Street West, Suite 209
Toronto, Ontario M6G 4A1
Phone: 416-538-0628
1-800-594-7514
Fax: 416-538-6737
Web site:
    www.childcareontario.org
E-mail: info@childcareontario.org

Work-Life Harmony Enterprises
601 – 207 Shaughnessy Blvd.
North York, Ontario M2J 1J9
Phone: 416-497-8942
Fax: 416-492-8799
Web site: www.worklifeharmony.ca

Grief/bereavement

Bereaved Families of Ontario
36 Eglinton Avenue East, Suite 602
Toronto, Ontario M4R 1A1
Phone: 416-440-0290
1-800-BFO-6364
Fax: 416-440-0304
Web site: www.bereavedfamilies.net
E-mail: prov.bfo@axxent.ca

The Compassionate Friends of Canada
P.O. Box 141, RPO Corydon
Winnipeg, Manitoba R3M 3S7
Phone: 204-475-9527
1-866-823-0141
Fax: 204-475-6693
Web site: www.tcfcanada.net
E-mail: tcflac@aol.com

Health

Bureau of Reproductive and Child Health
Reproductive Health Division
Health Canada, HPB Building 7
Tunney's Pasture, P-L 0701D
Ottawa, Ontario K1A 0L2
Phone: 613-941-2395
Fax: 613-941-9927
Web site: www.hc-sc.gc.ca/main/
    lcdc/web/brch/reprod.html
E-mail: CPSS@hc-sc.gc.ca

Canadian Dental Association

1815 Alta Vista Drive
Ottawa, Ontario K1G 3Y6
Phone: 613-523-1770
1-800-267-6354
Fax: 613-523-7736
Web site: www.cda-adc.ca
E-mail: reception@cda-adc.ca

The Canadian Dermatology Association

774 Echo Drive, Suite 521
Ottawa, Ontario K1S 5N8
Phone: 613-730-6262
1-800-267-3376
Fax: 613-730-8262
Web site: www.dermatology.ca
E-mail: contact.cda@
    dermatology.ca

Canadian Fitness and Lifestyle Research Institute

185 Somerset Street West, Suite 201
Ottawa, Ontario K2P 0J2
Phone: 613-233-5528
Fax: 613-233-5536
Web site: www.cflri.ca
E-mail: info@cflri.ca

The Canadian Institute of Child Health

384 Bank Street, Suite 300
Ottawa, Ontario K2P 1Y4
Phone: 613-230-8838
Fax. 613-230-0654
Web site: www.cich.ca
E-mail: cich@cich.ca

Canadian MedicAlert Foundation

2005 Sheppard Avenue East,
    Suite 800
Toronto, Ontario M2J 5B4
Phone: 416-696-0267 or
    416-696-0142
1-800-668-1507
Fax: 416-696-0156
Web site: www.medicalert.ca
E-mail: medinfo@medicalert.ca

Canadian Red Cross

National Office
170 Metcalfe Street, Suite 300
Ottawa, Ontario K2P 2P2
Phone: 613-740-1900
Fax: 613-740-1911
Web site: www.redcross.ca
E-mail: feedback@redcross.ca

The Hospital for Sick Children

555 University Avenue
Toronto, Ontario M5G 1X8
Phone: 416-813-1500
Poison Information Centre
    Phone: 416-813-5900
1-800-268-9017
Web site: www.sickkids.on.ca

Learning Disabilities Association of Canada/Troubles d'apprentissage-Association canadienne

323 Chapel Street, Suite 200
Ottawa, Ontario K1N 7Z2
Phone: 613-238-5721
Fax: 613-235-5391
Web site: www.ldac-taac.ca
E-mail: information@ldac-taac.ca

Mothercraft
32 Heath Street West
Toronto, Ontario M4V 1T3
Phone: 416-920-3515
Fax: 416-920-5983
Web site: www.mothercraft.ca
E-mail: office@mothercraft.org

Motherisk Program
The Hospital for Sick Children
555 University Avenue
Toronto, Ontario M5G 1X8
Phone: 416-823-6780 (M–F 9–5)
Fax: 416-813-7562
Web site: www.motherisk.org
E-mail: momrisk@sickkids.on.ca

Medical conditions

Allergy/Asthma Information Association
P.O. Box 100
Toronto, Ontario M9W 5K9
Phone: 416-679-9521
1-800-611-7011
Fax: 416-679-9524
Web site: www.aaia.ca
E-mail: national@aaia.ca

Asthma Society of Canada
130 Bridgeland Avenue, Suite 425
Toronto, Ontario M6A 1Z4
Phone 416-787-4050
1-800-787-3880
Fax: 416-787-5807
Web site: www.asthma.ca
E-mail: info@asthma.ca

Canadian AIDS Society
309 Cooper Street, 4th Floor
Ottawa, Ontario K2P 0G5
Phone: 613-230-3580
1-800-499-1986
Fax: 613-563-4998
Web site: www.cdnaids.ca
E-mail: casinfo@cdnaids.ca

Canadian Cancer Society
10 Alcorn Avenue, Suite 200
Toronto, Ontario M4V 3B1
Phone: 416-961-7223
Fax: 416-961-4189
Also Cancer Information
    Service: 1-888-939-3333
Web site: www.cancer.ca
E-mail: ccs@cancer.ca

Canadian Diabetes Association
National Office
15 Toronto Street, Suite 800
Toronto, Ontario M5C 2E3
Phone: 416-363-3373
1-800-226-8464
Fax: 416-214-1899
Web site: www.diabetes.ca
E-mail: info@diabetes.ca

Canadian Liver Foundation
2235 Sheppard Avenue East,
    Suite 1500
Toronto, Ontario M2J 5B5
Phone: 416-491-3353
1-800-563-5483
Fax: 416-491-4952
Web site: www.liver.ca
E-mail: clf@liver.ca

Canadian Lung Association
The Lung Association
3 Raymond Street, Suite 300
Ottawa, Ontario K1R 1A3
Phone: 613-569-6411
1-888-566-5864
Fax: 613-569-8860
Web site: www.lung.ca
E-mail: info@lung.ca

Crohn's and Colitis Foundation of Canada
60 St. Clair Avenue East, Suite 600
Toronto, Ontario M4T 1N5
Phone: 416-920-5035
1-800-387-1479
Fax: (416) 929-0364
Web site: www.ccfc.ca
E-mail: cctc@cctc.ca

Epilepsy Canada
1470 Peel Street, Suite 745
Montreal, Quebec H3A 1T1
Phone: 514-845-7855
1-877-SEIZURE (734-0873)
Fax: 514-845-7866
Web site: www.epilepsy.ca
E-mail: epilepsy@epilepsy.ca

The Kidney Foundation of Canada
5165 Sherbrooke Street West,
    Suite 300
Montreal, Quebec H4A 1T6
Phone: 514-369-4806
1-800-361-7494
Fax: 514-369-2472
Web site: www.kidney.ca
E-mail: webmaster@kidney.ca

Lupus Canada
18 Crown Steel Dr., Suite 209
Markham, Ontario L3R 9X8
Phone: 905-513-0004
1-800-661-1468
Fax: 905-513-9516
Web site: www.lupuscanada.org
E-mail: lupuscanada@bellnet.ca

Multiple Sclerosis Society of Canada
250 Bloor Street East, Suite 1000
Toronto, Ontario M4W 3P9
Phone: 416-922-6065
1-800-268-7582
Fax: 416-922-7538
Web site: www.mssociety.ca
E-mail: info@mssociety.ca

Thyroid Foundation of Canada/ La Fondation canadienne de la thyroïde
P.O. Box/C.P. 1919
Station Main
Kingston, Ontario K7L 5J7
Phone: 613-544-8364
1-800-267-8822
Fax: 613-544-9731
Web site: www.thyroid.ca

YWCA of/du Canada
590 Jarvis Street, 5th Floor
Toronto, Ontario M4Y 2J4
Phone: 416-962-8881
Fax: 416-962-8084
Web site: www.ywcacanada.ca
E-mail: national@ywcacanada.ca

Multiples

**Multiple Births Canada/
Naissances Multiples Canada**
P.O. Box 432
Wasaga Beach, Ontario L0L 2P0
Phone: 705-429-0901
1-866-228-8824
Fax: 705-429-9809
Web site:
    www.multiplebirthscanada.org
E-mail: office@
    multiplebirthscanada.org

Nutrition

Dietitians of Canada
480 University Avenue, Suite 604
Toronto, Ontario M5G 1V2
Phone: 416-596-0857
Fax: 416-596-0603
Web site: www.dietitians.ca
E-mail: centralinfo@dietitians.ca

National Institute of Nutrition
265 Carling Avenue, Suite 302
Ottawa, Ontario K1S 2E1
Phone: 613-235-3355
Fax: 613-235-7032
Web site: www.nin.ca
E-mail: nin@nin.ca

Parenting

Dads Can
St. Joseph's Health Care
268 Grosvenor Street
Box 34
London, Ontario N6A 4V2
Phone: 519-646-6095
1-888-DADS CAN
Web site: www.dadscan.org
E-mail: info@dadscan.org

Family Service Canada
383 Parkdale Avenue, Suite 404
Ottawa, Ontario K1Y 4R4
Phone: 613-722-9006
1-800-668-7808
Fax: 613-722-8610
Web site:
    www.familyservicecanada.org
E-mail:
    info@familyservicecanada.org

**One Parent Families Association
of Canada**
National Office
1099 Kingston Road, Suite 222
Pickering, Ontario L1V 1B5
Phone: 905-831-7098
Fax: 905-831-2580
Web site: www.hometown.aol.com/
    opfa222
E-mail: opfa222@aol.com

Parent Help Line
(Kids Help Phone National Office)
439 University Avenue, Suite 300
Toronto, Ontario M5G 1Y8
Phone: 416-586-5437
1-888-603-9100
Fax: 416-586-0651
Web site: www.parentsinfo.
sympatico.ca
E-mail: vp.services@kidshelp.
sympatico.ca

Safety

Canada Safety Council
1020 Thomas Spratt Place
Ottawa, Ontario K1G 5L5
Phone: 613-739-1535
Fax: 613-739-1566
Web site: www.safety-council.org
E-mail: csc@safety-council.org

**Canadian Juvenile Products
Association**
10435 Islington Avenue
P.O. Box 294
Kleinburg, Ontario L0J 1C0
Phone: 905-893-1689
Fax: 905-893-2392

Canadian Toy Testing Council
22 Antares Drive, Suite 102
Nepean, Ontario K2E 7Z6
Phone: 613-228-3155
Fax: 613-228-3242
Web site: www.toy-testing.org
E-mail: cttc@cyberus.ca

**Infant & Toddler Safety
Association**
385 Fairway Road South,
Suite 4A-230
Kitchener, Ontario N2C 2N9
Phone: 519-570-0181 (hotline)
Fax: 519-894-0739

Safe Kids Canada
180 Dundas Street West
Toronto, Ontario M5G 1Z8
1-888-SAFE-TIPS
Fax: 416-813-4986
Web site: www.safekidscanada.ca
E-mail: safekids.web@sickkids.ca

Safe Start
BC's Children's Hospital
4480 Oak Street, Room B321
Vancouver, British Columbia
V6H 3V4
Phone: 604-875-2111
1-888-331-8100
Fax: 604-875-2440
Web site: www.bcchf.ca
E-mail: amckendrick@bcchf.ca

Transport Canada
Road Safety and Motor Vehicle
Regulation
Place de Ville, Tower C
330 Sparks Street
Ottawa, Ontario K1A 0N5
Phone: 800-333-0371
Fax: 613-998-4831
Web site: www.tc.gc.ca/roadsafety/
rsindx_e.htm
E-mail: roadsafetywebmail@
tc.gc.ca

Special needs/birth defects

AboutFace International
123 Edward Street
Suite 1003
Toronto, Ontario M5G 1E2
Phone: 1-800-665-3223
Fax: 416-597-8494
Web site:
www.aboutfaceinternational.org
E-mail: info@
aboutfaceinternational.org

Autism Society of Canada
P.O. Box 65
Orangeville, Ontario L9W 2Z5
Phone: 1-866-874-3334
Fax: 519-942-3566
Web site: www.autism.ca
E-mail: info@autismsociety.ca

Canadian Association of Speech-Language Pathologists and Audiologists (CASLPA)
200 Elgin Street, Suite 401
Ottawa, Ontario K2P 1L5
Phone: 613-567-9968
1-800-259-8519
Fax: 613-567-2859
Web site: www.caslpa.ca
E-mail: caslpa@caslpa.ca

The Canadian Association of the Deaf
251 Bank Street, Suite 203
Ottawa, Ontario K2P 1X3
Phone: 613-565-2882
TTY: 613-565-8882
Fax: 613-565-1207
Web site: www.cad.ca
E-mail: cad@cad.ca

Canadian Council of the Blind
396 Cooper Street, Suite 401
Ottawa, Ontario K2P 2H7
Phone: 613-567-0311
1-877-304-0968
Fax: 613-567-2728
Web site: www.ccbnational.net
E-mail: ccb@ccbnational.net

Canadian Cystic Fibrosis Foundation
2221 Yonge Street, Suite 601
Toronto, Ontario M4S 2B4
Phone: 416-485-9149
1-800-378-2233
Fax: 416-485-0960
Web site: www.cysticfibrosis.ca
E-mail: info@cysticfibrosis.ca

Canadian Down Syndrome Society
811 – 14th Street N.W.
Calgary, Alberta T2N 2A4
Phone: 403-270-8500
1-800-883-5608
Fax: 403-270-8291
Web site: www.cdss.ca
E-mail: dsinfo@cdss.ca

Canadian Hemophilia Society
625 President Kennedy Avenue,
    Suite 1210
Montreal, Quebec H3A 1K2
Phone: 514-848-0503
1-800-668-2686
Fax: 514-848-9661
Web site: www.hemophilia.ca
E-mail: chs@hemophilia.ca

Canadian National Institute for the Blind (CNIB)
1929 Bayview Avenue
Toronto, Ontario M4G 3E8
Phone: 416-486-2500
Fax: 416-480-7677
Web site: www.cnib.ca
E-mail: webmaster@cnib.ca

Canadian Organization for Rare Disorders
P.O. Box 814
Coaldale, Alberta T1M 1M7
Phone: 403-345-4544
1-877-302-7273
Fax: 403-345-3948
Web site: www.cord.ca
E-mail: office@cord.ca

Canadian Spinal Research Organization
120 Newkirk Road, Unit 2
Richmond Hill, Ontario L4C 9S7
Phone: 905-508-4000
1-800-361-4004
Fax: 905-508-4002
Web site: www.csro.com
E-mail: csro@globalserve.net

Cerebral Palsy Canada
c/o Cerebral Palsy Association of
    Alberta
8180 Macleod Trail S
Calgary, Alberta T2H 2B8
Phone: 403-543-1161
1-800-363-2807 (in Alberta)
Fax: 403-543-1168
Web site:
    www.cerebralpalsycanada.com
E-mail: info@cerebralpalsy.com

Easter Seals/March of Dimes National Council
90 Eglinton Avenue East, Suite 511
Toronto, Ontario M4P 2Y3
Phone: 416-932-8382
Fax: 416-932-9844
TTY: 416-932-8151
Web site: www.esmodnc.org
E-mail: national.council@
    esmodnc.org

Muscular Dystrophy Association of Canada
National Office
2345 Yonge Street, Suite 900
Toronto, Ontario M4P 2E5
Phone: 416-488-0030
1-800-567-2873
Fax: 416-488-7523
Web site: www.mdac.ca
E-mail: info@mdac.ca

Spina Bifida and Hydrocephalus Association of Canada
167 Lombard Avenue
Winnipeg, Manitoba R3B 0T6
Phone: 1-800-565-9488
Fax: 204-925-3654
Web site: www.sbhac.ca
E-mail: spinab@mts.net

Turner's Syndrome Society
814 Glencairn Avenue
Toronto, Ontario M6B 2A3
Phone: 416-781-2086
1-800-465-6744
Fax: 416-781-7245
Web site: www.turnersyndrome.ca
E-mail: tssincan@web.net

Web Site Directory

Don't forget to check out the dozens of Web sites listed in the Directory of Organizations (Appendix B). To save space, I haven't bothered repeating those Web site addresses here.

While the Web sites listed in this directory represent the crème de la crème of the sites that were available when this book went to press, it's likely that other equally good toddler-related sites will show up in cyberspace over time. If you know of a site that should be included in the next edition of this book, please contact me via my Web site at www.having-a-baby.com to let me know.

Note: The Canadian Web sites listed in this directory have been highlighted with a maple leaf.

Health

🍁 Canadian Dental Hygienists Association
www.cdha.ca
The official site of the organization of the same name. Contains useful tips on caring for your toddler's teeth and ensuring his good oral health.

🍁 Canadian Directory of Genetic Support Groups
www.lhsc.on.ca/programs/medgenet/support.htm
An online database maintained by the Canadian Association of Genetic Counsellors. A useful way of finding out about support groups of interest to parents with toddlers who have particular genetic conditions.

🍁 Canadian Family Physician
www.cfpc.ca
Contains articles from the medical journal of the same name.

❀ Canadian Health Network
www.canadian-health-network.ca
A Health Canada site designed to provide Canadians with access to reliable health-related information.

❀ Canadian Medical Association Journal
www.cmaj.ca
Contains excerpts from the medical journal of the same name.

❀ Canadian Organization for Rare Disorders
www.cord.ca
Contains links to support organizations that may be of interest to families whose children were born with rare disorders.

❀ Caring for Kids
www.caringforkids.ca
The Canadian Paediatric Society's Web site for parents. Packed with useful articles on a variety of child health and parenting-related topics.

❀ C-Health at CANOE
www.canoe.ca/Health/home.html
The health section of the huge Canadian News Online (CANOE) Web site. Features news, columns, and more.

DrGreene.com
www.drgreene.com
A highly comprehensive pediatric health site maintained by U.S. pediatrician Alan Greene.

FamilyDoctor.org
www.familydoctor.org
A health information site for parents that's provided by the American Academy of Pediatrics. Contains useful information on a variety of topics, including alternative and complementary medicine.

❀ Health Canada
www.hc-sc.gc.ca
The official site of Health Canada. Contains articles on a variety of health-related topics of interest to parents with young children.

Intelihealth
www.intelihealth.com
A health site developed in partnership with Johns Hopkins University. Contains plenty of useful information on parenting and child health.

Mayo Health Oasis (Mayo Clinic)
www.mayohealth.org
Features meticulously researched articles on a wide variety of health-related topics, including child health.

❋ Medbroadcast
www.medbroadcast.com
A high-quality site offering online health information to Canadians.

MedicineNet
www.medicinenet.com
Contains detailed information on a variety of health-related topics, including infant health. Features an online medical dictionary and more.

Medscape
www.medscape.com
Another major health site that offers detailed information on a variety of health-related topics, including child health.

The Merck Manual
www.merck.com
Contains the entire text of this highly respected medical manual.

❋ MochaSofa.ca
www.mochasofa.ca
A site for Canadian women that features health- and parenting-related content from such publications as Canadian Living *and* Homemaker's *magazines.*

PubMed
www.ncbi.nlm.nih.gov/entrez/query.fcgi
A database that allows you to search for abstracts from the latest medical journals.

Reuters Health
www.reutershealth.com
An excellent source of breaking news on the health front.

❋ Sympatico Health
www1.sympatico.ca/Contents/health
The health area of the massive Sympatico site.

WebMD
www.Webmd.com
One of the best health sites out there. An excellent spot to track breaking news stories on the health front.

Nutrition

Food and Nutrition Information Center's Resource List on Food Allergies and Intolerances
www.nal.usda.gov/fnic/pubs/bibs/gen/allergy.htm
An excellent source of information on food allergies and intolerances.

❋ Life-Threatening Food Allergies in School and Child Care Settings: A Practical Resource for Parents, Care Providers, and Staff
www.healthservices.gov.bc.ca/cpa/publications/food_allergies.pdf
Published by the B.C. Ministry of Health Services, this brochure is packed with practical tips on managing food allergies in both child-care and school settings.

Tufts University Nutrition Navigator
www.navigator.tufts.edu
Provides links to the best nutrition-related sites online.

Parenting

BabyCenter
www.babycenter.com
One of the leading U.S. pregnancy and baby sites. Packed with useful information on a variety of parenting-related topics. Features numerous bulletin boards devoted to a smorgasbord of parenting-related topics.

BabyZone
www.babyzone.com
A grassroots U.S. parenting Web site that features regional content for a few Canadian cities: Calgary, Halifax, Montreal, Niagara Falls, Toronto, Vancouver, and Winnipeg.

❋ Canadian Parents Online
www.canadianparents.com
An excellent source of information for Canadian parents.

❋ Canadian Toy Testing Council
www.toy-testing.org
The official site of the Canadian Toy Testing Council (CTTC). Features useful information on choosing toys and a directory of the addresses and phone numbers for the major toy manufacturing companies—useful information if you happen to lose a block or two from your toddler's shape sorter!

❋ Centre for Families, Work, and Well-being
www.worklifecanada.ca
An excellent source of statistics and other information about the work–life balance and child care–related issues.

Child Magazine.com
www.childmagazine.com
The Web site for the print magazine of the same name.

ClubMom.com
www.clubmom.com
A parenting Web site featuring checklists and interactive tools galore.

Family.com
www.family.com
The launching pad for the Disney Corporation's Web site for families. You'll find parenting articles, craft ideas, party planners, and recipes galore.

🍁 Growing Healthy Canadians: A Guide for Positive Child Development
www.growinghealthykids.com
A high-quality site devoted to promoting healthy child development.

🍁 Having-A-Baby.com
www.having-a-baby.com
The official site of pregnancy and parenting book author Ann Douglas. Drop by for updates on a range of important pregnancy and parenting-related topics.

iParenting.com
www.iparenting.com
Part of a network of more than 30 Web sites devoted to preconception, pregnancy, and parenting.

The Labor of Love
www.thelaboroflove.com
A parenting site that has all kinds of fun and unusual extras: belly photos, baby shower planning tools, and much more.

🍁 Lifewise Family Matters at CANOE
www.canoe.ca/LifewiseFamilymatters/home.html
The parenting area of the huge Canadian News Online (CANOE) web site.

Midlife Mommies
www.midlifemommies.com
A Web site for women who are embarking on motherhood a little later in life.

🍁 Mom to Many: Parents of Multiples Across Canada
www.mom2many.com
A friendly and supportive site for parents of twins, triplets, and more. You'll find parenting advice, a coupon exchange, discussion groups, and much more.

❋ Mother of All Books.com
www.motherofallbooks.com
The official site of the Mother of All Books series: The Mother of All
Pregnancy Books, The Mother of All Baby Books, The Mother of All
Toddler Books, *and—coming soon!*—The Mother of All Parenting Books.
*Features links to hundreds of Web sites of interest to Canadian parents, the
highly popular "Ask Ann Douglas" Q&A area, and much more.*

Myria
www.Myria.com
*Part of a network of sites created by two Web-savvy moms. Intelligent, thought-
provoking, and always entertaining. Definitely worth a visit.*

❋ Parent Help Line
www.parentsinfo.sympatico.ca
*The site for Parents Help Line, a national 24-hour-a-day confidential support
service provided by trained counsellors. Also provides a library of recorded
messages on hundreds of parenting issues for quick and easy reference.*

Parenting.com
www.parenting.com
The official Web site of Parenting *magazine.*

Parents.com
www.parents.com
The official Web site of Parents *magazine.*

ParentsPlace.com
www.parentsplace.com
*One of two iVillage sites devoted to parenting. ParentsPlace.com focuses on preg-
nancy to age three while a sister site, Parentsoup.com, deals with the concerns of
parents with older children. You'll find bulletin boards, interactive tools, and more.*

Pregnancy.org
www.pregnancy.org
*A not-for-profit parenting community built by and for parents. Expect the
unexpected!*

❋ Today's Parent.com
www.todaysparent.com
*Features articles from the magazine of the same name, bulletin boards, and
much more.*

Working Mother
www.workingmother.com
The official site of the print publication of the same name.

Zero to Three's Young Explorers
www.zerotothree.org
A site operated by a non-profit Washington-based organization that aims to promote the healthy development of babies and toddlers. You'll find detailed information on child development, choosing child care, and more.

Safety

🍁 Child and Family Canada
www.cfc-efc.ca
Packed with useful information on a variety of topics related to child safety.

🍁 Safe Kids Canada
www.safekidscanada.ca
Contains useful information on keeping your child safe.

🍁 Transport Canada
www.tc.gc.ca/roadsafety/childsafe/cindex_e.htm
An excellent source of information on the safe use of car seats.

Toddler activities

Coloring Book Fun.com
www.coloringbookfun.com
This site is packed with outline drawings for toddlers and older children to colour. If you're not a big fan of colouring books, you can find other ways of using the colouring pages, e.g., having your toddler practise cutting out shapes.

Crayola
www.crayola.com
A craft activity site for kids. Features a helpful guide to removing stains caused by various Crayola products!

GoAheadGetDirty Club
www.goaheadgetdirty.com
A Web site produced by the manufacturers of Sunlight laundry detergent that is designed to give parents the tools they need to promote learning through play.

Lego.com
www.lego.com
A fun site that allows kids to play with virtual Lego. Many of the games and activities are too difficult for toddlers, so you'll want to "pre-surf" this site yourself, zeroing in on activities that your toddler will be likely to enjoy (e.g., the online Memory game).

Nick Jr.com

www.nickjr.com

Games and activities for your toddler plus parenting articles for you.

PBS Kids

www.pbskids.org

Features games, stories, music, colouring pages, plus information about some popular U.S. children's television shows

Sesame Workshop

www.sesameworkshop.org

A Web site that features activities for toddlers and articles for parents.

❧ Treehouse TV.com

www.treehousetv.com

A popular Web site for toddlers that features music, online games, craft activities, and more.

Toddler Growth Charts

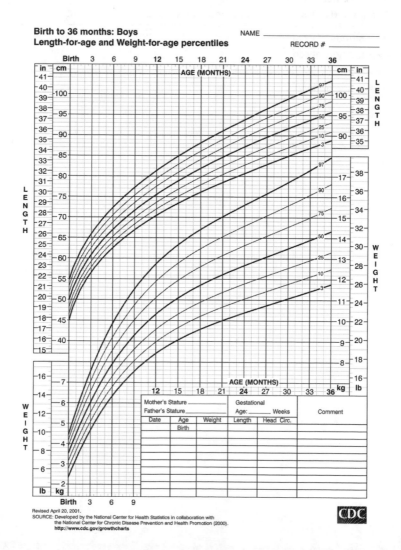

Birth to 36 months: Boys
Length-for-age and Weight-for-age percentiles

NAME _____

RECORD # _____

Revised April 20, 2001.
SOURCE: Developed by the National Center for Health Statistics in collaboration with
the National Center for Chronic Disease Prevention and Health Promotion (2000).
http://www.cdc.gov/growthcharts

CDC

Birth to 36 months: Girls
Length-for-age and Weight-for-age percentiles

NAME _____

RECORD # _____

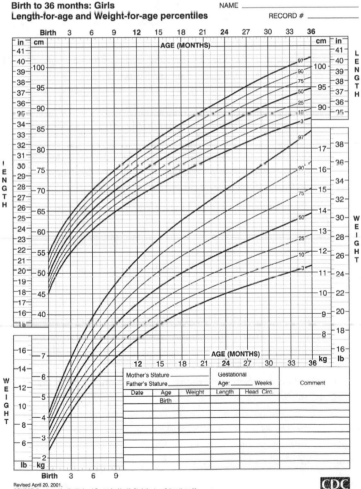

Revised April 20, 2001.
SOURCE: Developed by the National Center for Health Statistics in collaboration with
the National Center for Chronic Disease Prevention and Health Promotion (2000).
http://www.cdc.gov/growthcharts

Recommended Readings

Acredolo, Linda, and Susan Goodwyn. *Baby Minds: Brain-Building Games Your Baby Will Love*. New York: Bantam Books, 2000.

Adler, Bill, and Peggy Robin. *Outwitting Toddlers*. New York: Kensington Books, 2001.

Allen, K. Eileen, and Lynn Marotz. *Developmental Profiles: Birth to Six*. New York: Delmar Publishers Inc., 1989.

Apel, Kenn, and Julie Masterson. *Beyond Baby Talk: From Sounds to Sentences—A Parent's Complete Guide to Language Development*. New York: Prima Publishing, 2001.

Auerbach, Stevanne. *Dr. Toy's Smart Play: How to Raise a Child with a High PQ (Play Quotient)*. New York: St. Martin's Griffin, 1998.

Bennett, Holly, and Teresa Pitman. *Steps and Stages 1 to 3: The Toddler Years*. Toronto: Key Porter Books, 1998.

Boyd, Keith, and Kevin Osborn. *The Complete Idiot's Guide to Parenting a Preschooler and Toddler, Too*. New York: Alpha Books, 1997.

Butler, Shelley, and Deb Kratz. *The Field Guide to Parenting: A Comprehensive Handbook of Great Ideas, Advice, Tips and Solutions for Parenting Children Ages One to Five*. Worcester: Chandler House Press, 1999.

Canadian Institute of Child Health. *The Health of Canada's Children*. Ottawa: Canadian Institute of Child Health, 2000.

Canadian Paediatric Society. *Well Beings*. Ottawa: Canadian Paediatric Society, 1996.

Crary, Elizabeth. *Without Spanking or Spoiling*. Seattle: Parenting Press, 1993.

DeBroff, Stacy. *The Mom Book*. New York: Free Press, 2002.

Douglas, Ann. *Baby Science: How Babies Really Work*. Toronto: Owl Books, 1998. (For toddlers.)

_____. *Before You Were Born: The Inside Story.* Toronto: Owl Books, 1999.
(For toddlers.)

_____. *Family Finance: The Essential Guide for Canadian Parents.* Toronto:
Prentice Hall Canada, 1999.

_____. *The Mother of All Baby Books: An All-Canadian Guide to Your Baby's
First Year.* Toronto: Macmillan Canada, 2000.

_____. *The Mother of All Pregnancy Books: An All-Canadian Guide to
Conception, Birth, and Everything in Between.* Toronto: Macmillan
Canada, 2000.

_____. *Sanity Savers: The Canadian Working Woman's Guide to Almost
Having It All.* McGraw-Hill Ryerson, 1999.

_____. *The Unofficial Guide to Childcare.* New York: John Wiley and Sons,
1998.

Douglas, Ann, and John R. Sussman, MD. *The Unofficial Guide to Having a
Baby.* New York: John Wiley and Sons, 1999.

_____. *Trying Again: A Guide to Pregnancy After Miscarriage, Stillbirth, and
Infant Loss.* Dallas, Texas: Taylor Publishing, 2000.

Dowshen, Steven, Neil Izenberg, and Elizabeth Bass. *KidsHealth Guide for
Parents: Pregnancy to Age 5.* New York: Contemporary Books, 2002.

Eliot, Lise. *What's Going On in There?: How the Brain and Mind Develop in
the First Five Years of Life.* New York: Bantam Books, 1999.

Engel, June. *The Complete Canadian Health Guide.* Toronto: Key Porter,
1999.

Faber, Adele, and Elaine Mazlish. *How to Talk So Kids Will Listen and Listen
So Kids Will Talk.* New York: Avon Books, 1989.

Fancher, Vivian Kramer. *Safe Kids: A Complete Child-Safety Handbook and
Resource Guide for Parents.* New York: John Wiley and Sons, Inc., 1991.

Feldman, William. *The 3 a.m. Handbook: The Most Commonly Asked
Questions About Your Child's Health.* Toronto: Key Porter Books, 1997.

Fisher, John J. *From Baby to Toddler.* New York: Perigree Books, 1988.

Ginsberg, Susan. *Family Wisdom: The 2000 Most Important Things Ever
Said About Parenting, Children, and Family Life.* New York: Columbia
University Press, 1996.

Golinkoff, Roberta, and Kathy Hirsch-Pasek. *How Babies Talk: The Magic
and Mystery of Language in the First Three Years of Life.* New York:
Plume Books, 2000.

Gopnik, Alison, Andrew Meltzoff, and Patricia Kuhl. *The Scientist in the
Crib: Minds, Brains, and How Children Learn.* New York: William
Morrow and Company Inc., 1999.

Green, Christopher. *Toddler Taming: A Survival Guide for Parents.* New York:
Fawcett Columbine, 1984.

Health Canada. *For The Safety of Canadian Children and Youth*. Ottawa: Health Canada, 1997.

Herr, Judy. *Creative Learning Activities for Young Children*. Albany: Thomson Learning Inc., 2001.

Huggins, Kathleen. *The Nursing Mother's Companion*. Boston: Harvard Common Press, 1990.

Huntley, Rebecca. *The Sleep Book for Tired Parents*. Seattle: Parenting Press, 1991.

Iovine, Vicki. *The Girlfriends' Guide to Toddlers*. New York: Perigree Books, 1999.

Jackson, Marni. *The Mother Zone: Love, Sex, and Laundry in the Modern Family*. New York: Henry Holt, 1992.

Jhung, Paula. *How to Avoid Housework*. New York: Simon & Schuster, 1995.

Jones, Maggie. *Understanding Your Child Through Play*. Toronto: Stoddart, 1989.

Jones, Sandy. *Guide to Baby Products*. New York: Consumer Reports, 2001.

Jones, Teri Crawford. *As They Grow: Your One-Year-Old*. New York: St. Martin's Griffin, 2000.

Kaiser, Barbara, and Judy Sklar Rasminsky. *The Daycare Handbook*. Toronto: Little, Brown, and Company, 1991.

Kalnins, Daina, and Joanne Saab. *Better Baby Food*. Toronto: Robert Rose Inc., 2001.

Kennedy, Marge. *The Parents Book of Lists from Birth to Age Three*. New York: St. Martin's Griffin, 2000.

Kennedy, Marge, and Karen White. *Parents Play and Learn*. New York: St. Martin's Griffin, 2000.

Kopp, Claire. *Baby Steps: The "Whys" of Your Child's Behavior in the First Two Years*. New York: W.H.Freeman and Company, 1994.

Kuffner, Trish. *The Toddler's Busy Book*. New York: Meadowbrook Press, 1999.

Kurcinka, Mary Sheedy. *Raising Your Spirited Child*. New York: Harper Perennial, 1991.

Langlois, Christine, ed. *Growing with Your Child: Pre-Birth to Age 5*. Toronto: Ballantine Books, 1998.

Leach, Penelope. *Babyhood*. London: Penguin Books, 1983.

_____. *Your Baby & Child from Birth to Age Five*. New York: Alfred A. Knopf, 1977.

Leifer, Gloria. *Introduction to Maternity and Pediatric Nursing*. Philadelphia: W.B. Saunders Company, 1999.

Lerner, Harriet. *The Mother Dance: How Children Change Your Life*. New York: Harper Collins, 1998.

McKay, Sharon. *The New Child Safety Handbook*. Toronto: Macmillan Canada, 1988.

Miller, Karen. *Things to Do with Toddlers and Twos*. West Palm Beach: Telshare Publishing Co., Inc., 2000.

Minister of Health. *For The Safety of Canadian Children and Youth*. Ottawa: Minister of Public Works and Government Services Canada, 1997.

Newman, Jack, and Teresa Pitman. *Dr. Jack Newman's Guide to Breastfeeding*. Toronto: Harper Collins, 2000.

O'Connell, Diane. *As They Grow: Your Two-Year-Old*. New York: St. Martin's Griffin, 2000.

Offit, Paul. *Breaking the Antibiotic Habit*. New York: John Wiley & Sons, Inc., 1999.

Omichinski, Linda, and Heather Wiebe Hildegrand. *Tailoring Your Tastes*. Winnipeg: Tamos Books, 1995.

Orenstein, Julian. *365 Tips for the Toddler Years*. Avon: Adams Media Corporation, 2002.

Perry, Susan. *Playing Smart: The Family Guide to Enriching, Offbeat Learning Activities for Ages 4–14*. Minneapolis: Free Spirit Publishing, 2001.

Popper, Adrienne. *Parents Book for the Toddler Years*. New York: Ballantine Books, 1986.

Reichert, Bonny. *In Search of Sleep*. Toronto: Sarasota Press, 2001.

Reitzes, Fretta, Beth Teitelman, and Lois Alter Mark. *Wonderplay*. Philadelphia: Running Press, 1995.

Rogers, Fred, and Barry Head. *Mister Rogers' Playbook: Insights and Activities for Parents and Children*. New York: Berkley Books, 1986.

Rothbart, Betty. *Multiple Blessings*. New York: Hearst Books, 1994.

Satter, Ellyn. *Child of Mine: Feeding with Love and Good Sense*. Palo Alto: Bull Publishing Company, 2000.

Schiff, Donald, and Steven Shelov. *Guide to Your Child's Symptoms*. New York, Villard Books, 1997.

Sears, Martha, and William Sears. *The Breastfeeding Book: Everything You Need to Know About Nursing Your Child from Birth Through Weaning*. Boston: Little, Brown and Company, 2000.

_____. *The Discipline Book: How to Have a Better-Behaved Child from Birth to Age Ten*. Boston: Little, Brown and Company, 1995.

Segal, Marilyn. *Your Child at Play: One to Two Years*. New York: Newmarket Press, 1985.

_____. *Your Child at Play: Two to Three Years*. New York: Newmarket Press, 1985.

Segal, Marilyn, Wendy Masi, and Roni Leiderman. *In Time and with Love: Caring for Infants and Toddlers with Special Needs*. New York: Newmarket Press, 1988.

Settle, Miriam Bachar, and Susan Crites Price. *The Complete Idiot's Guide to Child Safety*. Indianapolis: Alpha Books, 2000.

Shelov, Steven, Editor-in-Chief. *Caring for Your Baby and Young Child*. New York: Bantam Books, 1991.

Shimm, Patricia Henderson, and Kate Ballen. *Parenting Your Toddler: The Expert's Guide to the Tough and Tender Years*. Cambridge: Perseus Books, 1995.

Spencer, Paula. *Parenting Guide to Your Toddler*. New York: Ballantine Books, 2000.

Stoppard, Miriam. *Complete Baby and Child Care*. Toronto: Macmillan Canada, 1995.

_____. *You and Your Toddler*. New York: DK Publishing Inc., 1999.

Thompson, Charlotte. *Raising a Handicapped Child*. New York: Oxford University Press, Inc., 2000.

Waldstein, Laurie, and Leslie Zinberg. *The Pink and Blue Toddler and Preschooler Pages: Practical Tips and Advice for Parents*. Chicago: Contemporary Books, 1999.

Wall, Kathleen. *Parenting Tricks of the Trade*. Golden: Fulcrum Publishing, 1994.

Watters, Nancy E., and Susan Hodges. *National Breastfeeding Guidelines for Health Care Providers*. Ottawa: Canadian Institute of Child Health, 1996.

Woolfson, Richard. *Bright Toddler*. New York: Barron's Educational Series, Inc., 2001

Zweiback, Meg. *Keys to Toilet Training*. New York: Barron's Educational Series, Inc., 1998.

Index

About the Author

Ann Douglas is the author of 21 books, including the highly popular *The Mother of All Pregnancy Books* and *The Mother of All Baby Books*. She and her books have been featured in *Parenting, Working Mother*, the *Chicago Tribune*, and *The New York Times*, and she has been invited to serve as a guest expert at such high-profile parenting and health web sites as BabyCenter.com, ParentSoup.com, and WebMD.com. Her articles and columns regularly appear in such publications as *Today's Parent, Canadian Living, Flare Pregnancy, Healthy Woman*, and *ePregnancy* magazine. Ann lives in Peterborough, Ontario, with her husband and four children, ages five through fourteen. She can be contacted via her Web site, www.having-a-baby.com.

Motherofallbooks.com

Just think of it as
The Mother of All Web Sites

Motherofallbooks.com is your launching pad to the very best Canadian parenting and pediatric health information to be found online.

You'll find

- an online directory of Canadian organizations of interest to parents with young children

- links to the most reputable Canadian parenting and pediatric health web sites

- a glossary of key pregnancy and pediatric terms

- articles and tools of interest to parents and parents-to-be

- regularly updated Q&As featuring Ann Douglas, Canada's foremost pregnancy and parenting book author and

- much more.

And, while you're visiting the site, be sure to sign up for important updates about future titles in The Mother of All Books series, including **The Mother of All Parenting Books** - Coming Soon!

Motherofallbooks.com
An all-Canadian web site for parents and parents-to-be

And **TODDLER** makes three...

**Mother of All
Toddler Books
ISBN: 1-55335-016-2**

**The Mother of all
Pregnancy Books
ISBN: 0-7715-7720-6**

**The Mother of All
Baby Books
ISBN: 1-55335-007-3**

Canada's best-selling parenting series
is available wherever books are sold.
Look for the *Mother of All Parenting Books*
coming soon.